C000171431

This is an essential book for anyone seeking t[...] threat today is to Jewish university students and [...]

> Anthony Julius
> Professor, Faculty of Laws, University College London; deputy chairman, Mishcon de Reya LLP; author, *Trials of the Diaspora: A History of Antisemitism in England*

Free speech is a central issue on American campuses today, and Israel, Zionism, antisemitism, and the BDS movement provide much of the substance of the ongoing debates. In this wonderfully well-informed and liberal-minded analysis, Cary Nelson constructs guardrails for the ideological combatants and suggests ways to keep the arguments civil. What kinds of resolutions and policies are protected by our free speech rights, and what kinds aren't? When do the acts of student groups or university authorities cross the line into antisemitism, and when not? Which types of boycotts constitute legitimate protest, and which types don't? Nelson is studiously careful, fair, and smart in making the necessary distinctions. If you plan to join the debates, read this book first.

> Michael Walzer
> Institute for Advanced Study, Princeton, NJ; author, *The Struggle for a Decent Politics: On "Liberal" as an Adjective*

Let me state outright: *Hate Speech and Academic Freedom* is the most comprehensive study of the topic ever published. In fact, there is nothing like it. For Nelson, the campus occupies hallowed ground precisely because it is intended to provide sanctuary—indeed, encouragement—for people who care about ideas. But ideas matter only when their validity can be ascertained through debate and discussion. For a narrative without evidence, no matter how often repeated in an increasingly networked world, elides its history into mythology. What should be happening on campuses regarding the Middle East conflict—meticulous research with a careful examination of data and events aiming for clarity—has too often been discarded for an advocacy that masquerades as scholarship with books and articles feeding each other in a cul-de-sac-like echo chamber. Cary Nelson has put together an exhaustive analysis of the serious narrowing of academic work on Israel.

> Donna Robinson Divine
> Morningstar Professor Emerita of Jewish Studies and Professor Emerita of Government, Smith College; coeditor, *Word Crimes: Reclaiming the Language of the Israeli-Palestinian Conflict*

Academic freedom, as traditionally understood, guarantees the right to pursue research in pursuit of the truth, independently of whether its results happen to be acceptable to ideological interests either inside or outside academia. This remarkable book asks what is to become of that guarantee, not only when ideological commitments based essentially on falsehood and bad argument become consensual within sections of the scholarly world itself, but when, as in the case of much current academic writing about Israel, the resulting "scholarship" plays a leading part in promoting hostility and violence against Jews (but not, significantly, to any great extent against non-Jewish supporters of Israel) both within and beyond academia. Nelson's background, as president of the American Association of University Professors in 2006–2012, and as a leading figure on the academic left, who has worked tirelessly in the cause not only of academic freedom but also of equal treatment for all members of the academic community, uniquely qualifies him to comment on these questions. He has produced a richly detailed and informative but also stringently and acutely argued book, which should become essential reading for anyone concerned about the present state of our universities.

Bernard Harrison

Emeritus E. E. Ericksen Professor of Philosophy, University of Utah; emeritus professor in the Faculty of Humanities, University of Sussex; author, *Blaming the Jews: Politics and Delusion*

HATE SPEECH AND ACADEMIC FREEDOM

The Antisemitic Assault on Basic Principles

The ISGAP Book Series on Critical Contemporary Antisemitism Studies is an interdisciplinary book series that explores the context of contemporary antisemitism studies as it relates to this longest hatred, otherness and belonging in the age of neoliberal globalisation. The series responds to the urgent need for interrogation and theorisation of particular forms of ideologically driven social movements and intellectual environments of increasing marginality and discrimination. The series utilises an interdisciplinary approach which includes sociology, anthropology, economics, psychology, history, political science, social theory and cultural studies, to analyse, map and decode contemporary antisemitism, especially the attack on notions of Jewish peoplehood, marginality and discrimination in various forms, with a focus on assessing the complex and entrenched genealogies of antisemitism and its contemporary manifestations. The series aims to explore the intersectional composition of antisemitism and marginality and to examine how these phenomena operate globally across societies and institutions. Through its interdisciplinary approach, the book series transcends narrowly conceived notions of boundaries, without neglecting peculiarities specific or unique to national histories and cultures. In the current intellectual environment, where there is a reluctance to *confront the multifaceted nature of antisemitism, this book series is most relevant, as it addresses the re-emergence of antisemitic discourse and violence, fostering interdisciplinary knowledge of this deeply rooted form of hatred.*

Series Editor: Charles Asher Small, Founder and Executive Director, Institute for the Study of Global Antisemitism and Policy (ISGAP); Director, ISGAP-Woolf Institute Fellowship Training Programme on Critical Contemporary Antisemitism Studies, Human Rights and Discrimination, Cambridge, UK. He is a graduate of St. Antony's College, Oxford University.

ISGAP / THE INSTITUTE FOR THE STUDY OF GLOBAL ANTISEMITISM & POLICY

HATE SPEECH AND ACADEMIC FREEDOM

The Antisemitic Assault on Basic Principles

Cary Nelson

BOSTON
2024

Library of Congress Cataloging-in-Publication Data

Names: Nelson, Cary, author.
Title: Hate speech and academic freedom : the antisemitic assault on basic
  principles / Cary Nelson.
Description: Boston : Academic Studies Press, 2024. | Includes
  bibliographical references and index.
Identifiers: LCCN 2023046658 (print) | LCCN 2023046659 (ebook) | ISBN
  9798887194196 (hardback) | ISBN 9798887194202 (paperback) | ISBN
  9798887194219 (adobe pdf) | ISBN 9798887194226 (epub)
Subjects: LCSH: Antisemitism in higher education. | Zionism--Public
  opinion. | Academic freedom. | Education, Higher--Political aspects. |
  Hate speech.
Classification: LCC LC212.4 .N45 2024 (print) | LCC LC212.4 (ebook) | DDC
  378.0089/924--dc23/eng/20231106
LC record available at https://lccn.loc.gov/2023046658
LC ebook record available at https://lccn.loc.gov/2023046659

Book design by Lapiz Digital Services
Cover design by Ivan Grave

Published by Academic Studies Press
1577 Beacon Street
Brookline, MA 02446
Tel: 617.782.6290
press@academicstudiespress.com
www.academicstudiespress.com

Contents

Acknowledgements

Hate Speech and Academic Freedom has benefited from careful and immensely knowledgeable comments and suggestions from a number of friends and colleagues. Many people read several chapters; several read the entire manuscript. Remaining errors or misjudgments remain my responsibility, but there are certainly far fewer of those because of the generosity of the following people: Yuval Abrams, Ronnie Fraser, Daniel Gordon, David Greenberg, Alan Johnson, Steven Lubet, Kenneth Stern, Paula A. Treichler, Jim Wald, and Jeff Weintraub. A number of other people answered specific questions: Russell Berman, Matthew Finkin, Richard Herman, John Hyman, Günther Jikeli, Anthony Julius, Marcia Kupfer, Jeffry Mallow, David Matas, Stan Nadel, Alvin Rosenfeld, Richard Ross, Tammi Rossman-Benjamin, Lev Topor, Gabriel Weimann, and Michael Whine. Special thanks for their thoughtful advice also goes to Alan Johnson and Lesley Klaff, the editors of *Fathom* and the *Journal of Contemporary Antisemitism*, where earlier versions of several of these chapters appeared. I also owe special thanks to my copy editor, Daniel Stephens, who knows the field well and did exceptionally fine and careful work. Finally, I am grateful for ISGAP's endorsement of the project and for the generous material support provided in aid of its publication.

On style, I use "antisemitism," which now seems to be the consensus spelling of the term, except when a quotation uses "anti-Semitism." That makes for awkward juxtapositions, but I don't see an alternative. Notes are numbered consecutively throughout the book. Finally, although I have tried to minimize repetition throughout, some topics recur in order to make individual chapters independently coherent.

Introduction

Antisemitism is on the rise worldwide, and academia plays an important role in rationalizing and normalizing its character and application, indeed in applauding and promoting antisemitism's cultural and political strategies. One can argue, as Charles Small did at a 2022 conference on antisemitism organized by the Institute for the Study of Global Antisemitism and Policy (ISGAP), that universities are the premier source of contemporary antisemitism.[1] At the same time, "Jews are more likely to suffer reported hate crimes at American institutions of higher education when compared to other minority groups" (Feinberg 2021, 7), a pattern of creating hostile environments that applies to British campuses as well. That is largely because antisemitism has become deeply entrenched as radical anti-Zionism in a number of academic disciplines.

As David Hirsh writes in a recent essay, "From a Critique of Zionism to an Anti-Jewish Worldview," an intensely hostile version of anti-Zionism has gained influence over several decades since 1967. This radical anti-Zionism "draws on its own grotesque caricature of Zionism as a single, monstrous, universal evil, and it constructs a whole worldview or ideology, in relation

---

1   ISGAP-Woolf Institute International Conference, Global Antisemitism: A Crisis of Modernity Revisited, Cambridge University, July 31–August 2, 2022.

to that demonic fantasy of Jewish nationhood" (Hirsh 2023, 5). While this "irrational, phobic response" (8) to the very idea of Jewish nationhood has always been a part of anti-Zionism, it acquired a different character in response to the creation of an actual Jewish state in 1948 and became still more aggressive as Israel consolidated its status as a regional power through the latter part of the twentieth century. For some constituencies, including part of the international left, Israel has become a demonic other, an opponent of humanity and an apartheid state.

It is often either NGOs or academics who not only explain the claim that Israel is an apartheid state but even say polemically that Israeli apartheid is worse than that long practiced in South Africa. It is academics, among others, who shamelessly repeat the lie that Israel is the world's worst violator of human rights, ignoring or discounting the overwhelming human rights abuses of such countries as China, Iran, Myanmar, North Korea, Russia, and Syria, among many others. It is academia that helps keep alive the slander that Zionism is a form of racism. It is academics who write at length to sustain the antisemitic fiction of a vastly powerful "Israel lobby." It is academics who try to justify not just comparisons but equivalences between Israel and Nazi Germany. It is academics who not only post concise lies about Israel online but also write books and essays with elaborate antisemitic fictions. It is academics who help turn young students into continuing opponents of Israel. It is academia that helps seed professions with college graduates convinced that Israel is a force for worldwide evil. Unlike many areas of academic writing, academic anti-Zionism has a sequential social impact. Faculty help mainstream antisemitism on campus, and the campus then helps mainstream it in society as a whole.

It is academics who are thus the major theoretical advocates for antisemitism. They have, for example, been leaders in elaborating the claim that Israel has been a settler-colonialist enterprise since Jews immigrated there to recover their ancient homeland in the nineteenth century. It is academics especially who make anti-Zionism the principle rationale for decolonization, thereby turning decolonization into an antisemitic project. Many academics, on the other hand, work hard at developing a theory of antisemitism in projects aimed at understanding and critiquing it, but their opponents in the academy are devoted to the contrary project, elaborating accounts of anti-Zionism that cross the line into antisemitism or, worse still, invoke a demonic, unreal Zionism detached from the historical record. Off-campus, far-right antisemitism presents a physical threat to Jews throughout the West. On campus, it is left-wing antisemitism that dominates, and the threats instead are cultural, political, polemical, religious, communal, and interpersonal. The challenges the left can present on campus are enhanced by the presence of radical right politicians in the Israeli government, politicians whose views most campus Zionists find reprehensible. The degree to which those Israel government ministers will succeed in determining policy remains to be seen, but they will surely be quoted on campus and be treated as broadly representative of the Israeli electorate.

The spread of antisemitism both on and off campus is relentlessly promoted by hate speech in both attenuated and elaborate forms, from tweets to full-length publications. Hate speech can clearly signal what or why someone hates, but that can also be unclear. A speaker can willfully seek to inspire others to share his or her hatred or can do so inadvertently. A speaker may alternatively concentrate on convincing others that *they* are hated. Hate speech can explicitly vilify "a person or group of people because they belong to a group or share an identity" (Benesch et al. 2021, 7), or it can do so implicitly, as hate speech directed at Jewish businessman and philanthropist George Soros often does. In 1990, the Canadian Supreme Court stated that "'hatred' connotes emotion of an intense and extreme nature that is clearly associated with vilification and detestation," adding that it is "predicated on destruction ... if exercised against members of an identifiable group, [it] implies that those individuals are to be despised, scorned, denied respect and made subject to ill-treatment on the basis of group affiliation."[2]

The increasing antisemitism we now face has been years in coming. Awareness of the evolution of anti-Zionist hate can help us understand where we are now and confront present conditions realistically. My own experience of confronting academic anti-Zionism dates to the early 1980s, specifically to the international teaching institute and conference that my colleague Lawrence Grossberg and I organized in 1983. At that point, at least for the international Marxist left, the injustice and fundamental perfidy of the world's only Jewish state was a matter of wide consensus. Opposition to Israel, a significant component of radical left ideology since the 1967 Six-Day War, had steadily grown into a priority. But it competed with race and gender for personal and group commitments. Now these competing priorities have begun to coalesce under the banner of anti-Zionism. Activists press their intersection. Until the fall of Saigon in 1975, moreover, the Vietnam War had overshadowed all other international political issues. The end of the Vietnam War opened space for a basic

---

2   Quoted in Walker (2018). Some analysts prefer the descriptive term "hateful speech" over the more categorical "hate speech." For most of the examples I consider, I find the stronger "hate speech" to be more appropriate.

reconfiguration of left-wing priorities. We had not yet fully entered the era of identity politics, but that trend was already in evidence.

Among the priorities being reconceived was the long-standing need on the left for a community of pure victims who could be idealized and seen as incapable of evil. The Palestinians did not at first fill that slot decisively, partly because the North Vietnamese played that role, but Palestinians have widely done so at least since the First Intifada. Yet being incapable of evil does not actually mean that everyone believes they are transcendent beings; it means instead that some people, especially in academia, believe it is politically incumbent on them to treat the Palestinians that way. And of course their opponents, Zionists in Israel and worldwide, have to be seen in contrast as irredeemably misguided or demonic.

Lawrence Grossberg and I organized the aforementioned 1983 events around the theme of Marxism and the Interpretation of Culture. We were among those interested in promoting what the Jamaican-born British scholar Stuart Hall characterized as a "Marxism without guarantees." It would no longer claim confidence in long-term historical predictions. It would no longer have faith in a proletarian revolution. But it would remain persuaded that class conflict has considerable explanatory power, and it would emphasize the cultural front in political struggle. The summer would be devoted to debates about these issues. It included four weeks of courses taught by faculty from Britain, Germany, Yugoslavia, and the United States, and a concluding five-day conference with a still more international audience. There were conference speakers from China and Latin America and attendees from Africa. The French government chartered a flight from Paris to bring people to the conference.

Already the congruence between scholarship and activism that so occupies the contemporary academy was defining radical left-wing academia, and it was linked both to political analysis and personal identity. In fact, we had seen the scholarship/activism convergence over Black Studies in the 1960s and feminism in the 1970s, convergences that are still with us, nowhere more intensely on campus today than in debates over Israel. In each of these areas we saw as well the emergence and prioritization of symbolic politics of the kind that so preoccupies contemporary anti-Zionist movements, the Boycott, Divestment, and Sanctions (BDS) movement among them.

This historical perspective suggests we should set aside surprise and outrage as reactions and ask instead what can be learned from this repeated political dynamic. At the 1983 events, there were competing constituencies in favor of feminism and anti-Zionism. Students and faculty felt they had to choose between these commitments. The feminist group held in-class demonstrations to pressure the faculty to revise their syllabi to include sections on feminism. Some faculty complied and some refused, among them Fred Jameson, who made the astonishingly outdated but classic Marxist argument that the full achievement of women's rights would have to wait until after the revolution. In any case, it was the responsibility of individual faculty to decide how to respond to the challenge. The anti-Zionist group instead organized a general campaign demanding that we cancel all classes for a week to address the moral and political "crisis" in Israel and the West Bank. Since that demand targeted all the teaching faculty and the program administrators, we had to respond.

Anticipating that political demands might arise, Larry and I had built support for student-initiated events into both the funding and the schedule. Thus, when the demand to cancel classes arose, we had reasonable alternatives to offer, namely student-organized evening and weekend teach-ins and symposia on topics of their choice. No classes or seminars met at night or on the weekends, so two days out of seven, along with all evenings, were free for other activities. We made funding available for travel and honoraria for outside speakers, film rentals for special showings, photocopying for distributing literature, and so forth. We reserved meeting spaces in advance. The funds could be had simply by asking— hardly a typical academic arrangement. There was little off-campus entertainment in the middle of Illinois in those days, so there were no distractions.

I pointed out that there really was no immediate crisis in relationships between Jews and Palestinians, and there was certainly no Middle East war at that moment. Nonetheless, then as now, the practical, non-radical alternatives we offered met with scorn because they had no overriding symbolic power to demonize Israel. Reason proved to have no leverage unless its rejection was combined with material consequences, a lesson that remains true today. We made it clear that funding for additional events was only available if it was used in the designated time slots. We would not fund outside speakers scheduled when their presentations would disrupt classes. We also faced the fact that a couple of the teaching faculty were competing for leadership of the student group by advocating for more disruptive actions, just as some do today. Only American faculty joined that competition. Other faculty, among them Stuart Hall, appealed for help in resisting demands to cancel their classes to "prove" their political commitment. As director, I agreed to cover additional faculty expenses if a prominent faculty member gave up that demand. We often confront a similar political dynamic today. Thus proposals to take practical steps to promote Palestinian freedom and well-being meet with disdain because they lack the appeal of symbolic action.

If you don't want anti-Zionist actions to compromise educational rights and opportunities, you have to be prepared to counter political manipulation. I learned that lesson in 1983. In the end, we held a weekend teach-in on Israel, with the schedule being set entirely by the anti-Zionist constituency. But the regular classes went on uninterrupted. I wanted to honor the anti-Zionist group's academic freedom, but not their lust for coercion. Today we face still more destructive anti-Zionist and antisemitic tactics, including targeted personal aggression, character assassination, and challenges to academic freedom and institutional integrity. Such tactics must have consequences. Political conviction does not warrant tolerance for ad hominem violations of academic standards. Faculty and administrative cowardice is the predictable response to political intimidation, but people must find the backbone to resist.

Documentation of highly personal antisemitic assaults in the academy since 2000 is now quite extensive, ranging from news reports to detailed academic studies. Both students and faculty have been targets. You can read their stories in scholarly research, the most important resources including collections coedited by Doron Ben-Atar, Corinne Blackmer, and Andrew Pessin—*Anti-Zionism on Campus* (2018) and, most recently, *Poisoning the Wells* (2021), along with Richard Landes's *Salem on the Thames* (2020). As these books demonstrate, administrators are often willing to investigate manufactured complaints against Zionist faculty, complaints that are fundamentally antisemitic. Both the hate campaigns and the investigations can go on for many months, turning the lives of campus Zionists into nightmares. Colleagues turn against each other in the process. Moreover, even when the accusations are proven to be fabricated and complainants are shown to have lied, there are rarely any negative consequences for those who organize these campaigns. When demonization campaigns are organized against students, like Rose Ritch at the University of Southern California, administrators express their regret but typically take no meaningful action.[3]

There is another historical lesson applicable to the present scene. When I became involved in public debates about Israel in the 2006–2007 academic year, they seemed to be only about Israeli history and policy. But those of us allied with Zionism were actually defending Israel's right to exist. Over the years, the fact that the BDS movement sought to eliminate Israel, not merely reform its

---

3   For details, see Ritch (2020).

policies, became increasingly clear. That made contesting claims about the historical record and correcting factual errors a priority. But by 2014, as positions increasingly hardened, that was a project with limited returns. Anti-Zionists were again unwilling to agree about facts when performative gratifications and symbolic victories were really at issue.

The arguments that proved most successful, indeed sometimes the only ones that made a difference, addressed matters of principle and avoided engaging with the Israeli-Palestinian conflict directly. Faced, for example, with the demand for an academic boycott, members of the Modern Language Association and the American Historical Association, as well as faculty in other professional groups, have prioritized the principle that such boycotts undermine the open exchange of people and ideas across national borders, a central tenet of academic freedom. Those devoted to a symbolic anti-Israel victory are typically unmoved, but those on the fence about Israel can sometimes be reached. From the vantage point of more cynical realism, one may conclude that those on the fence prefer to preserve their ignorance about the conflict, rather than combining their defense of principle with an understanding of Israeli history. But if that is the reality, we have to deal with it. Unfortunately, as in politics generally, the number of people who are undecided about Israel has dwindled. Polarization over the Israeli-Palestinian conflict preceded the wider phenomenon, but comprehensive political polarization now also empowers opinion about Israel. We have come to expect hardened views on all fronts.

Symbolic victories play a significant role in the battle for hearts and minds, a battle that we realized by 2015 was at the heart of debates over Israel in the West—for Britain, Canada, Europe, and the United States. What we did not quite see then was that anti-Zionist activism could do both immediate damage to individuals and long-term damage to the institutions of the West. An additional nine years of struggle has made that clear. Numerous efforts to disrupt duly invited Israeli speakers or actually prevent them from speaking gradually convinced some that long-term damage to academic freedom was underway. Of course, interruptions of speakers are time-specific events, so once the occasion passes supporters of Israel can convince themselves that things have returned to normal. That remains the case even though cancelling Israeli speakers is part of the ongoing, comprehensive BDS anti-normalization campaign.

Student government debates over boycott and divestment resolutions also seem to pass, though in two different ways. A number of those debates have resulted in the defeat of the resolutions. Even when they pass, administrators have indicated they will not honor them. They are not going to give students power over endowments. They are not going to cancel research collaborations with Israeli faculty and their institutions. They are not going to close study abroad programs. Unfortunately, a toxic campus atmosphere over Israel will dissuade some faculty and administrators from initiating new or expanded programs. That toxic climate makes Jewish students feel unwelcome on campus. Meanwhile, these campus conflicts do win hearts and minds. Some carry anti-Zionism into their professional careers. And we have examples of student or faculty anti-Zionist resolutions being defeated one year only to return the next and sometimes over and over again, resolutions at the University of Michigan and the Modern Language Association being prime repeat examples.

A major countermove came when numerous campuses adopted the 2016 International Holocaust Remembrance Alliance (IHRA) Working Definition of Antisemitism, a subject I discuss in Chapter One and in this book's final chapters. As additional nations, campuses, and other groups consider adopting the IHRA Definition, we are likely to see it continue to be intensely debated. I offer here my model text to accompany the adoption of the IHRA Definition. The debates and applications covered in what follows can be read in its light. Some of the controversy surrounding the IHRA Definition, especially regarding the risk of its abuse as outlined by its opponents, could be addressed by a clear statement defining why it is being adopted and limiting how it will be used:

> The university formally adopts the IHRA Working Definition of Antisemitism as its official guide to identifying, analyzing, and combatting examples of antisemitic speech and action. In doing so, we endorse the Definition's important qualification that full understanding of potentially antisemitic statements requires an account of the context in which they were made. That will often require knowledge of the long history of what has been called "the longest hatred," its strategies, metaphors, consequences, and contemporary manifestations. We also join with the International Holocaust Remembrance Alliance in specifying that the Definition is a "non-legally binding" document. Thus it will not be used on campus as a quasi-legal invitation to disciplinary proceedings against students, staff, or faculty. Nor will it be used to justify cancelling events arranged by student or faculty groups. However, we believe its eleven examples provide an extremely helpful guide to

the main forms of contemporary antisemitism and thus offer substantial assistance in understanding their growing presence both here and abroad. The goal of the working definition is not to shut down conversations but rather to illuminate them with understanding. The definition cannot be used to prevent antisemitic speech from occurring, but it can be used to help reach consensus about which statements merit condemnation. That will help alert us to broader patterns of antisemitic speech that require a coordinated response.

Meanwhile, ignorance about the nature of contemporary antisemitism continues to be widespread, and the IHRA Definition's examples give people ways to provisionally identify and categorize antisemitic acts and statements. They also provide a starting point for analyzing the complex versions of antisemitism that appear in some faculty publications, where antisemitic statements may be embedded in elaborate arguments and pages of false evidence. Without detailed analysis, this can be quite confusing. Faculty publications, moreover, are layered atop the great variety of antisemitic incidents, accusations, and purported evidence people confront throughout the culture.

The IHRA Definition is frequently misrepresented not only by BDS but also by members of the Jewish community who consider themselves sympathetic to Israel. Nonetheless, organizing to support the adoption of the Definition is a major way to install long-term education about antisemitism on campus. Falsifications of the Definition belong to the category of statements that are repeated no matter how many times they are disproven. This is a characteristic of antisemitism that has been around for thousands of years. Lies get repeated over and over again. I continue to be astonished that faculty members can publish books and essays that invent false claims about Israel. If you call them out by publishing the proof that they are lying, it has no effect. Their anti-Zionist and antisemitic colleagues will praise them and reward them for being courageous and original. In his essay "Apartheid / ~~Apartheid~~ / [   ]," UCLA English professor Sari Makdisi (2018) claimed that Bedouins in the Israeli town of Arab al' Na'im (near Haifa) live in tin shacks. I visited the town, met Bedouin residents, and photographed their masonry homes, then published the photos in *Israel Denial*. In the same essay, Makdisi said Israel has no laws guaranteeing equality for all citizens, so I quoted the laws and the court decisions reinforcing or in fact expanding them. In spite of this, he was subsequently named English department head at UCLA.

Documenting the antisemitic views and activities of faculty is nonetheless necessary and important work. It is not a form of harassment or a curtailment of speech rights. I think the role played by Canary Mission in creating profiles of faculty antisemitism, so long as they include links to the faculty member's publications, is both acceptable and useful. Conversely, both the Alliance for Academic Freedom and I condemn their practice of creating student profiles. It is inexcusably malicious to try to block BDS-allied students from all potential employment, including employment unrelated to Israel. Student views can change rapidly, and student activism can disappear after graduation, so it is irresponsible and unethical to call them out in a national public forum. Some students do become long-term opponents of Israel, but national debates about their individual politics should await their acquiring relevant professional responsibilities. Canary Mission should delete its existing student profiles and stop creating them.[4]

A more recent problem is with antisemitic statements by faculty on social media. For many years, key leaders of the American Association of University Professors (AAUP) took the position that public statements related to a person's areas of teaching and research—including tweets, Facebook posts, and contributions to all other online platforms—are part of their professional profile and can have professional consequences. The AAUP reversed that view in 2015 in its report on the Salaita case at the University of Illinois, in which it defended an antisemitic job candidate, in part by arguing that academic freedom protects all social media posts from evaluation or professional consequences (AAUP 2015a). This means that historians can engage in Holocaust denial on Facebook but cannot face sanctions unless they do so in class or in scholarship. As I detail in Chapter Two, "Social Media, Anti-Zionism, and the End of Academic Freedom," I believe that is absurd. There are contexts in which public statements can be included in professional evaluations. Job candidates, for example, can be rejected if they have public histories of racist or antisemitic statements on social media. In the first chapter of this book, "Does Academic Freedom Protect Antisemitism?," and well as in Chapter Two, I argue that online antisemitic statements by both job applicants and candidates for tenure should be considered part of their professional file if those statements fall within their areas of teaching or research. As will become clear in Chapter Two, the new world inaugurated by social media has made the cultural context immensely more perilous for all of us.

---

4   The problem is not solved by tracking changes in students' views. See Alliance for Academic Freedom (2016).

We have to fight back against the AAUP's misguided position, which is fueled by the anti-Zionism of some AAUP staff and leaders. Anti-Zionism in academia has escalated in recent years and is certain to increase still further. Online antisemitism has been surging for several years. The AAUP has now provided a protected online space for academic antisemites to disseminate their hatred. That is not a problem for higher education alone, as the academy is a source of antisemitism throughout Western culture. Moreover, faculty members' online presence is generally far more visible than anything else they do.

We do not have to tolerate an antisemitic climate on campus. Because of the assistance it offers in evaluating and categorizing statements and actions, the IHRA Definition has helped people recognize that an apparently isolated series of campus incidents might actually represent a pattern of antisemitic behavior and a pervasive bias. Prior to the adoption of the Definition, assaults on individuals that crossed a line between anti-Zionist debate and anti-Jewish verbal assault were often treated as exceptional behavior and denied their status as evidence of a broader antisemitic bias. On a few campuses at least, there is growing recognition that a pattern of antisemitic aggression represents not simply the collateral effects of anti-Zionism but something more pernicious, the corruption of fundamental community standards. The Louis D. Brandeis Center for Human Rights Under Law initiated a student complaint against my own campus, the University of Illinois at Urbana-Champaign in 2020, based on a collection of documented incidents.[5]

Here are ten examples of conduct that merit being studied together, evaluated for antisemitic effects, and considered worthy of a collective response. Many are faculty activities, but some can be carried out by students as well:

1. organizing character assaults on or harassment of individual students, faculty, or staff;
2. organizing campus-wide campaigns to condemn Israel through boycott or divestment resolutions;
3. promoting antisemitic beliefs and theories in the classroom;
4. pursuing pseudo-research embodying antisemitic tropes;
5. intentionally hiring antisemitic faculty;
6. defunding pro-Zionist student groups;
7. carrying out antisemitic property damage, such as scrawling swastikas on buildings;
8. distributing antisemitic literature on campus;

---

5   See Louis D. Brandeis Center (2020).

9. scheduling antisemitic speakers; and
10. constructing antisemitic public structures, such as apartheid walls.

Some of these tactics are or should be prohibited. Others are protected by academic freedom or, in the United States, by the First Amendment to the US Constitution, but all can contribute toward the creation of a hostile climate.

The combination of many or all of these instances of antisemitism creates a hostile campus environment for members of the Jewish community. One-off events like bringing a Zionist speaker to campus will not suffice to counteract such a hostile climate. A pattern of antisemitism requires a substantial long-term commitment in response. That can mean hiring faculty willing to teach more historically responsible courses. Condemnations of antisemitism play an important role, but they are not a sufficient means of education.

As I report in detail in Chapter One, a major escalation and turning point in campus antisemitism took place in May 2021, immediately after Israel's war with Hamas in Gaza. Over one hundred academic departments in Britain, Canada, the United States, and elsewhere, led by Women's Studies and Gender Studies programs indifferent to Hamas's views on women's rights, signed statements demonizing Israel and claiming academic unit endorsement for comprehensive programmatic opposition to the Jewish state (Palestinian Feminist Collective 2021). There was nothing ephemeral about these declarations. They encouraged anti-Zionist teaching and research that had no expiration date. Prominent university programs endorsing this statement included those at or in Berkeley, Chicago, Duke, London, Ottawa, Stanford, Texas, Toronto, UCLA, Virginia, and Yale.

As time passes and faculty and students begin to act on such declarations, matters will get worse. The expectation that "this too shall pass" has expired. We are in new territory, as academic departments set about institutionalizing anti-Zionism and antisemitism. We can safely assume that some departments believe that they now have a moral right to make admissions decisions using anti-Zionist litmus tests. Faculty will increasingly feel that political and ethical anti-Zionism is a professionally approved teaching principle. Fellowship and sabbatical applications, along with requests for research funding, will meet the same tests. Is there any chance that departments will ignore the values embedded in their anti-Zionist statement of principle when they assign merit to people and projects? In 2022, the City University of New York (CUNY) School of Law became the first higher-level academic unit (above departments) to adopt an anti-Zionist program. There is a need for faculty senates to consider adopting policies directed against academic unit politicization. Here is a sample of such a draft policy:

> The university/college prohibits academic departments, programs, and other administrative units from issuing collective statements on contested political topics. Of special concern are issues about which not only the country but also many college campuses are deeply divided. This policy is designed to protect the right of individual faculty members and voluntary faculty groups to issue such statements without the coercive effect produced by formal department endorsement of one political perspective. The right of individual faculty and voluntary faculty groups to express political opinions is guaranteed by academic freedom. Faculty should continue to fulfil their important role of advising both legislatures and the general public about matters of public policy related to their academic missions. However, administrative units do not possess the same freedom to address contested topics in their official capacity. This policy also guards against the possibility that members of the public will conclude that administrative unit statements on contested political topics represent the view of the institution as a whole. Disclaimers included with such political statements will prevent neither of these consequences.

In a fall 2021 letter to the chair of the Academic Freedom Committee of the senate of the University of Illinois at Urbana-Champaign, my colleague law professor Richard Ross succinctly demolished the unwarranted confidence in the power of pro forma disclaimers:

> Allowing political advocacy behind a disclaimer provides protective cover that encourages continued action of this type. Disclaimers do not convince instructors and students that a department's political commitment expressed on its website is anything other than a political commitment to be defied at one's peril. Moreover, it makes no sense for a department to say that it is "not speaking for the institution." Faculty commit a department to their favored opinions precisely in order to put an institution behind their personal politics. Making the

department as an institution speak is the whole point of the exercise.[6]

Developments like the aforementioned May 2021 statements are only partly about Israel. They are also part of an organized attack on the academy. To a significant degree, this is about where BDS is now, fostering a mounting assault on academic principles that will also deliver programmatic anti-Zionism, that is to say, antisemitism built into department missions worldwide. Outside the academy too, assaults on Western institutions often predominate over direct attacks on Israel, though there the potential for political damage is also real. The bottom line is that the struggle against anti-Zionism must be a dual struggle. We need to combine defending the Jewish state with determination to preserve the integrity of the institutions in which we live and work. In a Western country, you can no longer do one effectively without the other.

My book *Israel Denial* focuses specifically on the content of anti-Zionist teaching and research. In *Hate Speech and Academic Freedom*, my attention shifts to the damage that anti-Zionism and antisemitism do to people and institutions. As Yehuda Kurtzer (2022) pointed out at a November 2022 conference, the battle between BDS and its opponents has more to do with the identities of those in the West than it does with the Israeli-Palestinian conflict. At stake throughout this book are the nature, limits, and misrepresentation of academic freedom within our politically divided campuses. The book opens with a pair of chapters that address the basic problems of defining and applying academic freedom when the humanities and interpretive social sciences are widely riven by politics. The hard science departments have so far escaped political schism, though they need to think about developments elsewhere on campus. I track one disappointing example of politically compromised academic debate regarding Israel in the chapter on the "Word Crimes" controversy, a case that suggests that, at least in the near term, the prospects for rational academic debate about Israel and the Israeli-Palestinian conflict are dim. "Is BDS Antisemitic?" attempts to provide a concise answer to one of the most contested issues in the politicized academy.

My focus on issues of principle results in chapters that discuss urgent matters not addressed in detail by other scholars. This is apparent from the outset in the opening chapters, the first of which asks a question—"Does

---

6 Ross's letter is unpublished. It was distributed on campus by email and is quoted with permission.

Academic Freedom Protect Antisemitism?"—that should have already been the subject of discussion and debate. The second chapter also addresses a critical issue where adequate debate is lacking, namely the professional status of online remarks by faculty members. The chapter comparing secular and religious anti-Zionism considers a topic where comparisons are almost nonexistent, examining a fundamental institutionalized divide that is usually ignored. The chapter on Valentina Azarova, which offers a close reading of one faculty member's research, does so in order to answer an urgent institutional question—should a university hire a career anti-Zionist to administer an academic program?—on which detailed discussion cannot be found.

The Azarova chapter sets a standard for reviewing the publications of a finalist for a faculty position that is not currently met by any university I know of. Publication reviews for internal tenure candidates are also unacceptably brief. Indeed, universities typically set page limits for tenure files that would make it impossible to submit a review of the kind I have conducted, though nothing prevents a department from performing a thorough written review to inform its own decision making. Tenure or appointment papers amount to brief summaries interspersed with praise from outside evaluators. For politically compromised humanities disciplines, the resulting document may well be altogether unreliable. Such departments require a higher standard.

That standard begins with honoring the basic research principles that should apply in all faculty evaluations. In *It's Not Free Speech*, Michael Bérubé and Jennifer Ruth ask whether tenure "necessarily protects misinformation, discriminatory distortions of the historical record, and claims made with complete disregard for, or reflexive dismissal of, a settled body of knowledge built on well-documented scholarship and research" (Bérubé and Ruth 2022, 6). But the problem begins long before tenure; it is grounded in politically based hiring and tenure decisions, most broadly in those disciplines where anti-Zionism and antisemitism are now so thoroughly baked in that they represent unquestioned truths.

The issues and conflicts this book addresses frequently cross international boundaries. To reinforce that awareness, I have included representative case studies from several countries. There are examples from the United States throughout, as well as a chapter about University College London and another about the University of Toronto. In another chapter, I compare the legal context for hate speech and academic freedom in Britain, Canada, and the United States. Yet another chapter takes note of developments in religious anti-Zionism in both Britain and the United States. A full review of the international academic scene would be a project for another book and for multiple contributors, but this book at least brings several countries into view, thereby reminding readers that the strategies available for addressing these challenges can differ from country to country. Nevertheless, the misrepresentation and instrumentalization of academic freedom in the service of anti-Zionism and antisemitism merits increased attention and action wherever it appears. *Hate Speech and Academic Freedom* aims to contribute to both.

Chapter 1

Does Academic Freedom Protect Antisemitism?

Introduction: anti-Zionist and antisemitic research and teaching

> Genuine boldness and thoroughness of inquiry, and freedom of speech, are scarcely reconcilable with the prescribed inculcation of a particular opinion upon a controverted question.
>
> AAUP, "1915 Declaration of Principles on Academic Freedom and Academic Tenure"[1]

The most troubling and potentially destructive anti-Zionist or antisemitic conflicts on campus are generally those that cause the most distress and receive the most widespread publicity. Those incidents include controversial social media posts by faculty members; student government, faculty, and union debates over academic boycott and divestment resolutions; and group assaults on the integrity of individual Jewish students and faculty. Antisemitic assaults on individuals are and should be especially disturbing. All three categories of events are shaped by two sources of campus conviction and ideology that receive almost no public

---

1   Unless otherwise specified, all quotations from American Association of University Professors (AAUP) documents are taken from AAUP (2015b).

attention: the views promoted in anti-Zionist classrooms and the content of anti-Zionist faculty publications. Both can cross the line into antisemitism, yet both are routinely protected by academic freedom.

Meanwhile, the growth of social media blurs the difference between academic publication and extramural or public speech, speech that faculty members offer in their capacity as citizens. Publications are now shared on the internet and on Facebook; concise position statements in areas of a faculty member's professional expertise are disseminated publicly as tweets or threads and can reach far larger audiences than academic publications ever do. Even classroom assignments and observations can be circulated electronically, regardless of whether the professors prefer to see them shared only among their students.

In separate sections below, I discuss two cases of faculty anti-Zionism or antisemitism; the phenomenon of pervasively anti-Zionist academic disciplines and their role in teaching and research; the distinction between advocacy and indoctrination; and, in the final section, how professional standards influence the search for the truth. So far as I know, no one has yet directly addressed the troubling question at the center of this book: does academic freedom protect antisemitism? This is one of a cluster of interrelated questions, some of which have been subjects of continuing debate.

In April 2019, Hebrew University business professor Yaacov Bergman published an essay in the Hebrew-language edition of the Israeli newspaper *Haaretz*. The essay's title can be translated as "Does academic freedom allow the spreading of blood libels?" Bergman's essay was written in response to a lecture that Hebrew University social work professor Nadera Shalhoub-Kevorkian had presented at Columbia University. In the lecture, she claimed that Israel tests weapons systems on Palestinian children. In his essay, Bergman argues that her allegation belongs in the long tradition of blood libels. While Shalhoub-Kevorkian's claim is antisemitic, Bergman concentrates on whether the fact that it is false is a reason that she should be sanctioned by the university. Like other anti-Israel libels, it has the potential to encourage retaliatory violence against Jews. I would argue that it qualifies as hate speech. After first discounting her remarks as merely representing her opinion, the university's president and rector later labeled them baseless but protected by academic freedom.

A recent American case also raises the question of whether academic freedom protects the right to make false statements that have the potential to encourage physical harm. In 2020, Hoover Institution health policy fellow (and former chief of neurobiology at Stanford) Scott W. Atlas was serving as a White House coronavirus task force member. After he had repeatedly advised people to reject the medically recommended practices for protecting themselves from infection, Stanford's Faculty Senate condemned him. The resolution cited him for "discouraging the use of masks and other protective measures, misrepresenting knowledge and opinion regarding the management of pandemics, endangering citizens and public officials, showing disdain for established medical knowledge and damaging Stanford's reputation and academic standing" (Chesley 2020). The resolution specifically condemned Atlas's tweet urging the people of Michigan to "rise up" and combat their governor's anti-COVID health measures (LeBlanc and Diamond 2020). There is good reason to believe Atlas helped contribute to the deaths of thousands of people who failed to follow medical advice. Nonetheless, some faculty members were convinced the Senate had compromised his academic freedom.

These examples intersect in some ways with the question this chapter addresses, namely whether academic freedom protects antisemitism. While only the first example implicates antisemitism, both raise the general issue of whether promoting falsehoods should have professional consequences. Shalhoub-Kevorkian's lecture can lead us to consider whether campuses should hold faculty members harmless for expressions of hatred or racism that enjoy First Amendment protection. It also suggests that faculty antisemitism merits related consideration. But recent faculty antisemitism has a distinctive history and distinctive effects. All hate speech that can encourage violent action merits institutional attention, but each example requires contextualization within its history and present manifestation.

This chapter explores the problem of faculty antisemitism through a sequence of interconnected topics. Debate about one would be hampered by a lack of knowledge about the others:

1. The comparative legal and professional context for faculty speech;
2. Jasbir Puar, Rabab Abdulhadi, and faculty antisemitism;
3. When academic disciplines embrace anti-zionism;
4. When disciplinary politicization escalates;
5. The challenge of personnel decisions;
6. Advocacy versus indoctrination; and
7. Professional standards and the quest for the truth.

1. The comparative legal and professional context for faculty speech

In the next chapter, I will discuss what I consider to be the misguided position that the American Association of University Professors (AAUP) has taken about faculty statements on social media platforms, insisting that even online statements within a faculty member's areas of expertise are immune from professional evaluation and consequences. Here and elsewhere in the book I will take issue with other recent AAUP actions. For definitions of academic freedom, I nonetheless rely on the statements and investigative reports the AAUP has issued since 1915. I served as president of the AAUP from 2006 to 2012, completing 20 years in the organization's elected leadership. No other organization has a comparable record for defining and applying academic freedom. The AAUP's work has substantially influenced definitions of academic freedom worldwide, though autocratic governments often pay it lip service without honoring its principles. Europeans may prefer to cite UNESCO's detailed Recommendation concerning the Status of Higher-Education Teaching Personnel (1997). Its core goal of protecting the freedom of faculty to teach and to conduct and disseminate research parallels the aims of the AAUP principles.

But neither the AAUP's nor UNESCO's influence on contemporary views is absolute. Like it or not, we are now in the cultural context Edward Said described some years ago, when he argued that "each community of academics, intellectuals, and students must wrestle with the problem of what academic freedom in that society at that time actually is and should be" (Said 1996, 216). Despite being grounded in a basic commitment to faculty freedom in teaching and research, definitions of academic freedom are now a site of cultural struggle. I take up a number of those battles in this book. Nonetheless, I believe Said's embrace of cultural relativism about academic freedom is dangerous and should be resisted.

The legal framework for academic freedom varies across the world and limits or expands it in ways that are not universal. Sixteen European countries, along with Israel, have laws against Holocaust denial. Some countries have wider prohibitions against genocide denial. A majority of developed democracies worldwide ban hate speech, with broad application to antisemitism. Yet the utility of these laws has been substantially curtailed by the evolution of online hate. Holocaust denial is rampant on Telegram, a multi-platform encrypted messaging service that protects the anonymity of its 700 million monthly users. Holocaust denial, antisemitism, and hate speech proliferate on the dark web. As Lev Topor writes, "the illegality of certain manifestations such as Holocaust denial is, in fact, almost useless by now" (Topor 2023, 7).

After a summary of hate speech law in Canada, I will use Britain—specifically England and Wales—to represent the general willingness across Europe to limit free speech and academic freedom in order to discourage hate speech, racism, and (at least in principle) antisemitism. The United States has proven notably less willing to limit speech for these or other purposes because of its

First Amendment guarantees. Yet there are growing efforts in the United States to challenge campus speech that creates demonstrably hostile environments for Jewish students and call for remedies under the law.[2] The corrosive effects of hate speech disseminated on social media, addressed in the next chapter, may lead to other changes in the law. The legal status of academic freedom in the United States remains unresolved, since the Supreme Court has never ruled on the matter.[3] When academics worldwide object to limits on antisemitic speech or action, they typically invoke an absolutist version of academic freedom, unencumbered by responsibilities, that does not in principle obtain even in the United States.

Matters are different in Canada. In the United States, the First Amendment has been prioritized to protect individual agency in speech from government restraint. The Canadian Charter of Rights and Freedoms (1982) also makes freedom of expression a fundamental right, but it allows for restrictions when words "are uttered with the express intent of inflicting harm on others—especially those belonging to minority groups" (Kang 2018, 5). Canada has developed an egalitarian-driven understanding of hate speech focused on its effects in the public sphere. This model is attentive not only to short-term psychological injury but also to the potential long-term damage to social relationships. Section 319 of Canada's Criminal Code makes public expression that incites hatred against an identifiable group of people a punishable offense. The Criminal Code also makes advocacy of genocide punishable by imprisonment.

"The Supreme Court of Canada has remained hypervigilant against the destructive power of hate speech to create and accumulate a corrosive socio-political environment" (Kang 2018, 6). Speech with such effects is "perceived as a menace to the collective moral fabric of Canadian society" (8). But the Court makes it clear that the relevant laws "require that a balancing act be performed between the objective of eradicating discrimination and the need to protect free expression," adding that only speech of an "ardent and extreme" character qualifies legally as hate speech. Speech that is merely "belittling or

---

2   For an overview of actions brought by the Louis D. Brandeis Center, see https://brandeis-center.com/resources/case-materials/.

3   There are some Supreme Court decisions that raise the possibility of regulating faculty speech, including *Garcetti* v. *Ceballos* from 2006, in which the majority ruled that when public employees speak "pursuant to their official duties, the employees are not speaking as citizens for First Amendment purposes, and the Constitution does not insulate their communications from employer discipline." The AAUP (2009) issued a detailed report on the case, which I participated in drafting, warning about the implications for public colleges and universities, though so far the danger has not been realized outside Florida.

affronts the dignity of a person" does not (Walker 2018). To offer a clear contrast: Canadian courts would not have matched the 1978 US court decision according to which a group of neo-Nazis could march through the Jewish community of Skokie, Illinois, wearing SS uniforms. In the United States, only the prospect of the march inciting or producing imminent lawless action could have forced its cancellation. The reasoning prevailing in Canada is worthy of reflection when universities in other countries, including the United States, think about the kind of communities they want to establish and the impact of faculty speech on social life more generally.

Anthony Julius (2022) writes that "the charge of hate speech ... should be one of last resort—when no other explanation makes sense," and that itself makes sense as a general cultural proposition. Indeed, there are casual forms of racism and antisemitism to which we should instead apply contempt. There are also subversive forms of racist rhetoric wielded against racism that are common in the arts. The charge of racism, however, justly applies to many of the academic practices criticized here.

Although the elements of campus life cited above can have powerful consequences, their different national legal contexts and the cultural assumptions they create will shape and limit how campuses respond. Yet the two less visible features of the campus environment—publications and pedagogy—can have serious impacts on a community regardless of what the national laws do or do not restrain. Neither in teaching nor in writing, however, should criticism of Israeli government policy be considered inherently anti-Zionist or antisemitic, a position mirrored in the IHRA Working Definition of Antisemitism. The anti-Zionism that matters here includes demonstrably false accusations against Israel, attacks on Israel that employ established antisemitic rhetoric and stereotypes, insistence that Israel was founded illegitimately, and demands that the Jewish state be eliminated. Less common in Western countries but deeply troubling are attributions of supposed Israeli wrongdoing to its purported Jewish "character."

Academic freedom includes the right of faculty to say that their own country lacks the moral legitimacy to sustain its existence. That is a test of academic freedom that many societies fail. Yet to claim that Israel is the only nation that categorically lacks moral legitimacy is fundamentally antisemitic—notably so, among other examples, for an American, given that the horrific scale and duration of the genocide against Native Americans and the equally horrific history and continuing legacy of slavery so thoroughly dwarf anything one can say about Israeli history as to make any moral comparison between the two countries unintelligible. To avoid a charge of antisemitism one must allow that Israel's moral legitimacy can be regained by changes in policy and status while it remains a Jewish state. Achievement of a two-state solution should be recognized as sufficient to resolve any questions about Israeli legitimacy. Offered as an immutable existential fact, an accusation of Israeli illegitimacy crosses the line into antisemitism. Often such categorical claims are tied to the founding of the country, suggesting its illegitimate character is irreparable and can only be addressed by elimination.

The more elaborate versions of these views in faculty publications help establish what people in individual disciplines or groups of related disciplines go on to internalize as verified truths and subsequently communicate to others, including students. Convictions in one discipline's body of research often spread to those of neighboring disciplines. Specialists in a given discipline or group of disciplines frequently influence what faculty members and the general public believe.

2. Jasbir Puar, Rabab Abdulhadi, and faculty antisemitism

Anti-Zionist pedagogy and pseudo-scholarship are routinely defended by claims they are protected by academic freedom, rather than by defending their content and arguments. When complaints about Rutgers University's women's studies professor Jasbir Puar's 2017 book *The Right to Maim* surfaced from both Duke university faculty and others, Duke University Press defended its decision to publish the book by invoking Puar's academic freedom. The book promotes a series of undocumented and unproven slanders against the Jewish state, slanders that I elaborately disprove in *Israel Denial*. Puar's right to express her views does not cover Duke's failure to fulfil its editorial responsibility to carry out careful fact-checking and apply professional standards that discourage the publication of outright falsehoods. Academic freedom protects the right of a faculty member to pursue opportunities for publication, but it is no guarantee that anyone will choose to publish what a faculty member writes. Nor does academic freedom confirm that what anyone writes is true.

Puar claims that Israel denies Palestinian children sufficient food and thereby intentionally stunts their growth. Palestinian health officials state that this is not the case. The UN and the World Health Organization state that it is not the case. All these authorities conclude that stunting is not a major problem either in Gaza or on the West Bank. And indeed Puar cites no scholarship, no medical reports, and no statistics to back up her claim. No matter. Some people want to believe it is true, so they do. She received an award from the National Women's Studies Association and was made head of graduate studies in her Rutgers program. As I document in considerable detail in *Israel Denial*, the evidence that refutes her claims is readily available online.

When career anti-Zionist professor Rabab Abdulhadi scheduled and internationally promoted a September 2020 "open classroom" Zoom event featuring terrorist airplane hijacker Leila Khaled,[4] president of San Francisco State University (SFSU) Lynn Mahoney disingenuously defended the event as an innocent effort to expose students to an alternative point of view, a practice protected by academic freedom: "An invitation to a public figure to speak to a class should not be construed as an endorsement of a point of view."[5] But Abdulhadi does endorse Leilah Khaled, celebrating her as a feminist heroine. "We really idolize somebody like Leila Khaled," Abdulhadi told her student newspaper, "somebody who actually stands up for herself, actually goes to a plane and hijacks it" (Ramirez 2020). Zoom cancelled the event, citing the law against providing aid to terrorists, leading some to object and argue falsely that even a private company like Zoom was bound to honor academic freedom. The event was titled "Whose Narratives? Gender, Justice, and Resistance: A Conversation with Leila Khaled" and featured additional speakers who had participated in "revolutionary violence."[6] Except for Khaled's participation, this event was typical of other anti-Zionist events Abdulhadi and her colleagues regularly organize.

Mahoney addressed the Zoom cancellation in detail in an open letter of September 23, 2020, saying that while "we disagree with, and are disappointed

---

4 Khaled was part of a team from the terrorist Popular Front for the Liberation of Palestine (PFLP) that hijacked TWA Flight 840 en route from Rome to Tel Aviv on August 29, 1969. The flight was diverted to Damascus. After the passengers were allowed to disembark, the front of the plane was blown up. The following year, Khaled and a PFLP accomplice attempted to hijack El Al Flight 219 from Amsterdam to New York. Her accomplice was shot after a flight attendant was wounded and Khaled was overpowered. Given that Khaled has personally described her participation in both hijackings, it is absurd that some allies describe her as an "alleged" hijacker.

5 "San Francisco State University President Stands Behind Terrorist Leila Khaled Speaking Appearance," *Forward*, September 3, 2020, https://forward.com/fast-forward/453867/san-francisco-state-university-president-stands-behind-terrorist-leila/.

6 In addition to Khaled, the participants were to be Laura Whitehorn, sentenced to fourteen years in prison for her involvement in a 1983 US Senate bombing; Sekou Odinga, sentenced to twenty-five years for his involvement in the prison escape of Assata Shakur and a Brinks armored car robbery; Rula Abu Duhou, a PFLP member who spent nine years in an Israeli prison after being convicted for participating in the Jerusalem murder of Yigal Shahaf, a civilian; and Ronnie Kasrils, active in uMkhonto we Sizwe (Spear of the Nation), the armed wing of the African National Congress (ANC) from its founding in 1961 until 1990. Whitehorn was active in the Weather Underground; Odinga was active in the Black Liberation Army.

by, Zoom's decision not to allow the event to proceed on its platform, we also recognize that Zoom is a private company that has the right to set its own terms of service in its contracts with users." Trying to strike a balance among competing constituencies, she added that "Zoom's cancelation of the event will be deeply wounding to some members of our community who will feel themselves and their dissent silenced once again, just as the participation of Leila Khaled in a class panel discussion is deeply wounding to others in our community. And many across the University and beyond may fear the further erosion of the rights of faculty and see this as damaging to the role of the university in a liberal society" (Mahoney 2020).

But in May 2022, when Mahoney referred to Zoom's action as "deplatforming," using the contemporary term of art (Mahoney 2022), that was too much for Abdulhadi: "President Mahoney's labeling of the censorship of Professor Kinukawa and myself, along with our international luminary guests, as 'deplatforming,' is telling. It betrays President Mahoney's mindset and her political and ideological Islamophobic, anti-Arab, and anti-Palestinian bias, which she probably views as business-as-usual in everyday administrative politics." Deplatforming, she explained, is "a term that has been repeatedly employed by Israel lobby groups and their right-wing and white supremacist allies—to camouflage the silencing, bullying, and big private tech veto over the content of our classroom." This stream of invective came in an open letter by Abdulhadi published by *Mondoweiss* (2022) on September 12, 2022. By then, Abdulhadi's demands went beyond calling for Mahoney's resignation. She wanted two new tenure-track faculty appointments in her program, with her position as search committee chair confirmed. We can assume that anti-Zionism would be an unwritten requirement for the job.

After the 2020 cancellation, Zoom announced it would honor universities' own decisions about which events to allow, which represents a preferable position. Universities must assume responsibility for their own houses. The Khaled webinar was rescheduled for April 2021, but Zoom cancelled it, again citing the law making it a crime to knowingly give material support to a terrorist group. This time the University of California's Humanities Research Institute was added to the webinar's cosponsors. The Institute's long-term director David Theo Goldberg also has a long record of anti-Zionism.[7]

Khaled is an unrepentant terrorist. She remains active in the Popular Front for the Liberation of Palestine (PFLP), a designated terrorist group revived and newly funded by Iran since at least 2013 (Spyer 2020). Khaled is thus barred from

---

7   See, for example, Rossman-Benjamin (2009).

entering the United States. Founded in 1967 by George Habash, the PFLP was for years the second-largest group within the Palestine Liberation Organization (PLO). For a time, the PFLP seemed a diminished relic of the Cold War, but Iranian support has revived it and enabled it to recruit new members to its West Bank network. Iran formed an alliance with the PFLP because the group consistently supported Syrian president Bashar al-Assad during the Syrian civil war. Unlike some other terrorist groups, the PFLP makes no pretense of separating its military and political wings. Although the PFLP remains strongly committed to violence, Khaled assures us that it no longer carries out suicide bombings.

From a US perspective, academic freedom would allow the SFSU Zoom event to proceed, with people free to condemn it both beforehand and afterward. Despite claims to the contrary, condemnation of an event is not equivalent its prohibition. Such condemnation does not violate academic freedom. The free speech principle prohibiting speech urging imminent violence likely does not apply to US audience members in this case, but it would justify Israel blocking access to the panel, on the grounds that "calls to action originating in one country turn into actual shooting sprees in another" (Topor 2023, 140). I cannot find academics in the United States who believe that the planned international audience for the Khaled panel placed an ethical burden on US sponsors to consider whether the panel would encourage international violence. The crowded theater in which one might yell "fire" is now a global podium.

England's laws regarding academic freedom are different. In March 2018, the UK Parliament's Joint Committee on Human Rights (2018) published a document entitled "Free Speech: Guidance for Universities and Students Organising Events." This was an effort to gather together all the laws bearing on sponsored academic events. The document points out that sections of the 2000 Terrorism Act prohibit "incitement to commit acts of terrorism overseas," "inviting support for a proscribed organisation," and "encouragement of terrorism, including the unlawful glorification of the commission or preparation of terrorism, whether in the past, the future, or in general." Were the panel to be organized in England, these prohibitions could apply to both Khaled and Abdulhadi. On April 1, 2021, the UK Home Office published an updated version of its "Prevent Duty Guidance: For Higher Education Institutions in England and Wales" based on the 2015 Counterterrorism and Security Act: "when deciding whether or not to host a particular speaker RHEBs [relevant higher education bodies] should consider carefully whether the views being expressed, or likely to be expressed, constitute extremist views that risk drawing people into terrorism or are shared by terrorist groups. In these circumstances the event should not be allowed to proceed except where RHEBs are entirely convinced that such risk can be fully mitigated without cancellation of the event" (UK Home Office 2021). The mitigation must be "part of that same event, rather than a separate forum." That rule eliminates the standard US university strategy, which is to compensate with a balancing event sometime later. While including competing views within a given event is an honorable tradition, I oppose mandating it. The requirement would violate academic freedom.

The UK Public Order Act 1986 additionally bars "acts intended or likely to stir up hatred on grounds of race, religion, or sexual orientation." Racial hatred is defined as "hatred against a group of persons defined by reference to colour, race, nationality (including citizenship) or ethnic or national origins." British institutions must perform a risk assessment on these grounds, taking a speaker's prior acts and statements into account; they must also balance actions based on the risk assessment with the requirements of academic freedom and the obligation to guarantee freedom of speech. Because radical anti-Zionism transgresses the UK rules on several counts, the entire Khaled panel would be at risk of cancellation.

The SFSU College of Ethnic Studies' Arab and Muslim Ethnicities and Diasporas Program (AMED), the event's cosponsor, is hardly neutral about Zionism. Abdulhadi was AMED's founding director. In 2013, Khaled declared at a conference that armed struggle against Israel is the only route to Palestinian liberation.[8] In November 2013, AMED cosponsored the 6th Annual Palestinian Mural Celebration, where students used stencils to create placards and T-shirts boasting the image of a keffiyeh-clad Khaled holding an AK-47 rifle and the message "Resistance is not terrorism." Other stencils, all featured on Facebook, declared "My heroes have always killed colonizers."[9] However ignorant the students may have been about the significance of the slogans they were championing, the slogans certainly justified the murder of Israelis. These cheerful and self-congratulatory celebrations of terrorism create a hostile environment for Jewish and non-Jewish students, faculty, and staff. Moreover, this kind of mob embrace of menace is a tradition at SFSU. In February

8   See "Leila Khaled—Return and Liberation: Conference of the Palestinian Shatat," YouTube video, June 23, 2013, http://www.youtube.com/watch?v=vSfvBKGWDLk. In a 2014 interview, she said, "I would advise violence." See Paula Schmitt, "Interview with Leila Khaled: 'BDS Is Effective, But It Doesn't Liberate Land,'" +972 Magazine, May 17, 2014, https://www.972mag.com/interview-with-leila-khaled-bds-is-effective-but-it-doesnt-liberate-land/. In a 2016 interview, she stated, "I choose arms and I believe that taking up arms is one of the main tools to solve this [conflict]." See "[Interview] Meet Leila Khaled, the First Woman to Hijack a Plane," Euronews, June 30, 2016, https://www.euronews.com/2016/06/30/interview-meet-the-first-woman-to-hijack-a-plane.
9   For photographs of the stencils, see https://amchainitiative.org/wp-content/uploads/2020/09/Stencils-11.7.13.pdf.

2018, President Leslie Wong waffled on the issue of Zionists on campus, declining to say categorically that they were welcome. But public pressure led her to apologize and announce that "Zionists are welcome on our campus" (Waxman 2018). Abdulhadi condemned her: "I consider the statement below from President Wong, welcoming Zionists to campus, equating Jewishness with Zionism, and giving Hillel ownership of campus Jewishness, to be a declaration of war against Arabs, Muslims, Palestinians and all those who are committed to an indivisible sense of justice on and off campus."[10]

While Abdulhadi has the right to make an antisemitic statement about campus access, even though it violates academic freedom, anti-discrimination laws, and expectations for public institutions, it has to be condemned. Moreover, it indicates her comprehensive anti-Zionist bias, a bias that once again constitutes antisemitism. A state institution that barred Zionists from campus would be subject to severe sanctions in both England and the United States, even though, as I document in my book *Not in Kansas Anymore*, there are Palestinian institutions like Birzeit University that do exactly that. In the West, the only option for Abdulhadi and others who share her views is to make Zionists unwelcome once they arrive, though that too would run afoul of anti-discrimination laws.

SFSU has long proven itself adept at surrounding Jews with an atmosphere of intimidation. This dates back to the 1990s. As Tammi Rossman-Benjamin (2013) reports, in 1995 former student body president Troy Buckner-Nkrumah published an op-ed in *Golden-Gater*, the SFSU student newspaper, that declared "I do believe the only good Zionist is a dead Zionist, as I believe the only good Nazi is a dead Nazi, or the only good racist is a dead racist." In line with other provocations, the campus Pan-African Student Union in 1997 arranged a lecture by Khalid Muhammad, former national assistant to the Nation of Islam's leader Louis Farrakhan. His presentation, "Who Is Pimping the World?," included such passages as these:

> The practice of those freakish Rabbis [circumcision] is that they place their lips on the penis of these young boys and after they have cut the foreskin back, suck the blood from the head of the penis of their own young boys.

---

10 See reply of Rabab Abdulhadi to statement by Leslie E. Wong, February 23, 2018, posted by AMED Studies at SFSU, Facebook, February 23, 2018, https://www.facebook.com/AMEDStudies/posts/573870589632199.

> The white man is not only practicing racism and Zionism, and with the prostitution ring, the so-called Jew man with the Jew woman all over the world to make a few dollars, he is also practicing sexism. He's a racist, he's a Zionist, an imperialist. He's a no-good bastard. He's not *a* devil, the white man is *the* Devil.[11]

Although the combination of vulgarity and hostility here is appalling and exceptional, I still consider the lecture covered by academic freedom in the United States and would not prevent it from taking place. But such an event calls for significant counterprogramming and campus education. The Muhammad lecture represents moral depravity, not merely prejudice. Equal time spent opposing antisemitism would not suffice. A campus should aim to purge the community of such a presentation's hateful effects by mounting an extensive educational program on the history and contemporary manifestations of antisemitism. After detailing antisemitic remarks by Bristol University's David Miller, David Hirsh (2021b) argues that "a university which judges David Miller's freedom of speech to be a priority, also has a responsibility to employ genuine scholars of antisemitism and to fund scholarly journals of antisemitism in order to counter his conspiracy fantasy." The Muhammad statements are still more disturbing, magnified by their enraptured reception.

Significant legal responsibilities would apply as well. Section 149 of the UK Equality Act 2010 mandates that "a public authority must, in the exercise of its functions, have due regard to the need to—(a) eliminate discrimination, harassment, victimisation and any other conduct that is prohibited by or under this Act; (b) advance equality of opportunity between persons who share a relevant protected characteristic and persons who do not share it; (c) foster good relations between persons who share a relevant protected characteristic and persons who do not share it." The protected characteristics include race and religion or religious belief. Events that victimize, harass, or urge discrimination against Jews are not acceptable, nor are events that promote hatred between Jews and Muslims. The Muhammed lecture presents a severe challenge to free speech absolutists. The British requirement to "foster good relations" exists only as an occasional ideal in the United States, one explicitly rejected by the anti-Zionist anti-normalization agenda.

Although the general legal framework against racial and ethnic discrimination and harassment in Britain is robust, the laws provide no guidance to help identify specific forms of discrimination, whether antisemitic, Islamophobic, or

---

11 Quoted in Rossman-Benjamin (2013).

anti-Black, among others. Lesley Klaff (2019) documents several instances in which responsible officials rendered uninformed or biased judgments because they knew little or nothing about antisemitism. The IHRA Working Definition provides the initial guidance necessary to motivate further inquiry about anti-semitism. Colleges and universities can adopt the Definition's examples as an authorized guide to potentially verifiable forms of antisemitism without incor-porating it into disciplinary codes or declaring that it settles the character of individual statements without further analysis. A similar document addressing Islamophobia would be helpful and may be forthcoming. A general statement about racism would also be valuable, but it cannot replace the specific guidance the Definition offers.

The lack of such guidance too often means that a climate of antisemitism develops and receives reinforcement over time. Thus, over the years, other antisemitic SFSU campus events followed the Muhammed lecture. Consider "Genocide in the 21st Century" from 2002. A flyer promoting the event featured a dead baby as part of a soup can label. Framed with Israeli flags, it declared "Made in Israel—Palestinian Children Meat—Slaughtered According to Jewish Rites Under American License" (Rossman-Benjamin 2013, 497). The flyer revived the centuries-old blood libel that Jewish dietary laws entail the religious practice of murder; it made an appalling contribution to a hostile environment for Jewish students. Abdulhadi did not arrive until 2007, but she had a local tradition to sustain, one that would underwrite her own antisemitic initiatives. She would make herself an exceptional figure in US higher education, dedicating every feature of her campus work to hostility toward the Jewish state.

Despite this pattern of severe bias—or rather because of it—Abdulhadi received the 2020 Georgina M. Smith Award for "exceptional leadership" from the national AAUP. The award praised her for exemplifying "courage, persistence, political foresight" and for transcending "the division between scholarship and activism that encumbers traditional university life" and advancing "the agenda for social change in Palestine" (AAUP 2020). It is not clear that such a division between scholarship and activism any longer obtains throughout the humanities, but that division does not necessarily "encumber" those who choose to honor it. Abdulhadi did not "transcend" the division between scholarship and activism, a locution that suggests she ascended to a higher principle; she obliterated the distinction. The AAUP's award unasham-edly calls for the wholesale politicization of the academy. The organization thus endorsed the belief there is one transcendent cause, anti-Zionism, that actually warrants the transformation of the mission of higher education. It would be absurd to imagine the AAUP could honor Abdulhadi's activism and not its antisemitic objective. Reviewing the controversy over the Khaled webinar, Hank Reichman, the chair of the AAUP's Committee A on Academic Freedom and Tenure, described the PFLP as "a group deemed 'terrorist' by the U.S." (Reichman 2021b). How much mayhem would a terrorist group have to impose on Israel before an AAUP leader would remove the quotation marks from "terrorist"? It's not your grandparents' AAUP.

The Puar example represents publication, while the Abdulhadi example represents pedagogy. Academic freedom largely gives Puar the right to promote falsehoods in her publications, but it does not protect her or Duke University Press from professional criticism and consequences. The AAUP's 1994 "On the Relationship of Faculty Governance to Academic Freedom" explicitly states that "academic freedom does not protect plagiarism and deceit." Knowing dissemination of falsehoods in publications is professionally actionable (AAUP 2015b, 125). Yet it is possible Puar believes everything she says. She claims that Israelis are deliberately stunting the growth of Palestinian children. As suggested above, an internet search for health reports from the WHO, the UN, and the Palestinian Authority itself would have identified an international consensus that stunting is not a serious health problem either in Gaza or on the West Bank. Puar is unable to cite any medical authorities to support her assertion. International health authorities consider stunting a serious health problem when it affects 20 percent of young children. The average stunting rate in Gaza and the West Bank amounts to 7 percent. Rates in area nations during the same period include Algeria (11%), Kuwait (3%), Lebanon (12%), Libya (15%), Saudi Arabia (7%), Syria (23%), and Yemen (44%).[12] Puar's publisher should have pressed her to supply evidence or withdraw the claim. Reviews that identified errors and false claims might have led to the book being withdrawn, but that did not happen. I do not know of any academic publication that has been withdrawn over issues of anti-Zionism or antisemitism. None are listed in the Retraction Watch database.[13]

Given the politicization of the humanities, the only consequences Puar has faced so far are increased status and rewards. *The Right to Maim* received the 2018 Alison Piepmeier Book Prize from the National Women's Studies Association, the same group that in 2015 passed the most wide-ranging academic association boycott resolution against Israel, declaring Israel an

---

12 This is just a small sample of the stunting rates from health authorities documented in *Israel Denial*.

13 See http://retractiondatabase.org/RetractionSearch.aspx.

apartheid state within its pre-1967 borders and endorsing the BDS movement (Redden 2015). In theory, Abdulhadi could teach in such a way as to treat Zionist students with respect, welcoming their views in the classroom. But if a class is only assigned anti-Zionist books and essays, a Zionist student will have no shared resources to use in defending the Jewish state. Given the consistently anti-Zionist lineup of Abdulhadi's Zoom speakers, the event itself would likely have embodied unqualified hostility toward Israel and its allies. Zionist students participating worldwide by Zoom would not have felt tolerated; they might well have felt personally condemned. Abdulhadi is not simply an activist; she is a zealot. Her record demonstrates she does not observe the constraints on classroom advocacy that have guided the professoriate for more than a century.

Although criticism of Israel is commonplace and, in many cases, unobjectionable, the anti-Zionism that Puar and Abdulhadi embrace—which goes beyond routine or even harsh criticism to assert the illegitimacy of Jewish national identity or Israel's very existence—is a cover for antisemitism. Even when such statements are permitted by academic freedom, they deserve to be condemned. Nonetheless, many who advance anti-Zionist arguments do not recognize their antisemitic effects.[14] That both Puar and Abdulhadi are committed practitioners of antisemitism is apparent from both the ferocity of their politics and the literal falsehoods they promote. We do not need to look into their hearts and decide whether to call them antisemites. Their practices make their antisemitic impact clear. Similarly, their self-understanding, whatever it may be, is also irrelevant. Puar's anti-Zionist arguments are often strikingly idiosyncratic, amounting to hostile speculations presented as fact, among them the slander that Israelis harvest Palestinian organs. Moreover, both she and Abdulhadi, along with many other faculty members, often make statements that implicate the examples listed by the IHRA Definition. Although I discuss the IHRA Definition in detail in the final two chapters of this book, I want to point out that the IHRA examples are a good starting point for a more thorough discussion of the work of these two faculty members. Academic freedom allows Puar and Abdulhadi to make the claims they do, even if they are unwarranted, just as it gives me the freedom and the responsibility to criticize and condemn prejudice and false claims.

---

14 Bernard Harrison's *Blaming the Jews* (2020) goes beyond the definition of antisemitism as hatred of Jews to examine the body of theories that inform structural and ideological antisemitism.

3. When academic disciplines embrace anti-Zionism

The fields most vulnerable to wholesale anti-Zionist takeover are often those most recently given academic recognition. They often lack the guard rails established by history, methodology, and tradition. Their standards may be so thoroughly in flux that they are easily co-opted by a political mission, especially if they reject or disparage scholarly norms of evidence and documentation. I've been active in more than one of these emerging areas, enough so to value their immensely transformative achievements but also to shudder at the collective errors they can make, errors that can shape both teaching and research. Unfortunately, as we have found with the spread of anti-Zionism, a field in the grip of one illusion can gradually extricate itself just in time to fall prey to another.

Some relatively new disciplines, including women's studies and African-American studies, grew out of social movements informed by centuries of lived experience. Without those social movements there was no prospect of eliminating continuing discrimination against and assaults on the populations the movements represented. The need for social justice activism has not diminished. But some academic disciplines founded with a specific social mission have now embraced secondary social justice commitments where no lived experience, indeed little if any historical knowledge, underwrites their virtuous identification with the new cause. It should have been relatively easy to resist adopting causes with no disciplinary warrant. Instead, the slippery slope progression proved irresistible, and commitments migrated to issues where disciplinary ignorance reigned, and academic analysis was exchanged for political passion. Those supplemental social missions can function as unquestioned, unexamined truths, rather than as subjects of continuing reexamination and research. Foremost among the radical causes embraced in ignorance and disinformation is anti-Zionism. The disciplines entirely given over to anti-Zionism have found it easy to cross the line into antisemitism. Group solidarity focused on anti-Zionism easily turns into coerced conformity.

When a field has been thoroughly co-opted by a radical agenda, it ordinarily means that faculty members or students adopting the agenda will not be punished by their colleges or universities for doing so, though actions taken in support of such views could have consequences. This roughly parallels the US Constitution's First Amendment prohibition of state punishment for hate speech. Indeed, both the IHRA Definition's standards and widespread Jewish student and faculty experience confirm that the Definition's examples can represent instances of hate speech, though that judgment requires that actual instances be analyzed and contextualized. When the University of Michigan's John Cheney-Lippold refused to write one of his students a letter of recommendation to study at Tel Aviv University, telling her meanwhile he would write her a recommendation to any institution outside Israel, he was taking a discriminatory action in support of the American Studies Association boycott resolution. He violated widely recognized professional norms and was punished by the college dean (Kozlowski 2018). Colleagues in anti-Zionist fields across the country pledged to follow his lead. His case will be discussed in detail in Chapter Three.

AAUP leaders have long used the criterion of prevailing disciplinary consensus to decide whether certain views are protected from professional consequences by academic freedom. When disciplinary consensus doesn't exist or controversy dominates, one may look to the range of prevailing disciplinary opinion for guidance, though the principle of disciplinary consensus itself has been subject to continuing redefinition and debate. In its founding Declaration of Principles of 1915 and for decades thereafter, the AAUP saw religious and proprietary institutions and outside interference by politicians and business leaders as the major threats to academic freedom: "their purpose is not to advance knowledge by the unrestricted research and unfettered discussion of impartial investigators, but rather to subsidize the promotion of opinions, held by the persons, usually not of the scholar's calling, who provide the funds" (AAUP 2015b, 5). Those threats remain real, but today the practices of those supposedly "of the scholar's calling" are also at issue. Some faculty and their disciplines are dedicated to political activism aimed at imposing anti-Zionist narratives on colleagues and students alike. When scholars sharing a particular political agenda-driven mission so dominate a field that the agenda alone determines scholarly merit, the field functions as if it has been captured. The line between advancement of knowledge and promotion of political convictions has in some arenas been obliterated. The disciplinary pretense to objectivity then disappears.

As recently as Matthew Finkin and Robert Post's *For the Common Good* (2009), a book by two highly respected long-term members of the AAUP's Committee A on Academic Freedom and Tenure, followed by Post's *Democracy, Expertise, Academic Freedom* (2012), the disciplinary commitment to advance the "sum of human knowledge" seemed unshakable. Finkin and Post grounded their confidence in what they believed was a "commitment to the virtues of reason, fairness, and accuracy" (2009, 43). Such values formed the "framework of accepted professional norms that distinguish research that contributes to knowledge from research that does not" (54). They quote fellow Committee A member Joan Scott's unwarranted confidence that "disciplinary communities" protect "a place for criticism and critical transformation at the very heart of the conception of a discipline" (56) and former Committee A member historian David Hollinger's idealized assurance that "any particular disciplinary community exists within what we might see as a series of concentric circles of accountability" (57).

Finkin and Post trace their position to "John Dewey's observation that indoctrination consists in dogmatically promulgating '*as truth* ideas or opinions' that a discipline does not regard as dogmatically true" (84). They phrase their admonition accordingly: faculty should not "impose a '*truth*' of a matter as to which there is a dispute within the discipline" (86), a standard that no longer applies. They again quote Hollinger, who argues that we should judge a department's reliability in terms of "the fidelity of the department to the broad contours of the learned discipline it is charged with representing on a given campus" (100). Finkin and Post offer a concluding admonition: "Academic freedom obliges scholars to use disciplinary standards, not political standards, to guide their teaching" (104).

Yet they give no serious consideration to those disciplines whose standards have themselves become increasingly political. In the concluding pages of *Democracy, Expertise, Academic Freedom*, Post references "healthy disciplines" (2012, 97) but nowhere explores what the reverse might mean, other than suggesting that we might need to differentiate between those disciplinary practices that promote democratic competence and those that do not. Instead, throughout the book, he repeatedly and unreflectively tells us that disciplinary practices create expert knowledge. Since these people published their work before the serious problem with politicized teaching about Israel was widely recognized, I do not fault them for their views. I merely point out that *For the Common Good* and its sources no longer offer an adequate guide to politicized teaching and research or to the principles that motivate some disciplines. The confidence exuded by Finkin and Post and those they cite is no longer warranted. Hollinger's concentric circles of accountability have dissolved. A department's fidelity to an academic discipline can now demonstrate its intellectual bankruptcy.[15] Anthony Julius (2022) asks what the consequences should be if faculty "violate the discursive norms of their disciplines" but does not consider

---

15 Disciplines can be compromised when they are captured by a specific methodological approach. Political science has been diminished by the hegemony of "rational choice" theory. History is suffering from the marginalization of military, diplomatic, and "high" political history.

what should be done if antisemitic anti-Zionism is one of those disciplinary norms. Similarly, Liviu Matei and Shitij Kapur (2022), writing about British legislation, point out that academic freedom entails "the obligation to abide by disciplinary standards of rigour," a principle with both tragic and absurdist implications when contemplating contemporary academic disciplines. "The nature of disciplinary expertise," writes UC Davis law professor Brian Soucek (2022), "is to put some ideas beyond the pale." Well, yes, like the idea that the earth is flat, but not ideas grounded in political groupthink or in disinformation that the discipline embraces.

Yet faith in disciplinary consensus persists. Former Committee A member Michael Bérubé invoked it in a 2021 interview with Mark Dery about conspiracy theorist and NYU faculty member Mark Crispin Miller. Miller endorses the vicious and fundamentally immoral claim that the 2012 Sandy Hook Elementary School shooting in Connecticut was faked, defending himself by invoking both his free speech rights and academic freedom. According to Bérubé, "the real problem is Miller's disdain for the epistemological norms of his discipline" (Dery 2021). But the norms that discredit Miller's conspiracy theories are not discipline-specific. They are general norms for distinguishing between true and false statements. Miller works in media studies and communications. Would academic freedom apply if the field of communications reached consensus and endorsed several lunatic conspiracy theories? Should all communications faculty consequently be held harmless for holding those views? Is the unsupportable claim that Israel is committing genocide in Gaza, common in some disciplines, superior to, more accurate than, the delusional views Miller holds?

Bérubé's confidence in disciplinary norms continues in *It's Not Free Speech* (2022), coauthored with Jennifer Ruth, in which they urge the establishment of campus-level academic freedom committees that would judge faculty members accused of white supremacy, a claim that anti-Zionists frequently lodge against Israel and its faculty defenders. The campus committee would be charged with "evaluating competence in standard disciplinary terms" (Bérubé and Ruth 2022, 241). They "propose that faculty and professionals *with expertise in the relevant areas* be the primary drivers of any committee or review panel" (8–9). The italicized passage is highlighted in the original; it is their way of assuring us that disciplinary perspectives will shape the adjudication of cases. Ad hoc committees, "a panel of experts in the area in question" (228), would evaluate the political views of the faculty under review. Such occasions for review, they speculate later, might well have to be continuous, not simply limited to the established periods for review like tenure and promotion, thereby subjecting faculty to nonstop political surveillance.

Moreover, they are blind to the fundamental political corruption of a number of academic disciplines, including Middle East studies and women's studies. They think there is a safeguard built into their proposal. The committee would be "consulting the relevant professional organization and its standards of professional ethics" (246). Unfortunately, for some disciplines that would mean consulting the Middle East Studies Association, the National Women's Studies Association, or one of several other academic associations committed to fierce anti-Zionism and antisemitism. The only examples of antisemitism that Bérubé and Ruth charge with rising to the level of white supremacy are Holocaust denial and the Holocaust itself. Apparently they feel that concession will protect them from charges of bias or insensitivity. Bérubé has kept his distance from debates about Israel, but Ruth signed a 2022 "Statement in Support of *The Harvard Crimson* and Palestinian Liberation" and circulated it on the blog of the AAUP's *Academe* magazine.

Brian Soucek (2022) tries to apply reason to this crisis by recommending that departments ask "whether the statement's topic falls within the department's distinct disciplinary expertise." He then concludes "it's hard for me to imagine the UC Davis School of Law making a statement on Middle Eastern politics." His essay was published in spring 2022, but the CUNY School of Law had already adopted a resolution "proudly and unapologetically endors[ing] the Palestinian-led call for Boycott Divestment, and Sanctions (BDS) against Israel." Soucek notes that "any number of departments study power or systems of oppression," but doubts that gives "certain departments free rein to weigh in on any and all of the world's injustices."

4. When disciplinary politicization escalates

The politicization of several humanities and social science disciplines underwent a dramatic escalation in the spring of 2021. On May 21, the day after a ceasefire was announced in the war between Hamas and Israel, a coalition of women's and gender studies departments and programs made it clear that, for their part at least, the war of words would not stop. More than 100 such academic programs signed a statement entitled "Gender Studies Departments in Solidarity with Palestinian Feminist Collective." This statement condemned Israel's "indiscriminate bombing" of Gaza, thereby endorsing the accusation that Israel's conduct constitutes a war crime. Signatories ranged from departments at small liberal arts colleges (Amherst, Bryn Mawr, Carleton, Middlebury, Smith, Williams) to those at major universities in Canada,

Britain, and the United States (Arizona, Berkeley, Chicago, Columbia, Duke, Leeds, NYU, North Carolina, Ottawa, Pennsylvania, Rutgers, Stanford, Toronto, UCLA, University of Illinois, University of London, USC, Virginia, Warwick, Wisconsin, Yale, York).[16] Gender and women's studies programs from a few other countries also signed the statement.

In an analysis that aims to track reasons for and against departmental political statements, Daniel Gordon points out that such a "declaration appears to discourage any research or public statement that might contradict the party line decreed in advance" (2023, 142) and details some of its troubling epistemological consequences:[17]

> When the representatives of a discipline deploy their *collective* academic authority to endorse a political message, they are suggesting that there is only one uniquely correct way to look at a political situation through the lens of their discipline.... Does political opinion really emanate from the empirical facts which a discipline establishes? If it does not, then is it not dishonest to pass off one's political values as if they were the logical corollaries of an academic discipline? Is it not common for people to agree on certain facts but to draw different lessons from them? Is it reasonable to presume that all the members of a discipline will draw the same political conclusions from the academic knowledge generated by the discipline? (141)

The women's and gender studies (WGS) departments that signed the statement dramatically expanded their social justice mission beyond the discipline's founding commitments to purported intersections with causes worldwide. In so doing, the departments embraced political commitments having no inherent relation to their mission or to the discipline as a whole. The long history of feminist movement solidarity had been transformed by the 2015 anti-Zionist resolution of the National Women's Studies Association

---

16 See Joe Lockard's (2021) letter protesting the Arizona departmental signatures. Faculty members at UC Davis, UCLA, and the University of Illinois at Urbana-Champaign all wrote to senior administrators to protest campus departments signing the statement and ask that the statements be removed; none received adequate responses.

17 Gordon falsely asserts that the AAUP's support for faculty political advocacy is primarily due to my influence. I was a member of the AAUP Committee that wrote the policies, but the policies represented a consensus in a group of accomplished, rather strong-willed people. I was not the primary author. Gordon was not a member of Committee A. He comes to his irresponsible conclusion because of the arguments I mounted in my own publications.

(NWSA) from an enabling organizing resource and form of identity rein-forcement to an abstract principle. The 2021 statement reaffirms NWSA's anti-Zionism and imposes it on individual departments.

I have no problem with disciplinary involvement in issues clearly related to their mission. National women's studies groups had reason, for example, to support the Equal Rights Amendment to the US Constitution, and they have reason to support reproductive rights now. But individual departments should avoid taking official positions on even those issues, though faculty in the pro-gram could sign a statement on those or any other issues.

Long-term AAUP activist John Wilson (2021) worries that, once universities prohibit department political declarations, restrictions on individual political speech will soon follow. But advocates of such a university policy universally affirm the individual right. His fear is without merit. Academic freedom protects the right of individual students and faculty to take aggressive political stands. Departments and programs, in contrast, speak for the institution. University of Chicago president Robert Zimmer's 2020 open letter to members of the university community reinforced the core focus of the Kalven report in warning "against University positions on political and social action, with the exception of matters that threaten the very mission of the University, its commitment to freedom of inquiry and its basic operations." Departments, schools, centers, and divisions of the university should likewise not adopt political positions. Political advocacy by individuals "must be distinct from expression advanced by official units of the University."[18] A department's adoption of a coercive polit-ical stance has implications for all who work with that department. It creates a political litmus test for new appointments and a continuing loyalty test for existing employees.

Documents like the WGS statement amount to mission statements. Departments will not file them away for recollection in tranquility but will implement them, carrying them out in policies and actions. WGS faculty members could sign such a statement without invoking departmental authority, thereby impinging on the academic freedom of others. When departmental

---

18 Robert J. Zimmer, "Reinforcing the Chicago Principles and the Kalven Report," Office of the President, University of Chicago, October 5, 2020, available at https://president.uchicago.edu/page/reinforcing-chicago-principles-and-kalven-report. The full title of the Kalven Report is "Kalven Committee: Report on the University's Role in Political and Social Action." See https://provost.uchicago.edu/sites/default/files/documents/reports/KalvenRprt_0.pdf. The full title of the Chicago Principles is "Report of the Committee on Freedom of Expression." See https://provost.uchicago.edu/sites/default/files/documents/reports/FOECommitteeReport.pdf.

politicization has discipline-wide endorsement, the coercive potential is considerably enhanced.

Departmental commitment to anti-Zionism also empowers unrestrained student expression of a sort most faculty would avoid. It encourages a level of classroom and campus vituperation that will make Jewish students feel unwelcome. And it will spill over into other settings, like dormitories, that will drive some students to withdraw from school. Imagine, if you will, a Black Jewish student subjected to both racist and antisemitic verbal assault in a dorm, both forms of speech supposedly protected by academic freedom. A faculty member making such remarks in a department meeting or a student repeatedly making them in a dorm or a classroom need not be tolerated in silence. It is possible to defuse tensions around a single unacceptable remark and turn it into a teachable moment. A relentless pest can be asked to leave the room. Academic freedom does not protect personal aggression.

These are among the reasons universities place restraints and regulations on political expression by departments and other administrative units. Some require administrative approval for official statements. Some have policies addressing political activity. Others create advocacy guidelines. Many, like the University of California, at least until 2021, have specified that "the name, insignia, seal, or address of the University or any of its offices or units shall not be used for or in connection with political purposes or activity." Those restrictions apply to departmental political announcements on university web sites or disseminated by university email.[19] Some universities, the University of Arizona being an example, state explicitly that "university units may not engage in political activities or take positions on public policy controversies."[20] Arguing that the United States should condition or withdraw its financial support for Israel is obviously a public policy issue. To be clear: statements purporting to speak for a unit of a private university are subject to regulation by the president, chancellor, and board of regents. Even at a public university, the limit is not a constitutional problem. A governmental entity can impose rules on its own pronouncements.

The "Gender Studies Departments in Solidarity with Palestinian Feminist Collective" statement is far from the generic, anodyne calls for decency, sensitivity, or basic fairness that university bodies often issue. On the contrary,

---

19 Restrictions on the Use of University Resources and Facilities for Political Activities, September 18, 1970, https://policy.ucop.edu/doc/1200368/FacilPolitActiv.
20 University Handbook for Appointed Personnel (UHAP): Political Activity, policy number UHAP 2.10, last revised January 2016, FAQs, https://policy.web.arizona.edu/employment-human-resources/political-activity-uhap.

it uses incendiary rhetoric not just to support the rights of Palestinians but also to condemn Israel by taking sides in the political struggle: "We do not subscribe to a 'both sides' rhetoric that erases the military, economic, media, and global power that Israel has over Palestine." The statement characterizes the 2021 war with Hamas as part of an ethnic cleansing program that began in 1947, thereby condemning Israel's whole history. "We call for the end of Israel's military occupation of Palestine," the statement continues, "and for the Palestinian right to return to their homes." Their attack applies not just to "settler colonialism" in the West Bank but to Israel itself. In a final gesture of disingenuous bravado, the signers declare "we will not tolerate any censorship of nor retribution against Palestinian scholars, activists, and those openly critical of the Israeli state." In practice, this statement actually endangers the academic freedom of those who support Israel.

Almost immediately after the WGS statement was shared, the pattern of disciplinary politicization began to spread. Other disciplines either signed or issued statements of their own. Ethnic studies departments on three California campuses—UC Berkeley, UC Santa Cruz and UCLA—and elsewhere issued similarly politicized statements firmly rooted in the anti-Zionist tenets of their discipline. Several Asian studies programs, conventionally grouped with ethnic studies, signed, as did several anthropology departments and departments of architecture and urban planning. Anti-Zionism thus became a cross-disciplinary movement. In turn, the movement became global.

International efforts to commit entire academic disciplines—teaching, research, policies, and administration—to anti-Zionism represent a dangerous new phase in the politicization of the academy. In the absence of an explicit departmental or discipline-wide position on anti-Zionism, individual faculty members in these departments have academic freedom; they have the right to express political views without being sanctioned. Likewise, both faculty and students have the right to study, debate, and dispute the views on the subject. But once a department officially adopts one position on anti-Zionism and presents it as a collective view, debate and dissent can be problematic for the individual and the institution. A department is an administrative entity, an arm of the university. Academic and professional standards for departments typically hold that students and faculty members with opposing views will be free to adopt their own positions and be treated with respect. Departments and their administrators are responsible for numerous professional decisions presumed to be politically neutral. If departments violate that principle, as some departments do, then university leaders and governing bodies can reasonably move to defend the integrity of the institution, for example by restricting the authority of those departments to make academic and personnel decisions.

Once a department and its chief administrator sign on to a set of political positions, the academic freedom of those who disagree is compromised. Students who hold other views can face the bullying power of their professors and classmates. Dissenters—whether faculty, staff, or students—who may remain in perfectly good standing as scholars and teachers become formally defined as outlaws, members neither of the department nor of a discipline collectively committed to anti-Zionism. Furthermore, it would be delusional to suppose that this commitment will not influence decisions by a department or department head.

The University of California Press provides a remarkable example of this. In the wake of the anti-Zionist statement by WGS programs and other disciplines, the press adopted an official political mission, turning an implicit bias into an explicit public priority:

> We want to recognize the powerful expansion of international solidarity with Palestinians in their fight for liberation and stand with them. We support scholarship that confronts all forms of settler colonialism, US racial formations including Islamophobia, and prioritize pedagogies that reflect intersectional, anti-colonial, anti-racist action. As a university press, it is our responsibility to disseminate scholarship that challenges dominant narratives and makes understanding these injustices possible.[21]

Writers sympathetic to the Jewish state need not waste time submitting a manuscript to Berkeley. Meanwhile, anti-Zionist authors no longer have the imprimatur of a politically neutral and objective publisher. If administrators and dissenting faculty do not find the courage to resist this trend, it will spread. The Israeli-Palestinian conflict will not be the last divisive political issue on which departments and disciplines will take sides.

The University of California responded to the need to codify its policy on departmental political statements in a May 2022 draft report distributed that September. A divided ad hoc working group tried to balance competing interests by asking that all political statements representing academic units be signed by those individuals endorsing them and that space for dissenting views be provided. The report helpfully declares that academic freedom "does

---

21 "Solidarity and Support for Palestinians in their Fight for Liberation," UC Press blog, May 21, 2021, https://www.ucpress.edu/blog/56253/solidarity-and-support-for-palestinians-in-their-fight-for-liberation/.

not apply to the speech of corporate entities such as departments" (University of California 2022, 6) and that "departments *as entities* cannot validly represent themselves as holding or espousing views on issues other than the department's policies, narrowly defined" (8). Nonetheless, it empowers departments to issue political statements with the gratuitous advice that such statements should be "issued sparingly." In fact, this advice would only heighten the exceptional moral and political force of statements like the May 2021 declarations of anti-Zionism.

The report then embraces the collective illusion that faculty self-governance can and will be governed by restraint and sweet reason. Political statements on controversial issues, it tells us, should be made "with great thought and care about their possible effects—including harm and hurt to members of the university community and reputational damage to the university" (15). The advice is quite simply obsolete. In his dissent to the report's recommendations, Assistant Chancellor Dan Mogulof warns that "we will tie ourselves in knots, and potentially tear ourselves apart, trying to explain to our stakeholders, and ourselves, why a departmental or school statement on a departmental or school website signed by those presumed to be leaders is not somehow an expression of an institutional position" (22).

With notable understatement, the report warns that "signing onto a majority statement or voicing dissent are not always a simple matter for members of a department, especially those with less power or seniority" (16). In the letter quoted in my introduction, Richard Ross argues that "such statements intimidate dissenters and encourage self-censorship, withdrawal from politicized departments or, perhaps worse, insincere mouthing of the 'approved' view." Would it help if the campus dissociated itself from a department statement? As Ross asks, would a

> graduate student or assistant professor feel reassured if the Chancellor issued an email dissociating the university from the History Department's official commitment to "solidarity with Palestine?" Would the dissident graduate student or assistant professor now have confidence that the senior faculty would evaluate their work fairly? Would they believe that a single email emitting from the distant Chancellor in [the] Administrative Building would protect them from senior colleagues who work with them every day, writing letters of recommendation and voting on tenure, all the while irritated by failure to adhere to the "true" and "good" political stance collectively announced by the department?

As David Bell (2023) writes, "The fact that academic units are themselves political power structures means that these pressures operate regardless of the conscious intentions of chairs and tenured faculty." Indeed, "the more a statement is presented as self-evidently necessary, as an act of sheer moral obligation, the harder it is to leave room for significant deliberation, disagreement, or dissent." This is the world in which senior faculty members delude themselves that vulnerable colleagues are free to exercise their full political and expressive agency. It is not so much a brave new world as the one we have lived in throughout and beyond living memory. It is a world in which all solutions for dissenters come with professional risk. We are, however, adding anti-Zionism to its ruling coercions. One partial but important solution is to adopt the policy document against departmental political statements included in this book's introduction.

5. The challenge of personnel decisions

The use of disciplinary consensus as a standard presents higher education with additional challenges in personnel matters. While faculty members in many disciplines would reject the polemical claim that Israel is the world's most egregious violator of human rights or "the new Nazi Germany," faculty in other disciplines now embrace these very accusations (and not merely as deliberately exaggerated rhetoric mobilized to make a political point). At least three questions arise from reflection on the disciplinary standard: (1) Is it unprofessional or unethical to reject a job applicant because his or her views qualify as antisemitic once analyzed in terms of the IHRA Definition's examples? (2) Does it violate academic freedom to deny tenure to an assistant professor whose publications embody antisemitic convictions? (3) Might an institution decide that a faculty member holding antisemitic views cannot teach courses on the Israeli-Palestinian conflict or the history of Judaism? I know faculty members who would give different answers to all three questions. While each of the questions can only be answered on a case-by-case basis, I could see myself answering "no" to the first two questions and "yes" to the third. Academic freedom does not require us to hold job applicants harmless for their views, ignore the persuasive power of tenure candidates' published arguments, or guarantee faculty members a right to teach any course they want.

Disputing dominant accounts of the 1948 war, advocating for Palestinian rights, condemning the occupation of the West Bank and the expansion of settlements, urging changes in Israeli law, objecting to Israeli policy toward Gaza: those positions and many others would not justify opposing a job applicant or a tenure candidate. But encouraging belief in worldwide Jewish conspiracies, questioning the reality of the Holocaust, or reinventing the blood libel accusation would warrant rejecting a candidate. In certain cases, however, faculty members may endorse conspiracism through what appear to be rational arguments. As Bret Stephens points out, antisemitic conspiracy "theories that are themselves profoundly irrational … are still ideas, and, as such, intelligible, coherent, self-interested, and often instrumentally rational" (2023, 3).

A striking case of faculty antisemitism expressed during an appointment process is Cornel West's 2021 response to being offered a ten-year endowed chair at Harvard, "a position of extraordinary privilege in the academic world, and indeed in the world" (Harpham 2021). Offended that the offer, which entailed a substantial salary and employment until age 77, did not include tenure, West gave an interview to Maximillian Alvarez (2021) in the *Chronicle of Higher Education* unreservedly expressing his confidence that a Jewish conspiracy had blocked a tenured offer:

> My controversial and outspoken views about and critiques of empire, capitalism, white supremacy, male supremacy, and homophobia are tolerated, but any serious engagement around the issues of the Israeli occupation are rendered highly suspect and reduced to anti-Jewish hatred or prejudice.… I surmise it must be my deep Christian witness based on the idea that an ugly Israeli occupation of precious Palestinians is as wrong as any ugly Palestinian occupation of precious Jews.

West followed up in a 35-minute interview with Tricia Rose on "The Tight Rope," a podcast in which he carefully dances around laying the blame on Jews.[22] He invokes the wider cultural disrespect for Black intellectuals, then migrates to his certainty that the occupation "is a taboo issue among certain circles in high places," referring first to Jewish administrators, then says "it's also I think possibly tied to the donors," quickly adding "it's not just Jewish donors," but the damage had been done.

West offers no evidence for this slander other than an appeal to the kind of antisemitic beliefs the IHRA Definition warns us against. It's fundamentally the same reasoning an AAUP staff member offered me as evidence

---

22 "Cornel West—'My Ridiculous Situation at Harvard.'" The Tight Rope (podcast), February 23, 2021, available as YouTube video at https://www.youtube.com/watch?v=PQCsMxhB9ms.

that Jewish donors had forced the Steven Salaita appointment denial at the University of Illinois: "It's what Jews do." As I detail later in this book, accusations about Jewish donor influence also proliferated during the controversial 2020 effort to appoint Valentina Azarova as a University of Toronto administrator. West has long been critical of Israel and has sought to dramatize his views with memorable rhetoric. He had flirted with antisemitism before, calling Lawrence Summers "the Ariel Sharon of higher education" in a 2002 NPR interview. The remark is unacceptable despite Summers's career of saying decidedly objectionable things.[23] Why emphasize his Jewish status? What relevance does it have, for example, to his offensive view of women? In any case, West's casting of himself as the personal victim of an invisible Jewish conspiracy is antisemitic. Moreover, it helps authorize African-American, Palestinian, and anti-Zionist faculty generally to believe the same and publicize their own unprovable Israel-based victimhood, their personal grievances against invisible Jews.

This personalized form of victimhood amplifies a standard anti-Zionist campus fantasy—that the expression of pro-Palestinian sentiments is constrained by a pervasive atmosphere of fear—and turns it into a serious general accusation. West repeated the more common claim in a remark quoted in a piece by Ben Samuels (2021) in *Haaretz*: "You could hardly get a faculty member to raise a public voice being critical of Israeli occupation, they're scared.... There's this fear among the faculty, and among the staff." This is frankly nonsense; condemnations of the occupation are commonplace at Harvard and throughout higher education here and abroad. Surely West knows that. Nonetheless, in a resignation letter distributed in July he reiterated his claim that "the Harvard administration hostility to the Palestinian cause" was behind the decision not to offer him a tenured position.[24]

West's complaint about his own situation is nonsense of an especially dangerous kind: the difference between a tenured slot and the Victor S. Thomas Professorship of Public Philosophy that Harvard offered him is basically meaningless. As a colleague suggested, nobody outside of academia would even know the difference between his ten-year endowed-chair contract and a tenured position, much less care.[25] The professorship offered is an honor.

---

23 West also said of Obama: "He feels most comfortable with upper middle-class white and Jewish men who consider themselves very smart, very savvy and very effective in getting what they want" (Walsh 2011). The gratuitous inclusion of Jews in this remark carries an antisemitic implication.

24 For West's resignation letter, see Shivaram (2021).

25 Steven Lubet (2021) makes a comparable argument.

What Zionist would care about the one offer and not the other? Would I have voted against a tenured appointment were this interview in evidence? Probably. I am torn because West can be an inspiring presence. I would not vote to fire him were he already under contract, but I might well oppose a tenured appointment. I would not want to empower an antisemitic campus voice with tenure. West's arguments about Israeli policy can be debated, but accusations about an invisible Jewish conspiracy cannot be put to rest. As Bret Stephens writes, "The most important element of any conspiracy theory is that it is unfalsifiable — impervious to logical or evidentiary refutation. To the conspiracy theorist, contrary evidence doesn't diminish his argument; it thickens the plot" (2023, 7).

West pairs statements that indict Jews with statements affirming them, so that he can disclaim antisemitic intent. That is a common strategy for those concerned about the social impact of their speech. Former British Labour Party leader Jeremy Corbyn did it all the time: make an antisemitic accusation, then discount its obvious meaning (Johnson 2019). With Corbyn, I believe the strategy is cynical. With West, it is part of rationalization and self-persuasion. West also wants to spin his personal campaign to condemn Harvard as a social good, an effort to defend tenure and the speech rights of vulnerable faculty, but it is difficult to disguise the sense of offended entitlement.

There are different standards and principles at stake in answering the three questions raised above. Hiring committees can decide against a candidate because of the impression he or she makes in an interview; a wide range of judgments can be in play that would be unacceptable in a tenure decision. A hiring committee may make subjective decisions about what sort of colleague a person might make. They might ask whether a person's key views would prove a productive addition to the department or campus. They might decide, for example, not to hire a dedicated internet troll. West thinks his earlier tenure should automatically apply to the new appointment, but the system doesn't work that way. He turned himself into a job candidate. Harvard avoided the special constraints on tenure reviews by offering a term-limited contract instead.

We need to understand that under many circumstances academic freedom protects antisemitism. Tenured faculty are protected from severe sanctions for publishing antisemitic statements. But that doesn't protect them or untenured faculty from criticism for doing so, or from other consequences. You can call out antisemitism, just as you can call out misstatements or poor reasoning. Moreover—and this is important and not always understood—there are decision points in faculty careers when antisemitism can have serious consequences.

First, you do not have to hire an antisemite, a white supremacist, or a Nazi sympathizer. An antisemitic or white supremacist public social media profile is grounds for rejection quite apart from a job candidate's teaching and research record. Academic freedom does not bar us from concluding that such beliefs do not contribute to the search for the truth. Of course some social media activity, such as posts to private Facebook groups, is likely to be invisible to search committees, no matter how invidious the activity may be, but much of what is posted on Twitter and Facebook is public. One can gain some indication of how much traction a candidate's posts have had by noting how many followers they have or by feeding distinctive tweets into Twitter's advanced search function. At the same time, not all followers are fans; not all share the tweeter's viewpoint. Many platforms have their own search engines. Third-party software may be more versatile but can also be more challenging to use. Comments appended to forwarded posts can be a useful guide to their impact.

Committees evaluating a candidate's presence on social media may need to consult specialists outside the candidate's field. Purveyors of racist or antisemitic hate speech have developed coded language to signal their views to people of like minds. Some of the codes are specialized language ("Skypes" stands for "Kikes"), while abbreviations include the familiar "88" (HH or Heil Hitler) and the less familiar GTKRWN (Gas the Kikes, Race War Now). These are digital dog whistles, easily recognized by those familiar with the code. As the Perspective API (internet programming interface) becomes more sophisticated, people can type a statement into the program to see what its toxicity score is.

The character of a candidate's teaching and research, in any case, is always at issue and both components are necessary bases for professional evaluation. You are deciding in part what impact a job candidate will have on the campus, what international impact his or her research will have, and what impact his or her work will have on the institution's reputation. Nothing requires participants in a search process to declare their reasons for voting one way or another. But many faculty will want to know what bases for action are ethical. It should be clear that it is not ethical to require that a job candidate be an anti-Zionist, no matter how quietly such expectations have been imposed in the past. Later in this book, in the chapter on Valentina Azarova, I will consider another vexed question, namely whether a campus should hire an anti-Zionist or antisemitic candidate for an administrative position that entails setting policy and practice for an entire academic unit.

You do not have to award tenure or promotion to an antisemite or white supremacist who is already a member of the faculty if there is evidence of bias in his or her teaching, research, or public presence. The grounds for refusal are narrower than with job candidates, but academic freedom does not protect a tenure candidate whose professional activities are compromised by racism or antisemitism. Yet some of the criteria available to a hiring committee (at any rank) are no longer applicable. You may not like the impact an assistant professor has on the campus climate, but, once he or she has been hired, you do not have the opportunity to second guess your judgment about political commitments that were in evidence during the hiring process. Moreover, tenure decisions need to be based on the written file accumulated during the review process. Thus, if racist or antisemitic bias has substantially compromised a tenure candidate's teaching or research, the evidence for that conclusion has to be fully documented in the tenure papers. The same requirement obtains for other prejudicial beliefs.

You also do not have to give a sabbatical or a salary raise to someone pursuing an antisemitic or white supremacist research project or antisemitic or white supremacist teaching. Benefits like these are subject to professional evaluation. Academic freedom does not protect faculty members from all professional consequences. Except for demonstrable incompetence, unethical conduct, or violations of law, tenure does protect faculty members from being fired, but not from a variety of other consequences. A faculty member who adopts reprehensible views after tenure is subject to a variety of sanctions and restrictions short of termination, including limits on course assignments. The BDS movement often tries to repress charges of antisemitism by falsely claiming that they violate academic freedom. There is pressure from outside higher education to terminate antisemitic tenured faculty, but there is too great a risk that the precedent would encourage termination for other unpopular political beliefs. That is not to say we should be hopeful about the future of department hiring and promotion practices. It is rather to say that those who are concerned about the matter should know what their rights are and what constraints apply.

6. Advocacy versus indoctrination

Faculty members are generally protected from sanctions for expressing views prevailing in their discipline. But those views are not above criticism. Disciplinary consensus does not trump all other ways of reaching agreement. Disciplinary agreement does not mean that each discipline gets to have its own exclusive truths, or that there are no transdisciplinary standards. There are norms at departmental, campus, disciplinary, national, and international level that customarily constrain professional practices, even though anti-Zionist departments and disciplines have largely ceased to constrain individual conduct that reinforces their ideology. These norms are thought to be included in disciplinary training, though in some disciplines they are now explicitly discounted. Academic disciplines are not mutually exclusive conceptual universes. Blind adherence to a standard that institutionalizes disciplinary independence suggests that every discipline can maintain its consensual truths with indifference or hostility to counterevidence. This can lead to disabling professional incoherence; that is where many practices stand today.

Once an antisemitic belief is enshrined by its elevation to a disciplinary truth, it is difficult to discourage pedagogical practices that perpetuate it. And if the dissemination of antisemitic beliefs becomes foundational or pervasive in a particular field it may turn into indoctrination. A claim stated once in a class does not constitute indoctrination, but a claim repeatedly invoked or embedded within a discipline can rise to that level. That parallels the AAUP's 1970 clarification of its 1940 statement on academic freedom—that *persistent* intrusion of unrelated political matters is the standard for concern. Accepted truths, moreover, require less evidence, if any evidence at all, to be promoted in the classroom. Counterevidence comes to be regarded as irrelevant or misleading. Why assign Zionist course readings when such readings are, by definition, false or misguided? So there would be academic protection for Puar or Abdulhadi insisting that Israel's practices are comparable to those of Nazi Germany. The equation of Israel and Nazi Germany or the claim that Israel is engaged in genocide in Gaza are slanders without merit. Yet they are pursued nonetheless, and they help create a hostile campus climate for Jews who form their identities in part around commitment to Israel.

Over the last generation, classroom political advocacy has won wider acceptance in AAUP policy statements. I endorsed those efforts as AAUP president. In 2013, I published "Advocacy Versus Indoctrination" in the *Journal of College and University Law*. It was written in response to Kenneth Marcus's "Academic Freedom and Political Indoctrination." I argued for the value of carefully reasoned political advocacy in the classroom, so long as students were encouraged to hold or present opposing views. I was writing in general agreement with the AAUP's 2007 report "Freedom in the Classroom." Professors, I believed, could model political advocacy that was respectful of evidence and respectful of alternative views. My own practice was always to reward undergraduates who did a good job of disagreeing with me. Given what too often passes for acceptable argument in Congress, on television, and in social media, the observance of better standards in academia can be socially beneficial.

Yet that does not solve the disciplinary problem. "Freedom in the Classroom" states that "It is not indoctrination for professors to expect students to comprehend ideas and apply knowledge that is accepted as true within a relevant discipline" (AAUP 2007, 54). This argument again reflects an unwarranted faith in the character of all academic disciplines, some of which are pervasively dedicated to indoctrination, even if they see it as disseminating truths. I did not see that at the time. The report cites Dewey's certainty that "such consensus cannot be found in 'political economy, sociology, historical interpretation,'" but we were wrong (55). It is roughly there, in the humanities and social sciences, that an anti-Zionist consensus about what is true can be found. Marcus takes issue with the AAUP report's contention that "indoctrination occurs only when instructors dogmatically insist on the truth of such propositions by refusing to accord their students the opportunity to contest them" (55). I realize now that he is right. If the class exists in an Orwellian conceptual world where all the evidence is anti-Zionist, it will seem sweet reason to concur. The theoretical opportunity to contest course dogma becomes meaningless.

The case against classroom political advocacy was ably made by Max Weber in a 1918 speech at Munich University, first published the following year. Like the AAUP Declaration that is its contemporary, Weber's "Science as a Vocation" (*Wissenschaft als Beruf*) invokes the search for truth as the primary value underwriting the academic mission. And he comes to a conclusion in harmony with the AAUP's 1915 "Declaration of Principles on Academic Freedom and Academic Tenure": "the primary task of a useful teacher is to teach his students to recognize 'inconvenient' facts ... that are inconvenient to their party opinions" (Weber 1946, 14). If a teacher "introduces his personal value judgment, a full understanding of the facts *ceases*" (14). Even if students want absolute conviction from their professors, faculty should resist the attempt to become "petty prophets in their lecture-rooms" (18). Otherwise, we shall fail in our duty to help empower students to give themselves "an account of the ultimate meaning of their own conduct" (18). Self-clarification and responsibility cannot develop unless students are encouraged to think independently. Weber is on target when advocacy done poorly is at issue. Intellectual integrity is destroyed when a secular version of "unconditional religious devotion" takes the place of education. Weber's depiction of professorial zealots is eerily predictive of some ideologues in classrooms today, more than a hundred years later.

A consensus still prevails against using a classroom to indoctrinate students. But faculty members in some disciplines can forthrightly condemn indoctrination while nonetheless teaching that "Zionism is racism," that "Israel is an apartheid state on both sides of the green line," that "Israel is the world's worst violator of human rights," that justice requires that "the grandchildren of 1947 Palestinian refugees have the right to Israeli citizenship," that "Israeli Arabs have no human rights whatsoever," and so forth. They assign "research" papers and exam questions demonstrating the supposed truth of these propositions.

Naively, when I wrote my 2013 essay, I still thought the standards I had in mind were essentially universal in the academy. I had not yet confronted anti-Zionist pedagogy, with its secular version of unreflective religious devotion—one-sided syllabi, promotion of falsehoods, and indulgence in what amounts to hatred for credit. We now face advocacy run amok. In "Freedom in the Classroom" we declare that "it is a fundamental error to assume that the assignment of teaching materials constitutes their endorsement. An instructor who assigns a book no more endorses what it has to say than does the university library that acquires it (AAUP 2007, 55)." We cannot, indeed, assume endorsement on the basis of a single reading assignment. But when an entire syllabus embodies a particular political point of view and the instructor echoes that point of view in his or her publications, we have a clear indication of what conclusions a class will encourage. As *Israel Denial* documents, we have the example of teachers at Berkeley and Riverside instilling anti-Zionist convictions in undergraduates who went on to teach similar one-credit courses on their own.

Israel Denial includes a detailed chapter on anti-Zionist and frequently antisemitic pedagogy. *Not in Kansas Anymore* reports on still more degraded examples of antisemitic advocacy in Palestinian classrooms. The ideal I endorsed in my 2013 essay is often more dishonored than observed.[26] Rather than bar advocacy, however, I would argue for better standards for its implementation, including professional consequences for those who betray the search for the truth in their zeal to disseminate their views. Appropriate steps could include assigning a faculty member to other courses. When entire departments are dedicated to anti-Zionism, their hiring rights might be curtailed either by assigning that responsibility to another faculty group or by cancelling it entirely until a department is able to reform its practices. Colleges and universities, moreover, need to make certain that different cultural and political perspectives on Jewish and Israeli history are available in other departments, being ready to fund additional positions if necessary. While inviting alternative speakers to campus and bringing in visiting faculty can help, these are not adequate long-term counters to pervasive departmental anti-Zionism. Addressing that problem is an upper administration and faculty senate responsibility, not one a corrupted department would honor.

7. Professional standards and the quest for the truth

Antisemitism now has an academic mandate. The efforts to delegitimate Holocaust memory, to declare Israel the world's worst human rights violator,

---

26 I continue to support several of the arguments in "Freedom in the Classroom," including its critique of "balance" as a pedagogical necessity.

to invoke an absurd fantasy of limitless Jewish lobbying power—the fact that these demonic tropes and others are academically validated makes their threat to higher education's mission all the more dangerous. They have made antisemitism the equivalent of a social good within anti-Zionism's alternative academic universe. At least one conclusion is inescapable: disciplinary consensus no longer consistently safeguards academic freedom.

Addressing these problems is a campus-wide challenge. Countering the trend toward disciplinary politicization will require that the hard sciences and other departments not part of the trend participate in a dedicated conversation about the problem. Otherwise, practices will continue to degrade, and resistance to reform will grow.

The AAUP's 1915 Declaration of Principles gave academic freedom a purpose—to protect faculty members in their search for the truth. That standard reflected the organization's definition of the primary aim of higher education—"to promote inquiry and advance the sum of human knowledge" (AAUP 2015b, 7), a goal requiring faculty members "trained for, and dedicated to, the quest for truth" (6). The AAUP's 1940 "Statement of Principles on Academic Freedom and Tenure" reaffirms that the "common good" served by academic freedom "depends upon the free search for the truth and its free expression" (14). The imposition of preexisting anti-Zionist convictions does not qualify. Some conventional standards can substitute for ideological solidarity in making professional evaluations, among them whether political arguments are supported by sufficient evidence. We also need to rethink the relationship between academic freedom and antisemitism more broadly.

We generally accept, for example, that fierce accusations against the Jewish state should not be used as weapons against individual students and faculty— and yet they routinely are. If Zionism is racism, then every Zionist is a racist, and harassment on that basis can seem virtuous and ennobling. Anything less than relentless application of that anti-Zionist standard is taken to be a moral failure. Prohibitions against harassment would help if they were rigorously applied and came with meaningful sanctions.[27] Except that they are almost never applied, and the sanctions are rarely if ever meaningful. A university president merely expresses "regret" at the effort to cast a student or faculty member out of the campus community. Academic freedom is not a defense against a campaign of

---

27 The Office for Civil Rights of the US Department of Education (1994) offered this definition of harassment in a 1994 investigative guidance on how hostile environments are created: "harassing conduct (e.g., physical, verbal, graphic, or written) that is sufficiently severe, pervasive or persistent so as to interfere with or limit the ability of an individual to participate in or benefit from the services, activities or privileges provided by a recipient" of federal funds.

antisemitic vilification. It is not a defense against generating fabricated accusations and providing false witness. Harassment curtails academic freedom; it is not protected speech.

Casual antisemitic statements by one person may be less serious and damaging to a community than antisemitic group actions, but the two phenomena are connected. Incidents of group harassment—sometimes encouraged by faculty, condoned by administrators, and mistakenly considered protected by academic freedom—turn campuses into hostile environments for Jews. When a herd mentality empowers antisemitism and antisemitic statements become forms of virtue signaling, a hostile environment results. Collective anti-Zionism can empower antisemitism, and persistent antisemitic rhetoric by individuals can provoke group aggression.

Recent examples make this clear. In 2020, a USC student initiated a social media campaign against Rose Ritch, a Jewish member of the student government. He urged fellow students to "impeach her Zionist ass," and some joined the effort (ADL 2020). A group assault on a UCLA student, sophomore Rachel Beyda, was videotaped in 2015 when the student council debated whether to exclude her from the Judicial Board. "Given that you are a Jewish student," the interrogation proceeded, "how do you see yourself being able to maintain an unbiased view?" As Adam Nagourney (2015) wrote, the debate "seemed to echo the kind of questions, prejudices and tropes—particularly about divided loyalties—that have plagued Jews across the globe for centuries." Two years later, a Jewish undergraduate at my own campus who actively supported Israel and opposed BDS faced an almost identical antisemitic student government grilling. After a 2012 BDS debate at UC San Diego, professor Shlomo Dubnov was falsely charged with "verbally attacking and assaulting" the president of the Arab Student Union. A page attacking Dubnov was established on the university website, and a number of faculty members added personal letters demanding punitive action. Videotape evidence eventually surfaced revealing the accusation to be a complete fabrication. Dubnov was cleared, but no action was ever taken against those who had lied (Pessin and Ben-Atar 2018). Details of other incidents are provided in Chapter Three.

In its 1915 Declaration, the AAUP linked the purpose of academic freedom to its implementation: supporting a social good—the pursuit of the truth—by preventing faculty members who voice unorthodox and controversial opinions from being sanctioned. No one anticipated that academic freedom would instead be used to protect inaccurate herd opinion from analysis and critique.

Teaching and research that contribute to understanding and the pursuit of truth are essential to maintaining the academy's productive role in society.

It's not a flawless process; mistakes are made, but the principle is sound. A misguided version of academic freedom—used to discredit the professional evaluation of teaching and research—weakens the mission of higher education. Elements of the AAUP's 1915 Declaration have become dated, including its pre-radio, pre-television, and pre-internet warning that students are vulnerable and need protection from controversy. But its determination to put the search for truth at the center of the academy's mission remains crucial. Even if we are in a post-truth world politically, we need to resist that fact in the academy. It is not true that Israel is perhaps the world's worst violator of human rights or that Israel emulates the inhumanity of Nazi Germany. These claims are not "alternative facts." They are delusions.

As I have argued, there are decision points when lies can matter—during job searches, third-year reviews, and tenure and promotion decisions. Oberlin's Joy Karega did not make it to a tenure decision. As a probationary faculty member, she was suspended earlier because the pattern of her research, teaching, and public statements demonstrated that a positive tenure decision would be impossible. Her advocacy of wildly antisemitic conspiracy theories played a role in that process. She taught a course entitled "Writing for Social Justice" that emphasized anti-Zionism and covered the use of social media. Examples of her own 2015 Facebook posts include "ISIS is not a jihadist, Islamic terrorist organization. It's a CIA and Mossad operation" and "It seems obvious that the same people behind the massacre in Gaza are behind the shooting down [of Malaysia Airlines Flight] MA-17."[28]

Karega, moreover, was not just teaching *about* social media. She was teaching a practicum on how to do political advocacy through social media. Her own social media conspiracism was clearly relevant to the course. Karega embraced a series of bizarre conspiracy theories, casting doubts on her ability to adjudicate evidence and engage in rational thought. There are faculty members who cling to one conspiracy theory but are otherwise rational, but someone who maintains several delusional beliefs raises concerns about fitness. Ill-informed about (and unwilling to consider) the social consequences of spreading conspiracy theories online, the AAUP's Henry Reichman (2019) speculated that "a strong case can be made that Karega did not deserve to be dismissed" (59).

Although Bristol University sociologist David Miller was tenured prior to being fired in 2021 (losing an appeal in March 2022) and had a much more extensive publication history, his case in one respect parallels Karega's. Like

---

28 Karega's case is discussed in detail in my book *Israel Denial*.

Karega, Miller also promoted antisemitic conspiracy theories, though his more resembled the conspiracy theories that other anti-Zionist faculty spread. Among other claims, however, he added to more familiar positions the claim that Jewish interfaith work is really a deceptive effort to normalize Zionism. Similarly, "his position is that Jews who allege that there is antisemitism on the left, or on campus, are acting as part of a deliberate and collective conspiracy to lie" (Hirsh 2021b). He lectured accompanied by a slide linking Jews and their organizations in a conspiratorial network. No matter whether they are on the right or the left; they are all the same. In a valuable analysis, Keith Kahn-Harris (2021b) argues that this "constructs a kind of 'flatland,' a world in which networks of power and influence are so intricately connected that they form a seamless system ... every bit of the British Jewish community that has any kind of relationship with Israel and Zionism is all the same. There is no politics, no conflict, no tension.... The slightest contact with Zionism and Israel poisons all those who touch it even slightly." Kahn-Harris argues that this "makes a mockery of the discipline of sociology," which depends on drawing distinctions, not obliterating "the complexity of individual identity and commitments."

Anthony Julius places Miller's conspiracism in the context of conspiracy theories in the academy and in the general culture, where they represent "the discursive form taken by populist politics" (2022, 26). In conspiracism both within and outside academia, "we find a certain coexistence of scepticism and gullibility," a preference for "simplicity of motive over complexity of motive" (32). "A conspiracy theory makes use of random coincidences that become dense with meaning, and of connections between completely unconnected facts.... The more paranoid the conviction, the more the person in its grip seeks the evidence of conspiracies to conform its truth" (33). These are among the reasons why calling them "theories" is misleading and why the academy has a particular responsibility to discredit them.

Julius argues that antisemitic conspiracy theories are paradigmatic. "The conspiracy theories that have generated the *most* catastrophic counter-conspiracies, in addition to other, similarly catastrophic political actions, are the antisemitic ones.... They are the ones to which conspiracy-theorists graduate. They are all iterations of the one thesis: The Jews are a malign collective, acting in their own interests and to the detriment of the non-Jewish world. That is to say: antisemitism is one giant meta-conspiracy theory" (34). All this comes together in Miller's career, which embodies "everything that an academic should shun: extravagant claims, unmoored from evidence; the antisemitic premises of the work; the verbal assaults on Jewish students—assaults which are the inevitable outcome of his writing and speech-making" (38).

Where Miller most decidedly crossed the line was in claiming that Jewish students active in campus organizations were essentially serving as agents of Israel. Miller was nonetheless supported by a number of British faculty members who maintained that academic freedom protected his antisemitic speech despite its loathsome character. Others—among them Anthony Julius, David Hirsh, Keith Kahn-Harris, and Dave Rich—argued that his work did not deserve the protections of academic freedom. Whether Miller would have lost his job at a US campus would have depended on the specific institution, but it is likely that a number of major US universities would have deplored his statements but preserved his job.

Despite her wildly irrational conspiracism, Karega had significant student support. But she was a distinctive case, not an embodiment of disciplinary consensus. The issues at stake when an academic discipline has gone off the rails and made political advocacy a central raison d'être are still more difficult. The way academic dossiers are assembled makes objective review very difficult if the discipline as a whole has embraced anti-Zionism, since it is easy to gather a set of rave external reviews for an anti-Zionist or antisemitic candidate from an anti-Zionist discipline. This situation argues for additional faculty committee and administrative review for candidates from identifiably problematic fields. Such reviews should extend to new course proposals and to publication reviews at academic journals and university presses. Some will certainly object that such extra attention is discriminatory. Why Middle East studies deserves more scrutiny than chemistry is an answerable question. Position papers documenting why that is the case would be useful on multiple campuses. Review committees do sometimes solicit additional outside reviews to compensate for bias. We need to institute that requirement for anti-Zionist and antisemitic disciplines.

The AAUP does not maintain that academic disciplines are always right. No long-term historical vantage point could argue otherwise. What the AAUP maintains instead is that academic disciplines are self-correcting. But do politically compromised disciplines have dependable self-correcting mechanisms? If they hire, review proposed publications, train students, grant support, and award tenure on the basis of commitment to the field's political mission, what internal mechanisms would support reform? As David Hirsh (2021b) writes in "The Meaning of David Miller," "If Sociology is incapable of recognising antisemitic conspiracy as being outside of its own boundaries, then what does that tell us about the state of Sociology today?" The time frame for self-correction in our current anti-Zionist disciplines is not merely unpredictable; it is thoroughly uncertain and will leave more than a generation of current and future students condemned to antisemitic indoctrination.

Some disciplines repair themselves when there is sufficient internal debate and external critique, though the process is gradual and discontinuous and typically leaves behind some faculty who live out their careers holding discredited beliefs. The current generation may need to retire before reason can prevail, though of course the current generation is in the midst of training the next one. If academic antisemitism were primarily a function of hating Jews, as some definitions maintain, change would be easier. People can unlearn their hatreds. But antisemitism in the academy is not primarily a social prejudice. As Bernard Harrison has helped us understand, it is above all a political prejudice, a body of theory that helps explain the world, which helps account for its hold on people. As Bret Stephens puts it, antisemitism is "a political ideology—because it sees Jews as representing a self-interested political force disingenuously disguised as liberalism, socialism, globalism, or Zionism" (2023, 5). Since antisemitism in the academy is not primarily a social prejudice, anti-Zionists as different as Rabab Abdulhadi and Cornel West can assure us that some of their best friends are Jews or, more distressingly, that we must distinguish between good Jews and bad Jews. An implicit good Jews/bad Jews distinction is firmly installed on the academic left.

Although these exclusions may purport to rest on a principled political difference unconnected to religion, ethnicity, or nationality, in practice they amount to the denial of opportunities to Jews and Israelis, the great majority of whom do not wish to—and should not have to—renounce the Jewish state. We need to reduce our reluctance to make judgments about other disciplines. Before voting for antisemitic candidates, chemists and physicists need to be convinced that what Middle East specialists, literary critics, and women's studies faculty say about Israel and Zionism is true.

There are criteria that can be applied fairly. Does the person being reviewed provide sufficient (or any) evidence to support his or her conclusions? Does the candidate use the unsupported opinions of others, rather than evidence, to support his or her arguments? Are there reasons to conclude he or she is promoting demonstrable falsehoods? These may seem like understated challenges to wield against morally abhorrent claims, but they are effective places for academic evaluation to start. That obtains both for faculty evaluations and for student debates dominated by passionate anti-Zionism.

It is probably neither possible nor necessary to enlighten perpetrators of lies and modify their views. Those whose relentless critiques of Israel cross the line into antisemitism have been down a rabbit hole too long. If they are denied rewards for their antisemitism, they will likely feel resentment, not remorse. But it may be possible to establish a public climate in which antisemitism is judged socially and intellectually unacceptable. Academic freedom will still protect a faculty or student right to say Israelis are the new Nazis, but a campus majority will condemn the statement as false and deplorable. Faculty and students can still say Zionists should be barred from progressive campus groups or campus governance, but the weight of collective opinion will reject those demands as reprehensible. Universities will enforce the principle for groups seeking formal recognition.

In the summer of 2022, a complaint was filed with the Department of Education's Office for Civil Rights on behalf of two Jewish undergraduates at the State University of New York at New Paltz, Cassandra Blotner and Ofek Preis. Filed on their on their behalf by the Louis D. Brandeis Center for Human Rights under Law, the complaint alleged that they were expelled from a student group devoted to helping sexual assault survivors because they support Israel, which would constitute a violation of Title VI of the 1964 Civil Rights Act (Louis D. Brandeis Center 2022; Ain 2022). As the Alliance for Academic Freedom (2022) notes, "The exclusion of students and student groups from campus organizations, projects, and other opportunities because of their support for Israel represents an unconscionable development on North American campuses.... Although these exclusions may purport to rest on a principled political difference unconnected to religion, ethnicity, or nationality, in practice they amount to the denial of opportunities to Jews and Israelis, the great majority of whom do not wish to—and should not have to—renounce the Jewish state." The student group's action in expelling Jewish students contributed to a broader discriminatory atmosphere on campus, including Jewish and Israeli survivors of sexual assault. In failing to respond adequately, the suit alleges, SUNY New Paltz denies "Jewish and Israeli survivors of sexual assault on campus equal access to the educational opportunities and services they need, on the basis of their shared ancestry, ethnicity and national origin in violation of Title VI." Ad hominem anti-Zionism, the use of anti-Zionism to harass individual students and faculty, needs to be more than discouraged. There should be punishments for harassment based on race, gender, and national origin. The SUNY New Paltz events featured a campaign of harassment.

In August 2022, nine student groups at UC Berkeley School of Law adopted bylaws declaring that they would "not invite speakers that have expressed and continued to hold views or host/sponsor/promote events in support of Zionism, the apartheid state of Israel and the occupation of Palestine." As the school's dean Erwin Chemerinsky pointed out, that would bar most Jewish students and even himself from speaking before the groups. Indeed, it would bar Zionists from speaking on topics unrelated to Israel and thus went beyond viewpoint discrimination to impinge on identity (Patel 2022). Student and faculty groups in the United States have a right to invite or not invite the speakers they choose, but these student bylaws had antisemitic consequences.

BDS advocates claim that condemnation of anti-Zionist and antisemitic views suppresses academic freedom, whereas academic freedom actually requires robust debate and evaluation. Condemnation of BDS by university presidents and other senior administrators meets with loud protests that BDS faculty are being silenced and suppressed. Manufacturing lies about Israel meets with the same protest when the lie is criticized. As Steven Lubet (2022a) notes, "Shortly after the vicious stabbing of Indian-British-American author Salman Rushdie in 2022, Prof. Nader Hashemi, a specialist on Islam-West Relations, opined on the Iran Podcast that Israel was probably behind the life-threatening attack." When Hashemi's institution, the University of Denver, delivered the mildest imaginable warning against issuing dangerous speculations without evidence, in this case Hashemi's suggestion the Mossad could be behind the attack, the Middle East Studies Association (2022) condemned the university for violating Hashemi's academic freedom. MESA justified Hashemi's antisemitic remark by calling it "legitimate speculation about the politics surrounding the attempted assassination of Salman Rushdie." As David Schraub (2022) writes,

> The reason why utterly unfounded speculations about the Mossad is considered fair game, while utterly unfounded speculations about, say, antifa is not, is because for some Israel is at least on the suspect list for any evil that occurs in the world until proven otherwise. This is why lack of evidence makes it legitimate to "speculate" about Israel's involvement. No matter how seemingly distant or fanciful, Israel is always guilty till proven innocent. In a world where we know nothing, Israel is responsible for everything.

Far from being repressed, in actuality, some redouble their vocal anti-Zionism in response to criticism. But when the university distances itself from irresponsible faculty remarks, it establishes the institution as a site for rational discourse, protecting its right to defend academic freedom. The University of Denver properly imposed no sanctions on Professor Hashemi.

Universities need not treat all faculty statements as viewpoints meriting equal respect. False statements of fact are not viewpoints. Incitement to violence is not a viewpoint. People merit respect; viewpoints may not. Students and faculty who originate and promote demonstrable lies about other people should be punished, as they were not in the Dubnov case. Character assassination of the sort that Connecticut College philosopher Andrew Pessin was subjected to by a mob of students and colleagues is also not a viewpoint.

The available sanctions for tenured faculty involved in such actions do not, however, include termination of employment, except in cases where professional incompetence has been subjected to due process and proven. There are continuing demands from the public—in 2021 directed at a British faculty member, Bristol University sociologist David Miller—to fire tenured faculty who celebrate their antisemitism in public statements. The fact that Miller and other faculty engaged in antisemitic hate speech should be condemned. Irresponsible pedagogy should be addressed as well. When Wellesley College tenured African studies professor Tony Martin in 1993 assigned (and endorsed) the antisemitic book *The Secret Relationship Between Blacks and Jews*, Martin's department chair called the book "pernicious." The school's president Diana Chapman Walsh announced "We will not censor him [Martin] in any way. But we will censure him" (Dorning 1993). The book was compiled by followers of the openly antisemitic Nation of Islam leader Louis Farrakhan.

The long-term health of the academy requires that we maintain a broad understanding of academic freedom that includes speech we find abhorrent, save when we are evaluating the quality of a faculty member's teaching and research, not merely deciding what is permissible. There are very different standards and consequences at stake when the boundaries of the permissible are being defined and adjudicated. The threat of faculty terminations for unpopular speech—in the United States most widespread during World War I and during the McCarthy period—is always with us. But that does not mean the campus should be a welcoming environment for racist or antisemitic rhetoric, or that racist and antisemitic actions should be tolerated.

Our understanding of academic freedom is in flux and undergoing considerable debate. It is not clear whether a universal understanding of academic freedom can be restored. As one of my colleagues wrote to me, academic freedom is now being used in defense of things "to which the label cannot attach no matter how much an autonomic academic reaction it is to assert its being so." The AAUP has tried to counter the recognition that its view of academic freedom has changed over the years by insisting that its ongoing statements and reports have provided clarifications, not modifications. The general principle that academic freedom protects faculty publication and teaching remains intact. But confusion about whether this is primarily an individual right or a protection for higher education as a whole is widespread. Finkin and Post (2009) endorse the second view.

In summary, the answer to the question posed in the title of this chapter—"Does academic freedom protect antisemitism?"—is a qualified "yes," under circumstances I have tried to detail. Despite claims to the contrary, few faculty have suffered for holding antisemitic views. Academic freedom protects the right to say things others find loathsome or inexcusable. Despite claims to the contrary, anti-Zionist or antisemitic speakers are not being "silenced." Anti-Zionism flourishes. That is the reality. The main reason my "yes" is qualified is because of the theoretical basis for sanctioning some antisemitic actions. Yet campus antisemitism almost never entails consequences.

As a result, academic freedom has become a cover for malicious conduct, something it was not designed to be. Critiques of faculty publication and pedagogy do not violate academic freedom, though claiming they do is a regular tactic of boycott movement advocates. Continuing debate and critique are an expectation for responsible members of the academy; they are protected, not prohibited, by academic freedom. Academic freedom is simultaneously being misrepresented and undermined, and anti-Zionism and the BDS movement are at the forefront of both efforts. The BDS movement aims to normalize antisemitism on campus. Matters are likely to get worse. Those who want to prevent this must get involved.

Chapter 2

Social Media, Anti-Zionism, and the End of Academic Freedom

_____

1. Reality overtakes fantasy

As the new millennium began, it was no longer easy for everyone to sustain the utopian, democratizing fantasies that fueled early speculation about the internet and social media. Nevertheless, as late as 2017, as Max Fisher documents in *The Chaos Machine*, despite some national networks being deluged with calls for genocide, Mark Zuckerberg predicted that Facebook would end terrorism, fight climate change, lift people out of poverty, and prevent pandemics (2022, 171). Social media would engineer a new, more enlightened society. It would create "happier and freer souls" (11). We may see comparably unrealistic projections of our desires onto the metaverse.

Zuckerberg knew better, and soon the truth was revealed indelibly to others. The 2017 Rohingya genocide in Myanmar was promoted on Facebook. In Sri Lanka, Facebook drove the violent 2018 anti-Muslim riots "every deadly step" of the way (168); Facebook hate pages operated as openly as newspapers, encouraging the mobs carrying out mass murder (174). Both countries saw social media overwhelmed with "a rising chant for blood, explicit and in unison" (315). A 2018 UN report confirmed Facebook's role in promoting and organizing group violence, indeed of fomenting genocide. In Germany, 64 percent of people in extremist groups had been led to them at Facebook's suggestion (134). Launched in 2006, Twitter by 2015 was suffused with revenge fantasies and conspiracy theories, establishing a culture of provocation (82). In 2021, US president Biden would bluntly declare that Facebook was "killing people." Zuckerberg nonetheless maintained the utopian stance because it discouraged government regulation and distracted public attention from his unprincipled drive for profits and the reality of social media. Instead of a better world, unregulated online hate confronts us with "the 'democratic' rise of evil" (Topor 2023, 4).

Skepticism about inflated hopes for new and enhanced technologies is warranted by the dismal history of such predictions. Yet few if any predicted precisely the dark turn these new online communication methods would take. Every technological innovation for over a hundred years had been greeted with both high hopes and predictions of disaster. The world did change dramatically each time, but even as usage increased and the technologies evolved, neither a new Eden nor a new Hell materialized, at least until now. As we proceed through the third decade of the new century, we appear to have broken the pattern. The transformative benefits of the internet, digitization, social media, and AI are real, but so too are their immense capacities for destruction, perhaps even for evil, as hate speech proliferates and inspires violent action. Social media is now responsible for "enabling the community's collective id" (Fisher 2022, 72). Group online hate provokes the psychological state of deindividuation displayed in mob violence. As Lev Topor writes, "the online domain has become the main operational platform of extremists worldwide, upon which they structure their social network of hate" (2023, 4). He concludes that "online users are radicalized to the point that they leave their keyboard to take to the streets and murder people they dislike" (21). Hate speech is the glue that binds such people into communities.

The wider social effects of social media are becoming clear, and they are weighted toward disaster. Imagined to be a force favoring democracy, it has rapidly evolved to be the opposite. As a consequence, it is both irresponsible and delusional to view social media simply—as the AAUP does—as a neutral space for expressing personal opinions, a public square where an absolutist version of academic freedom should prevail. Professional standards reflecting the medium's power to harm must govern online faculty speech. How many lives were lost to COVID after the Hoover Institution's Scott Atlas discouraged the wearing of masks and tweeted his November 2020 plea for Michigan residents to "rise up" against Governor Gretchen Whitmer's COVID-19 mitigation policies?

Although most of us do not encounter them, we know that sites for child pornography, racism, and antisemitism proliferate. We know that the

January 6, 2021, assault on the US Capitol was partly organized through social media. We are learning that human trafficking and drug trafficking groups use the same resources. Can we have the benefits without the dangers? Not without standards for practice and regulation, better law enforcement, and appropriate constraints. We need more effective content moderation with public monitoring of private companies. But in the end, only fundamental repurposing and restructuring of social media will suffice to reform it. So long as the current business model—which maximizes advertising income by driving user participation through limited content moderation—is in force, hate speech will prevail.

The first wave of internet platforms (YouTube, Facebook, Instagram, and Twitter) is widely known. The growing second wave (TikTok, Telegram, Threads, 4chan, the 4chan spinoff 8chan, BitChute, Discord, Reddit, Parler, Snapchat, Twitch, WhatsApp, and others) may be less familiar. Some websites, 4chan and 8chan among them, provide message boards for anonymous, violently racist, and antisemitic memes and images. People post them without risking personal consequences. As Weimann and Masri (2022) point out, TikTok has good guidelines for the elimination of hate speech; it just doesn't apply them. It does, however, seem adept at removing material critical of the Chinese government. TikTok has tremendous reach among young people and has created a spiral of antisemitic journalism and media. A US Congressional committee found that it took only 75 minutes of random scrolling for a TikTok user to encounter pro-Nazi propaganda (Rawnsley 2023). At an October 19, 2022, Berlin conference on "Decoding Antisemitism," Weimann pointed out that TikTok distributed 11,200 versions of a song calling for the slaughter of Jews.

The academy needs principles to guide it in evaluating how our online liberties reshape academic freedom. Faculty so far face few consequences when they contribute to social media's "system-wide reality distortion" (Fisher 2022, 135), its "identity-affirming falsehoods" (144), its "subcultures of toxicity and hate" (71), its "doom-loop of polarization and misinformation" that culminate in calls for violence (98). This chapter will explore the academic consequences; it is a companion to "Does Academic Freedom Protect Antisemitism?"

Early concern about faculty forays into social media often stemmed from intemperate out-of-character moments. Annoyed or inspired, a faculty member would hit "send" and disseminate an ill-considered remark, then realize too late it was on its way before better judgment could prevail. As more users signed up to social media and shared messages proliferated, intemperate messages increasingly went viral and became people's signature statements. Rational observers realized that faculty should be forgiven occasional errors of judgment. Yet calls for forgiveness may decline now that there is a brief window of time when some emails can be cancelled, allowing a moment for reconsideration. But by the 2010s a more persistent phenomenon arose: the use of social media to create a parallel persona. It could present an identity unrelated to a faculty member's professional responsibilities. But for many it was an avatar embodying their areas of teaching and research. People also began to take liberties on social media in their areas of expertise that they would not take in their formal publications. Some faculty treated online comments as polemical addenda to their scholarship. Some supplement anti-Zionist views with more aggressive antisemitism. Lara Sheehi at George Washington University persistently used tweets that way.

The global reach of viral online hate exponentially exceeds anything we have confronted before. Antisemitism eliminated from one platform quickly spreads to another. Elon Musk's acquisition of Twitter (since renamed X) in October 2022 and his advocacy of unmoderated free speech has rapidly increased the site's dissemination of hate speech and disinformation. Indeed, parts of Twitter have already become the "hellscape" Musk declared he wished to forestall. In November 2022, the national director of the US-based Secure Community Network announced that "Twitter has an antisemitism problem—with hashtags such as #holohoax [Holocaust Hoax] and #killthe-jews abounding on the site" (Grant 2022). Whatever Twitter/X's future as a platform may be—given not only Musk's erratic leadership but also Twitter's competition with Zuckerberg/Meta's new 2023 app Threads— its failure to moderate content is a lesson for the entire industry. Alternative social media sites like Mastodon, which offers user networks where content moderation can eliminate the frenetic, abusive character of the Twitter environment, hold some promise (Chayka 2022).

Faculty members who contribute to online hate can reach tens of thousands of people. It is impossible to estimate the public impact of faculty speech without taking the internet into consideration. But there is one vast domain of online speech that will likely remain beyond the reach of peer review: the deep or dark web. It represents as much as 95 percent of web content overall, but it is not indexed by search engines and is virtually impossible to explore with any thoroughness. It is largely anonymous. As Lev Topor writes, there "antisemites can express their racist ideas with almost complete anonymity and security, and with no shame at all" (2019, 25). A faculty member could do so by creating an avatar to express unreserved antisemitism. Gabriel Weimann informs me that a highly skilled professional could track a person's dark net activity, but it is unsafe even to do a general search for antisemitic material there if you are unable to hide your identity. Downloading hate speech or illegal material from the dark web increases the risk of personal exposure.

The main dark web browser, Tor (short for The Onion Router), was developed by the US Navy, and it remains US-maintained and controlled but unregulated. Instead of being directly connected to a server, a user passes through several IP addresses, assuring their anonymity and making the routine indexing that Google and other sites carry out virtually impossible. This facilitates the invisibility that intelligence operations demand but also enables neo-Nazi, antisemitic, and other hate groups to operate without consequences. "The dark web acts as a cloud of ideas that float around without any particular association with the users who are their proponents" (Topor 2023, 95). The massacres in Jewish institutions and elsewhere that were live-streamed on Facebook by the murderers themselves were soon taken down, but they are preserved on the dark web, apparently forever. We may never know who transferred them there.

This argues for greater faculty care in posting intemperate or hateful remarks. Moreover, it warrants weighing faculty social media activism more heavily in personnel decisions if the activism implicates the person's areas of teaching or research. This is especially true for faculty members who become superposters—superspreaders who "pull the platforms toward these defining tendencies of dogmatism, narcissism, aggrandizement, and cruelty" (Fisher 2022, 189). Faculty superposters are not necessarily thoughtful, a criterion you might expect for faculty, but superposters drive engagement nonetheless. Faculty tempted to achieve that status are not necessarily guided by rational calculation. Anti-Zionists propelled by moral outrage may feel psychologically justified in denying their need for social media celebrity. The drive for celebrity is rationalized as righteous political action.

When it can be shown that a faculty member's social media activity may be helping to build hate groups and fuel incitement to violence, it is essential to engage with the problem. The first step is education, showing the faculty member that the particular online activity carries that risk. If the faculty member persists despite evidence, then more serious interventions may be required. Faculty members are entitled to their opinions, but online speech that incites violence can constitute unlawful conduct, not simply expressive speech protected by the First Amendment or academic freedom. Widely disseminated hate speech becomes a form of consequential action.

That brings us back to the question posed in the first chapter: does academic freedom protect antisemitism? Consider this reformulation: if the members of an academic discipline widely embrace anti-Zionist and antisemitic rhetoric and convictions, should they be protected from negative professional consequences? Others would include faculty members with no professional responsibilities related to Jewish culture or the Israeli-Palestinian conflict. The views of those unconnected to the relevant fields can be classified as extramural. The AAUP has long held that extramural remarks unrelated to a faculty member's field are protected from institutional discipline by academic freedom. Thus some of the IHRA Definition's examples of antisemitic speech would be protected from university sanctions if a paleontologist tweeted statements embodying them, though not if he or she repeatedly made the statements in class.

2. Amplification by algorithm

Critically important for aggressive posts is the widespread use of algorithms that automatically distribute additional disinformation and racist or antisemitic hate to users who show an interest in them. If you display any interest in online antisemitism, whether that interest is sympathetic or opposed, you will soon be flooded with more examples. Algorithms decide what you want to see and provide it. "The relationship between a Facebook algorithm and the user is bidirectional. Each trains the other" (Fisher 2022, 121). As Gabriel Weimann (2022) points out, if you are studying online hate, an algorithm becomes your research assistant. But if you are sympathetic or impressionable, it can drive you involuntarily into the dark realm of hate and disinformation.

Algorithms that distribute links to neutral subjects can be useful. Purchasing a book on Amazon will generate links to related titles. But the involuntary dissemination of hate speech can maximize its impact and social damage. "Through algorithm-driven technology, which serves to generate profit, the dissemination of hate thus got a major upgrade" (Hübscher and von Mering 2022, 5). Facebook, for example, "with the help of a 'stimulus-response loop,' prioritizes incendiary content, such as hateful speech and visuals, which subsequently becomes normalized" (7). Although the artificial intelligence (AI) that empowers algorithms is relatively simple compared to what awaits us, it has created "a curtain of illusions that increased societal polarization, undermined our mental health, and unraveled democracy" (Harari, Harris, and Ruskin 2023). When AI is fully integrated with algorithms, their combined power to saturate social life with hate speech and disinformation will be substantially magnified. Although algorithms can be tweaked to reduce their destructive potential, companies are well aware that doing so may decrease users' online time and thus reduce advertising revenue. I side with former Facebook employee Francis Haugen: turn off the algorithms. There is no other solution.

Social media drives attitudes, reinforces beliefs, and can intensify fear, anxiety, and hostility. It also cements personal identity. When social media integrates people into affinity groups, they no longer suffer resentment in isolation. "Hate websites often also include chat rooms and discussion boards where people discover the important fact that they are no longer alone" (Reichelmann, Vysotsky, and Levin 2021, 239). Group identification makes it possible to take pride in shared anxiety and resentment. Ferenc Huszár and his coauthors found that "in 6 out of 7 countries studied, the mainstream political right enjoys higher algorithmic amplification than the mainstream political left" (Huszár et al. 2021, 1). Pro-democracy groups also organize through social media, but their cultural impact is dwarfed by the flood of hate unleashed by platform algorithms.

The internet had already made it easier to find like-minded people and form hate-based alliances. That trend escalated after Twitter installed its personal algorithmic amplification system in 2016. In Brazil, algorithms were building a militia (Fisher 2022, 286), a force that tried to overrun the government in 2023. YouTube operates much the same way. Telegram is a favorite because it lacks meaningful content moderation. Moreover, what one user considers merely emotional or political venting can prove an inducement to violence to another. "Hate speech on social media can be a precursor to hateful violence in real life" (Hübscher and von Mering 2022, 6). Users can no longer control who receives their public messages. Forwarding messages has always been easy, as has adding comments that can intensify expressions of bias. But algorithmic dissemination vastly expands the audience for a Twitter, Threads, TikTok, or Telegram post. Retweets, too, can have very wide circulation.

Research makes clear that online hate speech can lead to real world physical violence. The same consequence obtains for spreading falsehoods online: "As false content propagates more and more widely online, it can lead to violence" (Benesch et al. 2021, 19). The incitement potential is increased by algorithms that spread hate and disinformation widely. These algorithms favor intense statements that attract attention and promote engagement. Incitement potential is maximized by repetition. This applies both to the impulse to condone violence and the willingness to commit it. Such statements require a receptive or susceptible audience, but those audiences exist whether or not someone posting hateful messages realizes this. Online hate that can incite violence includes updated versions of the conspiracy theories that have plagued Jews for centuries. The cycle of conspiracism that leads to violence is by no means limited to Jews and Israel; it pervades all contemporary politics. As Brian Hughes, cofounder and associate director of American University's Polarization and Extremism Research and Innovation Lab (PERIL), observes, "The conspiracy theory prompts an act of violence; that act of violence needs to be disavowed, and it can only be disavowed by more conspiracy theories, which prompt more violence" (Karni, Khurana, and Thompson 2022).

Existing algorithms favor emotionally charged expressions of moral outrage. Every single such word in a post increases distribution by 20 percent (Fisher 2022, 138). The contributing prejudices are typically already present, but the algorithms persuade more people of their validity. And they create new affinity groups by drawing together people with different conspiracist beliefs, "mashing hostile tribes together" into larger groups (143). The moral outrage against Israel that many faculty members expressed online during the country's recent wars with Hamas repeatedly propelled bizarre antisemitic fantasies. Rational critique of Israeli practices does not have the same power. The algorithms promote inflammatory rhetoric over reason.

This dark algorithmic universe has made the belief that fierce anti-Zionism and antisemitism can be segregated from one another obsolete. When evil intent is vehemently ascribed to the Jewish state, it implicates Jews worldwide. Israelis accused of committing genocide in Gaza are accused of engineering the COVID pandemic, and soon all Jews are implicated. The claim that the Zika virus was a Jewish plot had already done the rounds. "When Congress passed a stimulus package in 2020, for example, the most shared posts on Twitter reported that the bill siphoned $500 million meant for low-income Americans to Israel's government" (Fisher 2022, 98). From there the claim that the Jews aim to replace "us" and erase "our" culture requires no conceptual leap. The news about a Jewish plot to dilute the white race spread in company with hyperbolic anti-Zionism. The QAnon movement would lump together traitorous Democrats and Jewish financiers among the enemies to be eliminated. Reddit's hate communities include "WatchNiggersDie" and "GasTheKikes." The Southern Poverty Law Center calls Reddit "a worse black hole of violent racism than Stormfront," the notorious neo-Nazi website (Fisher 2022, 73).

3. The AAUP embraces social media

In 2015, the AAUP first gave definitive form to its evolving position by applying the principle that *all* extramural statements are protected to a controversial case. The principle developed in response to Steven Salaita's harsh tweets about Israel, but the AAUP concluded that all faculty statements on social media are protected by academic freedom.[1] Rebecca Ruth Gould has more recently articulated an absolutist version of this principle, asserting that extramural speech is protected for all employees: "It is necessary to distinguish between workplace-specific utterances, such as those uttered in a classroom context, and utterances made outside the workplace, which the employer has no right to monitor, let alone punish. Whether the employee in question is a university professor or a bus driver, what they do and say on their own time, outside workplace contexts, is their own business" (2023, 115).

Salaita was a prospective faculty hire at my campus, the University of Illinois at Urbana-Champaign. He had been writing about and would now be teaching the Israeli-Palestinian conflict in a course linking the treatment of indigenous peoples in Israel and the United States. He had also issued scores of anti-Zionist and antisemitic tweets about the Jewish state over a period of more than a year.[2]

---

1 In a March 2021 column about Yale University's dismissal of psychiatry professor Brandy Lee, Hank Reichman, the chair of the AAUP's Committee A on Academic Freedom and Tenure, argues in part that the action was inappropriate because the AAUP considers statements on social media protected. As Reichman (2021a) reports, "Lee charges that Yale fired her in response to a January 2020 tweet that characterized 'just about all' of former president Donald Trump's supporters as suffering from 'shared psychosis' and said that Trump attorney Alan Dershowitz had 'wholly taken on Trump's symptoms by contagion.'" The controversial Goldwater Rule claims that psychiatrists are barred from commenting on the mental health of people they have not examined. In my view, academic freedom protects a qualified faculty member who chooses to make a psychiatric evaluation of a public figure. That the vehicle was social media is irrelevant.

2 The University of Illinois at Urbana-Champaign's Chancellor Phyllis Wise only considered Salaita's aggressive tweets from the summer of 2014, during Operation Protective Edge, Israel's campaign in Gaza. That was the extent of the social media evidence her staff provided to her. Unfortunately, the AAUP compounded the error by declaring it had observed the same limit, indeed would only consider the same evidence the campus had. But then the AAUP added several tweets not part of the UIUC case. More problematically, the AAUP report cites its 1964 insistence that "a final decision should take into account the faculty member's entire record as a teacher and scholar" (AAUP 2015b, 12) but then asserts "it would therefore be presumptuous for this committee" to consider additional issues or evidence (14). As it happens, they did consider other evidence, including claims about donor evidence, but decided it would be more effective to omit committee member views on those matters from the report. Most importantly, the prospective department's and outside referee's comments on his publications were part of the dossier sent forward, as was his vita. His publications were not extraneous to the campus review; they were part of it. On the other hand, though his appointment papers were not complete, and the campus Academic Freedom Committee considered him to be suspended between a candidate and a serving faculty member, the AAUP's decision to place him in the latter category was not unreasonable. I considered him still a candidate, as that was consistent with advice the AAUP staff had given earlier when people facing similar crises requested assistance. Decades ago, a friend signed a contract for a new job, then resigned his current position. But financial constraints led the new campus to cancel the offer before the chair of the board of trustees added his signature to the contract. My friend was out of a job. The AAUP staff told him he had no recourse. For forty years I have advised people never to resign a current position, as Salaita did, until the new contract is finalized.

I had hoped never to write about this case again, but one cannot explain the AAUP's current position on extramural speech without delving into the organization's history regarding Salaita. As I document in *Israel Denial*, except for their occasional profanity or vulgarity, Salaita's tweets are often interchangeable with statements in his books and essays. They are part of a coherent professional profile that repeatedly mirrors the IHRA Definition's examples of antisemitism.[3] Of course, the IHRA had not yet adopted its Working Definition in 2014 and 2015 when the Salaita case was intensely debated. The Definition might have made it more difficult to defend him had it existed at this time.

Here are a few examples of sentences from his books that are politically consistent with his tweets:

- "Racism has always been fundamental to the Zionist Project."
- "Israel grants equal rights only to Jews."
- "Zionist colonization of Palestine started it. Only the decolonization of Palestine will end it."
- "Zionism, after all, has been responsible for innumerable atrocities."
- "It glorifies democracy while practicing apartheid."
- "Israel's soul died in the moment of its creation."
- "Israel's dead soul is the affirmation of life through its long overdue murder."
- "When Israel misbehaves, all Jews, no matter where, become responsible."
- "No ideology more than Zionism has the ability to make hypocrites of even the sincerest human beings."

And here are a few tweets embodying comparable beliefs:

- "Israel and ISIS are but two prongs of the same violent ethnonationalism."
- "Let's cut to the chase: If you're defending Israel now you're an awful human being."
- "Zionists: transforming 'antisemitism' from something horrible into something honorable since 1948."
- "If Israel affirms life, then why do so many Zionists celebrate the slaughter of children? What's that? Oh, I see JEWISH life."

---

3 See "Steven Salaita: The Fluid Line Between Anti-Zionism and Anti-Semitism," in Nelson (2019, 117–56).

In Britain, Salaita's tweets would count as harassment contributing to a hostile environment for Jewish students. Certainly they count as hate speech in both the US and Europe.

Although some faculty at the University of Illinois at Urbana-Champaign, including Michael Rothberg, my department head at the time (now at UCLA), tried to interpret a number of individual tweets to make them seem harmless, most of Salaita's campus supporters felt that the only relevant issue was that the administration and board of trustees should have honored the American Indian studies program decision to hire him, regardless of his views. My own problem was primarily with Salaita's scholarship, not with his tweets. I had read all his work and thought his standards for evidence did not meet those of a research university. My *Israel Denial* chapter on Salaita devotes much of its analysis to his books and essays, rather than to his activity on social media. Some of my critics prefer to ignore this, as they have not themselves read his publications. In fact, I had often voted against candidates for tenure when I believed their publications, having nothing to do with Israel or Judaism, were not first rate.

In a 2014 "Statement on the Case of Professor Steven G. Salaita," followed by a full report the next year, the AAUP argued that "while Professor Salaita's scholarship does appear to deal with the topic of Palestine, his posts were arguably not intended as scholarly statements but as expressions of personal viewpoint" (AAUP 2014).[4] Given that Salaita continually expresses his personal perspective on Palestine in his books and essays, the distinction is meaningless.[5] The AAUP's qualified and rather gingerly statement in its investigative report—it "has been alleged in this case [that] such speech relates to a faculty member's disciplinary expertise" (2015a, 11)— is rather odd, since Israel is the subject of the tweets and most of his books. His tweets proved to be anything but ephemeral: social media defined his public persona both then and now. The prevailing assumption about social media, that "this too shall pass," proved to be untrue. This adds a further challenge in evaluating the role social media that should play in personnel decisions.

In 2014, however, the university's major academic problem should have been the relentlessly antisemitic character of Salaita's publications. To say

---

4 For a detailed explanation of how the AAUP handles cases and develops investigative reports, see Nelson (2010).

5 The AAUP did not review Salaita's scholarship and thus could maintain the fiction that his tweets were separate statements of personal opinion. I served as AAUP president from 2006 to 2012 and on Committee A from 2006 to 2015. I dissented from the AAUP's 2015 report. It is important to note that the campus did not perform a sufficient review of Salaita's scholarship either.

Salaita "does appear to deal with the topic of Palestine" when it is the central preoccupation of his career is at best an empty concession. It reflected the AAUP's anti-Zionist motivation, its opposition to dealing forthrightly with his work. In the national Committee A sessions on Salaita, I appeared to be the only one who had read all his work. Salaita's obsessive attacks on Israel recur in *The Holy Land in Transit; Anti-Arab Racism in the USA; Israel's Dead Soul; Uncivil Rites*, and many of his other publications. His case highlights the problem with the AAUP's determination to separate social media statements from professional publications on the same subject. Social media statements are often made with great conviction, offering not mere "personal viewpoints" but ethical and political conclusions that apply to the areas in which faculty members publish and teach.

Writing a few years later in his book *The Future of Academic Freedom*, former AAUP Committee A chair Henry Reichman offered the same less than candid account of the relationship between Salaita's tweets and his formal publications: "his academic study of indigenous peoples can be said to be at least indirectly related to his views on the Israeli-Palestinian conflict expressed in his tweets" (2019, 59). Salaita was hired specifically to teach "comparative indigeneity," having previously covered only one such comparison in his academic work, namely the comparison between the history and treatment of Native Americans and Palestinians. This included repeated condemnations of Israel, including the unsupported claim that Israel modeled its practices after US history. "Indirectly related?" Why this reluctance to describe the reality of the appointment accurately? Obviously because the facts do not support the narrative Reichman wants to offer. In June 2014, Salaita tweeted, "At this point, if Netanyahu appeared on TV with a necklace made from the teeth of Palestinian children, would anybody be surprised?" Was it unreasonable to expect such views would affect his teaching about Israel?

The AAUP's position on the Salaita case ignored the impossibility of drawing a definitive line between published scholarship and social media posts—between speech directed toward the scholarly community and speech directed toward the general public. Max Fisher argues that the evolution of social media extremism has had the effect of "forever ending the separation between digital and nondigital spaces, between internet culture and culture" (2022, 41). Neither location nor audience provides a sound basis for drawing that distinction. Despite the AAUP's desire to sustain it, the distinction is now largely irrelevant. Nor does the difference in length and detail between scholarly publications and social media messages justify treating them as unrelated forms of communication. After noting that "the most theoretically problematic aspect of academic freedom is extramural expression," Finkin and Post reasonably deny externality to any expression implicating professional expertise: "This dimension of academic freedom does not concern communications that are connected to faculty expertise, for such expression is encompassed within freedom of research." Those communications must be considered contributions to research (2009, 127). In its Committee A report on the University of Illinois's 2014 Board of Trustees decision in the case of Salaita, a misguided AAUP withdrew that option: "the status of an utterance as extramural does not depend on its relationship to a faculty member's disciplinary expertise." Thus "Salaita's tweets were extramural, regardless of whether they were related to his area of expertise" (2015a, 11).[6]

The AAUP's efforts to hold faculty harmless for speech offered in their capacity as citizens have a long history. They are reinforced by the observation that faculty should have as much right to protected speech on matters of public concern as other Americans. Yet the AAUP is aware that employees in private industry are not so protected. Their tweets and Facebook posts can put their jobs at risk. As noted earlier, Rebecca Gould can wish it were otherwise, but that does not make it so. Indeed, faculty at private, not public, institutions also lack parallel First Amendment protections and require academic freedom guarantees against punishment by their employer.[7]

By the AAUP's 2015 standard, a historian who tweets that the Holocaust was a hoax would be protected. The same claim made to a history class would risk the ultimate sanction—termination of employment—following due process. That distinction is unworkable, an absurdity. By the AAUP standard that prevailed for more than half a century, a historian calling the Holocaust a hoax in any forum could be judged unfit to teach. Academic freedom would not have applied wherever the claim was made. The First Amendment protects a Holocaust denier from government sanctions but not from a university decision that he or she is not qualified to teach in a history department. Categorical opposition to Holocaust denial is not merely a disciplinary standard; it applies to the academy

---

6   The AAUP has a long history of seeking expanded protections for faculty speech, including by applying those protections to new means of communication, but I continue to believe it was its determination to defend Salaita in particular that led to the organization's 2015 views.

7   The 2006 US Supreme Court decision in *Garcetti* v. *Ceballos* ruled that "pursuant to their official duties, the employees are not speaking as citizens for First Amendment purposes, and the Constitution does not insulate their communications from employer discipline." Although the case did not concern faculty and although the majority set aside the decision's implications for academic freedom, the AAUP issued extensive warnings that speech protections for public university employees could be threatened. See AAUP (2009).

as a whole. But Holocaust denial is guaranteed to be professionally disabling only to a historian or another faculty member who studies or teaches about the Holocaust, whether in a dedicated course or as part of a broader survey. A specialist in Holocaust education in a college of education would also face dismissal for Holocaust denial. It could, however, also put at risk anyone whose expectations for disciplinary competence encompass modern history.

Fueled in part by the anti-Zionism of some Committee A members and national staff, the AAUP in 2015 was so focused on faculty speech rights that it failed to honor the organization's historic commitment to pairing rights with responsibilities. Faculty members have a responsibility not to promote gross falsehoods to their students. Holocaust denial qualifies as a gross falsehood. In one respect, however, I hold the organization harmless: in 2015 most faculty members did not yet know how pernicious the dissemination of false or malicious social media posts could be. Discussion of algorithms at that point was almost nonexistent. Businesses providing social media services knew the pitfalls, but the public did not. In 2015, we knew that internet campaigns could put individuals in harm's way, but we did not yet imagine internet trolls putting the country and the world in peril. We would learn that social media encourages intensified expressions of hate and enables people to create and join hate groups more easily. It draws people into hate-based alliances and overwhelms rational understanding with disinformation.

The challenge posed by faculty use of social media to disseminate hate was dramatized in 2023. Like many faculty whose social media activity gets them in trouble, Salaita deleted his Twitter account, making many of his tweets unavailable. So too did George Washington University (GWU) psychologist Lara Sheehi after the NGO StandWithUs filed a January 12 complaint against the university with the Civil Rights Division of the US Department of Education.[8] Filed on behalf of several female graduate students in GWU's professional psychology program, the complaint alleged that Sheehi had discriminated against them in her required course on diversity, then retaliated when the students raised their concern with the university. The university dismissed the Jewish students' complaint, instead pursuing Sheehi's retaliatory accusation of racism against them. This time, however, all Sheehi's tweets were harvested before she closed her account. I reviewed a file of 9,776 of her tweets issued between 2010 and January 2023, all consisting of original tweets or comments when retweeting.

Scores of her tweets include antisemitic insults about Israel itself and the Zionist project to reestablish a state in the Jews' ancient homeland. Her

---

8   The text of the complaint is available at https://online.flippingbook.com/view/536430327/.

vehement tweets are often sprinkled with profanity: "Palestinians have been telling us since its illegal inception that Israel is an ethnonationalist supremacist state whose very existence is built around ethnic purity to which they'll go to any end to achieve" (9/1/2019, 6:39 a.m.); "Zionism is literally predicated on settler-colonialism and the notion that a whole people is inferior and therefore worthy of extinction—my bad that I don't think that's progressive" (10/15/2018, 9:52:59 p.m.); "FUCK ZIONISM, ZIONISTS, AND SETTLER COLONIALISM using Palestinian lives as examples of their boundless cruelty and power. Anyone who can't yet get it, peddles 'both sides' bs and doesn't denounce this persistent violence is complicit" (10/24/2020, 11:48:18 a.m.); "the psychotic processing of settlers and Zionists truly has no bounds" (12/4/2021, 8:53 p.m.); "Zionists are so far up their own asses they don't see how this actually proves the point of undue and criminal force by occupying forces" (5/9/2021, 3:21:05 p.m.); "And fuckers are still arguing about whether or not zionism is a form of fascist white supremacy. Ok." (10/11/2022, 10:01:00 a.m.); "YOU CANNOT BE A ZIONIST AND A FEMINIST AT THE SAME TIME" (5/9/2021, 5:54:04 p.m.); "You can't be a 'zioness' and profess to have any ability to critically assess anything, ever." (1/29/2018, 10:12:52 p.m.). In addition to nearly 10,000 tweets of her own, she retweeted an equal number of tweets by others: "If you … STILL entertain for even a split second that Hamas is the terrorist entity, there is literally zero hope for you, your soul, or your general existence as an ethical human being in this world. There is no grey area here, I'm not sorry to report" (5/22/2021, 11:01 a.m.).

These tweets condemn Jewish and non-Jewish Zionist students alike. The problem will increase going forward because the tweets are now widely available in online essays (Mills 2023a, 2023b; Canary Mission 2023; Nelson 2023). The sentiments in the tweets are reinforced by numerous video interviews on YouTube and by the book-length anti-Zionist tract Sheehi coauthored with her partner Stephen, *Psychoanalysis under Occupation*. The StandWithUs complaint accounts in detail what her Jewish students endured in 2022 and suggests why students should be wary of her in the future. Sheehi presents a textbook case of the political triangulation of social media activity, classroom practices, and academic publications. At the very least, Sheehi's courses should not be required.

4. The consequences of unbridled hate

Antisemitism in the UK, a 2016 report by the House of Commons Home Affairs Committee, provides a preliminary picture of how unpleasant social media campaigns targeted against individuals can be, but some of the truly devastating examples occurred in other countries. Max Fisher (2022) describes a forbidding case in *The Chaos Machine,* in which he tells the story of a vicious and devastating social media campaign against Brazilian faculty member Tatiana Lionco, a campaign initiated by Jair Bolsonaro before he became president of Brazil. Internet conspiracy theories fueled both the 2021 assault on the US Capitol and opposition to vaccines—vaccines capable of protecting people from a deadly pandemic. With those events, many in the United States finally recognized the power of mass delusions that proliferate in what Tom Scocca calls a social media "dance of provocation and denial" (2020, 56).

"The context-collapsing and democracy-destabilizing nature of social media makes it extremely difficult to cling to the traditional liberal belief that the best remedy for hate speech is more speech" (Bérubé and Ruth 2022, 5). Likewise, the old confidence that lies would be discredited in the marketplace of ideas does not apply to social media. The flood of misinformation, hate speech, and conspiracy theories amplified by social media overwhelms efforts at rational correction. Delusions and moral outrage eviscerate the basic rationale behind responsible faculty reasoning. As Fisher argues, "on social media, a sober fact-check would never rise as high as a salacious rumor" (2022, 193). As Anthony Julius (2022) writes about the internet, "error does not collapse, exposed to truth; error overwhelms truth." The result, he writes, is "a collapsing of the disciplinary integrity of discourses; an erasure of demarcations between science and the Pseudosciences; and an equalizing of status of quack and expert." Joel Finkelstein and his coauthors ask "whether the best and most civic American inclinations can be empowered by social media in the same way that the worst inclinations have been" and conclude that "properly equipped digital Jewish citizens can exercise the power of free speech to challenge antisemitism at the speed of electrons and across the globe" (Finkelstein, Blackmer, and Rubin 2021, 83, 85), but that may be an empty fantasy.

Recognizing the special context of online speech, the US Defense Department revised its rules in late 2021 so that "reposting or 'liking' extremist content will be viewed as advocating the content" (Cooper 2021) and be subject to disciplinary action. While such disciplinary action is not appropriate in higher education, we should not hold faculty harmless for all public speech when they undergo professional evaluation.

My former chancellor Phyllis Wise's determination to impose a requirement of "civility" on faculty members' public speech was an ignorant violation of academic freedom. But we do need to think about faculty responsibilities in a public sphere now "driven by the production of 'high-arousal emotion' or 'activating emotions': curiosity, humor, 'lust, and nostalgia, and envy, and outrage'"

(Scocca 2020, 56; quoting Marantz [2019]). As Scocca writes, "the Internet and the devices and systems built on top of it have done something new and unsettling to the subjective experience of being human ... something has been damaged about the world in which people live" (55). As Anne Applebaum and Peter Pomerantsev write, "The voices of the angriest, most emotional, most divisive—and often the most duplicitous—participants are amplified," creating "internet mobs" in which people "are submerged in the logic of the crowd" (2021, 42). The AAUP's conviction that academic freedom protects faculty indulgence in broadcasting hate speech, antisemitism, and misinformation is worse than irresponsible. It does damage to the academy itself and to its own reputation.

"Online platforms are unmatched vectors for the rapid transmission of anti-semitic content" (R. Elman 2022, 110). Hate speech can magnify its political power through internet distribution. Both in the 2017 "Unite the Right" rally in Charlottesville, Virginia, and the 2018 mass murder of Jews at the Tree of Life synagogue in Pittsburgh, Pennsylvania, we saw antisemitism intensified online produce murderous action. "Tired of its online trolling," antisemitism "moved from the virtual world into the real one" (108). Another effect was unexpected: hate speech at the opposite ends of the political spectrum converged. Antisemites on the right and the left were "connected by the impression of themselves as rebels who speak truth to (Jewish) power" (111).

Does this mean that we should require what the AAUP advised in its 1915 Declaration? "In their extramural utterances," it states "it is obvious that academic teachers are under a peculiar obligation to avoid hasty or unverified or exaggerated statements, and to refrain from intemperate or sensational modes of expression" (AAUP 2015b, 10). Like the authors of the Second Amendment to the US Constitution, who never envisioned assault rifles, the authors of the Declaration did not foresee Facebook, Twitter, and YouTube a century later. A few pages earlier, the Declaration offers advice about faculty research: "the disinterestedness and impartiality of their inquiries and their conclusions shall be, so far as is humanly possible, beyond the reach of suspicion" (8). At least for the humanities, this amounts to a principle guiding the priesthood of a vanished religion. Reading that guidance only underlines the AAUP's disconnection from contemporary social practices. Faculty will not honor practices that so many online contributors have abandoned. But they should exercise special care in making statements that function as hate speech or discredit their own expertise.

The determination to protect online faculty speech at all costs poses a threat to the academy as a whole. One reason is that the public does not distinguish between professional and extramural opinion. Members of the public, including local and national politicians, will conclude more sensibly that the two categories of speech originate with the same person. Some people might be persuaded to accept such a division when social media remarks are clearly outside a faculty member's expertise. But there is no chance they will grant the distinction when compromising or hateful statements match the subjects about which faculty are expected to show professional judgment when teaching their children.

It's folly to think that a virulent online antisemite metamorphoses into an admirable person after crossing the campus threshold. To suppose that such a person teaches the Israeli-Palestinian conflict fairly requires blindness fueled by academic rationalization. The same is true of an online faculty racist who teaches or writes about the role of race in American or British society. Overt faculty racism, however, does not have the ideological support system that now exists for faculty antisemitism. Faculty members might indulge their hatreds online given the free pass granted to online statements, at the same time exercising caution on campus, thus creating two separate identities. Even absent such a willfully deceptive strategy, public acceptance of academic freedom will be undermined by the insistence that social media is beyond the realm of professional judgment.

The fragility of the current AAUP standard may have provoked a 2021 *Chronicle of Higher Education* essay by Feisal Mohamed, "I Love the Public Humanities, But…," which aims to buttress the AAUP principle by further expanding the faculty right to protect speech from professional judgment. Mohamed (2021) writes that "considering public activity as part of a faculty member's professional profile raises major academic-freedom concerns. Gone is the category of extramural speech." But that need not be the case. Finkin and Post (2009) sensibly limit extramural speech free from professional judgment to that outside faculty areas of official expertise, a position supported by many in the AAUP until 2015. Recognizing that not just social media posts but op-eds and other forms of public speech can be targeted for political attack, Mohamed urges that "we must recommit ourselves to the idea that faculty members as citizens have a right to speech beyond the scrutiny of the university." Indeed, faculty members "ought to be allowed to embargo certain writings, including social-media posts or entire social-media accounts, as not falling within the cognizance of their institutions." He includes opinion pieces, letters to the editor, op-eds, tweets, and other unspecified categories of writing among the works that could be self-embargoed, even during a tenure review. A person could exclude books and essays from evaluation.

Mohamed is frank in proposing that there should be no content limits on what can be protected: "a person can embargo ravings defending the cause of white nationalism." Only if classroom teaching could be shown to have the same bias could professional consequences obtain. But there could be public consequences if a university granted tenure to a faculty member who rants in favor of white nationalism online. The same consequences would apply to overt antisemitism from a faculty member who publishes about Jewish issues. No need any longer for faculty to prove anti-Zionism is not antisemitism. No need to hesitate over promoting hate speech. Feisal Mohamed is a former colleague for whom I have a great deal of respect, but I believe he is dead wrong. This plan would discredit academic freedom itself. Meanwhile, it would lend some academic credibility to the hatred it protected.

What do Mohamed and the members of the AAUP's Committee A actually know about hate speech on conventional social media or the dark web? Abstract references to hate speech can be misleading. The same can be said of Mohamed's reference to white nationalist ravings, despite the fact that he may have intended the phrase to have a sense of material reality. Social media "ravings" run the gamut from formulaic phrases to obscene videos to unimaginable creations. Consider what Gabriel Weimann and Natalie Masri (2022) found on TikTok: "In late April 2020, two Minnesota high school students were criticized for sharing a video titled 'Me and the boys on the way to camp,' which photoshops them dancing in a Nazi boxcar and happily skipping into Auschwitz" (171). "In another video, a young man drinks a milk-like liquid. As he complains about the strange taste, a friend explains to him that he had just poured Anne Frank's ashes from a container into his drink" (170). These were teenagers who could have such transgressions explained to them. Should we hold a historian harmless for posting comparable videos?

My own view, as detailed in Chapter One, contrary to Mohamed's, is that it is precisely at hiring and "during cases of tenure, promotion, or performance review" that "extramural" speech should be available for professional evaluation. Analysis of the relevant statements should be part of the written evaluation. For initial appointments the scope of relevant statements should be wider, since one is explicitly selecting a colleague. Academic freedom would protect speech widely considered reprehensible from university collaboration with ad hoc procedures triggered by either internal or external political opposition.

Matters change when the state adopts a regime of political terror, as the United States did during World War I and again in the leadup to and during the McCarthy period. Many institutions collaborated, including universities. But an alternative in which faculty members possess an untouchable discursive sphere—with no standards for truth, no consensual social values, no professional ethics, indeed no morality—would be especially dangerous for public higher education. Depending on the specific case, I might not deny tenure to a Holocaust-denying paleontologist who did not indulge those beliefs in teaching or publications, but I would not support his or her initial job application. I would deny tenure to a historian who promoted Holocaust denial, even if only on Facebook. Such standards have become even more necessary now than they were before. Otherwise, it will be impossible to defend academic freedom in either the courts or the court of public opinion. The AAUP's recent standard, worse still Mohamed's, will convince the public that universities are incapable of professional judgment. Far from protecting against externally forced political dismissals, Mohamed's proposal may make them more likely. Academic freedom will be decisively discredited and could come to an end.

The same is true of the proposal advanced by Bérubé and Ruth in *It's Not Free Speech* (2022), namely that campus academic freedom committees should have the power to recommend terminating tenured faculty who espouse white supremacist beliefs. Like Mohamed, they call for prohibiting professional evaluation of "extramural speech," saying that is necessary to protect academic freedom. Yet they believe in punishing people for supremacist speech—because they believe it undermines democracy. In other words, academic freedom protects speech on social media until it doesn't. In a book peppered with such unrecognized contradictions, they make it clear, for example, that Amy Wax's public racist remarks *are* nonetheless part of her professional profile. I would urge that Wax, a tenured University of Pennsylvania law professor be sanctioned, as I did when I appeared with her in a symposium. But I would not fire her, nor would I have fired tenured professor Ward Churchill from the University of Colorado for his antisemitic publications. If either were a job applicant or up for tenure it would be different. We need to condemn their views and sanction them in other ways, but not terminate tenured faculty. In order to preserve academic freedom, we must tolerate some loathsome tenured faculty.

Bérubé and Ruth want to redefine academic freedom so that it does not cover the ultimate crimes of racism and white supremacy. As their useful chapter on critical race theory reminds us, racism is part of the structural basis of American democracy. Rooting out racism should be America's foremost cultural priority. Yet the academy remains a place where racism and antisemitism can be countered by serious, long-term research and education. The corrosive effects of social media on the public sphere have eroded academic debate but not extinguished it. Bérubé and Ruth are confident a curtailed academic freedom will remain on the side of the angels. I am not so sure. Both the Red Scare and McCarthyism teach us otherwise. The faculty conviction that "Zionism is racism" is broad enough on some campuses that the academic freedom committee proposed by Bérubé and Ruth could well recommend that a dedicated Zionist deserves dismissal. The woke McCarthyism that Bérubé and Ruth advocate would produce results they might not welcome.

Conclusion

Journalists increasingly recognize that social media is a corrosive force across the world. Academics in the field of media studies and organizations working to combat the spread of hate speech and disinformation have reached the same conclusion. A rear guard in the academy has decided it is consequently time to double down on the faculty right to say whatever they please online, consequences be damned. Willful disregard for the responsibilities accompanying academic freedom will eventually prove unsustainable.

As the Center for Countering Digital Hate (CCDH) points out at the outset of its 2022 report on the STAR Framework, which aims to establish a global standard for regulating social media, "a handful of companies, owned by a small coterie of Big Tech billionaires, dominate internet content," and "the communities on these online platforms, their behaviors and beliefs, and the values which emerge from those spaces increasingly touch every aspect of offline society" (CCDH 2022, 2). "Hiding behind the techno-utopian halo of online technological innovation, they have both hidden the banal atavism of their core business models and avoided real scrutiny of the harms they cause" (3). For years, their CEOs, including Meta's Mark Zuckerberg, simply lied before the US Congress, promising a level of content management they never delivered, while proliferating hate drove online engagement and thus attracted paid advertisers eager to reach more consumers. "Harmful content, that is, hate and disinformation, is high-engagement content" (9). And it generates profits. Companies may even be unaware that their ads are placed on misinformation and hate sites. Elon Musk's erratic management of Twitter/X has drawn public attention to the role played by media CEOs, but regulation has not risen to the challenge.

The news media is aware of the harm done, but it nonetheless excuses Congress's aging leadership for its failure to act. That hides the strong American preference for not sanctioning the unregulated greed of late capitalism's new breed of robber barons. For that reason, along with absolutist American investments in the First Amendment, there is reason to look to the European Union for practical ways to regulate social media. The EU's Digital Services Act, which received parliamentary approval in October 2022, sets standards for disclosure of algorithms, elimination of disinformation, combatting harmful content, and regulating advertising on large platforms.[9]

---

9 For a concise summary of the Digital Services Act, along with links to news reports and comments, see the relevant Wikipedia entry at https://en.wikipedia.org/wiki/Digital_Services_Act.

CCDH argues that "we cannot continue on the current trajectory where bad actors opportunistically weaponize and poison the information ecosystem" (2022, 5). Some of those bad actors, witting and unwitting alike, are faculty members. CCDH argues that, for social media companies and their platforms, "self-regulation means no regulation" (4). Academia has long insisted it can and must regulate itself. It's not clear much longer we have to prove we can manage academic participation in the wild west of the internet. The future of academic freedom may depend on our acting now.

Chapter 3

Academic Freedom and the Israeli-Palestinian Conflict

———————

Introduction

No recent topic other than the Israeli-Palestinian conflict has occasioned comparably acrimonious campus debates. The founding of the Jewish state in 1948 met with more than its share of regional political hostility—from the outbreak of war to increased antisemitism, soon morphing into terrorism—but American and European campuses did not mirror those disputes. Relatively consistent public and campus support for Israel obtained until the consequences of the 1967 Six-Day War unfolded. Egypt had occupied the Gaza Strip until then, and Jordan controlled the West bank of the Jordan River. A national consciousness among the Arab refugees of the 1948 war had its first stirrings in the early to mid-1960s, but until 1967 it was an Arab, rather than a specifically Palestinian, phenomenon. Indeed, Egyptian and Jordanian territorial control of the two disputed areas were not widely condemned as "occupations." But what became internationally regarded as an occupation followed quickly upon the Israeli (and fundamentally Jewish) acquisition of Gaza and the West Bank.

Meanwhile, in American and European universities a series of evolving theoretical and political movements gained influence, postcolonialism being prominent among them. Adoption of "social justice" curricula in a number of US social science and humanities disciplines, impelled by civil rights and feminist movements originating outside the academy, helped prepare for the eventual intersection of these forces. Then in the new millennium identity politics became a defining feature of the academy, not only for many students but also for some faculty. The mix of these factors turned anti-Zionists and Zionists alike into aggrieved parties, rather than primarily advocates for intellectual and political positions. Accepted academic norms for debate and publication began to disintegrate in the humanities and social sciences, though not in the hard sciences. Suddenly we were where we now are, and where we are likely to be for some time—in an academy polarized over the Israeli-Palestinian conflict and defined by groups bound together by personal hostility.

In 2002, the first campaigns for academic boycotts of Israeli universities arose in Britain. The same year a few US universities, Berkeley and MIT among them, saw campaigns to divest from stock in companies doing business in Israel or the West Bank. Both agendas embodied the conclusions of an international United Nations anti-racism conference held in Durban, South Africa, the previous year. The conference reinvigorated the "Zionism is racism" slogan and helped launch an attendant movement. In 2005, the Boycott, Divestment, and Sanctions (BDS) movement became official and immediately gained influence on US and European campuses (Nelson 2016, 14–22). In 2005, responding to mounting calls to boycott Israeli universities, the AAUP's Committee on Academic Freedom and Tenure drafted an important policy statement opposing all academic boycotts. It was adopted by the organization's National Council in 2006, the same year that I became AAUP president, an office I held until 2012. Within a year, one of the statement's main authors, Joan Scott, reversed course and decided boycotts of Israeli universities were not merely acceptable but imperative. The statement makes it clear that all academic boycotts, not just those directed against Israeli universities, constitute fundamental violations of academic freedom, inhibiting the free international exchange of ideas and the freedom of faculty to collaborate across international borders, values the AAUP had championed since its founding in 1915 (Nelson and Brahm 2015, 31–38).

The AAUP realized that opposition to academic boycotts would either hold as a universal principle or its influence would soon be whittled away in fractious case-by-case debates. It was worthwhile honoring the principle even in the face of authoritarian regimes that eliminated academic freedom within their own borders. In Turkey, for example, President Recep Erdoğan demolished academic freedom with lightning speed, but boycotting Turkish academics would only make matters still worse for them. The AAUP understood that comprehensive economic and cultural boycotts, like that organized against South Africa's apartheid regime, would impact that country's universities, a consequence the organization accepted because universities were not being singled out and uniquely targeted. Meanwhile, it was widely recognized that Israel honors academic freedom within its pre-1967 borders; indeed, it is unique among area countries to do so. That helped sustain strong coalitions against academic boycotts until 2013, including many faculty and administrators opposed to Israeli government policies, at which point several academic associations broke ranks and voted to endorse the boycott movement.

While two of the largest of these—the Modern Language Association and the American Historical Association—stood their ground and rejected boycott resolutions, the American Anthropological Association reversed course in 2023 and voted for a boycott resolution that immediately instituted explicitly discriminatory practices. Among other rules violating academic freedom, Israeli universities are now barred from being listed in AAA's published materials, including AAA's AnthroGuide to Departments, from advertising in AAA publications, websites and other communications channels, including the AAA Career Center, from using AAA conference facilities for job interviews, from participating in the AAA Graduate School Fair, from participating in the AAA Departmental Services Program, and from participating in joint conferences or events with AAA and its sections.

Meanwhile, several smaller associations certified their deep anti-Zionism. The American Studies Association, the National Women's Studies Association, and the Middle East Studies Association (MESA) embraced boycotts. MESA's 2022 pro-boycott vote was facilitated by a 2017 decision to remove the qualifier "non-political" from its mission statement. In 2022, unfortunately, the MLA's Executive Council, acting with its Committee on Academic Freedom, endorsed a resolution condemning the IHRA Working Definition of Antisemitism. The MLA joined with the AAUP in repeating the lie that the IHRA Definition treats all criticism of Israel as antisemitic. Realizing that the members would likely vote down their statement, the members of the MLA bodies acted in secret, without notice and without membership approval. The AAUP had exceeded its mission, let alone what its modest expertise about antisemitism would warrant (Nelson and Lockard 2022).

The participation of the MLA's Academic Freedom Committee parallels an anti-Zionist trend to misrepresent or discount academic freedom. Increasingly, one hears claims that academic freedom is unfairly being given priority above other, more important, human rights (Salaita 2019). But academic freedom is a doctrine that applies only to colleges and universities, and it is in no way superior to a whole set of basic human rights. Nor does it compromise those rights. It is academic freedom, moreover, not some universal human right, that protects higher education's right to establish degree or exchange programs with other institutions in their own or other countries. It is academic freedom that gives students the right to apply to such programs if they so choose and to study in them if accepted. The BDS movement officially urges that all such arrangements with Israeli colleges and universities be closed. If academic freedom is higher education's core guiding principle, then movements that denigrate and disparage it represent a threat.

The international goal of discrediting academic freedom underwent some evolution at a Trinity College Dublin conference that produced a 2020 collection entitled *Enforcing Silence: Academic Freedom, Palestine, and the Criticism of Israel*, edited by David Landy, Ronit Lentin, and Conor McCarthy. While the authors need academic freedom's protections, their anti-Zionist political commitments drive them to claim it often "becomes a discourse designed to maintain situations of academic privilege" (Landy, Lentin, and McCarthy 2020, 3), basically "a selection of pieties used to legitimate a hierarchical system which has always carefully governed who is allowed to speak and who has been silenced" (2). Academic freedom therefore is "ultimately ... about capitalist elite cultures of obedience, about racism, about colonialism" (27). This claim becomes definitional: "academic freedom is a discourse and strategy of settler colonialism" (Schotten 2020, 296). These assaults on the principle of academic freedom that originated with anti-Zionism have now spread to other causes.

1. We support academic freedom but... —from anti-Zionism to cancel culture

On January 3, 2017, thirteen faculty members at the University of California at Berkeley sent a letter to their chancellor, Nicholas Dirks, with an unambiguous final line, isolated on the page above their signatures: "We urge you to cancel the planned speaking event for Milo Yiannopoulos as soon as possible." Ninety-eight faculty members subsequently signed on to both the original letter and a January 4 supplementary one restating the demand after Associate Chancellor Nils Gilman wrote to say a public university "may not engage in prior restraint of speech based on concern that a speaker's message may trigger disruptions."[1] Of the thirteen signatories to the original Berkeley faculty letter, five had previously signed public petitions endorsing boycotts of Israeli universities.

---

1 Transcripts of the first letter to Dirks and the second letter to Gilman and Dirks were published in the *Daily Californian*, see Members of UC Berkeley Faculty, "Open Letters Calling for Cancellation of Milo Yiannopoulos Event," *Daily Californian*, January 9, 2017, https://www.dailycal.org/2017/01/10/open-letter-calling-cancellation-milo-yiannopolous-event. The response from Gilman and the aforementioned two letters, as well as some additional communications, are available as a Google Doc, "Copy of Letter to the Chancellor re: free speech vs. harassment," created January 5, 2017, at https://docs.google.com/document/d/13mTOQ7wVst6voLMg6Pvr-3uJ2Fbn7zcXg_Bkx8mGDOk/edit.

A sixth signed a petition objecting to the University of California's Statement on Intolerance because of its inclusion of some forms of anti-Zionism as examples of prejudice. The opposition to Yiannopoulos's appearance on campus has no direct relation to debates about the Israeli-Palestinian conflict, but those debates have given anti-Zionist faculty warrant to violate academic freedom by shutting down events sponsored by those they perceive as their political opponents. This incident deserves detailed coverage here not only because it helped inaugurate a trend but also because the documentary record reveals arguments and motives underlying copycat events on other campuses.

The quote from Gilman above is from the conclusion of his letter, but he opened by pointing out that Yiannopoulos had been invited by a registered student organization, Berkeley College Republicans, which was exercising its right to invite speakers of its choice and to reserve space in which they could present their views. The university was hosting the event but was in no way endorsing the speaker (Dirks 2017). Neither, as Gilman properly declared, was the university willing to block or censor the event: "The First Amendment prohibits the University from censoring those events or banning speakers based on the viewpoints that might be expressed…. There is no general exception to First Amendment exception for 'hate' speech or speech that is deemed to be discriminatory."[2] In this case, academic freedom was supported by constitutional guarantees.

Gilman's arguments were definitive, but they did not dissuade Berkeley faculty members from reiterating the call for the talk to be cancelled. A number of the faculty members who signed are scholars with national reputations well beyond their areas of specialization. News reports highlighted literary theorist Judith Butler among them. Butler also gave a campus lecture defending her position (Friedersdorf 2017). All were, I suspect, well aware of the issues Gilman raised. Indeed, they could be guaranteed to make Gilman's arguments themselves in defense of speakers whose politics they endorsed. Politics trumped the principle of academic freedom. Some free speech rights were more equal than others.

In the rejoinder to Gilman, the thirteen letter writers made an argument more appropriate to a private religious community or a self-help group than a university: "Just because behavior isn't illegal doesn't mean it's appropriate. At the University of California, we hold ourselves to a higher standard and strive to promote a culture where everyone is supported to reach their fullest potential. To do that, we need to address problems before they hurt our community." One might warn in response that these Orwellian standards could not be widely

---

2 Ibid.

applied without suppressing much provocative campus speech, not only in public spaces but also in classrooms. Indeed, controversial and even outrageous speech can challenge assumptions and help people "to reach their fullest potential" by promoting critical analysis and self-definition.

The first faculty letter piously intones the very values the writers proceed to discard: "We support both freedom of speech and academic freedom on campus, and realize that controversial views must be tolerated in any campus community dedicated to open debate and opposed to censorship." But "Yiannopoulos' deplorable views pass from protected free speech to incitement, harassment and defamation…. Such actions are protected neither by free speech nor by academic freedom." This last passage comes from the third paragraph, but it is preceded by complaints clearly directed toward political opinion, including Yiannopoulos's castigation of Black Lives Matter and the fact that he "mocks campus cultures of inclusiveness." They go on to protest that he projects images of audience members onscreen, asserting a right that would disallow real-time news organization videos of campus audiences: "Students are not public figures, and they do not agree to have their likeness projected in public." Yet comedians frequently do the same, reasoning that audience members consent to be part of the show.

That Yiannopoulos, an alt-right provocateur and former Breitbart News editor, is an abusive speaker is not in question. He has been banned from Twitter and in February 2017 had a speaking offer withdrawn by the Conservative Political Action Conference (CPAC) after remarks surfaced that seemed to defend pedophilia. None of that, however, prevents a recognized campus group from inviting him. Some of his practices of singling out individuals might be considered intentional infliction of emotional distress or invasion of privacy, and legal remedies could be pursued after the fact.

But they are not typically enjoined in advance, as the group of Berkeley faculty urged. Slander is a subcategory of defamation, but it is not subject to prior restraint under the First Amendment. Insulting and vulgar speech cannot be punished, let alone restrained, though it can be energetically condemned. Private universities hosting an event before an invited audience could prohibit some practices as part of contractual conditions for a speaking engagement, but an open event at a public institution is more difficult to constrain.

The speech ended up being cancelled on advice of the police. Students and faculty staged a large public demonstration against the February talk. That was a perfectly appropriate expression of opinion, protected both by academic freedom and by the First Amendment. But, as Thomas Fuller (2017) reported in the *New York Times*, more than a hundred masked, black-clad off-campus political activists showed up to throw rocks, smash windows, and launch Molotov cocktails. At that point, public safety required that the event be cancelled (Marantz 2018).

The Berkeley effort to cancel a properly scheduled speech did not occur on the expected political terrain. It migrated from the usual arena of the heckler's veto, the Israeli-Palestinian conflict, to empower a quite different political agenda: the silencing of the alt-right. Those faculty who endorse the academic boycott of Israel are notably also those who support shuttering speech and freedoms they dislike. A commitment to opposing pro-Israeli speech becomes a "gateway drug" that leads to a broader rejection of traditional standards. By 2020, these left-wing practices had become common enough to merit condemnations of an emerging "cancel culture."

Cancel culture requires much less supportive reasoning than the Berkeley faculty provided. And sometimes the reasoning supplied is notably irrational. Thus, Tulane University on August 6, 2020, cancelled a presentation by Edward Ball based on his book *Life of a Klansman: A Family History of White Supremacy* (Soave 2020). Following his 1998 book *Slaves in the Family*, which traced the history of those his ancestors enslaved, Ball in *Life of a Klansman* condemns his family history of racism. The book tells the story of Ball's great-great grandfather (on his mother's side) Polycarp Constant Lecorgne (1832–1886), a nineteenth-century New Orleans, Louisiana, carpenter and KKK member who was active in Klan violence. With the coronavirus pandemic under way, the event was scheduled as an online presentation. This time the protest was largely student led, with the student government leading the way. People made it clear they knew Ball's politics were progressive and anti-racist. No one thought him a KKK advocate. Instead, social media promoted demands such as "Stop paying people who have profited off of their proximity to white supremacy and the literal Klan and replace this with a Black voice" and declarations the presentation would be "violent towards the experience of Black people in the Tulane community and our country."[3] The history of slavery is immensely violent and painful, but hearing a white descendant confront it provides a basis for reconciliation with one's contemporaries, not with the realities of slavery or its aftermath. What historical subject could be more urgent for Tulane? The letter cosigned by the student vice president for Academic Affairs and the student president of the School of Liberal Arts Government declared "this event is not only offensive and inappropriate but also undermines the efforts and experiences of Black people

---

3   For this and other representative social media comments, see Soave (2020).

at Tulane and in our country," an assertion that seems incomprehensible.[4] Ball, they complained, is "closely related to Klansmen." What "closely related" means after the passage of more than a hundred years is open to question. Many white Louisiana families have Klan members in their past, as do Black Louisiana families whose ancestors were raped by white slave owners.

Shamefully, Tulane cancelled the event, writing that "the event, as planned, has caused distress for many in our community, and we apologize" (Anderson 2020). The deplorable apology, acceding to a student demand, will be difficult to erase.[5] When it defined academic freedom in its 1915 Declaration, the AAUP insisted that education must challenge ingrained beliefs and be free to cause distress in doing so. Tulane left itself the out of saying that Ball's presentation was merely postponed, but the damage was done, both to academic freedom and to the university's reputation and educational mission. As a private university, Tulane, unlike Berkeley, would not likely be restrained by constitutional free speech guarantees. Its only bulwark against its bullies would have been academic freedom.

The background against which such abridgements of academic freedom take place includes repeated interruptions and cancellations of Zionist speakers. Despite the prevalence of claims that there is "a Palestinian exception to academic freedom," no comparable pattern of assaults on anti-Zionist speakers exists. Indeed, there have been cancellations of Israeli speakers based merely on a stated fear of BDS supporter protest, among them a 2016 Caroline Glick lecture at the University of Texas and a 2016 Shimon Dotan presentation at Syracuse University.[6] Again in 2016, Bassem Eid's University of Chicago lecture was shut down by police after protestors shouted him down.[7]

Efforts to shut down pro-Zionist speakers have flourished internationally. One unforgettable example, captured on video, occurred in 2014 when the editor of the British journal *Fathom*, Alan Johnson, was shouted down at the National University of Galway. When a student, Joseph Loughnane, heading

---

4   Originally posted on Instagram, the student letter is no longer accessible. For an account of the incident, see "Tell Tulane Student Leaders to Stop Trying to Cancel an Anti-Racist Speaker," New Tolerance Campaign, n.d., accessed August 2023, https://newtolerance.org/topcampaign/tell-tulane-student-leaders-to-stop-trying-to-cancel-an-anti-racist-speaker/ and "Tulane University Cancels Book Event Because Book Is on the KKK—Portraying It in a Horrible Light," Why Evolution Is True (blog), August 9, 2020, https://whyevolutionistrue.com/2020/08/09/tulane-cancels-book-event-because-book-is-on-the-kkk-portraying-it-in-a-horrible-light/.

5   See the accounts cited in the previous note.

6   See Speyer and Frommer (2016), Jaschik (2016), and Friedersdorf (2016).

7   See Pessin (2016).

a group of chanting protestors, moved forward—yelling "You Zionist pricks, fuck off our campus, now!"—the heckler's veto moved from incivility to outright physical intimidation.[8] King's College London had to evacuate a building in 2016 when protestors at a lecture by former Israeli Shin Bet head Ami Ayalon hurled chairs, smashed windows, and repeatedly set off fire alarms.[9] In 2018, Hebrew University philosopher Elhanan Yakira (2018) wrote:

> A few years ago I was invited to participate in a roundtable in the most prestigious French institute of higher education, the École Normale Supérieure in Paris. The topic was 'What is Zionism?' … The moment the person chairing the panel (a professor of political philosophy from the Sorbonne) began to talk, a group of youngsters rose up and began to shout slogans such as "Israeli murderer," "Child murderer," "Away with Israel!" and more. The youngsters—they all looked to me younger than twenty years old—were visibly organized. Three or four older ones, scattered in the hall, silently orchestrated the show, which lasted some three-quarters of an hour. The group then left, leaving almost no time and certainly no will for conducting a civilized and fruitful discussion. (349–50)

Protests over pro-Palestinian speakers have often failed to prevent events from taking place. In 2005 Harvard students asked Students for Justice in Palestine to disinvite Norman Finkelstein; SJP simply refused. The following year a protest against a Tony Kushner presentation at Brandeis failed as well. Jimmy Carter spoke at Yeshiva University in 2013 despite Zionist objections. Noam Chomsky's 2015 commencement address at Drexel University also proceeded despite objections, as did a 2015 Cornel West UCLA lecture. In 2019, students at the University of Massachusetts at Amherst filed a lawsuit to block a panel about the Israeli-Palestinian conflict and Palestinian rights featuring

---

8   On the Alan Johnson lecture event, see "Anti-Zionist Students Hurl Vicious Abuse at Professor," *Jewish Chronicle*, March 13, 2014, https://www.thejc.com/news/all/anti-zion-ist-students-hurl-vicious-abuse-at-professor-1.53132?reloadTime=1678060800011. On the Ami Ayalon protest, see Allison Kaplan Sommer, "Anti-Israel Protests Disrupt London Event with Former Shin Bet Chief Ami Ayalon," *Haaretz*, January 20, 2016, https://www.haaretz.com/jewish/2016-01-20/ty-article/.premium/anti-israel-protests-disrupt-london-event-with-former-shin-bet-chief/0000017f-dc63-d856-a37f-fde3cc220000.

9   For the King's College report on the Ayalon episode, see https://www.kcl.ac.uk/archive/news/kings/newsrecords/docs/investigation-report---19-january-2016.pdf.

the dedicated boycott supporter and Pink Floyd frontman Roger Waters and Palestinian-American activist Linda Sarsour; the suit failed.[10]

There have, to be sure, been many politically and culturally based cancellations of other prominent speakers over the years, among them speakers addressing abortion rights. Condoleezza Rice withdrew from plans to give a 2014 Rutgers University commencement address after faculty organized a protest; it may have been a negotiated decision.[11] But universities have also sometimes stood their ground. Germaine Greer delivered a 2015 lecture at Cardiff University despite demands it be cancelled because of her remarks about transgender rights.[12] In any case, the cancellations unconnected with Israel tend to be local events with sometimes confused agendas. The repeated cancellations of Israeli and pro-Israeli speakers embody an international movement supported by common arguments.

Unlike many other protests against campus speakers, anti-Zionist event cancellations and disruptions are not isolated incidents. They are part of an ideologically consistent and interconnected set of anti-Zionist political assaults against academic freedom and norms of professional conduct across a spectrum of campus activities. The closely related campaigns include those demanding divestment from stocks of companies doing business in Israel, those seeking to close down joint degree and study abroad programs in Israel, and those endorsing boycotts of Israeli universities. These mutually reinforcing projects collectively inform student and faculty political identities. The Black Lives Matter movement shows signs of comparable development, but, as with the Tulane events, the campus demands it makes are sometimes incoherent and counterproductive. A number of student groups have issued lists of demands centered on race that include items that compromise fundamental academic practices. Among them are demands that Black faculty be granted tenure without standard academic review. These demands contrast with some of the practical campaigns organized in the 1960s and later, including campaigns to create Black studies programs.

The attacks on Zionist events are merely the most prominent layer of relevant assaults on the professional norms governing academic freedom. A range of additional options are available to individuals seeking to redefine their academic duties for ideological purposes.

---

10 See Christensen (2019) and "Mass. Judge Refuses to Halt Pro-Palestinian Event at UMass Featuring Roger Waters & Linda Sarsour," Democracy Now!, May 3, 2019, https://www.democracynow.org/2019/5/3/mass_judge_refuses_to_halt_pro.

11 See Fitzsimmons (2014).

12 See Morris (2015).

2. Micro-boycotts, academic freedom, and professional responsibility

In the fall of 2018, University of Michigan American culture faculty member John Cheyney-Lippold generated wide publicity when he refused to write a letter of recommendation for a Michigan student who wanted to spend a year studying at Tel Aviv University (Nelson 2019, 44–45). Because he told the student that he would recommend her to universities in other countries, it was clear the standard, academically respectable reasons for refusing a letter—doubts about the student's abilities, lack of sufficient knowledge of the student's record, or even lack of time to write a letter—were not at issue. The only issues on the table were Cheyney-Lippold's objections to Israeli policies and his commitment to the American Studies Association's boycott of Israeli universities initiated in 2013. In a sign of political changes in the humanities, he defended his action as protected by his own academic freedom. He set aside the long-standing principle that student academic freedom gives them the right to apply to study at any program of their choice. And he rejected the idea that writing letters of recommendation is a standard academic responsibility to be honored except for the valid reasons listed above. Political objections to a student's choices are not a recognized rationale. Some would add that you could refuse to write a letter if you felt studying in a given location could place a student in serious danger.

As Steven Lubet (2022b) has detailed, Cheyney-Lippold's decision was further complicated by his other, related practices:

> Cheney-Lippold was actually sanctioned because he misled one of his students, promising her a recommendation that he never intended to provide, thus delaying her from seeking a willing recommender. Then he disingenuously claimed that he had not realized she planned to study at Tel Aviv University, when he was really waiting to pull the plug until after his impending tenure vote. He subsequently used class time to expound his political opinions to students, explaining his adherence to the BDS movement, which was a misuse of his authority as a faculty member. Cheney-Lippold told the dean that he devoted only fifteen minutes to his personal politics, but she determined it to have amounted to nearly a full session in two classes.

Cheyney-Lippold stated that his refusal embodied a principle most faculty would support, declaring that he was remaining true to his political convictions,

convictions that trumped his professional responsibilities. The national AAUP criticized his actions, but a reliably rogue AAUP chapter at NYU offered Cheney-Lippold its support. That reaction gained some national traction, at least for a time. This section reviews representative examples of personally initiated boycott actions—what I am calling "micro-boycotts"—as an increasing feature of academic life. I use the term "micro-boycotts" to signal the intimate, individual character of the decision to implement them and to differentiate them from the mass boycott movement that inspires them. Micro-boycotts include individual and small group actions, with some initiated by one person and joined by others. Micro-boycotts embody personal commitments and often represent actions by individual faculty members, but they do not take place in a vacuum.

The personal boycott actions against students that we know of begin with Oxford University's Andrew Wilkie, the Nuffield Professor of Pathology. He made news in June 2003 when he rejected an Israeli student who had written to explore the possibility of applying to work in Wilkie's lab because, like most young Israelis, the student, Amit Duvshani, had served in the Israeli army. Wilkie's letter to Duvshani made his motivations clear: "I am sure that you are perfectly nice at a personal level, but no way would I take on somebody who had served in the Israeli army" (Nelson 2019, 32–33). Yet most Israeli Jews serve in the Israeli army. It is clearly discrimination based on national origin and a violation of academic freedom. The Oxford University case acquired a counterpart on May 15, 2018, when a Yale University religious studies professor sent a recent Israeli PhD applying for a postdoc an email (I am withholding both names on request) again objecting to service in the Israeli army.

While some micro-boycotts, like Cheyney-Lippold's, violate academic freedom, other personal boycott actions are protected by academic freedom or free speech rights. That includes advocacy for some actions, like academic boycotts, that official university policy and many academic organizations would condemn. Individuals also are free to refuse to travel to conferences or other events at home or abroad; they can decline to establish research relationships with universities in their own country or elsewhere. They can boycott any domestic or foreign products they wish. In other cases, while individuals or groups are free to advocate for controversial policies, such as economic divestment or the cancellation of joint degree or study abroad programs, the campus should forthrightly reject such recommendations and proceed to foster the relevant programs. Some micro-boycotts can be devastating to people, whereas others are important mainly as indications that long-term norms for academic freedom and academic conduct are under assault.

For several years, faculty and graduate student groups at NYU have collaborated in efforts to shut down the university's programs at Israeli universities. All such efforts to implement academic boycotts of Israel subvert the scholarly and educational opportunities and curtail the academic freedom of colleagues and students who are members of our own campus communities. The Palestinian Campaign for the Academic and Cultural Boycott of Israel (PACBI) guidelines, which were expanded in 2014, object to "institutional cooperation agreements with Israeli universities or research institutes" and describe them as "schemes."[13] Yet the freedom to negotiate such interinstitutional agreements and research relationships and participate in them is fundamental to academic freedom. One may complain about them, but not seek to obstruct them.

Protest crossed the line into obstruction on March 2014 after Jill S. Schneiderman, a Vassar College geologist, led a class trip to Israel and Palestine to study water issues related to the Jordan River watershed. After a September 2013 informational meeting about the course, campus protests began because the trip would include a visit to Israel. In February 2014, members of Students for Justice in Palestine (SJP) picketed the course, thrusting fliers in the hands of students struggling to make their way into class: "Your participation in this class financially and symbolically supports apartheid and the degradation of Palestinians.... The indigenous people of Palestine do NOT want you to come!" (Schneiderman 2018, 327). Protests culminated in a mass meeting organized by the faculty Committee on Inclusion and Excellence (CIE), where the CIE chair announced that "cardboard notions of civility" would not guide the session. And, indeed, they did not: "belligerence, vilification, intimidation, and rage against Israel" dominated the meeting (324). Certainly Jewish students would have felt themselves victims of the speech. The trip took place as planned, but the protest produced a partial victory in which intimidation triumphed over academic freedom: a planned public display of student posters documenting the experience was cancelled to avoid further public conflict (320).

Protest has crossed a line several times since 2015 in a series of copycat assaults on the academic freedom qualified students have to run for office

---

13 PACBI Guidelines for the International Academic Boycott of Israel, July 9, 2014, available at https://bdsmovement.net/pacbi/academic-boycott-guidelines.

or be appointed to office in student government. The initial incident was a 2015 verbal assault on Rachel Beyda on the UCLA Undergraduate Students Association Council. As Adam Nagourney (2015) reported in the *New York Times*,

> It seemed like routine business for the student council at the University of California, Los Angeles: confirming the nomination of Rachel Beyda, a second-year economics major who wants to be a lawyer someday, to the council's Judicial Board. Until it came time for questions.
>
> "Given that you are a Jewish student and very active in the Jewish community," Fabienne Roth, a member of the Undergraduate Students Association Council, began, looking at Ms. Beyda at the other end of the room, "how do you see yourself being able to maintain an unbiased view?"
>
> For the next 40 minutes, after Ms. Beyda was dispatched from the room, the council tangled in a debate about whether her faith and affiliation with Jewish organizations, including her sorority and Hillel, a popular student group, meant she would be biased in dealing with sensitive governance questions that come before the board, which is the campus equivalent of the Supreme Court.
>
> The discussion, recorded in written minutes and captured on video, seemed to echo the kind of questions, prejudices and tropes—particularly about divided loyalties—that have plagued Jews across the globe for centuries, students and Jewish leaders said.

The video of Beyda's interrogation and the subsequent debate, with student BDS activists eagerly leading the charge against her, was chilling. The case against her, which was clearly hateful and antisemitic, produced a vote against her—until a faculty member later argued that "belonging to Jewish organizations was not a conflict of interest." Under pressure, students met again and approved her appointment to the board. Caught on video, then driven to reverse themselves, the UCLA students had, in effect, been publicly shamed and a public warning against comparable actions delivered. Or so one might have thought. But in the way that many stories are transformed in circulation, this one apparently arrived in some quarters as an inspiration to copycat action. Two years after the events at UCLA, Hayley Nagelberg, a Jewish undergraduate at my own campus who was an active supporter of Israel and opponent of the BDS movement faced an almost identical antisemitic grilling. With the campus meeting at this public institution, the University of Illinois at Urbana-Champaign, governed by the Illinois Open Meetings Law, the events once again played out in public.

As a member of the Campus Student Election Commission during a time when a divestment resolution was being debated on campus, Nagelberg was confronted with the accusation that she would be unable to make objective decisions about any issues that arose. They decided to remove her from the commission email list to guarantee she would have no input on any of their deliberations about the election. She reported meeting several times with the campus chancellor and a vice-chancellor, neither of whom would acknowledge that this in any way represented a violation of her rights, despite the fact that the Commission's charter prohibits it from engaging "in discrimination or harassment against any person because of race, color, religion, sex, national origin, ancestry, age, order of protection, marital status, genetic information, political affiliation, disability, pregnancy, sexual orientation including gender identity, unfavorable discharge from the military or status as a protected veteran."[14] They did nothing, and she has since graduated. Hostility toward Jewish identity trumped academic freedom and was a comprehensive disqualification from participation in all the committee's interactions and decision making, not just in votes related to Israel. Free speech rights should have assured her the ability to have a voice even in the divestment vote when it was discussed. Antisemitism seems the likely explanation for her global disenfranchisement.

In summer 2020, a similar campaign came to a head at the University of Southern California (USC). An antisemitic social media campaign against the student government vice president, Rose Ritch, culminated in her August 5 resignation by way of a letter posted on Facebook (Janofsky 2020). She had been elected that April, along with Truman Fritz, who ran for president. Fritz rapidly came under attack for supposed insensitivity about Black student interests, and his sometimes clumsy efforts to respond only fueled demands for his resignation or impeachment. Ritch remained silent rather than either defending or attacking her fellow student government officer, and that silence was taken as complicity. "Her silence aids and abets the already taxing oppression and microaggressions that Black students face at USC daily," wrote Abeer Tijani, an organizer of the effort to oust her

14 See the UIUC Student Election Code & Regulations (2000), available at https://studentelections.illinois.edu/docs/SP20-guide-to-student-elections.pdf.

(Bernstein and Timko 2020). The claim of complicity was amplified with anti-Zionism. As Ritch wrote in her resignation letter, "I have been told that my support for Israel has made me complicit in racism, and that, by association, I am racist. Students launched an aggressive social media campaign to 'impeach [my] Zionist ass.'" She decried the accusation that "my support for a Jewish homeland would make me unfit for office" and concluded that "my Zionism should not and cannot disqualify me from being a leader on campus, nor should others presume what that means about my position on social justice issues." She made it clear that the verbal assaults constituted antisemitism. She was slandered as a "Pro-Israel White Supremacist." USC president Carol Folt supported that conclusion in an August 5 statement. As the Alliance for Academic Freedom (which I chair) wrote after the story surfaced,[15] "The pernicious misconception that Zionism implies racism, white supremacism, theocracy, right-wing politics or anything other than a belief in the Jewish people's right to self-determination is a product of either ignorance or malice."

A petition calling for Ritch's impeachment was circulated, and a number of campus organizations endorsed it, including the local chapter of Students for Justice in Palestine. Ritch was a former head of the USC advocacy group Trojans for Israel, so her Zionist commitment was well known. Stephen D. Smith, executive director of the USC Shoah Foundation and an adjunct professor of religion stated that the social media campaign against Ritch embodied "pure blind hatred and ignorance" fueled by "a lack of critical thinking and a lack of curiosity" (Janofsky 2020). A scheduled hearing to consider her impeachment was cancelled after the USC administration ruled that the case against her was "insufficient to ensure integrity" of the process. Indeed, the only "evidence" was her Zionism, her silence regarding the accusations against Fitch, and her reluctance to participate in a recorded interrogation by those who had initiated the impeachment process. As Ritch wrote, "I am grateful that the University administration suspended my impeachment proceedings, but am disappointed that the university has not recognized the need to publicly protect Jewish students from the type of antisemitic harassment I endured" (Ritch 2020). The only way to bring an end to the campaign against her, she concluded, was to step down.

What is at stake? Academic freedom protects the right of qualified faculty and students to run for campus offices or be appointed to official committees,

15 See this and other Alliance for Academic Freedom statements at https://thirdnarrative.org/alliance-for-academic-freedom-statements/2/.

just as it protects the right of recognized campus groups to invite speakers of their choice. Campaigns to discredit people based in attacks on their race, religion, gender status, ethnicity, or national origin undermine that right in ways we must reject forcefully. The first step in combatting such behavior is for faculty and administrators to condemn it. With both the Tulane and USC stories, faculty silence no doubt reflected fear of being seen as opposing the growing Black Lives Matter movement on campus. The Tulane administration folded, while USC's in contrast eventually did its job, though it should have intervened earlier, rather than permitting an abusive campaign to go on for months without comment. More broadly, if student political movements are to serve an educational function, faculty and administrators must distinguish between productive versus destructive and ill-considered impulses and respond accordingly. Not all student passions are inspiring, even though some are.

The number and range of micro-boycotts are considerable. Many do not violate academic freedom, instead compromising standards for civility, collegiality, and truthfulness. But organized assaults can seriously abridge individuals' ability to exercise their academic freedom. And far too frequently passions over the Israeli-Palestinian conflict drive people to make false accusations against colleagues, which easily mushroom into group assaults on social media that then trigger unmotivated formal inquiries and investigations. Cowardly faculty and administrator silence in the face of what amounts to mass slander is now commonplace. *Anti-Zionism on Campus: The University, Free Speech, and BDS* (2018), edited by Andrew Pessin and Doron S. Ben-Atar, documents a number of such cases. Willingness to stand up for academic freedom in the face of prevailing political opinion is far too rare. Part of that prevailing political opinion in the academy relates to claims about academic freedom in Israel and Palestine that underwrite academic boycott campaigns.

There are a number of general lessons to be learned from the trend toward micro-boycotts and other local campus actions. First, we need to insist that a number of the local activities endorsed and encouraged by the Palestinian Campaign for the Academic and Cultural Boycott of Israel (PACBI) explicitly undermine student and faculty academic freedom. Those include:

- undermining a faculty member's collaborative research or teaching projects with Israeli universities and scholars;
- interfering with the equal, non-discriminatory treatment of all applicants for admissions to graduate programs;
- disrupting and shutting down events featuring Israeli leaders or scholars organized by their colleagues or students;

- working toward the closure of their own university's study abroad programs in Israel; and
- refusing to write letters of recommendation for their students who want to pursue studies in Israel.

In trying to deal with these and other local activities by groups and individuals, the limitations inherent in the current system become clear:

1. Universities too often have only the most rudimentary and flawed procedures for due process.
2. The individuals responsible for managing the campus investigative process too often have no clear understanding of academic freedom.
3. Cases that should be promptly dismissed will instead drag on for months and are themselves de facto forms of punishment for pro-Israeli faculty members and their families.
4. The unbridled passions that fuel anti-Israel politics on campus mean that people will readily lie to support charges against their Zionist colleagues, while others automatically assume pro-Israeli faculty are guilty of any charges leveled against them.
5. Unwarranted charges of racism are now a standard tactic to be used against pro-Israeli students and faculty; they need to be confronted.
6. A climate of fear and intimidation prevents sympathetic faculty from publicly supporting pro-Israeli faculty under attack; many are afraid even to offer private support.
7. Even discredited smear campaigns have a profound and sustained chilling effect on student and faculty speech.
8. Organized social support for anti-Zionist faculty rewards those who join the accusing chorus of voices.
9. In this, as in most other matters, administrators are not often sources of support for pro-Israeli faculty.
10. Sanctions against anti-Zionist students and faculty who lie in public or give false testimony in campus proceedings are unlikely.
11. Even a campus faculty association may not honor the principle of "innocent until proven guilty" when the campus climate is hostile to Israel and accusations are made against a Zionist faculty member.
12. A sometimes frightening mob mentality will drive anti-Zionist students when they are galvanized into protest or ad hominem attacks.
13. Administrators will often decide whether to investigate an accusation not on the basis of the evidence available but on the basis of the prevailing political climate on campus.

14. A pattern has emerged of local anti-Zionist groups creating an incident, then inventing an accusation that the real offense was perpetrated by the Jews in attendance.

15. Videotape evidence has been the only way that a number of pro-Israeli students and faculty have been able to get justice; people should routinely videotape public events, and those videotapes should begin before the event starts and continue until the audience has dispersed.

16. Some individual boycott actions clearly contradict existing university opposition to academic boycotts; administrators need to condemn such actions as violations of principle.

17. As virtually all the individually selected targets of these micro-boycotts are Jewish, they send a threatening message of antisemitism to the campus as a whole.

3. Academic Freedom in Gaza, Israel, and the West Bank

Boycotting universities in another country either limits or wholly curtails faculty communication and collaboration from both the countries involved. Such boycotts, often construed as a way to condemn government policy in the target country, inevitably treat the universities, faculty members, and students affected as unavoidable collateral damage. Ironically, those students and faculty members may well include many people who oppose the very government policies the boycotters want to protest. That is certainly the case with Israeli universities. Yet the arguments marshaled to support the boycott of Israeli universities include some issues unique to Israel, which occupies the disputed territory of the West Bank. Boycott advocates commonly claim that Israel seriously damages or denies academic freedom to West Bank universities.

During the twenty years in which Egypt occupied the Gaza Strip and Jordan occupied the West Bank, there were in fact no universities in either area. Egypt and Jordan feared that higher education would breed resistance to their authority. Within a few years of Israel taking over the two territories, however, the Jewish state approved the establishment of universities in both Gaza and the West Bank. What no one anticipated was the intense politicization of those institutions during the First Intifada (1987–1993). Palestinian universities became centers not only for the application of political theory to the Intifada but also for organizing demonstrations both on and off campus. That in turn led Israel to fear a violent uprising and to respond with campus closures designed to limit organizing. Palestinians are proud of the role their universities played, but consequences have included a continuing and less defensible impact on campus culture.

Israel's academic freedom policies and practices within its pre-1967 borders are consistent with those in the West. They are superior to those of any other country in the region. There is no question, however, that some Israeli practices curtailed academic freedom in the occupied territories, especially the repeated campus closures ordered by the Israel Defense Forces (IDF). Palestinian universities themselves opted for less extended closures as a way of handling internal conflicts, but the longer closures were imposed by the IDF. That said, it has been decades since the IDF ordered extended closures; the earlier history of prohibiting access to campuses does not justify current political actions.

At the time, Israel also tried other ways of micro-managing Palestinian higher education, although it made no effort to police courses or research agendas. The most notorious decision, one that failed completely, was the establishment of a list of books prohibited in Palestinian university libraries. The list was consistently ignored, and often the books were available in Israel in any case. That effort came to an end in 1994 when the Palestinian Authority took over the supervision of area higher education as an early step in the implementation of the Oslo Accords. Again, the issue is moot.

The only basis for claiming that the IDF or other security forces currently disrupt Palestinian academic freedom is the occasional campus incursions designed to capture student terror suspects or to investigate political activity aimed at incitement to violence. Most such raids, however, are conducted off campus, which is a much better tactic. Campus incursions do more to create ill will than they do to curb terrorism. Campus incursions by the Palestinian Authority are also frequent and equally counterproductive. Both the IDF and the Palestinian Authority practice administrative detention, including that of students.

Campus incitement to resistance took a transformative turn toward violence during the Second Intifada (2000–2005), thereafter fundamentally differentiating Palestinian higher education from anything people are familiar with in the West. My 2021 book on this subject, *Not in Kansas Anymore: Academic Freedom in Palestinian Universities*, for the first time draws together in one place the record of Palestinian student participation in suicide and other bombings, all of which has created a legacy from which Palestinian universities have yet to extricate themselves. Today's West Bank student terrorist cells, mostly organized by Hamas, plan conventional, not suicide, bombings, though they continue to target civilians. Arrests of students in such cells continues. An-Najah University in Nablus, the largest Palestinian university, has probably contributed the largest number of student suicide bombers, but participation in terrorist cells is much wider, including many documented arrests and indictments of Birzeit University students, among others (Levitt 2007).

Although the number of students involved in this violence has been relatively small compared to the total student population, it is not negligible. The planning and implementation of a bombing requires a whole network to recruit activists; sustain their commitment over time; purchase, build, and store bombs; plan operations; shelter participants; distribute propaganda; and do everything else necessary to maximize public impact. Unfortunately, the core activities are supplemented by continuing campus celebrations of student violence, including canonizing those who die executing bombings as *shahids* (martyrs), a form of political sainthood. Student and faculty academic freedom should enable criticism of such values, but engaging in such criticism can entail considerable personal risk.

Equally serious is the way in which interorganizational conflict among Palestinian political and paramilitary groups compromises academic freedom on Gaza and West Bank campuses. Especially during and since Hamas's defeat of Fatah in the 2007 civil war in Gaza, the conflict between the two groups has been regularly enacted on both West Bank and Gazan campuses. It has included efforts to kill faculty members identified with either faction and the violent policing of political expression by all campus constituencies. Student groups allied with competing factions are among those exacting punishments for opinion their faction considers unacceptable. Those who participate in dialogue with Israelis are considered to be "normalizing" the occupation and are vulnerable to violent sanctions from both factions. The result is that political and religious expression is not protected by academic freedom either in Gaza or the West Bank. Meanwhile, the Palestinian Authority has increased legal penalties for political expression it opposes. Recent laws are so vague that only vigorous self-censorship can protect students and faculty from reprisals. Academic freedom is not a controlling principle in either Gaza or the West Bank. But the major culprits are the Palestinians themselves.

Conclusion

If the test of academic freedom is the freedom to express political and religious views frankly in lectures, research results, classroom opinion, and public statements, it is a test higher education too frequently fails. Faculty expression is not without limits—advocacy of violence being the obvious exception—but even if maximized that freedom can have professional consequences. As detailed in Chapter Two, for years the AAUP leaders took the position that statements on social media in one's areas of teaching and research were part of one's professional profile and subject to professional evaluation, while statements outside one's areas of professional competence were protected. In 2015, the AAUP reversed itself and decided that all social media posts were protected by academic freedom. This means that a geologist could tweet that the earth is really flat and still not be judged unfit for service as a professor of geology. I choose an absurd example to demonstrate why I believe the AAUP's new position is a mistake. But there are more serious examples. A long-time engineering faculty member at Northwestern University near Chicago is a Holocaust denier. He can write or tweet that claim without fear of sanction. But until now a European historian could not deny the Holocaust without being judged incompetent and risk losing his or her job.

For those who teach and write about the Israeli-Palestinian conflict the matter is more complex and vexed. Can repeated and vehement Facebook posts or tweets excoriating Israelis or Palestinians suggest you may not be able to treat student opinion judiciously? If you have a history of demanding that Zionist or pro-Palestinian students or faculty be excluded from certain campus organizations or service on committees, is it reasonable for a hiring committee to conclude your voice might not make a productive addition to campus dialogue? If your advocacy for Israelis or Palestinians blinds you to the need to support your published claims and conclusions with evidence, should that effect your chance of being hired or promoted? The AAUP reversed itself while reviewing faculty social media statements about the Israeli-Palestinian conflict; in its effort to expand academic freedom protections, I believe the organization erred.

While tenured faculty members with strong opinions about the Israeli-Palestinian conflict can express them without fear if their universities honor academic freedom, untenured faculty, including those with contingent appointments, are far more vulnerable. The risk depends in part on departmental culture. It has long been true that humanities and social science departments worldwide that take pride in their liberal or conservative culture tend to reinforce that culture in hiring decisions. It can be the case whether the field is history or economics. Matters are much worse in Middle East studies. My advice to graduate students and untenured faculty over the last generation has been consistent: avoid taking public leadership positions in groups advocating for either Israelis or Palestinians. You can do advocacy work quietly in the background, but if you are on the job market or seeking tenure, caution and self-restraint are advisable.

While I did not honor this principle myself, I rose through the ranks in a different time. I took risks by publicly criticizing university policy, supporting faculty and graduate student unionization, and regularly expressing my opinion on controversial topics. I naively believed academic freedom would protect me, which it did to a degree. My tenure was approved over my department head's objections and never threatened thereafter. But the upper administration routinely refused every application for research support or other recognition. My college dean supported me because of my publication record. But I do not believe I would have survived in the current climate. I have followed a number of searches at research universities in the United States where I have learned the names and academic records of the finalists for an academic job. I have frequently seen the most qualified candidate rejected in favor of someone far less accomplished; the more widely published candidate has often been someone who is outspoken about the Israeli-Palestinian conflict.

Departmental culture partly shapes what is the last major issue I should address, one that is too widespread to cover here in detail: the relation between permissible faculty political advocacy in the classroom and academic freedom. Over the years, the AAUP has made it increasingly clear that faculty are free to express political opinion germane to the subject matter. But they must welcome alternative student opinion, which some faculty members evidently do not. As my book *Israel Denial* documents, many course syllabi on the Israeli-Palestinian conflict are so relentlessly one-sided that they more resemble indoctrination than an invitation to reasoned debate. In such cases, students have no assigned readings to draw on in promoting differing views. Academic freedom gives faculty wide latitude in designing courses, but colleges and universities have a responsibility to make sure that the overall curriculum includes courses embodying a variety of political perspectives.

Chapter 4

Is BDS Antisemitic?

Introduction

There has long been confusion about whether the Boycott, Divestment, and Sanctions (BDS) movement directed against Israel is fundamentally antisemitic, even though its ultimate goal, however obfuscated, is to eliminate the Jewish state. As Eric Alterman (2022) writes, BDS "demanded that the Israeli people turn over their country to their sworn enemies. Just how they might be convinced to do so, however, was a question for which BDS adherents had no coherent response…. All practical discussion tended to be replaced by rhetorical tropes such as the need to be on 'the right side of history.' … Its practical energies were exclusively devoted to inspiring a popular movement to consistently condemn Israel. It had no plans beyond that" (376–77). This "cloudy-to-the-point-of-nonexistent theory of change" has helped the BDS movement sustain a certain "idealistic varnish" that fuels recruitment (377–78). That has necessitated the creation of a category for those on the Zionist left who fail to see the light. They are branded "progressive except for Palestine."

At the same time, the continuing eagerness local BDS groups have shown to discredit or slander individual students and faculty opponents in Western countries repeatedly undercuts the movement's purported claim it focuses exclusively on institutions. And it makes the movement's motivations appear decidedly unidealistic. Indeed, the BDS movement has been "successful in fostering a politicized and hostile campus climate" that targets Jewish students and faculty (Oxnevad 2023, 14). Whatever efforts at denial or rationalization obfuscate that agenda—or at least hide its intent—it is difficult to hide its antisemitic effects.

It is easy enough, nonetheless, to meet students, faculty, and community members whose reasons for signing a BDS petition or joining a pro-BDS demonstration are either vague ("I want justice for Palestinians") or almost purely social ("All my friends were signing; it seemed like the thing to do"). People who cite these motivations are often comfortable with adding that they've never read much about the Israeli-Palestinian conflict, let alone studied it seriously. A similarly vague purpose defines those who insist that they are seeking to change Israeli policies through BDS activism but cannot specify what policies they want to see changed. It serves no purpose to characterize such peripheral BDS members or their reasons for joining the movement as antisemitic. But their casual commitment does not define either the movement's basic goals, its political and social impact, or the positions of its leaders and most influential advocates.

Moreover, as Bernard Harrison (2020) has helped us understand in *Blaming the Jews*, antisemitism as it is manifested in contemporary anti-Zionism and the BDS movement does not for the most part represent organized hatred of Jews as individuals. It is a set of beliefs, an ideology, a pseudo-explanatory system that manifests itself in hostility and animosity. It can prove lethal to groups or individuals, but it is first of all a set of political or religious convictions that believers may regard as necessary and virtuous. Some of those beliefs, like the fantasy that the pro-Israel lobby constitutes a vast, all powerful, and distinctly sinister worldwide conspiracy, are either counterfactual or delusional, but others, like resentment of Israeli military power, are partly tethered to reality. In any case, though BDS advocates may truthfully insist they harbor no hatred toward individual Jews, that ignores the antisemitism embodied in recurrent unsupportable claims, among them that Israel is the world's worst violator of human rights. Notably, however, some who despise Jews as people may use anti-Zionism as a cover for socially hostile antisemitism.

In some urban areas worldwide, there are numerous nongovernmental organizations (NGOs) and religious groups that promote the BDS agenda, but the most widely distributed BDS activity is in the academy. BDS is not a tightly controlled, hierarchical movement that issues directives from a central command source. Nevertheless, it achieves a high degree of policy consistency through leadership statements, op-eds, key news outlets, group meetings, websites, and exchanges on social media. The main BDS website provides a schematic recipe for movement goals or policy changes for those who want a concise answer but do not want to get into the weeds of detail. It lists three such goals:

- Ending its [Israel's] occupation and colonization of all Arab lands and dismantling the Wall.
- Recognizing the fundamental rights of the Arab-Palestinian citizens of Israel to full equality.
- Respecting, protecting, and promoting the rights of Palestinian refugees to return to their homes and properties as stipulated in UN Resolution 194.[1]

Even that much specification, however, presents major difficulties and potentially antisemitic implications:

1. There is intense debate about what constitutes "all Arab lands." For many in Arab countries, the existence of a Jewish state anywhere in "Arab lands" is an unsupportable affront. From that perspective, Israel was a colonialist project from the late nineteenth century when Jewish settlement increased and a colonialist entity from the moment of the nation's founding in 1948. Others regard the existence of a Jewish state as a fait accompli and consider only the territories occupied in the 1967 war to be effectively Arab or Palestinian lands. The BDS movement often characterizes this flexibility as a strength, as it appears to let people choose which position they want to adopt, but everything hinges on that distinction, and BDS's three demands are not actually ambiguous. They would eliminate the Jewish state. Signing on to a movement that misrepresents its most basic premise as reversible gives people a false sense of political self-confidence and leads to political manipulation by the movement's leaders.

2. Many in the West, find "tear down that wall" to be an emotionally gratifying demand. It suggests comparisons with the Berlin Wall. Some call Israel's barrier an "Apartheid Wall" to evoke an analogy with South Africa. Yet negotiators knowledgeable about the history of violence from all parties realize a separation barrier that divides the two peoples for at least a generation is a necessary component of any viable two-state

---

1 "What is BDS?," Palestinian BDS National Committee, accessed June 2022, https:// bdsmovement.net/what-is-bds.

solution. Otherwise, violence that will disable a peace agreement is virtually certain. We need to remember that barrier construction began in order to stop Palestinian terrorists from crossing from the West Bank into Israel to launch continuing suicide attacks against Israeli civilians. Less than 10 percent of the "separation barrier" is actually a wall; most of it is a fence whose route can easily be moved, as it has been in the past when problems with Palestinian access were recognized by the courts. Whether fence or wall, moreover, the structure represents a potential border between two states; its existence reinforces the logic of two states for two peoples, the guiding principle for negotiations since before Israel was established. For that reason, many West Bank settlers actually oppose the barrier, fearing they will be on the wrong side of it if it divides the two states.

3. Israel's founding Declaration of Independence and its Basic Laws have constitutional status and already guarantee full rights to all its citizens, Arab and Jewish alike, just as they assure freedom of religion to Christians, Druze, Jews, and Muslims. There are lingering elements of discrimination in Israel, but the arc of Israeli law has steadily been to eliminate them. Thus, legalized gender inequalities have been eliminated and full rights extended to the LGBTQ community, a process that has itself encouraged comparable protection for Arabs. Given that Israel is the only country in the area that assures this full range of rights, it is disingenuous at best for the BDS movement to "demand" them. Yet the insistence that Arab rights are not guaranteed often persuades audiences that are not knowledgeable about Israeli law. Since the BDS aim can hardly be to press Israel to pass laws that already exist, one is left with the obvious aim of delegitimization. Indeed, the false accusation about Israel's treatment of its Arab citizens fuels the powerful demand that Israel be branded a racist state.

4. Using rounded numbers, there are about seven million Jews in Israel and the West Bank and about two million Arabs within Israel's pre-1967 borders. With nearly four million additional Palestinians divided between Gaza and the West Bank, the demographics of one state between the Jordan River and the Mediterranean Sea preclude that state from being a Jewish one. Granting Israeli citizenship to several additional millions of descendants of Arabs worldwide who fled or were forced out during the 1948 war, as BDS insists, means that the resulting nation would be a Muslim-majority one. Jewish civil, political, and religious rights would not be secure. The entire arc of Middle East history confirms fear of

that outcome and its antisemitic consequences. BDS advocates like to assure us that a Palestinian-dominated state would be secular, not religious. But the existing Arab states in the region suggest otherwise. The BDS movement's third demand is thus one to which no imaginable Israeli government would agree. Despite the BDS movement's claim to nonviolence, only Israel's defeat in war could lead Israelis to accept a state with a Jewish minority.

Two separate states, conversely, would recognize each people's right to political self-determination. The BDS one-state model would eliminate the right of seven million Israeli Jews to political self-determination. It is an antisemitic agenda. Some people no doubt sign on to that agenda without understanding its consequences; they can do so without antisemitic intent. But that ignorance would not help those who would suffer from its antisemitic results.

If BDS's three declared policy objectives, detailed above, have antisemitic implications, BDS's tactics instead have real time antisemitic consequences. It should come as no surprise that the three terms that comprise the BDS movement's name and its anti-Zionist goals—boycott, divestment, and sanctions—are all hostile, all steps to punish Israel. All three tactics promote demonization of the world's only Jewish state.[2] While BDS campaigns routinely fail or have only limited impact, they inevitably recruit people to passionate anti-Zionism. The campaigns are pursued because they are effective in the battle for hearts and minds:

– Boycott: For a generation, a variety of organized campaigns have urged both individuals and organizations to boycott specific Israeli products (like Israeli hummus), businesses (including Israeli banks), sports teams and entertainment groups, and all Israeli universities and their academic programs, at times along with their students and faculty. These contemporary efforts cannot help but echo the boycotts of Jewish businesses initiated by the Nazis immediately after they came to power, as well as the Arab boycott of the *Yishuv* (the pre-state Jewish community in Palestine) of the 1920s and 1930s, or the boycott announced by the Arab League in 1945. However, a series of boycott campaigns since 2002 have failed to achieve their full purpose.

---

2 For more detail, see "The Goals and Tactics of the BDS Movement," in Nelson (2019, 18–45).

- Divestment: This term refers to the effort to convince groups and organizations to divest from (meaning sell) stock in companies doing business in Israel or "profiting from the occupation" of the West Bank. Resolutions to divest from selected companies doing business in Israel have been approved at the annual gatherings of several Protestant denominations and by a number of college student governments, but many such resolutions have been defeated. Frequent corporate targets have included Caterpillar, Hewlett Packard, and Motorola Solutions. No college or university administration, moreover, has abdicated its authority over investment decisions; no church divestment plan has had a significant economic impact.
- Sanctions: This term refers to organized, coordinated, international, government-initiated penalties and punitive actions against Israel. While the UN General Assembly would certainly endorse official sanctions by majority vote, Israel's allies would block their implementation. Short of full-scale war or substantial annexation of West Bank territory, an international sanctions regime is unlikely.

As the BDS movement has evolved, it has embraced another major tactic, an anti-normalization campaign—perhaps the most destructive element of the movement's agenda—along with a series of specific recommendations targeting higher education. Normalization, it is feared, would reinforce Israel's right to exist and demonstrate that it is like any other nation instead of an illegitimate and fundamentally evil entity. Anti-normalization supports the principle that dialogue with Israeli's Jewish citizens or its institutions is morally and politically unacceptable, even though no peace process is possible without it. The embrace of anti-normalization now increasingly entails rejecting interaction with Zionists worldwide. In the West, anti-normalization frustrates dialogue and is invoked to justify blocking Israeli speakers. On the West Bank and in Gaza, anti-normalization leads to assaults and killing based on accusations of collaboration with Israelis.[3]

In 2014, the Palestinian Campaign for the Academic and Cultural Boycott of Israel (PACBI) issued its "Guidelines for Academic and Cultural Boycotts," which not only provided the BDS movement with tactics for group activities but also with suggestions for a series of actions that individuals and

---

3 See the general discussion and specific accounts of violence justified by anti-normalization in Nelson (2019). For a detailed account of Palestinian and paramilitary involvement in violence, see Nelson (2021b).

small groups could take.[4] Both then and since, the movement disingenuously insists it targets institutions, not individuals, even though the guidelines demonstrate otherwise, explicitly stating that "common sense" boycotts against individuals are permissible. Thus, in 2018 when University of Michigan faculty member John Cheney-Lippold told his student Abigail Ingber he would not write her recommendations to study in Israel, he was following both the PACBI guidelines and the ASA boycott resolution.

Scores of such individual assaults are gradually being thoroughly documented.[5] Officially targeting students and faculty for their Zionism, these micro-boycotts are often carried out by means of virulently antisemitic social media assaults. In 2020, when University of Southern California student government vice president Rose Ritch was driven to resign by a campaign to "impeach her Zionist ass," she experienced it as an assault on her Jewish identity (Ritch 2020). She was one of several students on US campuses slandered with claims that being Jewish and Zionist meant they could not make objective judgments.

It is remarkable how rapidly and decisively all ambiguities about BDS's aims and tactics disappear when one shifts attention from the movement's followers to its national and international leaders. Their individual rhetoric varies, as each has his or her own favorite formulations, but the movement's major spokespersons have been explicit about wanting to bring the Jewish state to an end. Whether it is BDS movement founder Omar Barghouti (2007) declaring that "accepting Israel as a 'Jewish state' on our land is impossible" and that the only solution is "euthanasia" for Israel, California State University political scientist As'ad AbuKhalil (2012) maintaining that "Justice and freedom for the Palestinians are incompatible with the existence of the state of Israel," or *Electronic Intifada* cofounder Ali Abunimah concluding that "Israel's 'right to exist as a Jewish state' is one with no proper legal or moral remedy and one whose enforcement necessitates perpetuating terrible wrongs" and "therefore it is no right at all" (2014, 44), all the leaders of the BDS movement speak in modulations of one voice.

Even Judith Butler, whose solution to the conflict crosses a line into the bizarre is clear about her hostility to Israel's existence. Arguably she is the only major BDS spokesperson who is specific about how the Jewish state can be ended nonviolently. If Jews look into their hearts, she tells us in *Parting Ways: Jewishness and the Critique of Zionism*, they will realize they are a diasporic people destined to wander the earth who really do not want a state, and they

4 PACBI Guidelines for the International Cultural Boycott of Israel, July 16, 2014, available at https://bdsmovement.net/pacbi/cultural-boycott-guidelines.
5 See Ben-Atar and Pessin (2018), Landes (2020), and Blackmer and Pessin (2021).

will give it up voluntarily (Butler 2012).[6] This improbable scenario becomes less appealing when we recognize it is a variation on the antisemitic Christian myth of the wandering Jew, now rewritten, in Butler's case, as a sadomasochistic fantasy in which a Jew revives exile as the true condition of Jewish peoplehood.

In the contemporary world, the phenomenon of fierce and unrelenting BDS anti-Zionism constitutes antisemitism's new face, its political and social cover, its facilitator and enabler. It also supplies devotees of anti-Zionism with a rationale and reliable mechanism for rationalization and self-deception. Channeling objections to "injustice," it allows anti-Zionism to be fueled not just with moral righteousness but with rage. Anti-Zionism is the new mask of the world's oldest hatred.

1. Anti-Zionism as antisemitism

Butler is among those who have tried to deflect attention from the core BDS agenda of eliminating the Jewish state. She does so both by asserting that all nation states are obsolete and by claiming that accusations of antisemitism regarding anti-Zionism are really just efforts to protect Israeli government policy from valid criticism. Yet no national group is more contentious in debating Israeli government policy than Israelis themselves, and they do not have any illusion that doing so makes them antisemitic. Years ago, there was a significant Western contingent of Israel supporters who tolerated no criticism of the Jewish state, and some evangelical Christians still hue to that position, but fifty years of Jewish anguish at policies and practices in the occupied territories have left that position without a major constituency. Retired Israeli generals and security officers are but one of the groups putting forward serious criticism and reform proposals directed against government policy.[7]

Meanwhile, one group in particular has emerged to carry the burden of promoting the false claim that Zionists believe any and all criticism of Israeli government policy is antisemitic—Jewish Voice for Peace (JVP).[8] JVP is the BDS movement's main vehicle for this relentless deception. Founded in 1996, it took a decade before it rose to prominence. Now its representatives are front and center on stage at many BDS rallies, placed there to defend against the reality that it is the BDS movement's implacable hostility to all things

---

6 For a discussion of Butler's argument and citation of a number of commentaries by others, see "Judith Butler: A Philosopher Promotes a One-State Fantasy," in Nelson (2019, 68–116).
7 See, for example, Commanders for Israeli Security (2016).
8 For a detailed overview of JVP's history and tactics, see Elman (2015).

Israeli, not merely its objection to Israeli government policy, that crosses the line into antisemitism. At BDS events and during debates over anti-Zionist resolutions, particularly those at annual meetings of mainline Protestant churches, JVP is falsely treated as though the organization is the one true representative of the Jewish people, when it actually represents but one small faction of Jewish opinion. Despite being numerically marginal, however, JVP is extremely vocal and thus influential both on campus and in a number of Christian settings.

In 2019, JVP passed a certain milestone by formally declaring itself an anti-Zionist organization, pointing out that this new definition of JVP's mission would make it easier to establish alliances with other groups devoted to anti-Zionism.[9] In one respect, that merely codified what was already apparent, but the emphasis on coalition building meant JVP would be identified with troubling forms of virulently antisemitic anti-Zionism. It would also lose the most obvious basis for rejecting unsavory alliances. JVP's uncompromising anti-Zionism crosses the line into antisemitism.

At its most basic level, Zionism was the movement to establish a home and the right to national self-determination for the Jewish people in its ancient homeland. The return to Israel has been central to Jewish culture and Jewish prayers for nearly two thousand years. From the late nineteenth century on, some felt the search for a unique homeland and a return to Zion would undermine the still unfolding enlightenment project of securing full citizenship rights and equal opportunities for Jews wherever they lived. However, for those following the fate of the huge Jewish community in Russia's Pale of Settlement, among others, that would always have seemed a distant and unlikely goal. But after World War II, in the wake of the Holocaust, confidence that Europe could even protect its Jews, let alone integrate them, evaporated entirely. That confidence has been further undermined by the rise of antisemitism in the new millennium.[10] A nation state of the Jews had become an urgent need. After the creation of Israel in May 1948, following the adoption of the UN Partition Resolution in 1947, anti-Zionism was no longer a component of a hypothetical philosophical or political debate. With the military assault by the Arab states, anti-Zionism turned into a campaign to abolish the state of Israel and disenfranchise its Jewish citizens. Anti-Zionism had morphed into antisemitism. Those who try to maintain that anti-Zionism has the same character it had a hundred or more years ago are manipulating reality.

In embracing anti-Zionism, the BDS movement's most prominent advocates take the same step. BDS has struggled to maintain a public face that clings to the

9   See Jewish Voice for Peace (n.d.).
10 On the recent rise of antisemitism, see Rosenfeld (2013, 2015).

late nineteenth/early twentieth-century model of anti-Zionism as an abstract position within a political debate, but it has inescapably become a political agenda with material consequences. Its most popular slogan—"Palestine will be free from the river to the sea"—is a call for an utterly transformed polity grounded in a Palestinian majority with a disenfranchised or marginalized Jewish minority or no Jewish presence at all. That antisemitic eliminationist agenda is behind the entire BDS movement.

The ongoing debate over proposed academic boycotts of Israeli universities gives a clear indication of why the BDS movement's anti-Zionist tactics persist on college campuses and in academic professional associations—because the debates themselves turn some students and faculty members into lifelong anti-Zionists. There is reason to fear the long-term political effect of this battle over hearts and minds, as anti-Zionist student converts graduate and enter the professions. The irony that breaking relations with Israeli universities means isolating and distancing some of the most prominent Israeli sites of policy critique has not dissuaded academic BDS advocates from pursuing the strategy despite the fact that the American Association of University Professors (AAUP) has officially opposed all academic boycotts as a matter of principle since 2005.[11] Nevertheless, several relatively small academic associations, the largest of them being the 5,000-member American Studies Association (ASA), have passed academic boycott resolutions since 2013.[12] The National Women's Studies Association (NWSA) passed a far-ranging and unusually aggressive academic, political, and cultural boycott resolution in 2015.[13] But the largest and most venerable groups, among them the 12,000-member American Historical Association (AHA) and the 25,000-member Modern Language Association (MLA) have consistently rejected them.[14] The MLA defeated the most recent such resolution by a 2:1 margin in 2017. The 2016 membership-wide vote of

---

11 The AAUP statement "On Academic Boycotts" is reprinted in Nelson and Brahm (2015), along with a series of essays discussing the topic.

12 A number of essays in Nelson and Brahm (2015) focus on the ASA resolution.

13 For the text and an evaluation of the NWSA resolution, see "Campaign Highlights: National Women's Studies Association," Israel and the Academy, accessed March 2020, http://israelandtheacademy.org/campaigns-academic-professional-organizations/campaign-highlights-national-womens-studies-association/.

14 For the text of and responses to the AHA resolution, see "Campaign Highlights: American Historical Association," Israel and the Academy, accessed May 2021, http://israelandtheacademy.org/campaigns-academic-professional-organizations/campaign-highlights-american-historical-association/. For the text of and responses to a series of MLA resolutions, see "Campaign Highlights: Modern Language Association," Israel and the Academy, accessed February 2019, http://israelandtheacademy.org/campaigns-academic-professional-organizations/modern-language-association/.

the 10,000-member American Anthropological Association (AAA) was much closer, but it nonetheless settled the issue until the AAA voted on a boycott resolution again and approved it in 2023.[15] These debates can go on for years; the AHA, for example, rejected anti-Israel resolutions for the fourth time in 2020.

Other than the success at creating anti-Zionist activists—and certainly the success at making the Israeli-Palestinian conflict simultaneously a campus conflict—perhaps the most notable effect of the disciplinary association votes has been to convince faculty they have a right to teach ideologically committed courses. When your national academic discipline declares that "Zionism is racism," you may well believe it is no longer necessary to balance Zionist and anti-Zionist views in the classroom. (The "Zionism is racism" slander, adopted by the UN General Assembly in 1975, was revoked by the General Assembly in 1991. It was revived at a 2001 UN conference on racism in Durban, South Africa, an event that is credited with inaugurating the BDS movement.) Courses with uniformly anti-Zionist reading lists are now common in a number of academic disciplines, not only in Middle East studies but also in history, political science, and other humanities and social science disciplines, areas that are centers of BDS organizing.[16]

Despite years of BDS organizing on campus and in professional organizations, however, faculty and students in STEM fields (science, technology, engineering, and mathematics) continue to show no interest in anti-Zionism. The same applies to related fields like computer science and medicine, along with unrelated areas like business. This can be attributed not only to a stricter definition of professional responsibilities but also to different models of student and faculty identity. STEM faculty sometimes organize against campus divestment drives.

Academic freedom gives faculty members in humanities and other fields the right to teach one-sided courses if their departments assign them the subject area, though academic freedom does not protect faculty members from public criticism or the criticism of their colleagues if they teach in a propagandistic or antisemitic manner. The inherent danger in antisemitic courses includes the possibility that antisemitic claims amount to hate speech, a judgment that does not necessitate a conclusion about an instructor's intent, instead relying on an

---

15 The AAA resolution was accompanied by a substantial report endorsing it. For the report itself and responses to it, see "Campaign Timeline: American Anthropological Association," Israel and the Academy, accessed December 2016, http://israelandtheacademy.org/campaigns-academic-professional-organizations/campaigns-academic-professional-organizations-american-anthropological-association/.

16 For evaluations of anti-Zionist course syllabi, see "Anti-Zionist Hostility: Teaching to Delegitimate Israel," in Nelson (2019, 259–93).

analysis of discursive effects. Yet mounting alternative courses is the only other readily available counterstrategy.

Academic freedom also protects faculty members from official sanctions if their anti-Zionist pedagogy echoes the views prevailing in their disciplines. With the weight of opinion in some humanities and social science disciplines, unlike the sciences, having become predominantly anti-Zionist, those faculty have the warrant to treat such opinion as a consensus about what counts as the truth. Some BDS claims, such as the frequent accusation that Israel is an apartheid state or that it behaves like Nazi Germany, demonstrably cross the line into antisemitism, as there is no evidence to support the contention that Israel within its pre-1967 borders practices any form of apartheid or engages in any genocidal practices there or elsewhere. But a faculty member can safely promote those views if they are a disciplinary commonplace. A historian who engages in Holocaust denial, however, could well be terminated as unfit.

Most often the only direct evidence we have of a course's purpose, when it is available, is the syllabus. If virtually all of the assigned readings are anti-Zionist, opposing the existence of the Jewish state, that gives a clear indication of the instructor's views. Zionist students in such courses have no assigned readings to refer to in advocating for Israel's right to exist. AAUP principles since 1915 have required faculty members to permit student expression of alternative views, but when the playing field for classroom opinion is so tilted, that guarantee can prove hollow. Another indication of bias is found in faculty publications.

2. BDS pseudo-scholarship

Perhaps it was inevitable that the most intricate, obsessive, and distinctive expressions of BDS-linked antisemitism would come not in slogans, petitions, or organizational agendas but in extended examples of dedicated BDS scholarship. Writing substantial books and essays, or often enough a series of them, requires a deeper personal commitment. Like the BDS activists who commit themselves to a series of campaigns over a period of years—and unlike those who simply join a demonstration or sign a petition—people who write anti-Zionist books and essays cannot really do so casually. These deeper commitments become central to people's personal and professional identities, to their sense of who they are as people and as faculty members.

As a consequence, although they want to hail a sympathetic reader with anti-Zionism's established terms and arguments—declaring Zionism fundamentally racist, indeed a form of "white supremacism," labelling Israel a "settler colonialist" and apartheid society—they also feel a need to add their own claims to the growing body of what passes for BDS scholarship. That impulse comes in part from the standard academic pressure to produce original research, though in the case of BDS scholarship that often simply means "tell us something bad about Israel we didn't already know."

A number of established and highly regarded university and commercial presses—including California, Chicago, Duke, and Minnesota among the former—have built up significant anti-Zionist book lists or journals over a period of years. They do so in part by building a stable of readers who can be relied on to recommend anti-Zionist manuscripts for publication. The process is circular; people who publish anti-Zionist books or essays then serve as readers for other people's manuscripts. It is perfectly acceptable to seek out sympathetic readers. But those readers are expected to apply objective standards of evidence and argument. Indeed, a prospective author ideally wants them to do so. Far better to have your errors and weak arguments corrected than to have them glaringly evident in print. The baseline test in scholarship is whether the author has provided supporting evidence to prove a case. Unfortunately, in the echo chamber of academic anti-Zionism, evidence is no longer required. Absurd, invidious, and wholly unsupported claims now get published under the imprimatur of distinguished universities.

In *Palestine Inside Out*, published by W. W. Norton, UCLA's Saree Makdisi, an English professor and BDS leader, summarizes his wholly false account of the number of Israel's Basic Laws that guarantee equality (2010, 263):[17]

Inequality by the Numbers

- Number of Israel's Basic Laws that guarantee equality of citizenship: 0
- Number of Israeli High Court rulings upholding equality as a right: 0

Israel's Basic Laws have constitutional status and establish the principles that guide the government and the courts, so Makdisi's accusation would be quite serious were it true. In December 2017, the University of Chicago Press's journal *Critical Inquiry*, edited by W. J. T. Mitchell, himself a committed anti-Zionist, published "Apartheid / Apartheid / [   ]," Makdisi's third long essay about Israel featured in the journal, in which the author declares again that "nowhere in Israel law is the right to equality protected" (2018, 309), although an objective reading of Israel's Basic Law: Human Dignity and

---

17 See also "Saree Makdisi: Criminalizing Israeli Law and Culture," in Nelson (2019, 157–201).

Liberty (1992) proves otherwise. Its eight principles of equality cover basic freedom, the right to privacy and intimacy, property rights, freedom from illegal searches, and freedom of expression, among other topics. In my 2019 book *Israel Denial*, published by Indiana University Press, I devote ten pages to detailing the two major Basic Laws guaranteeing equality and the substantial number of Israeli Supreme Court decisions that repeatedly reinforce those guarantees, notably applying the principle in multiple decisions regarding women's rights and the rights of Arab minorities.

In "Apartheid / ~~Apartheid~~ / [   ]," Makdisi also emphasizes a claim that several Arab (actually Bedouin) villages near Haifa never received basic municipal services like sewer and water connections. He considers this "fact" key evidence of discrimination against Israel's Arab citizens. Yet the last of the villages he lists as being unrecognized, Arab al-Na'im, was recognized in 2000, at which point—like the others before it—it received the very services he claims it still lacked in 2017. Indeed, the neighboring Jewish village Eshchar had been supplying Arab al-Naim with water since 1993. Makdisi adds the painful information that the Arabs there live in crude tin shacks. A simple internet search reveals that masonry homes had been approved in 2013, with the first homes constructed the following year. My partner and I visited both villages in May 2018 and photographed several of the 140 masonry homes then inhabited or under construction in Arab al-Na'im. Several of those photos appear in *Israel Denial*. These are among the many false statements by Makdisi that could have been corrected by basic fact checking. Their publication by W. W. Norton and the University of Chicago Press constitute antisemitic slanders.

In October 2017, Duke University Press published *The Right to Maim* by Rutgers University women's studies professor Jasbir Puar. It was preceded by a well-publicized 2016 lecture at Vassar that presented her major accusations in abbreviated form; the lecture was transcribed and the text distributed. The book received an annual award from the now thoroughly anti-Zionist NWSA. Among Puar's many unsupported claims are that Israel has for years been stunting the growth of Palestinian children by preventing pregnant mothers and their young children (from birth through age five) from getting adequate nutrition. However, the World Health Organization (WHO), UNICEF, and the Palestinian Authority itself have elaborately documented that stunting is not a serious problem either in Gaza or the West Bank and that food supplies there are adequate, though food insecurity does exist both there and in the United States, for example, for those who cannot afford to purchase food at area stores. Puar offers no evidence for her claims, and neither Duke's readers nor the press itself apparently required her to do so. Indeed, she cites none of the standard international surveys on child health nor any data from the extensive worldwide medical literature about stunting. That anti-Zionism should fuel her promotion of medical fantasies is worse than deplorable. Amplified by her relentless conspiracism about Israelis, it constitutes a clear case of antisemitism.

The WHO considers childhood stunting rates below 20 percent to be a "low mild health problem." UNICEF gives the average rate for Gaza and the West Bank combined as about 7 percent, though some estimates are slightly higher. The 2017 version of UNICEF's *The State of the World's Children* lists childhood stunting rates worldwide, including for Saudi Arabia (9%), Lebanon (17%), and Egypt (22%). Rates are still worse elsewhere: Vietnam (25%), Philippines (33%), India (38%), Guatemala (47%), and Madagascar (49%), with many other countries falling in that range.[18] If Israelis are willfully stunting the growth of Palestinian children, they are doing a poor job of it.

Puar's accusations at Vassar were arguably still more ghoulish. Drawing on earlier accusations by anthropologist Nancy Scheper-Hughes (2011), Puar condemned Israel for harvesting the organs of Palestinians killed in terrorist actions and violent demonstrations. Harvesting major organs for transplantation, however, is impossible if the dead have been wounded; contamination and infection set in rapidly and render major organs unusable. Israel's Abu Kabir Institute for forensic science did violate Israeli law for a time by harvesting skin, inner ear bones, heart valves, and corneas from both Jewish and Palestinian cadavers; unlike major organs, those tissues can be sterilized for use. Many states in the United States, it should be noted, permit harvesting of corneas and heart valves without explicit consent. Those states have laws validating "presumed consent."[19]

In addition to sharing the belief that Zionism is racist at its core and that the very idea of a Jewish state is illegitimate, as I demonstrate with the case studies in *Israel Denial*, BDS academic authors hold a number of other views not typical of the movement's casual supporters: (1) that Israel is a fundamentally demonic, destructive, and anti-democratic country about which little or nothing positive can be said; (2) that Israel is perhaps the world's most extreme violator of human rights; (3) that there are no meaningful distinctions to be drawn between a given Israeli government and the Israeli people as a whole; and (4) that distinctions between what is true or false in scholarly debate can be set aside for purposes of political expediency. As a consequence, BDS faculty research and publications

---

18 See UNICEF (2017). See also the WHO's extensive Global Database on Child Growth and Malnutrition at https://platform.who.int/nutrition/malnutrition-database. *Israel Denial* cites a number of studies by Palestinians themselves that support the international conclusions. I confirmed those conclusions in personal interviews with Palestinian health officials from Gaza and the West Bank. For the data cited above, see UNICEF (2017).

19 See also "The Organ Harvesting Scandal," in Nelson (2019, 206–15).

often abandon the fundamental reason for the academy's existence and the societal basis for maintaining the commitment to academic freedom, namely the search for the truth. The combination of these factors marks a number of BDS faculty books and essays as both anti-Zionist and antisemitic. But any effort to list common features of BDS faculty ideology will fall short of the reality unless it notes what is, overall, perhaps the most disturbing feature of this work—the sheer ferocity of the hatred of the Jewish state.

That ferocity, both in academia and in the general public, gives the BDS movement its most tellingly antisemitic character. It led the German Bundestag to define the BDS movement as an antisemitic enterprise in 2019. When BDS advocates and allies assure us their problem is not with Jews but with Zionists, they omit the most pertinent fact—that the majority of Jews worldwide, whatever their objections to Israeli policy, support the existence of the Jewish state and thus qualify as Zionists. Moreover, as Harrison writes in *Blaming the Jews*, "the hostility of anti-Zionists … is virtually exclusively directed against Jewish supporters of Israel. The object is to create the entirely misleading impression that support for Israel is a new Jewish conspiracy" (2020, 125). When you add to this prejudice the vision of Israel as a uniquely aggressive, overmilitarized, murderous state, you bring on board the foundational Christian slander that Judaism is a religion founded in vengeance rather than love. That places us in the territory of the old hatreds that have plagued Jews for centuries. By reviving them, the BDS movement has helped position itself in the vanguard of the new antisemitism.

Chapter 5

The "Word Crimes" Debate: Assaulting Civility and Academic Freedom

———

Over a period of decades, key terms in the debate over the Israeli-Palestinian conflict have seen their meanings in anti-Zionist books, essays, and news reports shift to enable them to embody unqualified hostility to the Jewish state. In some constituencies, including many on the international political left, "Zionism" thus refers to a racist and imperialist venture, rather than the long-standing effort to give the Jewish people a means to realize their dream of political self-determination in their ancestral homeland.

In 2018 three academics—Donna Divine, Miriam Elman, and Asaf Romirowsky—launched a project to document this phenomenon, correct the misleading definitions attached to many of the key words at stake, and reclaim at least some of those words for more accurate political arguments. Analyzing the key terms associated with the Israeli-Palestinian conflict will not of itself complete the policy and political work necessary to redeem these terms and discredit anti-Zionism. There are terms like "occupation" that probably cannot be rescued without material changes in the West Bank. But the discursive and political analysis they undertook in a collective project is an essential component of the process.

The result was a special issue of the well-established scholarly journal *Israel Studies*, with essays from invited contributors each devoted to one influential word, including those just mentioned (Divine, Elman, and Romirowsky 2019).

The title of the issue, available from Indiana University Press, is "Word Crimes: Reclaiming the Language of the Israeli-Palestinian Conflict."[1] What no one could have anticipated was the passionate, organized opposition to the project that coalesced immediately upon publication.[2] As Ilan Troen (2019) noted in a response published in *Fathom*, it "is the only one of the 68 issues published by the journal over nearly a quarter of a century to become sensationalized, with criticism moved from the academy into the volatile public square" and escalating on social media. At the 2019 board meeting of the Association for Israel Studies, demands to withdraw the issue were accompanied by demands for the journal editors to resign. The journal's critics chose "Facebook as the platform to incite opposition to the special issue and gather names for petitions" (Divine 2020, 151). Unfounded accusations of secret funding for the issue circulated online. In a characteristic reversal, anti-Zionist critics of the journal issue claimed that *their* academic freedom had been violated, whereas the only real assault on academic freedom came in the demand that the journal and its editors be sanctioned.

In what follows I will analyze the source of that opposition and ask what the collection can teach us by bringing these essays together in one place. I will identify strengths and weaknesses in the book-length collection as I see them, as that is what academics are expected to do. It is depressing testimony to the polarized state of academic debate about the Israeli-Palestinian conflict—including the debate among specialists—that no one else was willing to conduct a rational discussion of the arguments the essays offered. As I will show, it is no great challenge to do so. But I also want to offer a theoretical reflection on the project's significance that none of those involved in producing or commenting on the collection were prepared to provide at the time.

In her introduction to the special issue, Donna Divine emphasizes the effect that language, especially key terms, can have on our understanding both of the Jewish state and of the Israeli-Palestinian conflict as a whole. The effect of labeling Israel as an apartheid or settler-colonial state combines rebranding and renaming. As Donald Ellis writes in his contribution on "Apartheid," such "labeling has been the primary weapon in the struggle for dominant meanings" ("Word Crimes," 69). Anti-Zionist vocabulary, in Divine's words, "delivers up a Jewish state that is, by its very nature, violent and racist" ("Word Crimes," 8). These highly charged words are more than definitional. They are a filter through

---

1 Hereinafter, "Word Crimes."
2 For a series of documents on the controversy, see Wallach (2019).

which Israel's opponents see the world, a screen through which evidence of all kinds—visual, verbal, emotional, psychological, historical, experiential, and statistical—passes to acquire its meaning. Such discursive filters are devices for outreach and political persuasion. They help teach students, faculty, community members, and politicians alike how to see the world.

The terms covered in the collection are omnipresent in policy debates, proposals, and social media statements about Israel. Because these terms are inescapable, policy-makers need to be aware how they shape comprehension. That means not only being self-aware but also being aware of how readers will perceive their meaning. There are no innocent uses of terms like "apartheid," "settlements," or "Zionism."

If individuals and social groups come to accept anti-Zionist reasoning, key words like those examined in "Word Crimes" become more than components of their beliefs. These terms are the primary vehicles for and embodiments of hostile conviction. Indeed, as people internalize them, they become elements of personal identity. Then this set of terms is all that is required to mobilize political passions. Nothing more need be said. Invoking colonialism or racism is enough to silence doubts and energize political solidarity. They become personal accusations that can be hurled at individuals to discredit them.

Divine imagines that the essays will "return sanity to the discourse on the Israeli-Palestinian Conflict" in the academy. I doubt that she would have made a wager on that prediction, but events since the special issue's 2019 publication have clearly put any such hope to rest. A group including some anti-Zionist faculty members allied with the BDS movement, along with accomplished scholars who are sympathetic to Israel, signed petitions or letters demanding that the three editors—Divine, Elman, and Romirowsky—be run out of town after being rhetorically tarred and feathered. The "Word Crimes" issue, they hyperbolically and unfairly declare, violates all standards for academic integrity; it should be withdrawn, remaining copies perhaps discarded. This unrestrained polemical outburst has intensified the unwelcome polarization of the field. I aim to show those who reacted quickly that there is genuine merit in the collection. The goal is to behave like faculty members, engaging with the substance of the essays, instead of demonizing the volume's editors.

Israel Studies is affiliated with the Association for Israel Studies (AIS), though AIS provides no funding to it and has no role in the journal's operation. AIS does not appoint editors or supervise submissions. But AIS members can subscribe at a discount, and AIS notices are published without charge. The protests against the publication of "Word Crimes" appeared so rapidly that it was clear many, including the original protest organizers, had likely not yet read the issue. Many who signed were not AIS members and certainly not subscribers. In today's academy, some faculty members will sign any petition about the Israeli-Palestinian conflict that mirrors their politics, even if they know nothing about the underlying facts.

For some of those protesting who do have AIS affiliations, the whole manufactured brouhaha was an opportunity to wrest control of AIS from Zionists and put anti-Zionists in charge. The largest block of AIS members are Israelis; while many are highly critical of the West Bank occupation and government policy more widely, they do not seek the dissolution of the Jewish state or its replacement by a single state dominated by Palestinians. For some of the protest organizers, among them Ian Lustick, the two-state solution is already dead.

Israel studies as a field has long struggled to maintain political neutrality, and many scholars in the field concentrate on historical and cultural analysis that predates the founding of the Jewish state, thereby maintaining a more non-political academic profile. It is more challenging to write about the Israeli-Palestinian conflict without sometimes taking sides, though focusing on historical facts rather than competing narratives makes it somewhat possible. Looking at those involved suggests that some felt the publication of "Word Crimes" risked compromising the field's apolitical posture and status. That, rather than any justifiable complaints about the essays themselves, may have motivated some to sign.

Though I have occasionally reviewed essays submitted to *Israel Studies*, I did not review any of the essays in "Word Crimes" and was not invited to contribute to the volume. I have, however, now read the entire issue carefully. I do know the editors personally; indeed, I know some of the contributors and protestors as well. Although there are tactical problems with the strategies some of the authors adopt, there is nothing outside the academic parameters established by the anti-Zionist publications issued by prominent university presses like California, Chicago, Duke, or Minnesota. The attack on the special issue was unwarranted, the attempt to slander its editors deplorable. *Israel Studies* would have welcomed the opportunity to publish rejoinders, but no other formal action was appropriate.

I will respond to the main lines of attack in detail, but I should first point out the absurd, feigned outrage at the title "Word Crimes"—that it literally criminalizes anti-Zionist writing and propaganda. The title is designed to be both playful and provocative, but it has a serious dimension. Responding to an essay I published in *Fathom*, Gershon Shafir (2019) takes particular umbrage at both the title and my comment. He expands on the claim by a group of scholars that their work had been "criminalized" (Wallach 2019):

> If the use of the 15 words from "colonialism" through "apartheid" to "human rights," in ways that differ from the issue's editors and contributors' preferences is a crime, then those using them are criminals: word criminals. Calling fellow scholars criminals is not an acceptable response; it is a threat. Criminals are locked up. Criminalising scholarship, as this issue does, crosses the line between legitimate criticism and incitement.
>
> The subtitle, "Reclaiming the Language of the Israeli-Palestinian Conflict," poses an equally grievous threat. Making a claim of "reclaiming" implies that the 15 chosen concepts have been usurped and will now be taken back by their rightful owners. It asserts that there is only one legitimate way of using them. By excluding other interpretations and analyses of these words, the editors and contributors threaten the freedom of scholars to engage in unrestricted and uncensored debate; they pose a threat to the academic enterprise and academic freedom itself.

Not only is this frankly silly; it is strikingly uninformed. Political struggles over the meaning of significant terms have a long public history and are unlikely to end. Scholars too debate the historical meaning of words and contest new meanings that change their traditional connotations. Giving words new political meanings can prevent them from being used for the purposes they have long served, affecting how they function politically and altering public understanding of the material conditions words characterize. Moreover, the word crimes targeted here are typically collective political strategies not attributable to individual persons. Thus, Shafir's manufactured distress that people are implicitly castigated as "word criminals" is overblown and misconstrued. In a political, religious, or cultural context, efforts to change the meaning of a key word that informs identity or understanding are proper subjects of controversy. Calling the falsification of existing meanings "word crimes" highlights the issues at stake by borrowing a legal term that the editors realize is not literally applicable.

As if that hyperbole were not enough, Shafir goes on to argue that "the attempt to describe dissenters as word criminals and suppress their voices within the AIS is a microcosm of the larger assault on liberal voices and institutions in Israel." The false "word criminals" charge has now become a fact, allowing Shafir to associate it with a series of repressive Israeli government actions, actions both I and others have contested, not endorsed. Shafir's rejoinder is itself a move in a political battle. As I write about the attack on the special issue in a piece coauthored with Paula A. Treichler, "the critiques have often come from those who want to maintain the power and influence of the anti-Zionist discourse the volume deconstructs" (Nelson and Treichler 2019). The special issue "sought to explore and explicate the sparring vocabularies of the Israeli-Palestinian conflict through a series of essays on selected words that have evolved over the decades into a familiar litany central to efforts to demonise the Jewish state." "Only by falsely reformulating objections to misuse and abuse of language as secret efforts at judicial repression," we conclude, "is Shafir able to tar the special issue with a nonexistent shared fascist mission by the Israeli right.... It is Shafir, with such accusations, not the 'Word Crimes' editors and authors, who is trying to stifle academic debate." But the consequences go beyond the academy: "Contrary to Shafir's claim, the volume does not argue that 'there is only one legitimate way of using' the words covered; rather, it makes the case that some uses have been misleading, incorrect, and have the potential to provoke increased antagonism in Israel Studies and in the Middle East." We go on to map how the struggle over meanings evolves:

> The late Stuart Hall used to argue that terms widely championed by the political right, like nationalism, should not simply be ceded to them. They should be the subject of intellectual and political debate, redefinition, and struggle; there should be forms of nationalism that progressives could endorse. Similarly, "human rights," "indigeneity," and "intersectionality," among the concepts covered in *Word Crimes*, should not simply be abandoned to the definitions promoted by anti-Zionists. That means contesting how they have been used, as the contributing authors do. And that requires recovery of the historical meaning of terms more recently criminalised by Israel's opponents, "Zionism" being the most obvious example. "Apartheid" is another key case here; its immensely important historical meaning in South Africa is seriously diminished by its inaccurate application to Israeli society west of the green line. Similarly, one does not want to cede the definition of "human rights" to the many UN members who see it only as a club to bash Israel with, while ignoring infinitely more serious violations elsewhere.

We then offer some general observations about contests over meaning:

> We typically think of meanings and definitions as referents to phenomena in the real world. But meanings are not stable, natural or inevitable, and nor do they map tidily onto the world or onto the definitions they may become. Contests for meaning do not take place in a vacuum, nor are they predictable at the outset. In fact, for a given meaning to become a formal definition—whether in a dictionary, law, statute, treaty, policy—that meaning must be fought for, compromised over, championed, and finally settled upon. Whose meaning is taken up and formalised in this way depends on the sponsor's authority and power, resources for promotion, elegance and clarity of formulation, strength and size of allied constituencies, source of the meaning, and other factors. But once formalised, it becomes difficult to revise or dislodge. *Word Crimes* offered a critique of some aspects of the currently dominant meanings routinely given to key words and concepts in Israel Studies.

Divine opens and closes her introductory essay by citing the deplorable and politically most dangerous anti-Israel word crime—the slander that Israel is engaged in genocide against the Palestinians. Given that the Palestinian population continues to increase, some have shifted their verbiage to claims of "slow genocide" or "delayed genocide" in an effort to sustain the slander, but the accusation remains false, unethical, and unprofessional. The Palestinian and Israeli deaths at every stage of this long-running conflict have been deeply disturbing, but they are overshadowed by the vastly superior number of regional casualties in Iraq, Syria, and Yemen. If the term genocide retains any of its original meaning, it cannot be responsibly applied to Israel's conduct. Yet you add genocide to the terminological field of anti-Zionism, and it is validated by all the other terms. The uneasiness about its plausibility—uneasiness reflected in problematic modifications like "attempted genocide"—is largely erased. Genocide is emptied of its immense, hard-won, transformative historical meaning to become just one more anti-Zionist complaint. The effort to empty genocide of its historical meaning, depriving it of the warranted political power it has wielded, justifies its designation as a word crime. Its misuse is increasing embraced by an anti-Zionist movement that takes its cues from the academy but extends beyond it. And the incorporation of genocide into the mix of complaints normalizes bogus claims that enact Holocaust inversion. Indeed, as Mor points out in his contribution

"On Three Anti-Zionisms," Holocaust inversion can even be combined with "a meaningless note of sympathy for Holocaust victims as an exculpatory addendum" ("Word Crimes," 211). As "Word Crimes" demonstrates, definitions are not merely a valid basis of struggle; they are the outcome of struggle.

"Word Crimes," it should be clear, is an effort to challenge the anti-Zionist consensus that now dominates some disciplines or subdisciplines. It is not designed as a pro and con debate, given that in some cases one already confronts an avalanche of anti-Zionist opinion. The effort to get people to think more critically about what they may perceive to be received truths that are deceptive, misleading, or even malicious required marshalling contributions that served that goal. Nevertheless, most of the essays are well-reasoned, adequately documented academic work. Thus, Miriam Elman offers a careful overview of "Islamophobia" that properly castigates the impulse to dehumanize and demonize Muslims and especially normalizes that hostility post 9/11. Yet she also faults "the unhelpful way in which Islamophobia is today wielded as a blunt cudgel to stifle critical analyses of Palestinian politics." The latter counts as the "word crime" she interrogates. Similarly, John Strawson interrogates uses of "Colonialism" that represent political rhetoric rather than historiography, such as those that "transform the Jewish population of Israel from an oppressed people fleeing persecution and genocide into an aggressive colonial settler." "The use of the crude colonial slogan," he concludes, "will not help solve the urgent problems of self-determination and democracy in Palestine." In his piece on the "Israel Lobby," Natan Aridan makes it clear that there is lobbying on behalf of the Jewish state; he shows, however, that its successes flow from mastering the formal and informal rules of US politics, not from "nefariously or unlawfully violating them." He recalls the history of antisemitic versions of Israel lobby accusations, among them Ilan Pappe's suggestion that American Jews have operated as a fifth column.

Many of the essays identify the weaponization of vocabulary that has fueled political polarization. The principle that draws these essays together is one that many academics recognize at some level, though not always with sufficient awareness of its significance. At least in the humanities and social sciences, certain words now carry almost talismanic power. Their use in academic writing, campus debate, or the classroom eliminates the need to supply evidence or develop persuasive arguments. This is a much broader and deeper problem than the one presented by the BDS movement, which is why BDS is not the focus of the special issue. The right term—whether racism, apartheid, or settler colonialism—can carry the day on its own. The anti-Zionist lobby has largely dominated the conversation, demonizing the term that designated the search for a Jewish homeland, Zionism, and widely discrediting the one accusation, antisemitism, that supporters of Israel long had in their arsenal.

The political success that earlier terms have achieved has helped empower newer ones and enabled them to be added to the mix. Thus, persuading people to filter everything they learn about Israel through accusations about colonialism and racism makes it possible to incorporate a more recent term like "pinkwashing" into anti-Zionism. Without the existing matrix, it would be inconceivable to convince people that Israel's culturally and politically LGBTQ-friendly environment is a project of deception and misdirection. Corinne Blackmer, who writes on "Pinkwashing" here, is addressing a subject she has addressed before. Moreover, she now has a single-author book, *Queering Anti-Zionism* (2022), about LGBTQ engagement in anti-Zionist politics. Like all of us who write about "pinkwashing"—as I have—Blackmer has to confront the exceptionally twisted logic that seeks to convert an Israeli virtue, well-established gay rights, into a liability.

If it seems unlikely that a verbal matrix alone could determine how objective social practices and even physical objects are perceived, consider two examples, the first serious, the second absurd. Despite the fact that more than 90 percent of it is a wire mesh fence, the security barrier is often falsely represented as a high concrete "wall" stretching hundreds of miles. Yet its obvious material and political meaning is as a barrier marking the dividing line between Israeli and Palestinian territory. As such, it suggests a possible division between two states, the one to the east constituting a potential independent Palestinian state. That reality is erased by the controlling verbal field of anti-Zionist rhetoric, in which the security barrier becomes the "Apartheid Wall" of Palestinian and BDS propaganda, replicated in Apartheid Walls constructed on campuses in the West. The absurd example takes form as the humble container of *Sabra*-brand hummus in a number of university cafeterias. The object of repeated protests and petition campaigns, it is taken to be the leading edge of Israeli power, a magical culinary repository of Israeli hegemony. We can take any other definition as evidence of the intrusion of the Israel lobby into our daily lives. The ultimate exaggeration of the power of *Sabra* hummus is Steven Salaita's absurd claim that the cultural appropriation of Palestinian hummus to make it Israeli hummus is the first step on the way to genocide.

Key terms also help empower slogans—"Zionism is racism"; "From the river to the sea, Palestine will be free"; "Anti-Zionism is not antisemitism"—and turn their components into charged signifiers. Some are persuaded that the very concept of freedom can only be applied to Palestine through the delegitimization of the Jewish state. Shany Mor describes sentences like these as "shields deployed in a rancorous conversation" ("Word Crimes," 206); they help people avoid thinking, indeed guard against it.

Throughout the special issue are scattered concise observations both about the psychological and political power of the terms being discussed and about the general character of ideologically charged rhetoric. Donald Ellis focuses his "Apartheid" essay on a general analysis of how words gain meaning, power, and influence through competitive political processes. The special issue empowers us to take this matter to the next level—to think about the relational and differential effects of these key terms conceived as a differential field. We know from the foundational work of Swiss linguist and semiotician Ferdinand de Saussure (1857–1913) that key terms operate within a field of similarities and differences, which is how they marshal their connotative effects. We need to study how apartheid, colonialism, human rights, occupation, pinkwashing, settlements, and other terms intersect and function collaboratively. The "Word Crimes" volume gives us the material we need to begin doing that work.

Writing on "Indigeneity," Ilan and Carol Troen thus trace the competing and surprisingly varied contemporary efforts to invent histories of indigeneity to gain political advantage and then offer the depressing but necessary conclusion: "Hitching a ride on this concept and using it indiscriminately obscures the complex issues that have to be addressed if the parties' conflicting claims are ever to be adjudicated." They show that the project of adapting the term "indigeneity" to the Israel-Palestinian conflict has entailed conflating a critique of Zionism with the earlier quasi-legal term "indigeneity" that was itself never definitively defined. The result is that, in the context of anti-Zionist politics, "indigeneity" invokes a belief that "Palestinian Arabs are the sole long-resident population with rights over the land, while Jews are but recent foreign conquerors" ("Word Crimes," 17). Because indigeneity so used "neatly defines Jews as invaders and the Jewish state as an intruding colonial-settler society in the service of an imperialistic mission" (20), all those other words become part of a connotative or associative field in which indigeneity is embedded. The pro-Palestinian claims about indigeneity are so thoroughly contradicted by thousands of years of Jewish history that the claims alone could not carry the day, but when powerfully linked with terms like apartheid and concepts like human rights, they become politically empowered.

Jonathan Schanzer, a former terrorism finance analyst with the US State Department and an author of several books on the Middle East, including one on Al-Qaeda and future trends in terrorism, offers a sober account of competing definitions of terrorism and the efforts by various constituencies to exploit them. He faults both Israeli and Palestinian Authority definitions and emphasizes the longstanding distinction between "*enforcement terror* (launched by those in power) and *agitational terror* (carried out by those who aspire to power" ["Word Crimes," 52]), making it clear that Israel targets the latter. He describes Israel's struggle to find a fully adequate definition, the Palestinian failure to establish a definition, and the US history of mounting inadequate definitions. His essay details the strategies and priorities these actors adopt in an objective account that does not really adopt a political vantage point. Instead, he tries to disentangle terrorism from the web of associations that compromise its utility, to take it out of the matrix in which it is currently embedded. It's as close to a politically neutral piece as one could ask.

Gerald Steinberg's essay "Uncivil Society: Tracking the Funders and Enablers of the Demonization of Israel" is quite factual as well. A political scientist at Bar-Ilan University, Steinberg has published widely on the Israeli-Palestinian conflict. Indeed, he is the premier authority worldwide on government and NGO funding of Israel delegitimization projects. His sixty-six footnotes are designed to help readers investigate the factual issues further. Since much such funding is hidden, researching it is very difficult, but Steinberg has persevered for years. His essay thus distills years of research into the role that NGOs supposedly apolitically devoted to human rights and humanitarian aid play in funding opposition to the Jewish state. They include a number of national and international church groups. He describes activities of both private and government-funded groups. The amounts at stake include many hundreds of millions of dollars annually.

Shany Mor contributes a position paper "On Three Anti-Zionisms." I have cited some of his earlier work on the Israeli-Palestinian conflict. The terms he uses here—alpha, beta, and gamma anti-Zionism—may not be universally adopted, and they may be intended more to be witty than definitive, but what he says about the historical transformation of Zionism is important. Among his aims is to discredit the link anti-Zionists have sought to make between opposition to Zionism before there was a Jewish state and the more recent anti-Zionism that arose once the state was founded. His second category refers to the Arab rejection of any Jewish presence in the Middle East, whereas the third identifies an Israel that "was created in sin and is tainted in its every action by sin." That is what Mor classifies as gamma anti-Zionism; it holds that "the establishment of the State of Israel in 1948 was an unconscionable crime against humanity." Mor seeks to help us avoid confusing these three types of anti-Zionism so that our understanding and analysis are improved. He does not do so in an effort to endorse Israeli government policy. "Israel as a state has its share of moral imperfections," he writes. "Some are the natural consequence of being a state and having to engage in difficult life or death choices and others are entirely inexcusable by any standard." Two things matter here: the classification system itself and his observations about the three types of anti-Zionism. As with the complaints that the issue's detractors have raised about other essays, the accusation about Mor's lack of documentation has the unfortunate effect of deflecting attention from the interesting content of his essay. Whether anti-Zionism can be similarly disentangled from its associational network is, at this point, impossible to say, but it cannot be done without supplying alternative meanings that can compete with those Israel's opponents promote.

Miriam Elman has two tasks in a piece on "Islamophobia"—to establish the pernicious character of the phenomenon, while condemning its use to silence valid criticism of Palestinian social practices, including honor killings of women. She calls Islamophobia "an affront to our common human rights and to human dignity" ("Word Crimes," 151) but faults "stretching of the concept ... to include critiques of religiously-motivated terrorism" (148). She devotes several pages to a detailed critique of anti-Muslim stereotypes and then gives the politically opportunistic applications of Islamophobia, including its anti-Zionist versions, equal time.

Donald Ellis writes on "Apartheid" not so as to summarize the existing debates, numerous examples of which are available online, but rather to explore how efforts to redefine and extend the concept's meaning have shaped its impact. He is thus applying his expertise as a widely published communications scholar to give us additional insight into the politics and semantics of this dynamic. Despite efforts to brand Israel an apartheid state, he reminds us, "apartheid is a system of institutionalized racial segregation and discrimination," whereas "the Israeli-Palestinian conflict is not about racial segregation but about land rights and occupation." It is worth noting that Ellis' blog includes a large number of concise essays about the Israeli-Palestinian conflict.[3]

Lesley Klaff, who is editor of the *Journal of Contemporary Antisemitism*, contributed an essay on "Holocaust Inversion," a subject that she has also addressed in full-length essays. One of her essay's initial contributions is a paragraph on dictionary and encyclopedia definitions of the Holocaust that vary widely on several details, including the time periods they cover. Several sections on the British context—from the Mandate years to the present—reveal disturbing examples of Holocaust denial and antisemitism likely to be new to anyone except a specialist. As she points out, Holocaust inversion has a dual

---

3   Peace and Conflict Politics (blog), http://peaceandconflictpolitics.com/.

effect: "By comparing Israel's behavior towards the Palestinians with that of the Nazis towards the Jews, any wrongdoing on the part of Israel is magnified and exaggerated and the crimes and atrocities the Nazis inflicted on the Jews are diminished." When combined with her history of the origin and evolution of Holocaust inversion, this straightforward conclusion highlights the challenge that all who are inclined to use Holocaust analogies should confront.

All these terms are part of the baggage any one word bears with it. Not that this list includes all the baggage at issue. You can enter the network at any point, say with "settler-colonialism" rather than indigeneity, with similar results. Consider how many of the terms in the "Word Crimes" lexicon are part of the connotative field of indigeneity: colonialism, occupation, apartheid, Holocaust, refugees, human rights, Zionism, Israel lobby, pinkwashing, settlements, to go right down the project's table of contents. Add some proper names: Jerusalem, Menachem Begin, Netanyahu, and so forth. Part of the point is that you do not need a present argument, thesis, or essay to get trapped in this associative nexus. All you need is the terms empowered over time and then invoked again.

The interrelationship between—or intersectionality of—these terms is why it is important to treat them together in one collection. That is part of the scholarly benefit of the special issue. Part of what is interesting and destructive about this anti-Zionist discursive field is that it is unstructured. There is no definitive hierarchy, really no hierarchy at all. The terms are all interchangeable. None of the accusations they wield against Israel are worse than any of the others. If you believe Israel is a settler-colonialist state, then you believe Palestinians alone are indigenous; then you believe all their human rights are being violated, that all the settlements are criminal ventures, that the Israel lobby promotes colonialism, that Israel practices pinkwashing, and so forth.

One of the most powerful features of the anti-Zionist discursive field or matrix is its success at countering the infinite interplay of similarity and difference characteristic of language as a whole. Within this mutually reinforcing field of terms, there is no variability of meaning. There is an iron law of equivalence operating to obliterate difference. It functions almost as counterevidence to what Saussure and his heirs, particularly the French philosopher Jacques Derrida (1930–2004), taught us about language. Instead of being vulnerable to a disabling form of inner contradiction, a politically motivated discursive field maintained by scores of true believers can evidently impose uniformity of meaning. In the case of contemporary anti-Zionism, demonization of the Jewish state is the uniform effect. I am not suggesting that entire anti-Zionist books or essays can be protected from destabilizing inner contradictions, but the force of the anti-Zionist core vocabulary can distract readers from recognizing the natural consequences of semiosis. The controlling field of terms functions as a kind of brainwashing for those whose politics it takes over. The rigid anti-Zionist convictions one sees on so many campuses are the most familiar consequence.

So far, the kind of conversation about a mutually reinforcing anti-Zionist discursive field that I am encouraging has not taken place. We have instead been diverted by the assault on the editors and contributors. We thus have a twofold responsibility—to account for the phenomenon of the organized opposition to the collection and to try to shift the conversation to a more responsible professional level.

We can do so while recognizing that some of the essays have a distinct political perspective. That's not surprising, since the collection is designed to interrogate and critique prevalent anti-Zionist definitions. Some contributors handle that task judiciously, others not. There are some people I would not have asked to contribute. Some critics of the enterprise may have thought the essays should have been staged as pro and con debates. In some cases—as with apartheid, Holocaust inversion, pinkwashing, and Zionism—that would have been to overturn the truth altogether, to give equal time and a false presentation of balance to views that do not merit any credibility. That said, the political commitments do lead to oversights that one can dispute without resorting to the unqualified condemnation in which the volume's critics have indulged.

In his entry on "Occupation," Efraim Karsh, a well-established scholar, works partly to recover a critical but often repressed historical fact—that the occupation of Gaza and the West Bank began, respectively, with Egypt and Jordan occupying them for twenty years. That process of repression is a word crime because it falsifies the historical reality and compromises what should be the full meaning of the word. He also emphasizes that, for many opponents of Israel, the "occupation" began not in 1967 but rather with the primal outrage—the land purchases of the *Yishuv* and the creation of the Jewish state in 1948.[4] He provides an informative list of the ways in which the occupation actually benefits Palestinians, but apparently chose not to document the evidence in support of his lists of economic and cultural improvements in the West Bank since 1967. I have cited some of the same facts in *Israel Denial* and felt it necessary to document them, in part because, unlike Karsh, I was criticizing the claims made by faculty members I was naming. Some of Karsh's evidence, like the establishment of seven West Bank Palestinian universities under the Israeli occupation, whereas the Jordanian occupation saw none created, should be well known. Others, like the huge improvements in West Bank health care, are not

---

4 The *Yishuv*, literally "settlement," denotes the body of Jewish residents living in the Land of Israel prior to 1948.

so well known, except to Palestinians themselves and some in the medical com-munity worldwide. But Karsh is *not* dealing in disputed facts; the information he offers is accurate but omits acknowledgement of the denial of the rights of political self-determination, freedom of movement, and the right to exploit the full resources of the land. The existence of separate West Bank legal systems for Jews and Palestinians meanwhile generates many inequalities he overlooks. He should have cited realities like fragmented territorial control and punitive policies like house demolition that have produced so much justified unrest. He is presenting the alternative case about the effects of the occupation, though I think the essay would have been more effective had he combined the positive with the negative.

Such omissions in a few essays are combined with strong rhetoric to make them polemical enough to undercut their effectiveness. The same thing might have happened with Asaf Romirowsky, who has written widely about the Israeli-Palestinian conflict, including a coauthored book on Palestine refugee relief, had he adopted inflated rhetoric. Instead, he contributes a well-researched piece on "Arab-Palestinian Refugees." Determined to counter the prevailing myth that Israelis are solely responsible for the plight of the 1948 refugees from then until now, Romirowsky details the ways in which the UN Relief and Works Agency for Palestinian Refugees in the Near East (UNRWA) has institution-alized refugee status, resisted solutions, and helped make "refugee" a "critical part of [Palestinian] national identity" ("Word Crimes," 91). In the process, UNRWA has promoted a unique multigenerational and multinational defini-tion of a Palestinian refugee that not only includes future generations but also Palestinians who are citizens of other countries. Whether out of conviction or strategy, however, Romirowsky frees Israelis of all responsibility for the *Nakba* and thus implicitly of the need to share now in matters like compensation for lost property. A couple of paragraphs adjusting his historical account would have better assured wide acceptance of his essay.

Rather than offer a skimpy sample of the vast debates about the refugees, Romirowsky emphasizes documentation about the factual issues at stake. He has been gratuitously criticized for not citing scholarly opinion, although it requires a good deal more knowledge about his subject to cite original evi-dentiary sources, as he does, than to cull opinions through an internet search. Here as elsewhere, the real objection is to Romirowsky's politics and his role in coordinating the activities of Scholars for Peace in the Middle East (SPME).

Similarly, historian Alex Joffe, author or coauthor of several books on the Middle East, provides both a historical account of the development of current human rights advocacy and a fierce but carefully reasoned critique of dominant human rights ideology as it applies to the Israeli-Palestinian conflict: "The concept of human rights as applied to the Palestinians deliberately blurs many legal categories. These include international humanitarian law, which aims at limiting armed conflict; international human rights law, which deals with refugees and migrants, as well as the treatment of women, children and others; and international criminal law, aimed at the conduct of individuals and regimes." As with many of the other essays here, the aim is to draw distinctions and thereby help us think more clearly. It is those distinctions that underwrite his political conclusions: "the 1975 UN resolution that declared that Zionism is racism, effectively convert[ed] the basic concept of Jewish autonomy and sovereignty into a human rights abuse against the Palestinians and the global order."

Joffe's essay thus takes up an important topic and offers a necessary critique of a concept whose influence can hardly be overstated. His account of how the concept has been elevated to near sacred status and weaponized to delegitimate the Jewish state is one that should be widely read. Perhaps because he is working to counter the dominant human rights industry, however, he omits any substantive account of the necessary work the concept does outside the Israeli-Palestinian context, which weakens the essay. At the very end he acknowledges that "building human rights into renationalized societies is critical" but allows that the odds of extricating the term from its abuses are poor. Along the way, the flamboyant claim that "all things unsavory, unhappy, and inconvenient are elevated to the level of human rights abuses" ("Word Crimes," 113) overstates matters, as does his critical definition: "human rights is a universal theology that describes, however vaguely, the eschatological condition of a stateless, borderless globe where individuals and communities are somehow both free to pursue their aspirations and be protected from one another" (112). I'll forgive him, however, the identification of human rights "seminaries formerly known as universities" (114) because it is an apt description of a minority reality in higher education. It describes some academic departments and the dominant forces in some fields, but not entire universities.

My own sympathies unsurprisingly do not match those of all the authors. Ari Blaff writes on "Settlements," arguing accurately that they "have become the rallying cry for international boycotts of Israel championed by BDS activists." "Refracting Palestinian grievances through settlements," he continues, and ignoring Palestinian intransigence, "an international consensus has prioritized their demonization over the conflict's roots." He is certainly correct that those who object to Israel's very existence on political, religious, or ethnic grounds are not in fact motivated by opposition to the post-1967 settlement movement. But he goes one step too far in asserting that the settlements are "a symptom, not a cause." Put simply, they are both. Settlement expansion beyond those settlements located close to the green line will eventually torpedo the two-state solution. So would annexation. I understand the anguish he feels when the Jews who returned to Hebron, one of the communities he cites, are deemed "illegitimate colonizers in their own ancestral lands," but Hebron is one of the communities that will have to be abandoned if Palestinians are to have political self-determination.

Among the contributions sure to remain controversial are Gabriel Brahm's on "Intersectionality" and Thane Rosenbaum's on "Zionism." Brahm's account of the benefits of traditional uses of intersectionality reliably summarizes those who have come before him. His critique of its current abuse combines wit and vigorous condemnation. He is admirably satiric when he describes "suffering ... tirelessly excavated by bureaucrats whose real job is *resentment management*." And he is at least close to being justified in saying "intersectionality is the sum-of-all-virtue-signals," the "Master-signifier of concern for every-injustice-all-at-once," though he recognizes it skips the injustice of the oldest hatred. Where he is on much shakier ground is in generalizing about this sequence:

> In a period when African Americans (of both genders) were classified as property and women across the board (of all races) were legally restricted from owning property and not yet allowed to vote in the United States, black women were doubly oppressed. Moreover, nowadays one certainly must add that black lesbians were trebly subordinated, disabled Third World women of color even more so, and non-white Muslim transsexuals (almost entirely officially erased at the time) suffered most of all. For *this* is the logic of intersectionality in practice: one is ethically bound to constantly take account of every variation in the vast menagerie of prejudice.

This passage exceeds warranted sarcasm to verge on the voice of an aggrieved white male. Where Brahm is on point is in warning that anti-Zionism is corrupting major components of contemporary feminism. The National Women's Studies Association (NWSA) fully merits Brahm's critique. But he is wrong to assert that feminism tout court is allied with BDS and lost to progressive liberalism. But the powers that control the NWSA are unflinching in their visceral hatred of Israel, as are the political activists who represent the majority of its membership.

If Brahm had confined his critique to the anti-Zionist wing of feminism, I would endorse what he says. But feminism, like Marxism, has fragmented since the 1980s. An intolerant wing now dominates women's studies and gender studies programs as well. But that is not feminism's entire legacy, and it does not represent the politics of all feminist scholars. It is difficult to support feminism's principled legacy when there is no major feminist political group devoted to it that does not also endorse anti-Zionism. But feminism's message about equal rights remains critical despite the corruption of the contemporary movement.

The portion of the movement that has embraced anti-Zionism with exceptional fervor also displays other troubling features. One anecdote may put the worst of its identity politics in a decisively disturbing light. When Brandeis University withdrew its 2014 offer of an honorary degree to Ayaan Hirsi Ali, a political activist who built her reputation condemning the genital mutilation of women, the opposition to the award was organized by the campus' women's studies program. Even though their protest was focused on her critique of Islam, it represented an assault on women's rights, a delegitimization of her life mission, and a betrayal of feminism's core commitment to the principle that women have authority over their own bodies. At some level, the women's studies faculty were enacting a ritual of self-hatred. For that constituency the women of Israel are now also expendable.

Thane Rosenbaum is another complex case. A New York University law professor who has written several novels, he is notably flamboyant in addressing the Israeli-Palestinian conflict. "Zionism is the one nationalism that dare not speak its name" is obviously witty but overstated, but the claim that "Arab-Israeli parties ... unleash oppositional invective that would constitute treason in most democratic societies" is actually irresponsible, especially from a law professor. And "arguably no other democracy would allow anything approaching some of the seditious rantings found in Ha'aretz" is no better. Calling Zionism "a cleansing agent for Jew-hatred everywhere" takes an important point and undercuts it rhetorically. Rosenbaum is often on target here, but his lapses into rhetorical overkill do damage to the overall project. Judicious editing would have helped.

A full account of each of these essays would be a substantially more elaborate undertaking. I will do that in what follows in the case of Valentina Azarova, but these were all word-limited projects. Thus, it is pointless to demand that they treat their own topics thoroughly. These brief entries are not fair game for a complete review of and conclusive judgment about the author's capacities and standards. Yet that judgment is what their critics undertook in what must be described as bad faith. They did so without actually engaging with the arguments mounted by the essays. I have seen none of the special issue critics engage in debates about the possible contributions any of the essays might have made to our understanding of the key terms they discuss. As others have pointed out, that would be the standard academic practice. The academic outrage proceeded in a notably unacademic fashion.

Contributors to "Word Crimes" did not have as much space for either argumentation or documentation as they would have had were they writing a full-length article or a chapter in a book, so they had to decide how many footnotes they could afford to provide. When I write concise essays for reference books or anthologies on topics I have already addressed in great detail elsewhere—topics like academic freedom, contingent employment, or many areas of modern poetry—I often use my available word length for my argument and omit documentation entirely. You can certainly do that if you write as an established authority.

A number of the contributors to *Word Crimes*, devoted more space to notes than I would have. Two chose to offer no documentation, which some critics, inappropriately, seem to feel discredits the whole issue. It has been pointed out that the fall 2018 issue of *Israel Studies* included six essays without footnotes, though no readers raised objections that time.

The attack on the credentials of the special issue's authors is at best disingenuous. They all have a history of writing about the Israeli-Palestinian conflict, though one (Ari Blaff) is a journalist and global affairs graduate student at the University of Toronto who has written for several news outlets. Most have previously written about the specific topic they address, though that is not always the best standard to apply in building such a volume. Sometimes you ask people to move out of their more narrow and familiar comfort zone to take on a related topic within the broader subject area. That helps generate some original thinking, rather than just a summary of people's earlier work.

Some of the protestors were agitated that "non-specialists" were invited to contribute. Over a period of years, when I several times debated the conservative activist David Horowitz in public, he argued that you could only validly write on a subject if you were trained in it in graduate school. Among my books are several each on higher education, the Spanish Civil War, and the Israeli-Palestinian conflict. My PhD in literature did not formally prepare me in any of these subjects. Some faculty members stay within a single area their entire careers; others acquire new interests and either move on or add them to their profile. They read in the new area, attend conferences, conduct original research, discuss the issues with colleagues, and eventually draft academic publications. At first no one credits you with any expertise when you enter a new field. And I suppose for David Horowitz my six books and many refereed essays on antisemitism and the Israeli-Palestinian conflict still leave me unqualified. But his disapproval does not keep me awake at night. Nor would any comparable judgment from those, including petition signers who've never written anything about Israel, who mounted the campaign against "Word Crimes."

Why the volume's detractors considered themselves authorized to police the discipline in the way they sought to do is difficult to say, though the range of contributors appears to violate their sense of who the canonical, authorized Israel studies scholars are. Even fluency in multiple languages, which is a tremendous asset, will not guarantee that you will produce compelling insights. There is more hollow posturing by people of all political persuasions about qualifications in Middle East and Israel studies than in many other fields. In all areas of academic life, the challenge is to exercise judgments about the research and insights themselves. In the case of "Word Crimes," the results are of demonstrable interest and utility and do not merit the hostility they received.

A number of us have detailed some of the political and institutional forces behind the recent "Word Crimes" controversy. Certainly, many of those who signed the petition denouncing "Word Crimes" did so before they could acquire and read the volume. They amount to a who's who list of committed anti-Zionists and antisemites. The more puzzling opponents are the credible scholars who joined in the campaign. Some of those are long-term anti-Zionists and supporters of the BDS movement. But that still leaves unexplained the participation of faculty who ordinarily avoid association with anti-Zionism. The campaign against the "Word Crimes" issue rapidly became part of the more general effort to delegitimate the Jewish state, an effort from which some of the more qualified critics would ordinarily want to keep their distance.

I characterized their participation in part as a struggle for power over Israel studies as a field and over the Association for Israel Studies (AIS) as an organization. It also reflected anxiety over changes in the field that are outside the control of AIS members, among them those who helped found Israel studies as what they thought could be an objective, apolitical area of academic study. Given that so much anti-Zionist scholarship—or what passes for scholarship from presses like California, Chicago, or Duke—is so ferociously partisan, and given how polarized public debate is over the Israeli-Palestinian conflict, it is not likely the field could remain indefinitely above the fray.

I am not suggesting that the field should be ruthlessly politicized. It is admirable to seek neutral scholarly standards, but much of what is said about Israel has political implications, and it is acceptable and even helpful to address them if you are able to do so. Yet political conviction can lead to basic confirmation bias in doing research, shaping arguments, and reaching conclusions, and that needs to be confronted both by researchers themselves and by reviewers. As I argue in *Israel Denial*, the echo chamber of peer review too often merely reinforces anti-Zionist confirmation bias.

The attacks on the "Word Crimes" issue were not a shining example of enlightenment reason. The attacks exhibited the familiar features of a moral panic, in this case a fervid anti-Zionist one. The sky was falling on Israel studies. Flee the cursed terrain of the special issue or see your career and the field damned to perdition. Not the most Jewish of concepts, perdition, but there are only so many tropes available to support moral panics. People in the grips of a moral panic do not retreat to sweet reason when challenged. They double down. They get louder.

The protest was fundamentally an example of irrational collective madness, albeit of the sort to which academics are especially disposed. They plea for moral panic solidarity. They sign petitions. They demand apologies. They threaten legal action. They call for resignations. They resign from the journal's editorial board themselves, then reverse course if the wind changes direction. They revel in mob action.

One distinction is that the critics didn't simply claim that the editors and contributors did substandard work, They wanted to go further and stigmatize it as unprofessional. They didn't want to have to prove the work was bad, because to do that they would have to contend with the pro-Israeli arguments people made, with the substance of the essays. Instead, they wanted to cast it out as rogue conduct. Their case is merely a series of overwrought accusations. The editors and contributors should apparently be abandoned on the campus of Birzeit University and left to see if they can safely hitchhike back.

"Word Crimes" should have started a fruitful discussion, not a defamatory campaign that urged professional sanctions for the journal and its editors, sanctions that would have compromised academic freedom in the field as a whole. Divine ends her introduction by declaring that "the essays should return sanity to the discourse on the Israeli-Palestinian conflict" ("Word Crimes," 15). There was faint hope of that then, less now. Most of the excessive rhetoric accompanying the controversy came from anti-Zionist writers. Scholarship can sometimes also amount to war by other means. Unfortunately, the whole controversy did not auger well for the ability of Israel studies as a field to sustain civil debate. The years since have reinforced that conclusion.

Chapter 6

Secular Versus Religious Anti-Zionism

―――――

The religious and secular campaigns to delegitimate the state of Israel have largely proceeded on separate but roughly parallel tracks during their activism in the new millennium. Although these movements know relatively little about one another, full understanding of anti-Zionism's cultural and political impact cannot be achieved without that knowledge. Nor can useful dialogue between Zionists and students and faculty who identify as Christians take place without understanding the movements that may be shaping their opinions. The most aggressive anti-Zionist Christian constituencies are quite capable of moving from anti-Zionism to antisemitism. In the process, they direct hate speech against the Jewish state. Christian hate speech can be a distinctive phenomenon when it combines anti-Zionism with revived supersessionism. Scholars need to pursue unflinching critique of those trends in anti-Zionist publications from religious groups while sustaining respectful and sympathetic conversations on campus.

Christian and secular anti-Zionism are each grounded in a Manichean ideology that divides the political world between good and evil, right and wrong, light and darkness. Christian anti-Zionism adds a spiritual dimension to the opposition, one paralleled by left-wing anti-Zionism's grounding in absolutist human rights condemnations of the Jewish state. Both the religious and secular versions of anti-Zionism have radical extremes that the more mainstream constituencies are not inclined to condemn. The radical voices have considerable online presence that inevitably establishes them as components of a spectrum, rather than as outliers beyond the pale of mainstream anti-Zionist ideology. Extreme religious anti-Zionism castigates its opponents as children of Satan, a connection that draws on centuries of Christian antisemitism. Secular anti-Zionism courts an eliminationist ambition that calls not just for political disenfranchisement but for death itself. Both consequently represent forms of antisemitic hatred. One does not often see or hear the extremist voices on campus, but they have a presence both in public sphere demonstrations and in social media.

Both secular and religious anti-Zionism gained inspiration from the notorious 2001 UN conference on racism held in Durban, South Africa, though, unlike the secular movement, religious denominations had been addressing the Israeli-Palestinian conflict for decades. Billed as a meeting to address multiple forms of racism worldwide, the Durban conference quickly devolved into an intense anti-Zionist rally and declared that "Zionism is racism." Both secular and religious versions of anti-Zionism are fueled by a relatively small core of activists who often attend annual organizational meetings en masse and dominate them. Both also embrace the BDS movement's three deceptive demands, including the demand that all several million descendants of Palestinians who fled Israel in 1947 or 1948 be allowed to return to Israel and claim citizenship, a development that would render Israel's continued status as a Jewish state no longer viable and which no Israeli government would accept.[1]

Activists in both camps also embrace the evolving ideological features of the anti-Zionist movement, such as the intensifying anti-normalization agenda that rejects any dialogue with individual Zionists or Zionist institutions. Increasingly, BDS activists see refusing to speak with or listen to Zionists as the observation of a high moral principle. The secular and religious wings of anti-Zionism both have significant constituencies that have grown disenchanted with the two-state solution. Both pursue boycott options and various forms of divestment from businesses operating in Israel or the West Bank. Both vehemently deny any element of antisemitism in their goals or methods. Both tend to disclaim pressures for ideological conformity within their groups. Both increasingly claim to uniquely occupy the moral and political high ground in debates about the Israeli-Palestinian conflict. And both proclaim themselves to be impeccably and devoutly nonviolent enterprises. The contrasting debates have played out most extensively in the United States, though I have addressed other countries where relevant.

---

1   For overviews of the BDS movement, see Nelson (2016, 2019).

During the new millennium, in particular, anti-Zionist constituencies in both secular and religious institutions have developed their own interest groups to promote their cause. In response, constituencies favorable to Israel have developed their own organizations within Christian denominations in some cases. The Episcopalians promote Palestinian advocacy through the Palestine Israel Network, which is part of the Episcopal Peace Fellowship. In the Presbyterian Church, the Israel/Palestine Mission Network was established to promote divestment in 2004; it is opposed by Presbyterians for Middle East Peace. United Methodists for Kairos Response formed in 2010 as an anti-Zionist activist group within that Church. It is opposed by United Methodists for Constructive Peacemaking in Israel and Palestine. Mennonites critical of Israel formed the Mennonite Palestine Israel Network in 2013. Among Catholics, several existing independent groups, among them Pax Christi and its affiliates, intensified their anti-Zionism, as did groups under the supervision of the Vatican or Catholic bishops such as the Pontifical Mission for Palestine and the Conference of Major Superiors of Men (Quer 2021). BDS targets religious groups because of the moral authority they wield and the high publicity value of their pro-BDS votes. Faculty members are active in several of these groups, often taking the lead in organizing anti-Zionist publications, comfortable that they can make antisemitic claims and be protected by academic freedom, as I pointed out in Chapter One. Secular BDS-allied groups have frequently taken their inspiration from the Palestinian Campaign for the Academic and Cultural Boycott of Israel (PACBI), which was launched in 2004 to define anti-Zionist goals and strategies. USACBI was established as a US affiliate in 2009.

Yet secular and religious enterprises have only a very limited number of participants in common. These are most often activists, such as members of Jewish Voice for Peace both on and off campus, who visit both local and national church meetings to support anti-Zionist resolutions but are not themselves Christian and do not otherwise participate in the denomination's activities. Overall, religious and secular anti-Zionists board different ships that merely pass in the night despite sharing parallel destinations. Within Christians denominations, debates about resolutions are largely conducted by Church members, including faculty. In some secular groups, such as faculty disciplinary associations, the self-imposed exclusivity is even more absolute: one discipline typically does not want to hear from members of another, even if they have special expertise in area history or on principles of academic freedom. On the other hand, faculty members commonly join and help lead city-wide BDS campaigns.

The lack of contact between secular and religious anti-Zionisms in part reflects the fact that, while some of their language and recent histories overlap, their long-term historical roots are very different. Those different histories sometimes manifest in different rhetoric and forms of self-understanding or self-representation. At times those differences open up alternative tactical and strategic options. There are also two very different time spans at issue. The secular BDS movement has antecedents like the Arab boycott movement and the nascent left-wing and Black anti-Zionism of the 1960s. The Soviet Union's turn from Jewish state advocacy to anti-Zionism informed the anti-Zionist left. Secular BDS has enduring intellectual heroes in academia, from Edward Said to Noam Chomsky. But Christian BDS has roots going back two thousand years, from the early Church fathers—through the Spanish Inquisition, Martin Luther, and supersessionism—to the present day.

There is no comparable lineage that can be constructed for secular BDS. It has no ancient history. Some Protestant denominations were debating and passing resolutions about the Israeli-Palestinian conflict fifty years ago. Omar Barghouti and his BDS allies were obviously not yet involved. Both the Catholic Church in Europe and at least one notable denomination, the Mennonites, have Holocaust involvement that historians have yet to fully document or resolve. A core group of Mennonite historians, Ben Goossen among them, have begun to document that involvement. A significant minority of Mennonites collaborated with the Nazis.[2] Mennonite theologians developed a racialist theology. There was a *Waffen SS* calvary unit in the Ukraine composed mostly of Mennonites. In the Catholic Church, debates about its role in the Holocaust have concentrated on the role of Pope Pius XII, who learned of the mass murder of the Jews by the fall of 1942 but chose to remain silent. The most recent examination is David Kertzer's *The Pope at War*. More broadly, the long history of Church demonization of Jews and Judaism helped make the Holocaust possible. If the Church thus brings some sense of historical guilt to present debates, secular BDS surely does not. Sensitivity to the Holocaust should give pause to campus secular groups demanding an end to the Jewish state, but it does not. Muslim antisemitism and anti-Zionism have long histories as well, but their contemporary avatars do not often acknowledge a burden of guilt, despite antisemitic passages in the Koran and the Hadith and despite the wartime collaboration of the Grand Mufti of Jerusalem, Haj Amin el Husseini, and the Nazis. In dreaming of the Holy Land, some Christians dream of its origins and the end of days. Most secular BDS advocates have more immediate interests, though students with strong religious convictions will make those associations whether or not they feel comfortable expressing them. One word for the core difference is theology, but where the Middle East is at issue theology cannot be altogether disentangled from politics.

2   See Goossen (2017) and Kampen (2021).

Taking two denominations as representative examples, I will describe the long-standing regional investments of the Presbyterian Church and the evolution of Episcopalian resolutions regarding the Israeli-Palestinian conflict.[3] Presbyterians and other denominations have been involved in missionary work in the Middle East for over a hundred and fifty years. They never succeeded in converting Muslims, but the Church did become part of Arab culture and eventually became allied with anticolonialism in the region. Those regional experiences and commitments had both theological and organizational impacts on the Church in the United States and Europe, including on religiously affiliated colleges and universities. To those experiences were added the accounts of Presbyterian missionaries who were among the denominational groups, including the Mennonites, that began to work with Palestinian refugees in 1948. The following year the Presbyterian Board of Foreign Missions submitted a report to the Church's annual General Assembly that was critical of Israel's displacement of those refugees. Other missionary reports urged not just the amelioration of Palestinian suffering but also the pursuit of long-term solutions. A split developed in the 1950s and 1960s between these missionaries and Presbyterian leaders who focused on interfaith alliances with the Jewish community. That division intensified after the 1967 war when the occupation emerged as an issue.

The Episcopal Church's General Convention (GC), which meets every three years, has been passing resolutions about the Israeli-Palestinian conflict for forty years.[4] The Executive Council meets three times a year in between the GCs and has issued statements as well. The 1979 GC began the process by affirming Israel's right to exist and urging the creation of a Palestinian state. The next three GCs passed similar resolutions, but debates started to become more fractious in the 1990s. The 1991 GC passed a resolution urging the United States to hold in escrow the amount of aid sent to Israel equal to what the Israel government spends in support of settlements in the West Bank and Gaza. The GC also expressed concern about the "*de facto* annexation of Palestinian land" (Robertson 2021, 239). The 1994 GC formally declared the settlements to be illegal. The 1997 GC recommended Jerusalem as the capital of both an Israeli and a Palestinian state. Thereafter internal Church debates over homosexuality and other issues turned into culture wars, and those engulfed the Israeli-Palestinian conflict as well, a pattern that applies to several denominations. The 2003 GC

---

3   For a series of essays detailing Presbyterian engagement with the Israeli-Palestinian conflict, see the contributions by Daniel Friedman, John Wimberly and William Harter, Michael C. Gizzi, and Cary Nelson in Nelson and Gizzi (2021, 318–421).

4   I am drawing on the account provided by Robertson (2021).

denounced the construction of Israel's security barrier. Debates in subsequent years, echoing secular activism, included disputes over divestment resolutions. At the 2018 meeting a resolution declaring Israel an apartheid state was debated but thereafter opposed by Episcopalian bishops.

In the wake of the 1967 war, a key theological issue began to occupy multiple denominations: Was the covenant between God and the Jews still valid, or had Israel's conduct invalidated it? That revived one of Christianity's oldest claims, one that had long shaped Catholic theology, namely supersessionism. This is the belief that the Church has superseded or replaced Judaism in the relationship with God and as a route to salvation. An important report issued by the Presbyterians in 1972, "Peoples and Conflict in the Middle East," declared that "the Abrahamic covenant is unconditional in that it is not based on the prior acts of the people nor can it be invalidated by any sin of the people."[5] The debates about the divine covenants with Abraham and Moses continue in multiple churches today, but the last decade has seen the emergence of anti-Zionist church constituencies that claim the covenant has been abrogated. A major figure in lending support to that thesis has been emeritus faculty member and United Church of Christ leader Walter Brueggemann. The central issue in debates about the status of the covenant is whether its dedication of the Land of Israel to the Jewish people still obtains. One anti-Zionist strategy, advanced by East Jerusalem Anglican cleric Naim Ateek, founder of the Sabeel Ecumenical Liberation Theology Center, and others, has been to argue that the covenant is no longer about land, about a particular piece of Middle Eastern territory. The new covenant with the Church is a universal covenant about salvation through Jesus Christ. The particularist covenant with the Jews has been superseded. Friends of Sabeel has local chapters worldwide that collaborate with national boycott initiatives.

The political actions that both secular and religious anti-Zionists undertake and agitate for are determined largely opportunistically, not by theology or abstract principles, though moral and political abstractions are certainly deployed in their service. Thus, religious denominations have anti-Zionist cohorts that campaign for divestment from businesses operating in Israel because the churches have relevant investments in stock. If they do not have any connections with Israeli universities there isn't much point in pressing for academic boycotts. Academic boycotts, conversely, are a continuing focus for multiple components of the academy—academic unions representing both faculty and graduate students, faculty disciplinary organizations, and various

---

5 Quoted in Nelson and Gizzi (2021).

campus groups. Students have campaigned against Israeli hummus when their local cafeteria or campus grocery offer it for sale. Local communities have initiated similar campaigns when their stores stock Israeli products. Some US ports in California have seen secular campaigns and demonstrations designed to prevent Israeli cargo ships from being unloaded. The project to harass Zionist speakers, interrupting them repeatedly or trying to prevent them from speaking at all, is pretty much exclusively a secular enterprise, as it runs counter to all Christian principles for dialogue. Religious groups, however, have often been willing to schedule substantially less time during debates for Zionist than for anti-Zionist speakers. For some, that preserves an illusion of nonviolence, though the members who are thereby denied opportunities to air their views certainly feel themselves to be targets of aggressive antisemitic action.

The secular anti-Zionist movement on campus has on numerous occasions organized what I term "micro-boycotts" against individual Jewish students or faculty, a trend I analyze more fully in Chapter Three.[6] The first such micro-boycott may well have been British faculty member Mona Baker's 2002 decision to remove two Israeli academics from the editorial boards of the journals *Translator* and *Translator Studies Abstracts*. In a characteristic example of the paradox of carrying out such actions against Israelis, one of those faculty members, Miriam Shlesinger, was a former chair of Amnesty International, a group often critical of Israeli policy. It is regularly pointed out that Israeli universities are sites of regular criticism of government policy.

As such micro-boycotts evolved, they became increasingly personal and aggressive. The political assaults on students have taken advantage of the opportunity to demonize individual students serving in student government. The following two examples are just a small sample of a much larger number. For six months in 2015, Andrew Pessin of Connecticut College was subjected to a manufactured faculty and student campaign to demonize him for his Zionist commitments. In 2020, Rose Ritch was hounded out of University of California student government, where she was serving as vice president, by a concerted anti-Zionist and antisemitic campaign. Such campaigns have repeatedly been based on false accusations. While those accusations have typically been disproven, exoneration often follows lengthy investigations that themselves do huge damage to those falsely accused. Jewish students at University College London have reported assaults that rise to the level of physical intimidation. Meanwhile,

---

6 For detailed accounts of numerous anti-Zionist attacks on individuals, see Ben-Atar and Pessin (2018) and Blackmer and Pessin (2021). For the most detailed treatment of one such incident, see Landes (2020).

as I have emphasized, there have been no punishments for those who invented the original lies or carried out physical threats. Universities must be pressed to apply punishments to those who instigate these attacks. Expressions of regret from university administrators are not a sufficient remedy. Once again, these are secular assaults. Campus religious groups generally do not encourage ad hominem assaults.

The similarities and differences between the secular and religious wings of anti-Zionism merit urgent comparison not so much because of the need to understand history but because both wings cast a shadow over contemporary politics. It is thus crucial to come up with strategies to counter their impact, which in turn requires an understanding of their beliefs, goals, and motivations. Even basic communication between secular Zionist and non-Zionist groups suffers severely from a lack of shared values. Meanwhile, estimating the long-term impact of either religious or secular anti-Zionism is at once important and yet entirely speculative. To a significant degree, secular and religious forces wield disparate impacts even with respect to the same political issues. For example, because there are constituencies within both secular and religious communities arguing for the elimination of US military aid to Israel, it is essential to track the sources of this impulse.

In the US Congress, the impulse is thus far limited to a small cohort of members of the House of Representatives. Whether and how rapidly that number will grow is impossible to say, but it is a source of serious concern among Israel's supporters. The BDS movement credits all political influence on military spending to the mythically powerful "Israel lobby," a lobby that is actually no different from or more influential than lobbies promoting legislation against global warming, promoting fossil fuels, or any other cause. Anti-Zionist groups succeed in exaggerating the Israel lobby's influence because it is fertile ground; such arguments play into existing antisemitism and conspiracy theorizing. While purportedly combatting the Israel lobby, they are actually using antisemitism indirectly to raise funds and maximize their own impact. Yet the real power behind Congressional support for Israel is not six million American Jews but sixty-five million US Christian evangelicals, some of whom have distinctive theological reasons for their Zionism. While evangelicals have steadily grown in number and influence, membership in mainline Protestant denominations has declined. Membership in the Presbyterian Church (USA) declined to about 1.25 million in 2020, a loss of about a million members over the previous fifteen years. Membership in the US Episcopal Church amounted to about 1.6 million at this time. Once virtually defining the religious character of the Republican Party establishment, it has lost much of its political cachet. Among smaller denominations, Mennonites number about 60,000 in the United States.

Britain has no comparably fierce or powerful pro-Zionist religious power, but it has had an important political vehicle for anti-Zionism. For a long time, the British Labour Party was galvanized by its leader Jeremy Corbyn's relentless but entirely secular antisemitic anti-Zionism. The prospect of Labour coming to power under his leadership thus held out the possibility of an abrupt reversal in British foreign policy, something the United States has not faced. Corbyn's removal from power in 2020 has given the party an opportunity to purge itself of antisemitism. Whether it will be successful in this regard remains uncertain. Jewish Voice for Labour, a group formed in 2017, supported Corbyn and decried his ouster.

In Britain, the most virulent religious anti-Zionist rhetoric has been that advanced by the Church of Scotland. In its much-critiqued 2013 report, "The Inheritance of Abraham?," it asserts that Jews during the time of Jesus "were not ready" for the "radical critique of Jewish specialness and exclusivism" he "offered" them.[7] The report rejected the view that the covenant with Abraham granted the Jews any special claim to the Land of Israel, a belief it once endorsed. The Scottish Council of Jewish Communities (2013) rejected the report for providing "a veneer of theological respectability for what is effectively a call for the destruction of the State of Israel." In 2017, however, the Church partly reversed course by rejecting the BDS movement and condemning Hamas for denying Israel's right to exist.

The only other Church in the United Kingdom involved in anti-Israel activism has been the Methodists, the fourth largest Christian Church in Britain. In 2006 it adopted an "ethical" investment policy toward Israel, and in 2010 it backed a boycott of products from West Bank settlements. In a report published two years later, it called for EU governments to ban the import of settlement products, including fruit and vegetables, textiles, plastic furniture, cosmetics, and some wines. The Methodist Conference called for an end to the blockade of Gaza in 2018. British and American Methodists have adopted similar policies regarding Israel. Their significance is enhanced by the size of the denomination worldwide, encompassing a membership of some 70 million people (Nelson and Gizzi 2021).[8]

As one would expect, the funding streams for secular and religious anti-Zionist groups are often quite different, with religious groups maximizing funding within their individual communities. But that distinction does not

---

7 See "The Inheritance of Abraham? A Report on the 'Promised Land,'" Church of Scotland, May 2013, https://www.scojec.org/news/2013/13v_cos/inheritance_of_abraham-original.pdf.

8 See also "The Methodist Anti-Zionist Agenda," in Nelson and Gizzi (2021, 73–81).

obtain as often as one might assume, and the exceptions involve substantial sums. With its broad international reach, the United Nations stands at the top of the list of organizations that are willing, however indirectly, to fund both secular and religious-based anti-Zionism and antisemitism, often, to be sure, on behalf of groups that put forward a secular face and announce a social justice mission. The European Union and some of its member countries also engage in dual funding—either directly or indirectly. Sometimes that is because funds that go to one group are then awarded to others. NGO Monitor has published numerous investigative reports detailing such funding over a period of years. These reports are readily accessible on its website.[9] Some of the denominational anti-Zionist groups are substantially better funded than their Zionist counterparts. Methodist and Presbyterian opponents of Israel are able to distribute color brochures at meetings and publish large-format anti-Zionist books.

With these distinctions in mind, it will be useful to track additional representative examples of secular and religious anti-Zionism to give a sense of timing. As noted at the outset, the 2001 Durban conference was the shared trigger for the most recent generation's activism. The BDS movement has promoted the myth that a 2005 "call" from Palestinian civil society organizations sparked the movement's inception, but both religious and secular calls for all three components of BDS's defining acronym—boycotts, divestment, and sanctions—were already well underway before then. In Britain, faculty members Hilary and Steven Rose launched a call for the boycott of Israeli universities in 2002.[10] Sanctions are a special category, as they entail punitive actions organized by nation states, and efforts to initiate them have often started within the United Nations. The United States has regularly blocked them from being carried out. Boycotts and divestment can be organized by non-state actors and have thus been the main focus of both religious and secular groups. Whether Palestinian NGOs were actually answering an implicit invitation to endorse Western boycott and divestment drives or whether a specific request from Western groups generated the "call" is still open to question, but the chronology is clear nonetheless. The advantage of the myth is that it suggests a selfless Western project inaugurated in the service of a Palestinian need, as opposed to a form of performative politics emanating from the Western desire for virtue signaling. Moreover, it is easier to justify a movement that accomplishes nothing if its justification is another people's putative call for help.

---

9 See https://www.ngo-monitor.org. For an overview of funding issues, see Steinberg (2019).
10 See Rose and Rose (2002).

Students for Justice in Palestine (SJP) was founded in Berkeley in 2001 and gradually spread to many other campuses. Jewish Voice for Peace was founded a few years earlier, in 1996, but its growth was also energized by Durban and the subsequent emergence of the formal BDS movement. In February 2002, both groups participated in a petition drive at the University of California at Berkeley urging the campus to divest itself of stock held in companies deemed as benefiting from their relationship with the Jewish state. That spring divestment drives followed at Harvard, MIT, and elsewhere. They have since spread along the East and West Coasts and throughout the Midwest. They have all failed, in part because boards of trustees and regents were not about to cede their fiduciary responsibilities to campus advocacy groups. But before long activists learned that these campaigns won hearts and minds and thus had significant political impact despite failing to achieve their formal objective. At that point the national movement to delegitimate Israel by promoting its economic isolation had no name and no formal organization apart from groups like SJP, but it was a national movement nonetheless. It was a rallying point for anti-Zionist activism in which local groups emulated each other's tactics and rhetoric and discussed strategies with one another. A similar pattern has obtained in Britain.

Some 35 Christian religious institutions attended the 2001 Durban World Conference against Racism and brought its propaganda home with them. But several denominations had already been debating the Israeli-Palestinian conflict and issuing statements or passing resolutions about it at their national and international meetings. Some denominations hold those meetings annually, while others do so in alternate years. The Episcopalians hold their General Assembly once every three years. Unlike the Catholic Church, which is substantially a top-down enterprise, Protestant denominations consolidate issues that arise and develop locally when they meet nationally. Unlike the campus anti-Zionist drives that erupted almost simultaneously in 2002, developments in the Christian churches were dependent on the opportunities provided by the schedule for their national meetings. Moreover, those meetings had to be preceded by local organizing. The US Presbyterian Church passed its first divestment resolution at its 2004 General Assembly. The United Methodist Church debated divestment resolutions in 2008, 2012, and 2016.

The Christian group with the most relentless anti-Zionist history is the once unequivocally pacifist American Friends Service Committee (AFSC), which actively supports BDS campaigns, trains students in BDS activism, and promotes anti-Israel rhetoric. AFSC pamphlets in the early 1970s expressed sympathy for Palestinian violence. In 1973, the AFSC called for a US embargo on military aid to Israel. It has been especially active in divestment debates at annual stockholder meetings (Nelson and Gizzi 2021, 67, 371).

There are theological issues that occupy or underlie church debates about the Israeli-Palestinian conflict that are so foreign to the secular controversy over Israel's status that they might seem to have arrived from a different planet. But there are also notable features that secular and religious anti-Zionism have in common. One of the oldest traditions in both Judaism and Christianity, drawing on and amplifying exhortations by the Jewish prophets and Jesus in the Christian Gospels, focuses on the need to redress inequities, minister to the poor and the oppressed, and defend them against wealth and power. The political left in both Europe and the United States has been shaped by those traditions whether or not there is much inclination to evoke that lineage. On the anti-Zionist left, however, that inheritance has been stripped of the practical commitments and traditions it still carries in some (though not all) Christian arenas. There is little interest on the left outside Israel itself in actually working with Palestinian communities to improve their lives and defend their interests. Instead, you minister to the poor merely by denouncing Israel and congratulating yourself for doing so. But the structural features of an ideology based on counterposing rich and poor, powerful and powerless, remain and are shared by both secular and religious anti-Zionism.

Once peoples are grouped together and branded as oppressors or oppressed, one group can be dehumanized, and justice and human sympathy can easily become justice and empathy for the oppressed alone. Both secular and religious anti-Zionism share that debased version of a Manichean world view. While many would resist explicitly referring to the Israeli-Palestinian conflict as a struggle between good and evil, that bald characterization nonetheless underlies much anti-Zionist passion and moral uplift, including on campus. It aims to marshal support for the anti-Zionist cause as if it were enlisting participants in a crusade.

As suggested above, to a significant degree, contemporary Christian Church advocacy for Palestinians resonates with well over a hundred years of missionary work in the Middle East. No such history obtains for the secular BDS. Rather, there is reason to believe that the Manichean left-wing political investment in Palestine stems instead from a long-running progressive need to identify with and idealize an oppressed population, whether it is the working classes under capitalism, the North Vietnamese in the Vietnam War, or the Palestinians on the West Bank and in Gaza. When a specific conflict is inserted into that recurring structure it can lose its specificity and its actual complexity and complication. Indeed, one of the rallying cries on the anti-Zionist left since 2020 has become "It's not complicated!" It is chanted at demonstrations, along with "Palestine shall be free from the river to the sea!" This recurrent structure does not guarantee that historical and political specificity will be eliminated, but it poses the risk that it will be. This tendency can only be countered by opposing the dichotomy by insisting on subtlety and complication.

Matters get worse when people insist that all political oppression is not merely subject to comparison and contrast but is actually intersectional, interchangeable, and fundamentally the same. Much of the anti-Zionist left has now succumbed to this anti-intellectual temptation. Accusations of racism in Britain, Canada, and the United States consequently become one with accusations of racism in Palestine. All anti-racist struggles are thus the same as well, which limits or eliminates the historical differentiation necessary to obtain tactical and communicative specificity. This makes condemnation easier but comprehension more difficult. A series of terms, categories, and definitions become unproblematic and universal. Thus Israel becomes a colonialist state even though it never served as an outpost of a European power, even though the Jewish control of territory first increased through legal land purchase, not military action.

Over the last half decade, religious anti-Zionism has drawn significantly closer to its secular cousin, losing some of its specific character as a consequence. In 2018, the primary anti-Zionist group in the US Presbyterian Church published *Why Palestine Matters: The Struggle to End Colonialism*, announcing with its title that standard moral and theological arguments about Israeli conduct and its impact on God's covenant with the Jews would be upstaged by a postcolonialist emphasis. Within the book itself, however, still more notable is the reliance—for the first time—on the left's claims of "intersectionality." "Intersectionality: Threads of Connection" is the heading for two pages of briefly invoked "intersections" such as: "Our liberation is intertwined, our stories are intertwined, our identities are intertwined" and "Islamophobia, homophobia, anti-Black racism, and antisemitism are all connected, and we cannot dismantle one without the other." The book repeatedly tries to link Native American opposition to the Dakota Access Pipeline with organized resistance in the West Bank and Gaza. The resulting confusion has no real bearing on Israel, but it does obscure the tragic and continuing history of Native American oppression and discrimination in the Americas, effectively exploiting the Native American story in support of the anti-Zionist agenda. *Why Palestine Matters* goes on to link the US mainland's indifference to Puerto Rico's multiple crises to Israel's purported indifference to Palestinian needs. It asks readers to see the US Civil Rights struggles of the 1950s and 1960s as intersecting with the Israeli-Palestinian conflict. And the book predictably aims to connect with the anti-Zionist constituency in the Black Lives Matter movement.

These multiple rhetorical claims of intersectionality, however, do not represent serious engagement with this range of indigenous and antiracist movements. As one would expect, the anti-Zionist left for its part shows no interest in embracing the traditional anti-Zionist tropes of its new religious partner. Debates about the validity of God's covenant with the Jews have no resonance with secular anti-Zionism. That intersection, at least, is unidirectional. What the future of this tentative alignment on or off campus may be remains to be seen. Actual organizational intersections would require serious commitment to each other's causes. Secular anti-Zionism, on the other hand, is being strengthened by its links to antiracism.

One obvious remaining issue is whether appropriate strategies to respond to and potentially discourage secular and religious anti-Zionism are similar or dissimilar. On the face of it, theological issues would seem to require altogether specific responses and arguments that would have no points of connection with secular movements. Yet in one respect they overlap, namely the degree to which antisemitism is a relevant charge worthy of emphasis. Even as a tactical matter there are points of convergence, such as what anti-Zionist audiences will tolerate as a challenge before they end the conversation. Unlike secular anti-Zionism, however, Christian anti-Zionism has the inescapable burden of long centuries of aggressive theological and state antisemitism for which to account. Secular anti-Zionism notably often revives tropes and stereotypes from the long history of antisemitism as well, a fact social media rhetoric has made increasingly apparent. The presence of antisemitic anti-Zionism cannot be discounted simply by arguing that criticism of Israeli government policy is not inherently antisemitic. There is plausibly an antisemitic element to assertions that the covenant with Abraham is void. Christian and secular anti-Zionism are both liable to the charge that it is fundamentally antisemitic to demand that the Jewish state actually be eliminated. An agenda that would eliminate Israel's Jewish character while preserving a putative Jewish right to live there is also inherently antisemitic, whether or not its advocates recognize this.

When anti-Zionism is deeply embedded in what amounts to either secular or religious zealotry, dislodging it may be virtually impossible. Certainly, no single righteous counterpresentation or conversation will have much if any impact. Zealots dismiss facts that disprove their beliefs out of hand. Gradual exposure to qualifying and complicating facts and arguments is the only option. Considerable patience from critics of anti-Zionism is an inescapable requirement because progress is slow and frequently undermined. Actual exposure to Israeli society may be the most reliable option for less indoctrinated people. Combating antisemitism has not proven to be a short-term project. Anti-Zionism has a shorter history, but its resilience seems comparably resistant to challenges. On the other hand, education about the history of antisemitism can take place without linking it directly to the Jewish state. Both secular and religious institutions have a responsibility to undertake this task. The same is true more broadly of Jewish history and culture.

Where a major difference obtains is in the realm of theology. Careful study, in-depth analysis, and an acceptance of complication are embedded in many theological traditions, even if unwarranted certainty is equally prominent. The first half of the previous sentence separates the study of theology from much debate about the Israeli-Palestinian conflict. Religious anti-Zionism has been at work to infuse theology with contemporary political passions, but they can be carefully disentangled. The effort by multiple Christian denominations to discredit or at least seriously qualify supersessionism since the Catholic Church issued its historic *Nostra Aetate* in 1965 provides a sound basis for undermining theologically grounded antisemitism. And it can help disable anti-Zionism.

There is a contemporary equivalent of supersessionism at work in both secular and religious anti-Zionism, namely the belief that the heroic representation of the founding of the Jewish state has been superseded by the higher morality and transcendent political virtues of anti-Zionism. Like Judaism itself, Israel was once worthy of admiration, but its place in our ethical and political firmament has been displaced by universalism and postnationalism. You can sign on to that conclusion whether you believe that Israel has betrayed its more egalitarian roots or that it was an imperialist and colonialist project from the outset. Christianity itself will likely never be entirely free of supersessionist convictions, but their amelioration opens opportunities for interfaith dialogue. Religious and secular anti-Zionism are similarly wedded to their contemporary versions of supersessionism. Unfortunately, its moderation therefore depends on treating Israel's current strengths and weaknesses like those of any other county, which is a tall order for the BDS movement.

Yet as both the general political environment and the contexts for discussion of the Israeli-Palestinian conflict become more fractious and polarized, opportunities for dialogue disappear. In the spring of 2021, following the most recent war with Hamas, over 130 academic women's studies programs and other departments across the world signed a statement condemning Israel and endorsing boycotts. Academia has always been one of the best arenas for BDS advocacy, but these statements crossed a line that had not been crossed before. Faculty members had always been free to form groups for political advocacy, but never before had administrative units of a university done so. Until then, the coercive and intimidating effect on students, faculty, and staff and the political impact on the university's public image had been enough to prevent this from happening. Meanwhile, for two years during the COVID pandemic, the annual meetings of both secular and religious groups had retreated online to virtual events that made debating resolutions about Israel or any other subject largely impossible. Among the first annual meetings to return at the end of 2021 was that of the Middle East Studies Association (MESA), a disciplinary faculty group. It voted overwhelmingly to approve a resolution calling for an academic boycott of Israel and sent it to the general membership for a vote in March 2022. Unsurprisingly, the resolution passed with 80 percent of MESA's members approving. Hostility toward Israel trumped the usual academic reluctance to block the free exchange of people and ideas among universities worldwide. As religious groups resume face-to-face meetings, we can expect to see further anti-Zionist resolutions there as well.

The lopsided character of the vote at MESA's annual meeting—in an audience of several hundred only three faculty members could be found to speak out against the resolution in the debate preceding the vote—replicated the scene at several such small academic association meetings, although larger disciplinary associations such as the American Historical Association and the Modern Language Association have rejected academic boycotts. Academic groups that represent indigenous peoples or minority groups or that see themselves as victims of discrimination, including the Association for Asian American Studies and the Native American and Indigenous Studies Association, which both voted in favor of an academic boycott in 2013, readily internalize the argument that the Palestinians are victims of discrimination or the only true indigenous people in the area. Other groups long politicized or long identified with postcolonial movements, such as the American Studies Association, operate from strong ideological assumptions. Britain's Association of University Teachers (AUT) voted to boycott two Israeli universities in 2005 but reversed itself following condemnation for violating academic freedom. Britain's University and College Union (UCU), however, has followed a different course. Since 2007, it has repeatedly debated or endorsed academic boycotts despite legal advice that it would be in violation of equality legislation if it actually implemented one. The union's executive has ruled that a decision to boycott will be declared null and void.

Similar lopsided votes are likely in the future as various secular or religious groups are overtaken by anti-Zionism. This includes religious denominations so riven by culture wars on other fronts that they see no option but to split into rival organizations. The United Methodist Church is expected to split into two separate denominations, one of which may—incidentally—be ready to support an anti-Zionist resolution while the other may not. Some labor unions have survived such divisions, as when a local chapter votes for a boycott of Israeli universities and the national union overrules the vote, as happened when the United Auto Workers chapter at New York University, which represents graduate student employees, endorsed an academic boycott and was overruled (Oster 2016).

The polarized cultural scene has also undermined something that could still promote reasoned discussion both of the Israeli-Palestinian conflict and of boycott resolutions that come before secular or religious groups, namely, as suggested throughout this book, the 2016 Working Definition of Antisemitism adopted by the International Holocaust Remembrance Alliance (IHRA). The brief opening definition has relatively little practical application, but the eleven examples that follow could help both secular and religious groups shift from accusation to analysis and negotiation. Instead of fighting over antisemitism in the abstract, people could talk, for example, about whether it is antisemitic to apply double standards by demanding that Israel conduct itself in a way "not expected or demanded of any other democratic nation" or to accuse "the Jews as a people, or Israel as a state, of inventing or exaggerating the Holocaust." They could discuss the historical and definitional problems associated with "drawing comparisons of contemporary Israeli policy to that of the Nazis." These and other instances of the eleven examples are quite common in both secular and religious settings. Despite the ways in which the IHRA Definition has been attacked, its examples offer specificity that promotes evidence-based analysis. And its insistence that analysis requires careful contextualization before concluding that a statement is antisemitic promotes the same practice. The IHRA Definition should be widely used. It is one of the few ways we have of moving forward with less rancor. That said, the debates in the academy over the formal adoption of the IHRA Definition have not taken place in the churches. Those churches that have struggled to define antisemitism since 2010 have found the only potential compromise with anti-Israel activists to be one that leaves clear space for anti-Zionism that is deemed not antisemitic. This has made it impossible to adopt new, more contemporary definitions of antisemitism that reference Israel. In the foreseeable future, the IHRA Definition is likely only to be useable in churches without formal adoption.

Chapter 7

The Valentina Azarova File: Should a University Hire an Anti-Zionist as a Senior Administrator?

Introduction

In the fall of 2020, a widespread national controversy erupted over the decision of the dean of the University of Toronto law school not to go forward with the appointment of Valentina Azarova as director of the school's International Human Rights Program (IHRP).[1] Azarova is an extensively published critic of Israel with considerable experience working with anti-Zionist Palestinian NGOs. She was born in the former Soviet Union and became a citizen of Israel.[2] The dean's decision was widely criticized as a violation of academic freedom by Azarova's supporters, a view I will dispute here. In June 2021, the search was reopened, with Azarova still identified as "the preferred candidate" and encouraged to reapply. In December 2021, Toronto announced that it had once again offered Azarova the job, but that she had declined it. That may have

---

1 At the time of her application, she was teaching online in Germany while living in Greece. I sent an earlier version of this chapter to each member of the Toronto law faculty. A series of email exchanges with several people followed.

2 Neither Azarova's place of birth nor her citizenship status are publicly listed anywhere, but they were noted on her employment application. A confidential Toronto informant provided me with the information. These facts, however, do not tell us anything about her ethnicity or the circumstances of her emigration from the Soviet Union.

left all parties unsatisfied, as their public comments suggested, but in truth it gave something tangible to both those in favor of and against the appointment (Arnold 2021). The anti-Zionist online outlet *Mondoweiss* claimed that she declined the offer "because she didn't want to be hounded by pro-Israel groups, and the University of Toronto couldn't protect her from attacks" (Engler 2021), but they supplied no direct quote, so the reliability of that report is uncertain. But she would certainly have faced greater scrutiny on the job, and, if she set up student internships with the anti-Zionist groups on the West Bank that she had established relationships with, thereby giving her Toronto academic program an anti-Zionist profile, there would have been complaints.

All full-time faculty make certain policy decisions that affect both colleagues and students. But the policy role is much larger, nonstop, and definitional for the administrator of an academic program. The power over the professional and personal lives of all department members is considerable. That is why the politically neutral character of university administration is, or should be, a requirement for the job, especially when direct program administration is at stake.[3]

The substantive issues to be decided in relation to Azarova's candidacy should have been what her publication record and political advocacy said about how she would administer the program and how they would reinforce or undermine public respect for the program. Those remain the issues. This chapter reviews Azarova's work and career in detail, as should have been done in 2020 but apparently was not, as a basis for assessing the controversy. A search process at a research university should include a very thorough and comprehensive review of a candidate's publications. I saw no evidence of that from either Azarova's defenders or her opponents. An undertaking like this one involves a great deal of work, but if all the members of a search committee do that work the resulting discussions are much more substantive. They can be the most substantive conversations you will ever have with colleagues. And of course they lead to a fully informed decision about a job candidate.

Even if the Azarova file had remained closed, it would have been worthwhile to have read all her work and written this chapter. Her identification as the candidate of choice set a standard and established a principle that heralds further politicization of the academy overall, not just in Canada but also elsewhere. Nonetheless, many if not all Toronto faculty members may feel I have no business commenting on the case, as I am not a Toronto colleague.

---

3 Another unresolved issue is whether the job required that the applicant be licensed to practice law in Canada or another jurisdiction. It is not clear that Azarova met this criterion.

But this is a case that matters to all of us in the academy. Higher education is at a turning point, on a precipice, when an increasing number of academic programs and departments are openly defining themselves in terms of an anti-Zionist political mission, something that would have been inconceivable as recently as 2020. Higher education as a whole needs to address the core question posed here: Should a dedicated career anti-Zionist be appointed as a senior administrator responsible for designing and running an academic program? Will she incorporate a variety of political views and work opportunities for student interns in the program or will she emphasize opportunities embodying her own convictions? Could her selection possibly be politically disinterested? Although her appointment as a senior administrator at the University of Toronto did not go through, it will not be the last highly politicized appointment of this kind we will see.

This chapter also adds to the detailed analyses of anti-Zionist scholarship I have been producing for a number of years. It is an addition to the series of very detailed portraits of individual anti-Zionist faculty published in my 2019 book *Israel Denial: Anti-Zionism, Anti-Semitism, and the Faculty Campaign against the Jewish State.* Summary, analysis, and evaluation of faculty publications is fundamental to academic freedom and to the collective search for the truth. It is a professional responsibility that should honor no institutional boundaries. Those who simply applaud or denounce Azarova's work have failed to rise to the necessary standard for academic evaluation. A full account of a career like Azarova's, that includes both longer research projects and numerous shorter, more argumentative pieces, requires careful analyses of both kinds of publications. Indeed, the clearest formulations of her positions are scattered throughout her work and often not repeated. Without a detailed review, one cannot reliably establish the values and conclusions that define her career or suggest how she would do her job.

In addition to drawing widely on conclusions from her publications, I will include detailed readings of several of them. After reviewing the appointment controversy that provoked widespread interest in the case, I proceed to an overview of the mix of publication and NGO work that define her career. This is followed by the core of the chapter a detailed review of her written work that establishes her professional identity and the values that have defined it. I open by focusing on one substantial essay—a coauthored essay on Israeli archeology. I follow with an overview of her publications, then concentrate on one of her recurrent topics, namely the potential impact of international law on corporations that do business with Israel. A section on her essays on Gaza and

West Bank legal issues is next, followed by some final reflections. Here is the sequence of topics:

1. The Azarova appointment controversy
2. An overview of Azarova's career
3. Imaginary antiquities
4. Azarova's publication pattern
5. Opposing West Bank business relationships
6. War in Gaza and the law of occupation
7. Final reflections

1. The Azarova appointment controversy

The University of Toronto's International Human Rights Program is distinctive because it combines course work with practical experience in legal advocacy at NGOs. Indeed, students receive credit for advocacy that is not connected to a given course. As the Canadian Association of University Professors would later observe, "the Director oversees the IHRP's advocacy initiatives, clinic, speaker series, working groups, publications, internship and mentoring programs. In addition, the Director is required to supervise students, develop and deliver clinical legal education programs, and organize and conduct workshops, conferences, and research." Depending on how you view academic political advocacy, Azarova's career is either a perfect match for such a program or one guaranteed to undermine the program by giving it an unqualified political orientation. Azarova has made it clear that she considers Palestinian human rights to be the only pressing human rights issue in the Israeli-Palestinian conflict. She would almost certainly identify the law school with one side of the conflict. I find it difficult to credit arguments to the contrary.

Although the position of IHRP director is clearly an administrative job and not a faculty slot, that fact has been lost in much of the controversy around the appointment. Azarova was told more than once that the appointment did not come with faculty status or tenure and would not lead to either. It is an eleven-month annual administrative appointment. She would serve at the pleasure of the dean. Nonetheless, Azarova expressed her wish to have "pseudo-faculty" status, a status that does not exist. Its benefits, she proposed, might include the right to annually spend two summer months abroad doing advocacy work, possibly the pro-Palestinian advocacy work she had done on the West Bank for years. Her request was turned down. She would be hired to be on campus eleven months a year. One benefit of doing that work on the West Bank would be the ability to maintain comparable NGO advocacy options for University of Toronto students. It was not clear that they could work for the Anti-Defamation League instead, let alone that the program under Azarova would establish opportunities with both Zionist and anti-Zionist organizations, along with robust options of many other forms.

Did the committee discuss how Azarova's previous experience would affect her work as IHRP director? Her vita makes such conversations inescapable.[4] Did they talk to her about the matter? It would be remarkable not to do so, given the job's responsibilities. We do not know enough about the politics of the three-person "selection" committee (Professor Audrey Macklin, Chair of the Faculty Advisory Committee to the IHRP; Vincent Wong, Research Associate at the IHRP; and Alexis Archbold, Assistant Dean at the law school) to make a definitive judgment about how their politics affected the decision-making process, but we are not without indicative facts.

Macklin, the chair of the search committee and, it is important to emphasize, its only full-time faculty member, had signed a 2009 letter stating that "It is crucial that forums for discussion of Israel's accountability to the international community for what many have called war crimes be allowed to proceed unrestricted by specious claims of anti-Semitism" (IJAN 2009). She signed a 2015 "Open Letter to university community regarding Palestinian Rights and Canadian Universities" that protests "increasing efforts to limit advocacy of Palestinian rights on Canadian universities" and issues a demand to "defend the right to freedom of speech about Palestine for all members of the university community, including freedom to use the term 'apartheid' to identify and debate certain policies associated with the state of Israel and the freedom to support, facilitate and participate freely in activities under the rubric of 'Israeli apartheid week'" (Faculty for Palestine Canada 2015). She also signed a 2020 open letter arguing that the IHRA Definition "is worded in such a way as to intentionally equate legitimate criticisms of Israel and advocacy for Palestinian rights with antisemitism."[5] Her overall support for the political views Azarova holds is thus a matter of record.

Wong taught a clinical course on media freedom and international human rights at IHRP. He resigned in protest against the decision to withdraw the offer

---

4 See https://cdn.ku.edu.tr/resume/vazarova.pdf. In addition to listing her publications, Azarova's vita details her employment history. I draw on it for a number of biographical details in this chapter.
5 See Independent Jewish Voices (2020).

and is now in private practice. He is also the only selection committee member to condemn the University of Toronto's process, something he has done in a detailed essay that characterizes it as "a nakedly political process obscured by legal rhetoric" (Wong 2021). He asserts that "Palestinian rights and international law with respect to the Israel/Palestine situation are now demonstrably a taboo subject in the law school," a conclusion that is hyperbolic and unfair, given that university faculty continue to possess academic freedom and that events criticizing Israel are common in Toronto. Wong reserves especially strong rhetoric for the role he believes institutionalized, structural racism and sexism—"the operation of intersectional power and privilege that continues to govern the legal academy, the legal profession, and the judiciary in Canada"—played in the decision: "this episode first related to improper conduct and influence by a powerful white male judge (Justice David Spiro), was bumped up to and decided upon by a powerful white male Dean of Law (Dean Ed Iacobucci, son of former SCC judge Frank Iacobucci), was mediated through another powerful white male investigator (former SCC judge Thomas Cromwell), and was then whitewashed by a powerful white male university president (President Meric Gertler) while all other voices have been sidelined." Finally, Wong attributes the sequence of events to a conspiracy between the Centre for Israel and Jewish Affairs (CIJA) and some of those just named: "an almost surreal story of what went on behind the scenes with Dean Iacobucci, the funding offices at UofT, Justice Spiro, and the CIJA, who found out about Dr. Azarova's candidacy and explicitly set out to put the brakes on it." There is some indication of where Wong's political sympathies lie.

As this was an administrative position, the Toronto selection committee's recommendation for the appointment was only advisory. The actual decision belonged to the dean. Although faculty position search committees also make recommendations, not appointments, their recommendations are most often honored. After all, they are evaluating a prospective colleague. But administrative positions entail issues and responsibilities faculty members are neither qualified nor charged to evaluate. Will the candidate support administration policies once they are adopted? Do other administrators find a candidate compatible? Will their public positions undermine their ability to do their jobs properly? Faculty members are free to adopt controversial public political positions, but administrators are expected to be neutral. It is much more difficult to insist that an administrator "does not represent the institution." Administrators are not protected by academic freedom. Few if any of Azarova's supporters seem to recognize that stark and compelling fact.

The advertisement for the IHRP directorship included a requirement that successful candidates be licensed to practice law either in Ontario or elsewhere. Details regarding Azarova's fulfilment of that requirement have not been released. Failure to meet that requirement would risk lowering the job classification to a lower salary level. As was suggested to me in a confidential interview, without that requirement in the job notice, additional candidates might have applied.

The sequence of events is fairly clear. The three-person selection committee recommended her unanimously. But she was living in Germany and was not a Canadian citizen. The administration then set out to find a way to bring her to campus by the start of the fall semester. When the lawyers involved made it clear approval from Canadian immigration authorities would take longer, the law school looked into the possibility of hiring her as an external employee and having her direct the IHRP program from abroad for a semester. Then the German authorities informed Toronto that such an arrangement would be illegal.

Meanwhile, someone leaked the news about Azarova's being the candidate of choice to David E. Spiro, a tax court judge, University of Toronto alumnus, and a donor who had given somewhere between $25,000 to $100,000 to the university. For a highly ranked research university, that is not a huge sum, though his family (in the person of his uncle Larry Tanenbaum) donated more, reportedly as much as $10 million to finance the university's Anne Tanenbaum Centre for Jewish Studies. It costs millions of dollars to endow one faculty chair, still more to fund a building and get your name on it. In any case, contrary to what some have claimed, Spiro did not contact the university to protest Azarova's appointment. At the end of a routine fundraising phone conversation initiated by a University of Toronto assistant vice president, Spiro was asked whether he had other issues of concern. At that point, he mentioned that the Azarova appointment would be controversial in the Jewish community, a factual statement. Under prevailing US judicial ethics, there would be no prohibition on Judge Spiro expressing a private opinion to the university administration. There is no evidence Spiro threatened not to make further gifts, though a number of people have decided a threat was surely implied. The dean of the law school decided the visa problems were unsolvable and notified Azarova they would not proceed with the appointment. At that point the Azarova case became a large public controversy.

The Canadian Association of University Teachers (CAUT), which serves as a union for almost all Canadian teachers, took up the case, supported the accusation of political interference even in the absence of direct evidence, and decided Azarova's academic freedom had been violated. CAUT issued a full report, as well as a news release. The executive director emphasized the conclusion "that the decision to cancel Dr. Azarova's hiring was politically motivated and as such constitutes a serious breach of widely recognized principles of academic freedom."[6] CAUT applied its most extreme remedy, formally censuring the University of Toronto. CAUT also insisted, contrary to academic tradition, University of Toronto policy, and the standards of the American Association of University Professors (AAUP), that administrators have exactly the same academic freedom as faculty. The AAUP specifies that administrators only have academic freedom when they are engaged in performing faculty responsibilities—teaching classes, advising students, and publishing research—not in the performance of their administrative duties. Azarova thus could not have comprehensive academic freedom. Academic freedom should not have constrained evaluation of issues affecting her fitness to be an administrator. CAUT notably acted before two important reports were issued.

The university insisted no formal offer had been made. It subsequently hired retired Supreme Court Justice Thomas A. Cromwell to investigate the matter and write an independent report. Crowell could find no evidence of political influence in the decision. His 78-page report detailed the law school's efforts to solve the visa problem in excruciating detail. He found no reason to conclude the dean was lying in reporting that neither Azarova's politics nor Justice Spiro's warning had played any role in his decision. Azarova's allies were not persuaded.

With David Spiro regularly vilified in the press and demands for his removal escalating, the Canadian Judicial Council appointed a Judicial Conduct Review Panel to evaluate his conduct in the Azarova case and decide whether he should be removed from office. The panel decided that "Justice Spiro was voicing his concerns about the potential impact of the appointment and associated controversy on the University and the Faculty, as opposed to actively campaigning or lobbying against the appointment."[7] He had avoided contacting the dean directly because he thought that would be inappropriate and did not wish to signal that level of concern. They noted that "before his appointment to the judiciary, Justice Spiro devoted a great deal of time to enhance his understanding of the Israel-Palestine conflict and to build bridges between the parties and the faith communities involved." They added that no reasonable person could "conclude that the judge is biased against Palestinian, Arab or Muslim interests. The fear of bias on the part of Justice Spiro is based

---

6   See CAUT (2021).

7   See CJC (2021).

on misinformation and speculation that is inaccurate." Nonetheless, they decided that, as a member of the judiciary, he should not have intervened in the appointment. Spiro expressed his regret, and he was not sanctioned. The panic in the press and among academics about Justice Spiro's phone call was unwarranted. Given that the accusations against Spiro have been discredited, one is left with the question of why it was so readily believed that one Jewish donor could dictate who the richest law school in Canada could or could not hire.

2. An overview of Azarova's career

On April 24 and 25, 2014, the UN Committee on the Exercise of the Inalienable Rights of the Palestinian People held a Roundtable on Legal Aspects of the Question of Palestine in Geneva. According to Human Rights Voices (2014), speakers at a closed session included Valentina Azarova, at the time a lecturer in human rights and international law at Al-Quds University in East Jerusalem, who "argued in favor of the Palestinian 'right to return' including 'Palestinian refugees in the Diaspora with a territorial link to Israel.' ... She also supported the 'BDS' (boycott, divestment and sanctions) campaign against Israel, pushing third states and international actors to adhere to 'the duty of non-recognition, non-aid or assistance ... the same goes for private entities like businesses.'" Except for the encouragement of third state action against Israel, these views are often not explicit in her published work, though she is sometimes clear about them in other contexts.

In a 2019 interview, she endorses the BDS movement and reports "there is promise in the mobilization of third-party enforcement action, including those by local councils, investment institutions, and supermarkets" to address "the ultimate subaltern case that Palestine represents" (Shokirova 2019). Indeed, she says, there is a "now-generally-accepted view amongst international lawyers and political analysts that few contemporary cases, aside from that of Palestine, make international law appear as morally and politically bankrupt." She argues that political activism is the only practical option now available, given that the International Criminal Court (ICC) has been constrained "through political and financial blackmail." Until the ICC can become "a law enforcement body in the proper sense, that is prosecutorial and operational," it will be limited to "a social mechanism symbolic and perceptional, or reputational," through "activities auxiliary to the investigation and prosecution of international crimes, such as the outreach it plans to conduct in the West Bank and Gaza." The ultimate point is that "Israel is illegally present in Palestine and has an obligation to withdraw from the territory."

Meanwhile, she has explicit advice to law students: learn "how to frame and address ongoing processes of structural violence and structures of complicity," as "in the case of Palestine": combine on-the-ground work with research to discover "how law can be brought to operate in disruptive and subversive ways." Of course, she said that before facing controversy over the Toronto appointment. Azarova calls herself a "practitioner-scholar"; she reports "having spent a considerable part of my professional life working with primarily local and regional human rights organizations, and then teaching and thinking about the law through and in order to refine my and others' legal practice." There is no doubt that she would have brought this paired commitment to anti-Zionist activism and analysis regarding Palestine to her role in mentoring students and designing programs at the University of Toronto.

Azarova's dual career moves beyond alternating between scholarship and activism toward an exceptional fusion of the two. She completed an LLB in European Legal Studies at London's University of Westminster in May 2008, meanwhile earning a Certificate in Transnational Law from the University of Geneva in 2006–2007. Those combined programs qualified her as an attorney, to which she added a summer 2009 certificate of attendance from the Hague Academy of International Law. She earned a PhD in public international law from the National University of Ireland after completing a two-and-a-half-year program in 2014. Her doctoral thesis was about contemporary forms of occupation and their regulation under international law.

Before then, however, she had undertaken a substantial amount of pro-Palestinian activism and work experience, first at HaMoked (an Israel-based NGO dedicated to defending Palestinians it regards as political victims) in 2007 and from 2008 to 2010 both during the time she studied for an LLB and immediately thereafter.[8] She was a senior legal researcher at Al-Haq from June 2010 to December 2011 and an external legal advisor to the same group from August 2013 to January 2014. In between, from July to October 2012, she was a research consultant at the Diakonia International Humanitarian Law Research Center in Jerusalem, which was founded to address international humanitarian

---

8   See NGO Monitor (2023). According to this profile, "While HaMoked states that its main aim is 'assisting Palestinians of the occupied territories whose rights are violated due to Israel's policies,' it regularly represents families of terrorists responsible for carrying out terrorist attacks against Israel." Among other things, the profile details HaMoked's legal activities and the European government funding it has received.

law violations in the Israeli/Palestinian conflict. Al-Haq is a leader in anti-Israel lawfare and BDS campaigns. Its general director, Shawan Jabarin, has been active in the Popular Front for the Liberation of Palestine (PFLP), a recognized terrorist group. In 2007, the Israeli Supreme Court characterized him as a "Doctor Jekyll and Mister Hyde, acting some of the time as the CEO of a human rights organization, and at other times as an activist in a terror organization which has not shied away from murder." From September 2013 to May 2014, while studying for her PhD, she was an associate at the MATTIN Group, which promotes human rights resistance to Israel within the European Union, a focus of Azarova's research.[9]

Although we do not have any information on the representation of clients during her NGO work, we know that a significant amount of her time was spent researching and writing reports, some of which were apparently distributed as bound pamphlets. They include four reports prepared for Al-Haq and three for Dakonia. All these reports are highly critical of Israel, sometimes appropriately, such as *Institutionalized Impunity: Israel's Failure to Combat Settler Violence in the Occupied Palestinian Territory* (2013). She later prepared several reports for Amnesty International on the 2014 war in Gaza.

Her essay "Making Human Rights Work for the Palestines of the World" (2013f) describes some of her work with the MATTIN Group. In the acknowledgements to "From Discretion to Necessity: Third State Responsibility for Israel's Control of Stay and Entry into Palestinian Territory," Azarova expresses "immense gratitude to Charles Shamas ... cofounder and senior partner of the MATTIN Group, whose methodology and work this article seeks to capture" (2014, 353). She also draws on work by Al-Haq and HaMoked. This essay condemns Israel's "de facto prohibition on virtually all movement between the two territories" (333), while failing to point out that Hamas organizes terrorist cells from Gaza and thus that movement from Hamas to the West Bank presents security risks. The Palestinian Authority is consequently unwilling to support free travel from Gaza to the West Bank.

Her first teaching experiences matched her NGO-based anti-Zionist advocacy. From 2009 to 2013 she was cofounder and director of the Human Rights and International Law Program at the West Bank's Al-Quds Bard College at Al-Quds University, simultaneously teaching such courses as "Human Rights in Armed Conflict," the topic of several of her anti-Zionist publications. She continued to teach the course there until January 2015,

---

9 NGO Monitor maintains online profiles on all the above-mentioned groups. See https://www.ngo-monitor.org/ngos/.

immediately afterwards spending a year as a research fellow at Birzeit University in Ramallah. Meanwhile she taught at Birzeit from 2014 to 2015. She went on to teach in a summer 2015 program at Bilgi University in Istanbul, followed by an academic year in Lebanon.

Azarova's first publications came in 2009 when she was working at HaMoked, partly overlapping with her summer at the Hague Academy. A series of essays followed in 2012 and 2013 while she was working for the anti-Zionist NGOs described above. She has neither abandoned nor significantly modified the views she expressed then. This consistent, devoted, and elaborate history of Palestine-based anti-Zionist NGO work and anti-Zionist writing and publication seems distinctive. Although a few of her essays take on other topics, notably a coauthored article on the enforced disappearance of migrants (Azarova, Brown, and Mann 2022), Israel is overall her main subject. As a first step in understanding what that means, I review her claim that Israeli archeology violates international law in the next section.

3. Imaginary antiquities

In 2013, as her online vita details,[10] in the midst of her PhD studies and while working for several Palestinian NGOs in Jerusalem and Ramallah, Valentina Azarova published an essay coauthored with David Keane, "UNESCO, Palestine, and Archaeology in Conflict" that seeks to apply political opinion and international law to the status of antiquities discovered in the West Bank and in waters off the coast of Gaza. They are not alone among anti-Zionists in castigating Israeli archeology, though they particularly emphasize legal arguments. "For more than a century," they argue, "Palestinian cultural heritage and property has been the subject of capture and destruction by other states" (Keane and Azarova 2013, 310). The claim that all area antiquities have a specifically Palestinian character is strikingly anachronistic, since a distinctly Palestinian, as opposed to Arab, identity did not exist until the late 1960s, a fact Azarova seems unable to acknowledge. Although Yasser Arafat announced the creation of a "State of Palestine" in 1988, this hypothetical entity only gained the status of a United Nations non-member observer state in 2012. The authors' 100-plus-year timeline dates the property seizure by "other states" to the period of the Ottoman Empire, an entity that did not survive the First World War. But Keane and Azarova extend a Palestinian cultural heritage to

---

10 See https://cdn.ku.edu.tr/resume/vazarova.pdf.

the Roman and Byzantine eras as well (318). When the Oslo Accords took effect in 1994 and the Palestinian Authority gained authority over Areas A and B, "for the first time the Palestinians could control part of their own cultural heritage" (315). In a highly debatable claim, they add that "the Palestinian Department of Antiquities and Cultural Heritage, re-established in 1994, is considered to be a revival of the Department of Antiquities that was established in 1920 under the British mandate and terminated by the political events of 1948" (316). In other words, the creation of Israel and the war that followed it temporarily broke the proper chain of custody over Palestinian artifacts. But the only legally credited chain of custody following the British mandate belongs to Israel, as both the local Arab population and the Arab states at war with Israel refused to accept the statehood offered by the United Nations in 1947.

In the world the Keane-Azarova essay evokes, Israeli archeology exhibits no cultural or historical virtues and delivers no academic benefits; every project is an appropriation of Palestinian property and a violation of Palestinian rights, what Rafi Greenberg, another critic of Israeli practices, calls "an archeological heart of darkness."[11] "The presence of archeological or biblical sites," they argue, "is used to justify confiscating Palestinian lands and building illegal settlements" (316). "In some cases, offences against cultural property can amount to crimes against humanity, in so far as these acts are part of a broader set of facts on the widespread or systematic persecution of a civilian population" (323). There is no disinterested historical research at issue, only the exploitation of the past.

They detail the existence of an illegal antiquities market supplied by Palestinian workers finding opportunities to loot the Israeli sites at which they work. But the workers are never motivated by greed. "Palestinian involvement in the looting stems from the alienation of the population from its own cultural heritage," since all antiquities are by definition artifacts of Palestinian history; moreover, "looting grows in line with unemployment" (330). Keane and Azarova are both law faculty specializing in international rights law. Neither is an archeologist. Far from being disabling for them, that status is altogether enabling. An archeologist might have to justify the invented, anachronistic notion of a *Palestinian antiquity*. For them it is not an historical category to be verified and defended. It is apparently validated by international rights law, by the belief that Palestine is occupied territory; the region's true history is therefore Palestinian, not Jewish. As a consequence of their unhistorical

---

11 Quoted in Keane and Azarova (2013, 315).

construction of ancient artifacts, their essay becomes a meditation on what amount to imaginary antiquities.

A series of elaborate legal arguments follow, which eventually enable Keane and Azarova to endorse the most provocative of all the claims in this long-running dispute in cultural politics, that the Dead Sea Scrolls are part of the Palestinian cultural heritage and thus legally Palestinian property (324–326). As people worldwide know, the first of the Dead Sea Scrolls were discovered by Bedouin goatherds in 1947. Israel gained control of most of them in 1967. After a long hiatus, additional fragments were found in caves in 2021. Political disputes over their ownership most often erupt when plans surface for the Israel Museum in Jerusalem to lend them to a museum abroad, at which point Palestinians demand they be seized and handed over to the Palestinian Authority. Jordan has also claimed ownership and demanded their return. When the German government declined to guarantee their return to Israel after a scheduled 2019 exhibition at a museum in Frankfurt, the exhibit was cancelled.

The scrolls and fragments are the earliest known material versions of the Hebrew Bible, the sacred text of Judaism, and thus carry immense religious significance for Jews. The scrolls include no Christian or Muslim texts. Few other artifacts thus belong more decisively to Jewish cultural and religious history. Israelis overall have no tolerance for the idea that they are part of Palestinian history and no intention to send them to Ramallah. Palestinian claims of ownership are little more than a gratuitous provocation, an instance of war by other means, which is evidently how Keane and Azarova deploy them. Indeed, they suggest circumstances could arise to justify a Palestinian case demanding their seizure before a US court. Remarkably, these two writers do not find occasion to mention, let alone debate, the unique place that the scrolls occupy in Jewish religious history. Indeed, they do not mention the fact that Jews lived in Palestine during the Roman period. Israel's Jewish character is not part of the Keane-Azarova analysis, but it must be part of any morally honorable evaluation of who has the deepest right to ownership.

In the opening pages of their essay, Keane and Azarova decry the fact that "this hemorrhaging of Palestinian property is occurring in a context where archeology has been used by Israel" as pretext to control territory and exercise its sovereignty over the West Bank and its resources (310). They conclude by pointing out that Palestinian efforts to gain control over archeological artifacts "not only constitute an expression of Palestinian sovereignty … but also represent a means of moving beyond the cultural property protection framework to propel the integration of the State of Palestine within the international legal order" (343). Their first passage stigmatizes what they consider a case of theft, the second endorses their view of political justice at work.

4. Azarova's publication pattern

Azarov's coauthored essay on archeology is characteristic of the longer single author essays she began to publish the following year, in 2014. She does not, however, typically publish in law reviews or produce the type of monograph-length research papers often seen there, sometimes preferring more political venues, especially when she wishes to be more polemical. Of the sixty-seven publications on her 2016 vita, ranging from essays and reports to blog posts, fifty-eight centrally address Israel. Others do so briefly, as with her piece on genocide in Bosnia. Israel is rarely far from her mind, since she often writes about a legal principle that she then applies to the Israeli occupation of the West Bank. Her 2020 essay "Adjudicators, Guardians, and Enforcers: Taking the Role of Non-Governmental Organisations in Customary International Law-Making Seriously" draws on her experience with Palestinian NGOs without mentioning any of their names or those of any other NGO. The essay is an effort to categorize the work that NGOs do to "mobilize international law with the hope of raising global standards of human security and offering greater protections to marginal and vulnerable populations" (Azarova 2020). She does not have to name Palestinians or any other group to make the context clear. Masha Gessen (2021) claims that "early in her career, she [Azarova] focused primarily on the Israeli occupation of Palestine," then moved on to other topics, which is manifestly untrue. *The New Yorker* could have easily fact-checked that statement and realized that it was false.

From the time Azarova began publishing in 2009 she intermittently addressed legal issues in other countries as well as Israel. But her career to the present day is single-mindedly devoted to the delegitimization of the Jewish state through legal analysis. She either writes about specific Israeli violations of international law or explores the ways a particular category of international law can used to sanction or condemn the country, as in these "reports and expert opinions" listed on her vita: "Unmasking the 'Freeze': Israel's Alleged Moratorium on Settlement Construction Whitewashes Violations of International Law," Al-Haq, September 2010; *Families under the Rubble: Unlawful Israeli Airstrikes Kill Entire Families, Destroy Homes,* Amnesty International, November 2014;[12] *Nothing Is Immune: Israeli Military Policy Results in Unlawful Destruction of Civilian Property,* Amnesty International, December 2014; and "Mapping

---

12 The published title is actually *Families Under The Rubble: Israeli Attacks on Inhabited Homes.* The 47-page report consists of eight individual reports on families killed in Gaza. See Azarova (2014c).

the Legal Framework of Israel's Occupation: How to Better Secure Rights," European Council for Foreign Relations & Human Rights Watch, October–December 2016. Azarova routinely sanitizes her research focus in her author notes, for example stating that "her research concerns the role of third parties and the contribution of domestic and transnational regulatory processes to the enforcement of international law." There is no mention of the fact that almost all this "research" is focused on Israel. Faculty members often concentrate their research on one country, but it is unusual to issue self-representations in the form of abstractions that omit that fact.

Azarova is something of a precocious anti-Zionist. Her five anti-Zionist pieces from 2009 were published the year following the completion of her first degree. As her vita details, two years earlier she had done a summer internship for a Palestinian NGO. Her ideological commitments coalesced when she was young. They have organized her life ever since.

Her 2016 vita includes forthcoming pieces and others "pending submission," so it extends beyond its date of composition. Her SSRN author page lists some of the publications in her vita, along with more recent ones, and offers PDFs of most of them. A Koç University webpage established during an extended position as a postdoctoral fellow in Istanbul, provided PDFs of several other essays and reports, including several written for Al-Haq, that are otherwise difficult to obtain.[13] I supplemented these resources with searches on Google and Chrome and several academic search engines in 2021. Given the number of her publications and the difficulty of locating some of them, it is entirely possible, indeed likely, that the 2020 Toronto search committee did not review her entire output.

Israel has been and continues to be the central preoccupation of her research and advocacy. Her recurring topic, how international law applies to a given set of Israeli policies and practices, is pursued with a political aim—in order to discover "the ways in which international law is capable of constraining political discretion" (Azarova 2014a). The aforementioned "UNESCO, Palestine, and Archaeology in Conflict" is one of several longer, self-contained pieces that address topics, in this case archeology, that she has only written about once, though they are often linked by anti-Zionism. In other essays, she takes up a topic briefly and tackles it again later in a different context. But opposition to

---

13 See https://ku.academia.edu/Departments/Center_for_Global_Public_Law/Documents?page=2. Last accessed May 2021. This webpage was maintained by the Koç University Center for Global Public Law. It included four of Azarova's course syllabi and a couple of posters advertising public lectures.

Israel and to the occupation continue to unify almost everything she writes. It would be easy to gather her chapter-length anti-Zionist essays into a book, something she may be planning to do. Indeed, their interlocking and mutually supplementary character means there is no one essay fully summarizing her position on Israel and the Israeli-Palestinian conflict. As the documentation in this essay suggests, one must read them all.

Some describe Azarova's preoccupation as obsessive, but many scholarly careers are defined by some narrow topic pursued over decades. Research is almost by definition obsessive. The issue is what she argues. A key question is whether her fierce anti-Zionism crosses a line into antisemitism. With some possible exceptions, I do not believe she crosses that line in her publications, though I cannot speak to how she conducts herself informally when she works with a series of anti-Zionist NGOs, an issue that is only relevant because NGO work will be part of her job. In any case, we don't have the evidence needed to decide the question. She is certainly capable of unpersuasive hyperbole, as in "Lost at Sea" when she asks regarding the Gaza blockade whether "the use of blockade terminology is indeed more appropriate than the law of siege warfare" (Azarova 2010). "The blockade," she has irresponsibly concluded, "is in fact arguably rather a siege." Well, it is neither the siege of Troy nor the siege of Leningrad. Israel facilitates delivery of food and materials, helps with electrical and gas supplies, and provides other services.[14] The blockade is more restrictive than it needs to be, but it is foolish to insist it is really a siege.

Most of what Azarova has written recently, however, is reasoned, not abusive or exclusively polemical. Her claims regularly omit counterevidence and are frequently misleading, but they are consistently debatable and cannot simply be cast aside as inexcusably false. She is invariably hostile toward Israel, having nothing good to say about the Jewish state. Israelis and Palestinians for her represent uniform, internally consistent categories. They are flattened and two-dimensional; you never encounter a fully realized human being in what she

---

14 The UN Office for the Coordination of Humanitarian Affairs (OCHA) tracks annual food and livestock deliveries from Israel to Gaza in its *Humanitarian Atlas*. Its statistics show, for example, a relatively steady increase in the number of deliveries, from 9,037 truckloads in 2007 to 26,268 truckloads in 2017, meaning that deliveries increased even during the 2014 war. The problems with food insecurity in Gaza, as I detail in *Israel Denial*, are not related to the supply of food but rather to poverty and unemployment, with people consequently being unable to purchase the food on sale in Palestinian markets. The irregular supply of electricity is a structural problem. As I recommend in the same book, Gaza would benefit from a substantial solar panel array. It could be built in Israel with international support if Hamas would cease hostilities. In 2023, Israel approved the development of a gas field off Gaza's Mediterranean coast. Again, obtaining international funding to connect Gaza to this resource would not be difficult, so long as Hamas would stop sending rockets into Israel.

writes. I realize some of her critics would prefer to believe otherwise, but careful distinctions regarding antisemitism are essential. There are faculty members whose publications clearly and repeatedly exhibit antisemitism. And there are cases like that of Azarova that establish themselves in a gray area and present real challenges to classification. Notably, in the scores of pieces written about her since 2020, both positive and negative, little if any detailed attention is devoted to her publications; it is not clear that many people have actually read any of them. The problem for her hiring, as I will show, is due to the way her previous and continuing anti-Zionist commitments intersect with a major administrative role implementing a curriculum and external work experience. I would not welcome her appointment as a full-time faculty member, as opposed to a senior administrator, but I would not campaign against it.

A recent essay that may cross the line into antisemitism is "The Pathology of a Legal System: Israel's Military Justice System and International Law" from 2017. It declares itself to be "a diagnosis of a wrongdoer's legal system," a system that "accepts, encourages, or even mandates conduct that is internationally unlawful" (Azarova 2017c, 6), indeed carries out "premeditated and deliberate internationally unlawful acts" (15). Israel's legal system not only operates "in contempt of" international norms, it aims to revise them; although she is unwilling to say so, not all of its efforts to do so are inherently destructive. The core of her accusation is the "unlawful re-definition of the internationally-recognized status of Palestinian territory," with Israel "arguing that there was no sovereign Palestinian state before 1967" (8), an issue taken up below. One example of a clear violation of those norms, she claims, is the decision "to detain inside Israel proper persons arrested in the West Bank" despite "the absolute prohibition of such transfers in international humanitarian law" (10). Although she predictably does not acknowledge it, Israel has to investigate actual terrorist cells in the West Bank, while building a prison in the West Bank would not be a politically applauded alternative to the use of facilities in Israel proper. Moreover, this concerns short distances, not removal to a distant country.

That said, I too think the present dual legal system on the West Bank is unacceptable, despite the expectations for military supervision of occupied territory. While Israel cannot simply incorporate the West Bank into its own legal system without provoking accusations of annexation, the current inequities must be ameliorated. But her complaint about "the threat that Palestinians are socially constructed to represent within the Israeli national system" (12) ignores the fact that a minority of Palestinians are a threat. Once you know Palestinians or Israelis personally, it is difficult to impose an identical social construction on all of them. Given that Azarova knows many personally, it is regrettable that she does exactly that herself.

Although her essay does not engage in any detailed analysis of Israeli law, she justifies this by noting that it is instead "directed at the social structure and cognition of the Israeli domestic system" (17). She "steps back from the classical approach to the assessment of violations" (17), she says, to expose the "deep structure of internationally wrongful acts" (20). Yet she never actually undertakes that ambitious task either. Nor, in a typical violation of the IHRA Definition guidelines, does she compare Israel's legal system to that of any other country. Where is the call for a structural analysis of the racialized US justice system, let along what counts for justice in China, North Korea, or Russia. The key point is that Azarova is very good at making such comparisons and contrasts succinctly, when she wants to do so, in a sentence or two. In this case, she prefers to depict Israel as an outcast within the community of nations, a particularly relentless violator of human rights. That stand is inherently biased; readers may decide themselves whether or not it qualifies as antisemitic.

5. Opposing West Bank business relationships

As an example of a recent essay by Azarova that is at once thoroughly opposed to Israel's presence in the West Bank and entirely rational, one can consider "Business and Human Rights in Occupied Territory: The UN Database of Business Active in Israel's Settlements," published in the *Business and Human Rights Journal* in 2018. In 2016, a UN Human Rights Council resolution requested the High Commissioner for Human Rights to create a database of companies doing business with settlements and to review it annually. Given the many years in which a wide range of groups have promoted organized boycotts of corporations conducting business on the West Bank, a reader might expect Azarova to do the same. Although she devotes paragraphs to a "wave of divest-ment decisions" (Azarova 2018a, 204) carried out by various companies, boy-cotts are not mentioned until the end of the essay, and BDS is never mentioned at all. In "Boycotts, International Law Enforcement and the UK's 'Anti-Boycott' Note," however, she does welcome the potential for public bodies refusing con-tracts with companies implicated in "Israel's internationally unlawful exercise of its domestic jurisdiction in occupied territory" (Azarova 2016d). Since such actions would not be "adopted on the basis of a sweeping, politically-driven boycott that targets commercial sectors, governments, or situations," they could escape the "long practice of executive branch monopoly over boycotts."

In the above-mentioned 2018 piece, she disassociates herself from the expec-tation that a database of businesses operating in occupied territory will inform boycott organizing: "Political narratives in the US, the UK and France have assimilated the database with 'boycotts' against Israel, which are prohibited under their respective domestic laws. The misconceived view of the purpose of this initiative as one that is intended to politically isolate and bully Israel has fueled state and business hostility towards it" (Azarova 2018a, 208). The database, she assures us—some will feel disingenuously—is not part of a political movement. She is aware that it will be used that way, but she claims the motivation for its creation is simply to enhance adherence to international law. Even if this line of argument is tactical, not principled, it governs the character of the essay and its scholarly status. Putting "boycotts" in quotation marks deftly distances her from the movement, stages a simulacrum of distaste for the phenomenon, and appears to render it illegitimate.

Azarova's aims for the project are both economic and political, and they would in reality be carried out in tandem with boycott and disinvestment initiatives, but this fact is bracketed and ignored. Indeed, boycott organizers can adapt their strategies and use Azarova's essay to advocate for multinational corporations and national governments to discourage business investment in West Bank activities. The essay amounts to a set of guidelines for rational persuasion to promote its political agenda. While most boycott pressure emphasizes morality, Azarova focuses on legality: "a home state could and should protect its domestic legal order and domestic subjects from contributions to illicit proceeds and financial flows in transnational contexts" (2018a, 208). That is the kind of advice a legislator might offer, or a risk assessment that a company's own lawyers might provide if confronted by third-state regulation of West Bank investment. The essay is a model of the way faculty research and analysis can contribute to a political project while claiming not to do so.

Yet Azarova is more forthcoming about her aspirations for the UN database in more polemical pieces for nonacademic audiences also published in 2018, especially "The UN Database on Business in Israeli Settlements" and "Tracking Business in Israeli Settlements." In the second of these pieces, she defines the UN database as "a mechanism to document, report, and engage primary interested parties" and specifies accurately that "it does not have the mandate to adjudicate the responsibility of concerned parties, nor to act as a coercive tool of law enforcement" (Azarova 2018e). She adds that "it cannot afford to alienate its target audiences by operating as an adjudicative or coercive body." A few sentences later, however, she expresses her wish for how the database will be used: "it could well become the first to function as a regulatory tool that gains support and encourages compliance with international law." In the first of these two essays, published by Al-Shabaka: The Palestinian Policy Network, however, she reminds us that "not only does the establishment and maintenance of the settlements constitute violations of international law, but so do all private transactions and business dealings in or related to the settlements" (Azarova 2018d). The UN Guiding Principles on Business and Human Rights, she insists, "require businesses to assess whether their operations have a harmful effect on human rights and to mitigate such harms," but warns us that "HRC resolution 31/36 affirms that a business undertaking operations in Israel's settlements is unable to mitigate the adverse impact of its activities on the severity and frequency of violations of human rights ... all business activities in settlements would contribute to the rampant human rights abuses caused by their existence and maintenance."

The range of those implicated is broad: "companies and individuals acting as procurers, investors, and consumers may contribute to and benefit from violations of international law in occupation." Consequently, "to guarantee their compliance with international standards, all businesses must therefore terminate all their business activities that extend to the settlements." We are in the presence of a political agenda. It would be misleading to tell students otherwise.

Azarova is correct that the UN database is not part of an enforcement regime. On the other hand, UN countries are implicitly encouraged to use it as one by her repeated emphasis on settlement engagement as a hugely serious human rights violation. In both "The UN Database" and "Tracking Business" she emphasizes that, since the database lacks enforcement mechanisms, it cannot be considered a blacklist. This is in response to all of those who complain that this is precisely what it is. Notably, blacklists are often quite independent of enforcement. The claim it is a blacklist, she writes, "is a semantic twist that is intended to undo the image of a soft mechanism with a mandate to document, report, and engage interested parties into a coercive tool that shames offenders into compliance" (Azarova 2018d). Her characterizations of the human rights violations intrinsic to all settlements turn the database into a means of shaming offenders into compliance. And the only way states can protect their constituencies from violating human rights is to opt for enforcement. The controlling logic of her argument might be characterized this way: "it's not a blacklist; it's a blacklist."

Azarova's dissatisfaction with the existing investment patterns and widespread indifference to what she sees as the legal demand to withdraw from West Bank entanglements was made clear in her 2016 essay "On Business and Human Rights in Illegal Territorial Regimes." "The track record on lawsuits for foreign business involvement in Israeli wrongdoing," she complains there, "is dismal" (Azarova 2016a). Moreover, states "have stopped short of enforcing international law-based obligations by adopting measures that could redress the immitigable business involvement in the harm resulting from operations under the auspice of Israel's illegal legislative and administrative regime." She points out that a 2016 Human Rights Watch report "requires states to stop or prevent their corporate nationals from becoming involved in settlements." Domestic law must be brought in line with public policy. Then laws barring doing business in settlements "would become as enforceable as any other domestic laws regulating corporate actors." Two years later she would turn to the UN database as an inducement to trigger action.

You could read "Business and Human Rights in Occupied Territory" in the *Business and Human Rights Journal* and conclude that Azarova is not interested in enforcement. But you would be wrong. She decides how forthcoming to be according to the audience she is addressing. It is at least a problematic strategy to teach to law students.

Azarova's deep commitment to enforcement is also evident in other pieces, among them the briefing paper "Taking forward the UN Commission of Inquiry Report on Gaza," in which she recommends consideration of more punitive actions: "suspending arms and defense exports to Israel," "adopting restrictions on travel and economic activities of individuals in the Israeli military or political ranks," and "preventing nationals, individuals, charities and other associations from lending support to unlawful Israeli acts" (2016b, 9). She considers such actions necessary because Israel's enforcement of international law is limited to "the 'bad apples' that Israel has sacrificed to maintain a pretense of house-keeping" (11). Appropriate principles must be "brought to bear on the perpetrators through criminal accountability and on Israel for state responsibility" (10). Ostensibly just a report on Gaza, this briefing paper implicates West Bank conduct as well.

Azarova's companion briefing paper on "The International Criminal Court, Israel/Palestine and EU Support" revisits this advice to give it more specificity, recommending that other countries "halt arms trade with Israel in light of the unlawful use of certain weapons by Israeli forces" and "review the travel to and economic activities in the EU jurisdiction of Israeli military and political officials suspected of international crimes (e.g. in relation to settlements and the conduct of hostilities)" (Azarova 2016c). She urges that EU countries "regulate private actors' activities in settlements." Some of the NGOs she has worked for, including Al-Haq and Diakonia, have compiled dossiers for submission to the ICC for possible prosecution. She highlights "individuals or entities involved in planning and ordering" actions by "violent settlers, military and political officials responsible for Area C destruction," and "charities funding settlements." Meanwhile, the character of several Palestinian human rights groups began to be intensely debated in 2022 due to Israel deciding to remove their recognition due to purported terrorist links.

Azarova's 2013 paper for the Palestinian NGO Dakonia, "Securing Injustice: Legal Analysis of G4S Israel Operations in Occupied Palestinian Territory," is more explicit in assigning responsibility to corporate "actors who benefit financially from the conflict, and who have altered their activities in order to gain from it financially, without taking into consideration the role they play in the conflict" (2013e, 4). G4S withdrew from all settlement business relationships in 2017, but the essay's general principles remain relevant. Companies engaged with settlement activities, she argues, "have a vested interest in the prolongation of conflict, as it allows them to maximize their profits" (5). Although she does not say so, business activity in the West Bank could well increase with the realization of a two-state solution, which suggests there is little necessary corporate determination to sustain the conflict. Since she accuses Israel of committing war crimes in the occupation, it follows that "those aiding and abetting, ordering, supervising, and jointly perpetrating can also be held individually accountable" (12). She adds that "case law has shown that corporate officers have successfully been prosecuted for international crimes" (24).

Returning, then, to "Business and Human Rights in Occupied Territory," it is less polemical, though the subject is the same as Azarova's more argumentative publications. The essay is carefully calculated to address concerns business representatives and business faculty would recognize and to employ rhetoric with which they would feel more comfortable. But she also wants to expand their horizons. The "internationally unlawful acts committed by Israeli authorities" begin with the physical establishment of West Bank settlements but implicate much more: "The non-physical infrastructure of the settlements include the legal and administrative acts that enable the establishment and maintenance of settlement-based entities, and thus that absorb the settlements into the economy, and social and political life in Israel proper" (Azarova 2018a, 190). This casts a wide net, implicating more than those companies actually operating in the settlements in "the rights abuses that result from the conversion of [Palestinian] property rights into revenues" (196). Settlement-based contributions to abuses of human rights "may be impalpable and unintended, often falling short of the standard of complicity, but nonetheless entail the conversion of wrongful rights and titles into financial gains" (197). The name for the "entire legal and political regime" that "underpins the creation and maintenance of settlements in occupied territory" can be identified in one word: Israel. Israel's very existence is grounded in illegality. Although Azarova does not say so, her analysis makes it difficult to rationalize any economic relationship with the Jewish state by claiming it has no entanglement with the settlements.

Tracking all the ways businesses "contribute to the chain of custody of the illicit financial flows generated by the settlements economy" (203) requires some new categories for evaluating economic activity. Her interest in this issue dates back to her 2013 paper "Backtracking on Responsibility," which found fault with a French court's decision regarding two French companies, Alstom and Veolia, that participated in constructing a light railway between West Jerusalem and East Jerusalem settlements (Azarova 2013b). The Court in part "concluded that the claimants failed to demonstrate the proximity and causal link of the company's actions to the Israeli authorities' internationally unlawful conduct."[15] To clarify that issue, she proposes a proximity-based classification system that can account for "a lower threshold of harm" (Azarova 2018a, 204). It is a three-part "typology of degrees of proximity" to the settlements. First-degree proximity characterizes companies actually based in settlements, including those operating franchises there. Second-degree proximity is reserved for companies "that buy or supply products, equipment and services to or from settlement-based companies," a much larger number. Finally, third-degree proximity is achieved indirectly by doing business with a company that itself does business with settlements. The UN database will not track or list those companies; nonetheless, Azarova believes companies have a responsibility to monitor their own relationships for third-degree proximity. The intrusive surveillance and research required to do so should not be underestimated. I would not want my department head urging students to institutionalize that agenda.

Published a year before, in 2017, "The Bounds of (Il)legality: Rethinking the Regulation of Transnational Corporate Wrongs" is very much a companion piece to "Business and Human Rights in Occupied Territory," as is 2018's "The Secret Life of Non-Recognition: EU-Israel Relations and the Obligation of Non-Recognition in International Law," which is about the European Union's

---

15 Veolia responded to Azarova's essay: "The Appeals Court of Versailles upheld the Nanterre Court's decision in a clear and unequivocal ruling that neither Veolia nor Alstom were breaching international law or the rules of the UN Global Compact by executing their contracts for the construction and operation of the Jerusalem tramway. . . . Ms. Azarov's describes the purpose of the tramway and of the contract to operate it, as being to 'facilitate the establishment of Israel's illegal settlements in occupied territory and the movement of Israeli Jewish settlers between Israel and their residences in occupied territory'. This is a political statement and view that we cannot agree with. . . . Along the 14 kilometres of the route which serves 23 stations, 7 are situated in or close by Arab neighbourhoods. . . . As part of its disinformation campaign against Veolia, the BDS movement has repeatedly portrayed every contract loss by Veolia as a result of its successful efforts. . . . [W]e are not aware of any contracts that have been lost as a result of Veolia's involvement in the Jerusalem tramway." See "Veolia's Response," Business and Human Rights Resource Centre, n.d., accessed June 2021, https://www.business-human-rights.org/en/latest-news/veolias-response/.

"obligations of non-recognition and non-assistance to Israel's serious breaches of peremptory norms under international law … such as the flagrant denial of the right to self-determination of peoples" (Azarova 2018c, 24, 25). The subject of "The Bounds of (Il)legality" is the lack of adequate home-country regulation and enforcement of corporate practices in foreign countries, particularly the failure to monitor and enforce indirect corporate human rights obligations. The body of the essay is mostly composed in the abstract; no specific corporations are mentioned.[16] Except for the 2013 tragic collapse of the Rana Plaza factories in Bangladesh, country-specific violations are not cited. Palestine is only referenced in the text toward the end. Unless you read the series of footnotes dealing with Israel, you might imagine the essay entailed no specific political commitments. But the Israel-focused notes are there; the 2017 essay underwrites the 2018 essay.

Azarova's opposition to the occupation unfortunately blinds her to some of the economic benefits Palestinians gain from foreign and Israeli investment in the West Bank, the most obvious one being better jobs than they could otherwise find. When the Israeli firm SodaStream abandoned its West Bank factory in 2015 under BDS pressure, some 500 Palestinians lost jobs paying about twice as much as Palestinian businesses paid. If the Palestinians are ever to get a viable state of their own it will require economic cooperation with Israel. For Azarova, unlike, say, for former Palestinian Prime Minister Salam Fayyad, all Israeli West Bank economic investment equates to exploitation.

6. War in Gaza and the law of occupation

Nonetheless, Azarova's more recent business-related essays are more rhetorically restrained than a number of her earlier publications. In her 2009 piece on an Israel Supreme Court decision, she claims, with a sense of injustice, that the Court "has virtually never upheld or referenced in any context whatsoever" the Palestinian "inherent right to self-determination" (Azarova 2009d). That right is a matter of principle, not of black-letter law. In neither case, moreover, would the right be "inherent." Yet the Court has recognized Palestinian rights many times and has regularly asserted equal rights for Israeli Arabs. Azarova partly concedes this in a 2014 essay. In "An International Legal Demarche for Human Rights?,"

---

16 For a discussion of two companies she considers involved in Israeli human rights violations, see Azarova (2013b, 2013d).

she writes that "the court has provided a remedy to Palestinians in few cases, in rulings that have not curtailed the general policy and practice responsible for the individual injury" (Azarova 2014a). Familiarity with the Court's history shows that under some chief justices it preferred to decide cases narrowly, while under others it was more activist and used rulings to establish or extend general rights. In "A Line of Selective Rhetoric," Azarova accuses the Court of rendering yet "another stultifying judgement" (Azarova 2009c). In "The Security Paradigm in the Israeli Supreme Court," she accuses the Court of "heedlessness towards international law" (Azarova 2009e); and in "An International Legal Demarche for Human Rights?," she condemns the Court for "providing a legal façade for illegal policies and practices" (Azarova 2014a). The Court in reality has sometimes acted as a check on Israeli policy. It has not always played this role, but it has done so frequently enough to earn it substantial international respect.

Azarova's 2013 piece "Israel's Loopy Logic of Exoneration" takes on the Israeli Military Advocate General's record of investigating potentially illegal fatal wartime attacks, arguing that "Israel's system of military investigation has created a closed circuit of impunity," embodying "the tautology whereby without investigation there is no evidence and without evidence there is no investigation" (Azarova 2013c). The result, she tells us, is "virtual impunity for its military and political officials" due to "Israel's deficient institutional and legal practice." Those political officials who have been convicted of offenses and sent to prison might beg to differ about their impunity. Only two years later, in "Palestine's Day in Court?," she reports that "Israel has embarked on a series of potentially resource-intensive, prolonged investigations into alleged wrongdoing by its forces in the Gaza Strip" (Azarova 2015c).

In any case, "Business and Human Rights in Occupied Territory" is politically and ideologically of a piece with everything she has published since 2009. Indeed, her controlling subject of Israel's "belligerent occupation" received its first definition and analysis in five brief essays she published in the *International Law Observer* that year. During that time, from June 2008 to March 2010, she was employed as a legal researcher at HaMoked: Center for the Defence of the Individual in East Jerusalem. As NGO Monitor notes, HaMoked defines its main aim as "assisting Palestinians of the occupied territories whose rights are violated due to Israel's policies." It regularly represents families of Palestinians responsible for carrying out terrorist attacks against Israel. Azarova had earlier served as a legal research intern at HaMoked in the summer of 2007.

In the first of her 2009 pieces, "Who Is a Civilian in Gaza?," Azarova insists on classifying Hamas as a "non-state actor," although the terrorist group has been governing Gaza since 2007. The main issue, however, is how to determine who is a valid target during hostilities. She argues for a clear distinction between combatants (members of the military wing of the armed group) and fighters ("those who sporadically participate in hostilities on an 'ad hoc' basis without being members of a brigade") (Azarova 2009a). The impossibility of realizing this distinction in the midst of combat in urban warfare is made considerably more difficult by Hamas's lack of military uniforms, a fact she fails to mention. How one is to know "whether the individual is performing a 'continuous combat function'" she does not say. Yet she suggests provocatively that, without observing the distinction, Israeli reservists could be considered valid targets. By 2015, in the wake of the 2014 war with Hamas, she writes in "A Healthy Dose of Wartime Normative Realism" that Israel "in effect eviscerates the category of civilians and undermines the principle of distinction" (Azarova 2015a, 214). She is arguably blunter still in "An International Legal Demarche for Human Rights?," saying polemically that Israel has "disposed of the international humanitarian law principle of distinction by classifying Gaza's civilian population as the enemy" (Azarova 2014a). That is a tendentious political argument masquerading as fact. Although it is a typical move for anti-Zionists to ignore Israel's elaborate efforts to limit civilian deaths, it is a more serious case of irresponsible slander for a specialist in international law to do so. In "A Healthy Dose," she writes, "A belligerent with a cumulatively scandalous record of in bello violations should be scrutinized for its liability for the fact of sustaining the war" (Azarova 2015a, 212)—scrutiny that among all participants apparently only Israel merits.

In 2015's "Exploding Civilian Involvement," an essay that pays "particular attention to the case of Israel," Azarova adds yet another requirement. Deciding whether a civilian is a valid military target, she asserts, "involves a two-part test, which requires both that their actions be 'crucial' to and concretely and causally linked to military operations, and that the individual made an objectively-determinable free choice to make such a contribution" (Azarova 2015d). She insists that Israel honor these criteria despite acknowledging that "in some cases civilians feel that they are subject to circumstantial coercion and socio-political pressures to support the fighting forces." From Nazi Germany to Hamas's Gaza, "circumstantial coercion" is a documented phenomenon. Yet there is no way to apply the two-part test in the midst of combat in any case. But more broadly she believes Israel has no right to claim self-defense to justify targeting combat units or rocket launch sites in Gaza. As Sharon Weill and Azarova write absurdly in "The 2014 Gaza War," "a State may not invoke self-defense against attacks originating from territory that it controls" (2015, 367). It is arguably morally corrupt to suggest a state cannot claim the right of self-defense when its citizens are subjected to lethal attack. They do have an alternative argument, but it is one only the most radical anti-Zionists offer: "it can be argued that the use of force by Hamas was not illegal ... because it amounts to legitimate resistance to illegal oppression. In that case, Hamas' acts would not constitute an (unlawful) 'armed attack' for the purpose of triggering Israel's right to self-defence" (372).

Azarova's insistence that Israel occupies Gaza through "remote control" has led to some strained reasoning. In her 2012 essay "Disingenuous 'Disengagement,'" she claims Israel maintains "its ultimate ability to reinstate its control over any domain of daily life whenever it so wishes" (Azarova, 2012b). Short of a massive invasion and permanent physical occupation by troops and bureaucrats, that claim is not based in reality. Yet she uses the following case in point:

> Take, for instance, the example of an occupier's responsibilities in the field of education. If the occupier does not have full control over the functioning of the education system in the occupied territory, in terms of the way schools are administered, curricula set and teachers hired, then the occupier cannot be held liable for defaults made by the local authorities. However, notwithstanding its limited control, the occupier remains fully charged with its responsibility to ensure the enjoyment of the right to education by the occupied population.[17]

Exactly how Israel could carry out that or any other on-the-ground responsibility in Gaza is not easy to imagine. For my part, although I believe Israel and Egypt have no choice but to continue maintaining a blockade that monitors and regulates imports into Gaza, I believe it comes with responsibilities. As I argue in *Israel Denial* and *Peace and Faith*, that includes expanding the fishing limit to 12 miles, supplying additional electricity to Gaza, freeing up and facilitating exports from Gaza, expanding work opportunities in Israel for Gazans, and many other practical actions. Azarova's focus on questionable or unrealistic responsibilities is immensely counterproductive. It does Gaza no good and confuses the debate.

In earlier pieces, such as "Al-Haq's Questions and Answers," she declares that "during occupation, the sovereignty over the territory remains at all times with the local population" (Azarova 2011, 5). In "Israel's Unlawfully Prolonged Occupation," she argues that an occupying power must be committed to

---

17 This passage also appears in Azarova (2015b, 963).

returning occupied territory to the ousted "'rightful sovereign' at the time when it was first occupied" (Azarova 2017b). In a 2019 essay, "Towards a Counter-Hegemonic Law of Occupation," she repeats but qualifies this principle to adapt the category of sovereignty to conditions in Gaza and the West Bank. The West Bank was occupied by Jordan from 1948 to 1967 and was part of the British mandate from 1923 to 1948. Gaza had a parallel history, save that Egypt filled the role held by Jordan on the West Bank. The only recognized sovereign in modern times was the Ottoman Empire, which was dissolved after its defeat in the First World War. Azarova therefore invokes the notion that the Palestinian people are actually the rightful sovereign, a principle implicitly supported internationally—but as an ethical and political principle rather than a historically based one. She now argues that the law of occupation applies to "self-determining peoples (West Bank and Gaza Strip)" (Azarova 2019, 119). That enables her to call for the international community "to expedite the return of the ousted sovereign" (123), defined as the Palestinian people. Granting Palestinians that status is at best speculative.

Azarova's reasoning requires some additional support. "As a corollary to the prohibition on the acquisition of territory by force, the right to self-determination—also a peremptory norm and a general principle enshrined in the UN Charter—was intended to protect the link between a self-determining people and a given territory" (135). Following standard anti-Zionist practice, she never suggests that Egypt or Jordan should have recognized the peoplehood or self-determination rights of the Palestinians under their control. She has pointed out elsewhere that the concept of self-determination evolved after the demise of the era of colonialization, and she repeats that point here, though decolonization was well under way in the 1940s and 1950s. "Before the decolonization era of international law," she writes, "the rules on occupation as a function of war were deemed inapplicable to 'colonial occupations', since 'civilised' nations allowed themselves to claim sovereignty and acquire parts of the uncivilized world" (122). She is aware, though she doesn't say so, that some see Israel's occupation of the West Bank as the last vestige of the era of colonialism. Although she never mentions the fact, here, as with her claims about antiquities, her argument is weakened by the relatively recent coalescence of Palestinians into peoplehood. So she invokes "the indigenous civilian population of the occupied territory" and argues that Israel "seeks the permanent erosion of the indigenous population's future rights to self-determination of peoples" (127), even though many Palestinians did not arrive in Gaza or the West Bank until 1948 or 1967. Historically, the people with the longest claim to indigeneity are the Jews. Perhaps that is why she does not explore indigeneity at length. I strongly agree that the Netanyahu government was determined to block Palestinian self-determination, a goal it shared with the settler movement, but such views do not have to gain their moral or political force through claims of indigeneity.

Instead, Azarova opens the essay by reminding the reader that "Israel's occupation of Palestinian territory ... is the longest occupation in modern times" (115). Some of us might afford that status to China's occupation of Tibet, which dates from 1951, rather than Israel's occupation of the West Bank since 1967. Nonetheless, it is the combination of a continuing 50-year occupation with settlement growth that justifies her saying "unlawfully prolonged occupations are no different from outright annexation, or other forms of aggression that may amount to so-called 'crimes against peace'" (136). Both here and in several other essays, she includes comparisons with or brief references to other international examples and in those cases, unlike others, thus violates the IHRA Definition's warning against "applying double standards by requiring of it [Israel] a behavior not expected or demanded of any other democratic state," though the other occupations she cites are not necessarily by democratic states. As she writes, "This is the case beyond Palestine and the Golan Heights, in northern Cyprus, Western Sahara, Transnistria, Nagorno Karabakh, South Ossetia and Abkhazia, and most recently Crimea" (115).

The occupations that may most deserve comparison, on the other hand, are those of Germany and Japan by the United States and its allies following the Second World War. In "Neo-Colonial Transformations of Occupied Territory," Azarova raises the possibility of comparing the West Bank and other current occupations with those of Germany and Japan (Azarova 2018b, 225) but dismisses the comparisons as invalid because they are out of date. She argues that too much of international law has changed since then. Those occupations actually proved beneficial to the "indigenous" peoples, not only because they did not restore the defeated governments (Nazi Germany and Imperial Japan), though Japanese Emperor Hirohito retained his symbolic role, but also because the United States helped mandate new institutions to transform the occupations into viable democracies in Germany and Japan. While the creation of the Palestinian Authority (PA) in the Oslo Accords did not achieve this goal, the PA remains the only vehicle in place. But Azarova wants to disallow all such interventions—"prohibiting revisions to the occupied territory's legal and political order as part of its [the occupying power's] conservationist premise" (Azarova 2019, 125)—and instead rely on a hypothetical independent process of self-determination. Azarova is what one could call a self-determination absolutist. Palestinians should be left on their own immediately to determine their own future. She has briefly endorsed a one-state solution, without offering any detail, but many of us believe that route would not end well for the indigenous Jew.

Azarova regularly invokes the notion of a "universal" conviction that the West Bank is occupied territory, rather than "disputed" territory, as many Israeli governments have maintained. But she fails to acknowledge that many use the designation "occupied" in this case descriptively and categorically, to make it clear that the West Bank cannot be annexed by Israel and that Israel at some point must withdraw from most of it. The descriptive element is thus paired with an aspirational one. But many who use the term "occupied" do not intend to impose the specifics of occupation law, as Azarova does; indeed, most are unlikely to know those specifics. The designation "State of Palestine," which some international bodies use, is also aspirational, given that the state in question cannot build an international airport, sign recognized treaties with other states, or establish a full-fledged army, and that its two halves have a substantially hostile relationship. Azarova likes to repeat that the 2011 vote admitting Palestine into UNESCO established its statehood, but in "ICC Jurisdiction in Palestine" she admits that "no objective definition of a state exists in international law" and thus that "states and international organizations are left to decide individually whether they treat an entity as a state for their specific purposes" (Azarova 2012a). She characterizes statehood as a "hollow shell" to be filled with what we choose. In "An International Legal Demarche for Human Rights?," she notes that "the determination of 'State' status and the emergence of States are perhaps two of the most indeterminate, tautological matters in international law" (Azarova 2014a). A state may hold rights in theory while having no capacity to exercise them.

In a detailed 2011 legal essay "Al-Haq's Questions and Answers," Azarova follows a shifting line regarding Palestinian statehood. One the one hand, she finds the 1947 General Assembly resolution 181 providing "for the creation of two States, one Arab, one Jewish" to be "supportive evidence of the international community's perception and practice in relation to Palestine's statehood" (Azarova 2011, 4). On the other hand, she insists that "neither is UN membership a requirement for statehood nor does the General Assembly have the powers to constitute a State" (8). Perhaps the verb "constitute" carries weight here; the General Assembly cannot magically and literally create a state, but it can give the establishment of one international warrant, as it did with Israel. One may be excused for suspecting that the UN's role in establishing the Jewish state is the unspoken issue here, just as Azarova would certainly make much of a General Assembly vote now to establish a Palestinian state in the West Bank. Similarly, she says "a refusal to recognize Palestine is a political act, which does not have any legal bearing on its statehood status" (5), though we recall the considerable significance that the United States' recognition of Israel carried in 1948. US recognition triggered a series of recognitions by other nations, without which Israel's statehood would have been uncertain at best. Turn the same group of recognitions into refusals, and history would likely have taken a different course. As Azarova notes here and elsewhere, "the existence of a State is not a legal, but a purely factual and political matter, and Palestine has been treated as a State over the years by the majority of States and international organisations" (1).

Remarkably, the only specific suggestion she offers about how to transition to one state between the river and the sea is the piece of rhetorical bravado she inserts into "The Trickle-Down Effects of Normative Power" and other essays: in order for the final status issues to be addressed, Israel must "first bring an end to its belligerent occupation" (Azarova 2015e, 85). She reinforces this stand in "Shifting Paradigms" by insisting that the Fourth Geneva Convention "entails the immediate removal of all Israeli settlements" from occupied territory (Azarova 2012c). Sudden and comprehensive unilateral withdrawal from the West Bank could well prove catastrophic. I say this even though I believe that targeted withdrawal from limited territory now to empower the Palestinian Authority to govern more contiguous areas would be welcome. The standard model is that negotiation would precede resolution of issues like "borders, natural resources, nationality and the return of refugees" (Azarova 2015e, 85). Withdrawal from the large settlement blocs near the Green Line will not happen; the model has been that those would be accommodated though negotiated land swaps.

All this raises an interesting question: who are the audiences for Azarova's detailed legal analyses and what do her publications aim to achieve? They may certainly be of technical use to those in the European Union, the UN, and elsewhere who seek legal arguments to buttress opposition to the occupation. But, while these publications may offer rational alternatives to anti-Zionism based in antisemitism, they are not likely to change existing views. Some undecided legal scholars may find Azarova's work persuasive, and that is not a trivial potential audience. But the large audience that simply does not read extended analyses will not be affected either way. The same limitation applies to detailed scholarship sympathetic to the Jewish state, including my own. But Azarova's work has not even been subjected to serious academic debate, only to attack and defense regarding her aborted appointment. People who find her persuasive and those engaged in the controversy over the appointment need to undertake more thorough analyses of her work than they have produced so far.

7. Final reflections

Azarova's publications may not have been evaluated as if she were a candidate for tenure. Ordinarily, she could have been hired in a purely administrative position even if it were decided that she did not meet the research standards for a full professorship or even for tenure. A strong publication record would be a plus for an administrator but not a requirement. The publication record would have to be respectable, but not stellar. As I said at the outset, the core issue to be decided was what her publication record and political advocacy suggested about how she would administer the program and how this would reinforce or undermine public confidence in the program. And that, in my view, is the problem. Given the nature of her writing and its direct entanglement with advocacy on the same issues, her publications needed the kind of detailed review I have carried out here. Assuming that the former dean is being truthful in saying he never considered the issue of her scholarship and activism, however pertinent to the job they were, I would say the dean failed in his oversight responsibility. I would argue that her entire career is critically central to her potential administrative responsibilities. In setting aside and not reviewing her publishing and NGO experience, the dean did an inadequate job. If, in reopening the search, Toronto believed it could appoint Azarova or someone like her in a disinterested, apolitical process, then those responsible for that belief were either self-deceived or disingenuous.

Azarova would have immediately given the program she was to direct an anti-Zionist public face and possibly followed through by adding anti-Zionist elements to the program itself. Would it have been reasonable to expect she would set aside the values she had spent years articulating and traveling the world to support and become a politically neutral administrator? The selection committee clearly found her programmatic political commitment appealing. Should there be testimony under oath to the contrary, I would take it seriously, otherwise not. Meanwhile, we are talking about a candidate who has displayed lifelong ideological rigidity in every part of her professional life. That includes her objection to a Zionist law professor being included in a 2018 conference on "The International Legality of Economic Activity in Occupied Territory."[18] Had

---

18 The conference was organized by the Asser Institute in The Hague. Eugene Kontorovich, Director of the Center for the Middle East and International Law at George Mason University, submitted a paper proposal for the conference, which was accepted. After a draft program was distributed, several participants with opposing views protested his inclusion and demanded his invitation be revoked (Mackenzie 2020). The organizers refused but made several concessions to avoid the protestors boycotting the event. As Kontorovich recounts in

the Toronto dean decided that Azarova's fixed ideological views were not appropriate to the job or to the public image of the university he would have been acting responsibly. Applying the same considerations to a faculty search would be unacceptable. This was not and is not a struggle over academic freedom; it was and is a conflict over an academic program's mission and identity.

The politicization of the academy that I warn about in this book is accelerating. Over a hundred women's and gender studies programs officially adopted an anti-Zionist mission statement during the 2021 war between Hamas and Israel. Several ethnic studies programs joined the movement, as did Asian studies on my own campus. Most unexpectedly, the University of California Press declared itself to have a political mission. I had already claimed that the press was biased in my 2019 book *Israel Denial*, but a public declaration by the press itself crosses a line that many of us thought was an impenetrable barrier. The Azarova file is thus not likely to be the last politically charged appointment file that is opened. The academic issues at stake in the controversy over her appointment were obscured by the reductive politics embraced by many of her defenders and opponents alike. If this chapter serves a long-term purpose, it will be to help people think about politicized administrative appointments more clearly next time. Meanwhile, a pretense that the decision concerning Azarova's appointment should have been apolitical prevails among many at the University of Toronto. But it was always a political matter: the selection of Azarova made it so.

---

an October 21, 2020, letter sent to Toronto faculty at their request, this included "cancelling the planned conference dinner, so that they should not have to break bread" with him. Before presenting her own paper, Azarova "got up and formally announced that her 'participation in the workshop does not constitute an acceptance of the unconditional invitation to Eugene Kontorovich.'" Azarova then refused to be published in the resulting book if Kontorovich were included. His paper was published there, but not hers. People who write about political issues often find themselves invited to speak at conferences or asked to contribute to books with people whose views they reject or even strongly dislike. One has to make a career decision about whether to demand ideological conformity from fellow speakers and contributors. The only people I have refused to share a stage with are Holocaust deniers. This anecdote about Azarova is significant because she was being considered for an administrative role that should welcome opposing opinion in scheduling events. Since Kontorovich lives part of the time in the West Bank settlement of Alon Shvut and is a major intellectual force behind anti-BDS legislation, it is unsurprising that Azarova dislikes him, but that does not justify demanding that he be excluded from an academic conference.

Chapter 8

Adopted but under Assault: The Status of the IHRA Working Definition of Antisemitism

———————

Introduction

Controversy continues to swirl around the Working Definition of Antisemitism adopted by the International Holocaust Remembrance Alliance (IHRA) in 2016 and subsequently endorsed by over 1,000 nations, agencies, and organizations.[1] The Definition opens with a brief summary definition of antisemitism and later lists eleven major categories of contemporary antisemitism, such as "accusing the Jews as a people, or Israel as a state, of inventing or exaggerating the Holocaust" and "using the symbols and images associated with classic antisemitism (e.g., claims of killing Jesus or blood libel) to characterize Israel or Israelis."[2] The Definition warns that its examples should not be applied to other statements without analysis that takes their specific overall context into account. Nor does the Definition claim that its list of examples is exhaustive; it does, however, encompass many varieties of antisemitism encountered in contemporary writing and daily life, including anti-semitism focused on the State of Israel and antisemitism that proliferates on the

---

1   A good, clear summary of the IHRA Definition and the criticism leveled against it, written for the general public, was jointly published by Dina Porat, Giovanni Quer, and Talia Naamat (2021).
2   Except within quotations, I use "Definition" in initial caps to refer to the entire document, not just the brief definition at its outset.

internet and through social media. Although many critics have chosen to discount the point, the Definition makes perfectly clear from the outset that it is not crafted to be a legally binding document. The introduction to this book presents a concise policy document that campuses could adopt when they endorse the Definition. It specifies how the Definition may and may not be used at the campus adopting it. US campuses that accept federal funds are, however, expected to give the IHRA examples careful consideration when reviewing complaints of antisemitism.

The history of the Definition dates to 2005, when the European Monitoring Centre on Racism and Xenophobia (EUMC) issued the first version. The EUMC working definition was "the first to offer concise reference points for interpreting an ideology that is not necessarily expressed in overt hatred but is rather characterized by codes and detour communication" (Arnold 2022, 1). From the outset, however, it provoked fears that it could inhibit free speech or even be used to sanction it. Indeed, in 2011, I coauthored an open letter (distributed by the AAUP) stating that the EUMC working definition should not be used "to censor what a professor, student or speaker can say." Hate speech is broadly protected by academic freedom, though it can have professional consequences. But debates about that potential intensified after the IHRA issued a reorganized version of the working definition that began to be both endorsed and adopted worldwide.

Widespread commitment to free speech, academic freedom, and the IHRA Definition's own guidelines have prevented the fears of pervasive restrictions on speech from materializing, though a growing chorus of dire warnings and unfounded complaints about the Definition persists nonetheless. The mounting number of attacks on the Definition suggest frustration at its increasing legitimacy. Its wide international adoption is a remarkable accomplishment. That international consensus comes at a time when social media have made antisemitism a pervasive global phenomenon.

Lara Friedman, who runs a left-wing organization called the Foundation for Middle East Peace, has been among the Definition's leading critics. At a 2022 symposium, she claimed that the IHRA Definition is being used exclusively to suppress criticism of Israel. Certain people, she added, place a higher value on protecting Israel from criticism than they do on our fundamental freedoms (Friedman 2022). Earlier that year, at a Harvard Divinity School roundtable, she went further, insisting that the Definition's supporters want to criminalize all criticism of Israel.[3] At the same event, Nadia Abu El-Haj cast a wider net,

---

3 For a video and transcript of the roundtable, see https://rpl.hds.harvard.edu/news/2021/05/17/video-politics-defining-roundtable-discussion-about-jerusalem-declaration-antisemitism.

declaring that the Definition was being weaponized—whether officially or unofficially—to shut down all kinds of speech. She added a concluding challenge, asking why it is "self-evidently antisemitic" on the face of it to expel all the Jews from Palestine?

Rebecca Ruth Gould's contribution to the debate, her book *Erasing Palestine: Free Speech and Palestinian Freedom* (2023), represents arguably the most extreme to date, invoking the "deception, manipulation, and antidemocratic coercion" (23) producing "the dead-end of silence and suppression to which the IHRA definition … leads" (128). She tells us it "has taken hold of UK universities with … disastrous consequences" (116–17). She purports to document "the sordid history of the IHRA definition's implementation" (111) that accompanies its "weaponization of fundamental rights" (58), but ends up instead often listing mere criticism of faculty, not the suppression of their views. She does more specifically say that "definitions like the IHRA's greatly contribute to the bureaucratization of debate" (99), which would be true if the Definition were misused as a disciplinary code, but is an unreasonable conclusion when its categories educate and increase understanding. It is also true that "no fundamental reworking of the social order has transpired" following the Definition's adoption (87), but her solution to the problem of antisemitism—to address the economic conditions that make discrimination possible—does not seem likely to be achieved any time soon either. She decides that "the IHRA definition, like the Balfour Declaration before it, has thereby become a means of papering over the entrenched structural inequalities that underwrite contemporary imperialism" (58), but I think we can be forgiven for believing that ending the Jewish state will not eliminate either antisemitism or imperialism. Should that argument fail to gain any traction, she has a less apocalyptic complaint: "Under the IHRA definition, fighting antisemitism has become an empty performance, undertaken for political gain" (24). It is too soon to know if any of these views will take hold, but I detail them to give fair warning.

A convenient way to keep track of these and other challenges to the IHRA Definition is to consult the regularly updated annotated list of anti-IHRA Definition publications. It has 21 entries for 2018, 23 for 2019, 41 for 2020, and 90 for 2021, but only 16 for 2022 (Friedman 2023). The 2021 increase is due in part to the publication of two new formal definitions of antisemitism, the Jerusalem Declaration on Antisemitism (JDA) and the Nexus Document, both adapting the structure of the IHRA Definition, but it also reflects a widening controversy. The drop-off in anti-IHRA Definition publications in 2022 may be evidence that the campaign against the Definition is running out of new arguments to present and losing steam, though events or new approaches like Gould's could revive it. At the Harvard event, Brian Klug said the Jerusalem Declaration was "an attempt to stop a runaway train," indeed, "to derail it," though admitting that these attempts to block the adoption of the IHRA Definition had failed. Atalia Omer suggested that all three definitions were fatally flawed because they promoted belief in an exceptionalist antisemitism that should instead be absorbed into a general commitment to antiracism. El-Haj agreed, bizarrely adding that this would "desexualize" antisemitism.

Like the IHRA Definition, the alternative definitions begin with a revised definition and general comments, then follow up with examples. Instead of just listing examples of antisemitism as the Definition does, however, they each offer two lists—with examples differentiated between those the authors consider antisemitic and those they think are not. The Jerusalem Declaration criticizes the IHRA Definition and aims to replace it. The Nexus Document has been described by its authors as complementing and clarifying the IHRA Definition, effectively positioning itself as a friendly amendment, despite the fact that it also aims to absolve much anti-Zionism of charges it is antisemitic. However, the Nexus Document had largely dropped out of the debate by mid-2022, perhaps because it is less hostile to the IHRA Definition and thus less appealing to the Definition's critics. The Nexus Document may receive a new lease of life now that it has been welcomed in the framework of the Biden administration's U.S. National Strategy to Combat Antisemitism, which was unveiled in 2023.[4] These competing definitions have generated a further round of critical debate and added to the confusion over what the IHRA Definition does and doesn't say or do. After giving an overview of the current state of competing views about the IHRA Definition, I will discuss the Jerusalem Declaration in detail, followed by comments on the Nexus Document. Friedman's list of anti-IHRA Definition publications in 2022 highlights the AAUP's intervention, which is discussed in detail below.

1. The IHRA Working Definition

There is some confusion as to what is meant by the "IHRA Definition." The document as a whole has three parts: (1) a brief definition of antisemitism; (2) a statement of principles about how the IHRA Definition should be applied; and (3) a series of eleven examples or categories of contemporary antisemitism. I use "Definition" (upper case) to refer to the document as

---

4   See   https://www.whitehouse.gov/wp-content/uploads/2023/05/U.S.-National-Strategy-to-Counter-Antisemitism.pdf.

whole and "definition" (lower case) to refer to the brief opening definition. The opening definition is often criticized for being too vague. It opens with this sentence: "Antisemitism is a certain perception of Jews, which may be expressed as hatred toward Jews." The emphasis on perception seems to some to emphasize personal psychology and set aside antisemitism that is based on conspiratorial bodies of theory.

Peter Ullrich's widely regarded 2019 critique makes a particular point about the term *perception*, noting that it "refers not least to sensory processes, such as seeing, hearing, smelling, and therefore its meaning extends at least to some degree into the empirical-sensory domain (despite also being somewhat applicable to collective processes of construction)" (Ullrich 2019, 11). As Dana Ionescu (2022) reminds us, the Definition also references stereotypes, myths, allegations, and claims, all of which are forms of social construction. Ullrich wrote in German and was responding to the German translation of the Definition. "The German word *Wahrnehmung* refers more strongly to the sensory dimension than does the English word 'perception'" (Jensen 2022, 2). Ionescu points out that "the meanings of 'perception' in English, 'percepción' in Spanish and 'perception' in French … are more multifaceted than in German. In addition to sensory perception, these terms can also refer to an apprehension, an image, a notion, an idea or a view" (Ionescu 2022, 2). Given that antisemitism for centuries has often been attributed to people who have never encountered a Jew, it would have been very odd indeed for those drafting the Definition to insist on sensory processes as its primary means of confirmation.

The crux of the issue, however, may be Ullrich's insistence that the heart of the matter is necessarily the opening definition and that everything else, including the eleven examples, is mere annotation. He sees the brief definition as a failed effort to "determine a widely accepted *core* of antisemitism" (10), "what antisemitism is understood to be at its core" (Ullrich 2019, 11), whereas I see it as a preface to the examples. He also takes the modifier "working" to be deceptive, since the Definition has never actually been revised. But the nations and NGOs that have adopted it would not have tolerated repeated review procedures for revised versions. The qualifications and additions would have to come in scholarly and political debate and publication, in the accumulation of a rich body of commentary, which is exactly what has happened. Sina Arnold writes that "the definition is intended for working *with* it and *on* it" (2022, 1), but both those activities take place outside the Definition itself.

In truth, there is probably no way to define antisemitism adequately in a few sentences. Historically, no other hatred has been so adaptable and shifting. I recommend considering several different short definitions so we can see what is at stake. A good place to start is with Helen Fein's well-regarded definition of antisemitism as

> a persisting latent structure of hostile beliefs towards Jews as a collectivity manifested in individuals as attitudes, and in culture as myth, ideology, folklore, and imagery, and in actions—social or legal discrimination, political mobilization against Jews, and collective or state violence—which results in and/or is designed to distance, displace, or destroy Jews as Jews (Fein 1987, 67).

In August, 2022, the well-known pro-Israel blogger Elder of Ziyon presented an alternative definition of antisemitism at a conference organized by the Institute for the Study of Global Antisemitism and Policy (ISGAP).[5] He offered it as a kind of algorithm, a definition one could reliably use to determine whether a statement is antisemitic. It is less helpful in understanding complex bodies of antisemitic theory. He offers it as an elaboration of Natan Sharansky's "3D" definition of the forms that antisemitism takes—delegitimization, demonization, and double standards. It has two columns. On the left are four types of antisemitism; on the right are their multiple targets:

Antisemitism is

(1)	hostility toward Jews;	(a)	as individual Jews;
(2)	denigration of Jews;	(b)	as a people;
(3)	malicious lies about Jews; or	(c)	as a religion;
(4)	discrimination against Jews	(d)	as an ethnic group; or
		(e)	as a nation (i.e. Israel)

Each of the four categories of aggression on the left can be combined with any of the five Jewish targets on the right, so there are a total of twenty possible combinations. It's a pretty good test, which is one of the things a definition can be. The IHRA Definition itself, however, doesn't seek to be a test. It seeks to be a guide to analysis. Its authors also chose not to use the eleven examples to list all the malicious lies you can tell about Jews or Israel. I'm glad to have all these definitions, in addition to others, though the so-called Jerusalem Declaration on

---

5 ISGAP-Woolf Institute International Conference, Global Antisemitism: A Crisis of Modernity Revisited, Cambridge University, July 31–August 2, 2022.

Antisemitism was drafted as an alternative to the IHRA Definition that widely absolves anti-Zionism of claims that it is antisemitic. The IHRA Definition is the only definition that has won broad international acceptance.

As Kenneth Marcus (2013b) writes,

> A theoretically sophisticated definition of this term must fully account for antisemitism's ideological, attitudinal, and practical qualities; its persisting latent structure within Western cultures; its continuities and discontinuities with analogous phenomena; its chimerical quality; its potentially self-fulfilling character; and its role in the construction of Jewish identity. Most importantly, the definition must account for the participation of antisemitic discourses and practices in the construction of the individual and collective "Jew," both as false image and as actual being (97).

Not a project for a typical afternoon. And not one a concise dictionary definition can encompass.

The reality is that IHRA Definition's brief opening definition, while much debated by academics, is often ignored. The second part, the principles regarding how the Definition is to be understood and applied, is very important. It is sometimes casually discounted, but it is at the heart of the Definition; to ignore it is to misrepresent the entire document. The eleven categories of antisemitism, however, are where the real battles have been fought. When people refer to the "IHRA Definition," they are often referring to all three sections taken together, though some polemically place most of their emphasis on the opening definition.

The second part, the principles, includes the warning that deciding whether particular statements are antisemitic requires taking the overall context into account. Context can mean in what circumstances a statement is made or what the history of the person or the group making a statement suggests about what the statement means. "The context also includes an understanding of the respective political (sub)culture and its historical development" (Arnold 2022, 3), though it doesn't take a whole lot of research to decide whether a neo-Nazi group's statements are antisemitic. Individual statements in such cases are often linked to dozens of others by the same person or group that render the meaning and purpose unambiguous. In such cases, the designation as antisemitic is definitive. Yet people do not always know why they say things or what the implications of their words are. A person's intent can be difficult or impossible to establish. A lack of clear context can lead you to decide that a statement has antisemitic effects that may not have been understood or intended. Then you are faced with an antisemitic statement, but not a fundamentally antisemitic person. Our concern is better concentrated on determining a statement's effects than on trying to look into someone's heart to determine their intent.

Some of the eleven IHRA Definition examples have their own complex and multifaceted contextual history, despite their contemporaneity. Thus, "accusing Jewish citizens of being more loyal to Israel, or to the alleged priorities of Jews worldwide, than to the interests of their own nations" has an ideological history that long predates the creation of a Jewish state. The concern that Jews constituted an alien "nation within the nation," one more loyal to itself, intensified in reaction to the Enlightenment in Europe in the nineteenth century. Similarly "the notion that e.g. a German Jew actually only represents Israel's interests— and is by extension not a 'proper' German" (Arnold 2022, 2) can hardly avoid comparison with the status of Jews in Nazi Germany.

There is another helpful distinction we can make—between how much context we need to decide whether a statement is antisemitic versus how much we need to more fully understand it. Sometimes it depends on how much your audience can tolerate or how much patience you have. The work of full contextualization is on display in Susie Linfield's chapter on Noam Chomsky in *The Lion's Den* (2019) and in my book *Israel Denial*. It features in this volume in the chapter on Valentina Azarova and in an essay I have published about Lara Sheehi. I continue to work both on contemporary antisemitism and on contextualizing antisemitism in Germany's Third Reich. What a statement from the Nazi era means can depend on the state of the regime's escalating assault on the Jews. The meaning of what was said about German Jews in 1935, two years after Hitler came to power, depends in part on what laws and actions were in effect at that point. As the flood of new laws and regulations continued, it changed the connotations that such statements acquired. As some antisemitic themes become normalized today, both intrinsic meanings and our judgment about responsibility for them may shift.

Debates about the IHRA Definition concentrate on the examples about Israel, which aim to help answer the challenging question about when anti-Zionism crosses the line into antisemitism. Two chapters in this volume address the relationship between anti-Zionism and antisemitism more fully: "Is BDS Antisemitic?" and "Academic Freedom and the Israeli-Palestinian Conflict." Instead of seriously engaging with debates over this issue, far too many misrepresent the Definition by claiming it says that *all* criticism of Israeli policy is antisemitic. By that standard, most Israelis are nonstop antisemites, since they complain about their government all the time. The Definition states clearly that "criticism of Israel similar to that leveled against any other country cannot be regarded as antisemitic." Among other examples of possible antisemitism, it mentions "applying double standards by requiring of [Israel] a behavior not expected or demanded of any other democratic nation." As a principle that should put us on the alert for antisemitism, this seems very reasonable. Yet it upsets people who themselves apply special standards to Israel or who invent Israeli crimes for which there is no evidence and of which no other nation has ever been accused.

It has now been more than fifteen years since 2005 and eight years since 2016. Yet the debate about the IHRA Definition has only intensified. But it is also now possible to document the ways in which the Definition has actually been used. The need for a contemporary definition was triggered by the fact that instances of antisemitism were increasing in Europe and that the nature of antisemitism was changing at the same time. Decades of antagonism toward Israel created a need for updated understanding of the oldest hatred. According to a recent essay by David Hirsh (2021a): "It was the new phenomenon of Israel-focused antisemitism that required the new definition." "Precisely because Israel-related antisemitism is widespread and influential in society," Ionescu argues, "it should play a key role in a definition of antisemitism" (Ionescu 2022, 3). As three of its original authors have testified, moreover, the Definition was understood from the outset to be considerably more than an aid to data collection and bureaucratic record-keeping. Its intended purpose was educational: to educate people worldwide about the nature of contemporary antisemitism in the service of combating it (Baker, Berger, and Whine 2021). Making antisemitic practices visible, the thinking went, would make people better able to reject them.

There have been some demands that both the EUMC and IHRA definitions be restricted to measuring trends in antisemitism and keeping records of them, but the IHRA Definition's transformative effects cannot be halted. Even the authors of a text cannot control the meanings or uses it will acquire over time. As the Definition circulated, new constituencies found uses for it in their areas of interest and responsibility. That is exactly what happened when the IHRA modified the Definition and adopted it. As David Matas and Aurel Braun (2022) remind us, the IHRA website intends the Definition "to fight (not simply monitor)" antisemitism. The limitation to collecting data did not have the character of an eleventh commandment, handed down from Mount Sinai, despite Kenneth Stern's repeated insistence to the contrary.[6] Indeed, even the record-keeping function could not operate without education to increase the knowledge and comprehension of the record-keepers. They have to think about and analyze the examples they encounter.

---

6 See Stern (2020a).

Just the project of categorizing thousands of antisemitic tweets and Facebook posts is now a complex interpretive task. The idea that everyone would maintain lists of antisemitic incidents without ever seeking to do something about them is fanciful at best. If a campus uses the Definition's examples to track local incidents and evaluate the severity of its problem, is it sensible, whatever the results, to conclude that nothing should be done? In *The Conflict Over the Conflict* Stern treats "data collection" in the case of antisemitism as if it were a neutral mathematical calculation and an end in itself, an accumulative list, something an accountant might handle. If it had been obvious what all the varieties of contemporary antisemitism were—how to identify, categorize, classify, and respond to them—we wouldn't have needed the IHRA Definition. Data collection by government ordinarily precedes policy formulation and implementation. The corrosive interpersonal and institutional effect of increasing antisemitic hate speech on social media has made that task still more urgent.

Stern's aim is not only to limit and minimize the valid uses for the IHRA Definition but also to trivialize it. In a November 2022 conference presentation, he repeated his recurrent quip about the Definition's origin: "there needed to be a guide for the bean counters to know what to include and what to exclude" (Stern 2022b). Stern's repetition of the data collection mandate has become a ritual incantation among opponents of the Definition. For example, Derek Penslar (2021) insists that "the IHRA definition was developed for the purpose of data collection, not policy making." That claim is typically underwritten with reference to Stern's insistence that he was the Definition's primary author or "the lead drafter," the phrase used on the jacket flap of his 2020 book *The Conflict over the Conflict*. He clearly contributed to, and, for a time, coordinated the EUMC drafting process, though he played no role in the final revisions of the IHRA Definition. In his book, he gives himself primary responsibility: "I set out to draft a definition and to get leaders in the field on board. Over the next months, I drafted, redrafted, and coordinated with antisemitism scholars and experts around the world" (Stern 2020a, 151). He then lists a number of people who were involved but gives no detail about how the process worked. Three of those Stern mentions as having been involved in the EUMC process dispute his account. Stern, they report, filled "the vitally important but limited role of being the communications hub as various drafts and proposed language were circulated, slowly moving toward a consensus agreement where his role ended" (Baker, Berger, and Whine 2021, 9). According to Rabbi Andrew Baker, Deidre Berger, and Michael Whine, they all participated in the drafting and Whine took responsibility for the final draft. Stern was in fact not present when the final revisions were made. As Whine informed me, those revisions included the addition of the phrase "depending on the context" and various additions to the examples addressing Israel. Matas and Braun (2022) are blunt: "Kenneth Stern is not the principal drafter of the IHRA definition he claims to be."

While I have known Stern for years and commented on a draft of his book at his request, he declined to discuss the matter with me. Stern frequently tries to deflect attention from specific questions about his role, saying that how the Definition is used is the important issue. Yet his asserted status gives him tremendous authority in the debate. People who celebrate his status typically do so because they agree with his anti-Definition stance. I assume he genuinely believes what he says, as do the three dissenters, though it is irresponsible to dismiss the account of the three other drafting participants. There is little chance the matter will be resolved. One reasonable way to proceed is to describe Stern as "*one* of the IHRA Definition's original drafters."

The data collection goal continues, but with the determination to use the information gathered to combat antisemitism. Identifying and categorizing instances of antisemitism has in fact become more critical, not only because of the rise in the number of antisemitic incidents throughout the West but also because of the emergence of online antisemitism as a major phenomenon. "Indeed, social media are by far the most important space for the spread of antisemitism today" (Andermann and Zizek 2022, 153). Furthermore, "It can be said that every manifestation of Jewishness on social media is a potential target for people who spread antisemitism" (Czymmek 2022, 187).

The IHRA Working Definition is proving the model of choice for recognizing, categorizing, making the phenomenon of online antisemitism intelligible, and empowering individuals and groups to combat it. Günther Jikeli and his collaborators have found that the Definition does a good job of making it possible to classify most antisemitic statements on social media, though additional work is necessary: "For example, the definition mentions 'classic stereotypes' and 'stereotypical allegations about Jews as such,' without specifying what they are" (Jikeli, Cavar et al. 2022, 195). They consult the scholarly literature to create an appropriate list. Weimann and Masri (2022) use the IHRA Definition as their classification system for antisemitic posts on TikTok. Sample posts from their work are quoted in Chapter Two. Jakob Guhl (2022) uses the Definition's eleven examples to organize his analysis of public Facebook pages supporting the UK Labour Party in 2015–2019. In *Phishing for Nazis*, Lev Topor (2023) uses the examples to investigate antisemitism on the dark web.

Jikeli and his team have an ambitious interdisciplinary project to create an annotated data set of antisemitic tweets that can be used to teach artificial intelligence (AI) software to determine the prevalence and character of antisemitism in large data sets like that of Twitter. Using a large database of 2019 and 2020 tweets, they extracted a working corpus based on keyword searches. Analysts trained in the history of antisemitism then decided whether each tweet qualified as antisemitic in terms of the Definition's eleven examples. The analysts could see the entire thread, including replies, likes, and comments. Disagreements were resolved through discussion or the tweets were discarded.[7] Although multiple tweets from particular senders were accessible, the concern throughout was to discount intent or motivation and instead focus on the meaning and impact of the tweet itself. The resulting dataset consists of 929 English-language tweets identified as antisemitic and over 5,000 identified as not antisemitic. Both are necessary for AI instruction, as many tweets with key words like "Jew" or "Israel" are not antisemitic, and many, including some with the key word "kike," are written to oppose antisemitism. On the other hand, "when using the term 'Likes,' the disseminators of antisemitic messages share an open hatred of Jews and spread conspiracy theories" (Jikeli, Axelrod et al. 2022). The Indiana group is also building comparable data sets for tweets in German.

Jikeli's team has continued to analyze new tweets since building the data set, assigning each tweet to one of the eleven examples with additional discussion as necessary. In the case of antisemitic tweets with the word "Jew,"

> "Making mendacious, dehumanizing, demonizing, or stereotyp-
> ical allegations about Jews as such or the power of Jews as a col-
> lective—such as especially, but not exclusively, the myth about a
> world Jewish conspiracy or of Jews controlling the media, econ-
> omy government or other social institutions" is the paragraph
> of the working definition section that both annotators assigned
> to about 62% of the antisemitic tweets in which both annota-
> tors agreed on the relevant Working Definition paragraph. The
> second most common annotation by both annotators (15%) for
> antisemitic tweets with the keyword "Jews" was the paragraph
> "Denying the Jewish people their right to self-determination,
> e.g., by claiming that the existence of a state of Israel is a racist
> endeavor." (Jikeli, Axelrod et al. 2022)

The IHRA features the Jikeli team project on its website (IHRA 2023), noting that "the dataset uses an annotation portal to classify tweets in their natural context and meaning. It also considers threads, images, videos, text, Twitter IDs, links, and other accompanying information to holistically understand

---

7   For a discussion of sample tweets and the issues involved, see Jikeli, Cavar, and Miehling (2019).

the message being conveyed," among the ways it honors the Definition's call for contextualization.

These are among a growing number of faculty research projects grounded in the IHRA Definition. Together they are developing a common language for investigation of the massive phenomenon of online antisemitism. The use of the Definition's examples makes it possible to compare results across different platforms carried out in a variety of countries. Contrary to what Definition opponents would like to believe, categorizing online messages through the Definition's examples is neither automatic nor the final product of their research. It is the step that precedes analysis. Guhl (2022) contextualizes the posts analyzed within the history of party leader Jeremy Corbyn's remarks about Jews. He then provides a separate analysis of each of the major groups of online comments he found—conspiracy myths, comparing Israeli policy to that of the Nazis, denying the Jewish people their right to self-determination, and holding Jews collectively responsible for Israel's actions.

Stern's overall hostility to the IHRA Definition is now complicated by his September 2022 *Times of Israel* column supporting the right of officially recognized and funded student groups to bar Zionists from membership. The issue arose as a debate about whether progressive student groups, like one supporting sexual assault survivors, could prohibit Zionists supporting the group's cause from joining. Stern believes that their constitutional right to freedom of association in the United States gives them this right. Presumably they could add that prohibition when they use university stationary. Many Jewish students see Zionism as meaning the right to a Jewish homeland, not a form of right-wing politics. Support for Israel is fundamental to their identity as Jews. I am among those who see Stern's position as having antisemitic, not just anti-Zionist, effects, though that is not his intent.

No one could have predicted in 2016 how widely the IHRA Definition would be adopted or the speed with which it acquired symbolic and canonical status. More than thirty countries and hundreds of local authorities and organizations have adopted it. Sociologist Keith Kahn-Harris (2021a) of Birkbeck College writes that it "has taken on such totemic significance" that "its adoption or non-adoption has become an existential question for institutions and individuals." As Sina Arnold puts it, "The litmus test, 'What is your take on the IHRA definition?,' has become a confessional rather than an analytical question" (2022, 2). In January 2021, the European Commission and the IHRA jointly published a *Handbook for the Practical Use of the IHRA Working Definition of Antisemitism*, which includes a substantial list of good practices and examples of how the Definition is being employed. It recommends the Definition's continued use as a guiding reference at educational institutions, including in curricula, for preventive and reactive purposes, in evaluating educational materials, and as a basis for support of academic research. It suggests it be used for training police, state attorneys, and judges and in manuals on addressing antisemitic hate crimes. Among some on the left, the fact that a document is used by the police makes it suspect or automatically worthy of condemnation. But these officials otherwise often lack any detailed knowledge about antisemitism—knowledge they require in their jobs. The Definition can also help agencies avoid unintentionally funding antisemitic groups and projects. It is also useful, the *Handbook* suggests, in providing "support services for victims of antisemitism, including legal and psychological counseling or intervening when expertise is needed" (European Commission 2021, 33). The Definition is no longer just a text to be debated in the abstract; it has a growing track record of applications.

Specific examples from the *Handbook* indicate the variety of these practical applications. European football clubs have offered it "as a specific reference point for employees, stewards and fans on what antisemitism is" (34). The Church of England's "interfaith team and national advisors use the Definition as the benchmark in their work and ministry" (35). UNESCO incorporates the Definition in a set of four framework curricula for teacher trainers (29). The American Jewish Committee's guide to the Working Definition of Antisemitism adds its own list of applications, noting that "the United Kingdom Judicial College included the Working Definition in its 2018 guidance to judges," that "the NGO CEJI–A Jewish Contribution to an Inclusive Europe holds an annual training for EU officials on antisemitism using the Working Definition," and that "the Mauthausen Memorial in Austria (at the site of the former concentration camp) uses the Working Definition in its police training" (AJC 2020, 4). I have not yet seen opponents of the Definition systematically address the range of verifiable applications already in place, its critics apparently preferring hypothetical concerns or unsubstantiated anecdotes.

2. Thinking with the help of the IHRA Definition's examples

Five of the Definition's eleven examples are listed below in order of what I estimate to be their relative frequency in faculty anti-Zionist polemics, starting with the most frequent. These examples can help readers identify the core antisemitic arguments in books and essays. Those readers can then determine whether or not a document's collateral arguments amplify or qualify the core claims.

Identifying those arguments also highlights which ones create reinforcing ideological networks among multiple writers. The first example (using double standards) is for all intents and purposes a universal feature of contemporary anti-Zionism. The second example (denying the right to self-determination) is widespread in BDS-allied literature, as are claims that the State of Israel is a racist endeavor. The claim of fundamental racism should be distinguished from arguments that particular Israeli policies are racist, a critique that can be leveled against policies of many nation states. The antisemitic claim is that the Jewish state is irredeemably racist in its essence. Some faculty, like Judith Butler, argue against a Jewish right to self-determination in a state of their own on the grounds that the age of the nation state is coming to an end. Little in actual history confirms that contention. Moreover, the antisemitic version of the conviction typically asserts that, while the nation state overall is dying, Israel needs to go first. The third and fourth examples, including comparisons between Israel and Nazi Germany, are increasingly common among faculty, but not universal.

The five examples from the IHRA Definition that I am highlighting read as follows:

- Applying double standards by requiring of Israel a behavior not expected or demanded of any other democratic nation.
- Denying the Jewish people their right to self-determination, e.g. by claiming that the existence of a State of Israel is a racist endeavor.
- Making mendacious, dehumanizing, demonizing, or stereotypical allegations about Jews as such or the power of Jews as collective—such as, especially but not exclusively, the myth about a world Jewish conspiracy or of Jews controlling the media, economy, government or other societal institutions.
- Drawing comparisons of contemporary Israeli policy to that of the Nazis.
- Accusing the Jews as a people, or Israel as a state, of inventing or exaggerating the Holocaust.

Some qualifications are necessary before calling these five examples hallmarks of faculty anti-Zionism that cross the line into antisemitism. The estimates of relative frequency could well be different were I to try to take full account of posts on social media, where people feel more freedom to indulge in examples three, four, and five. The first and second examples may be accompanied by other beliefs that identify a move into antisemitism, such as that there are no meaningful distinctions to be drawn between a given Israeli government and the Israeli people as a whole, that Israel is a demonic or colonialist political entity about which nothing positive can be said, or that normal relationships with any Israeli institutions or organizations that fail to condemn the occupation are morally unacceptable. In applying the example of "inventing or exaggerating the Holocaust" to faculty teaching and research, it is important to point out that, although faculty anti-Zionists frequently say Israel exaggerates the impact and contemporary relevance of the Holocaust, they rarely engage in the kind of explicit Holocaust denial that claims the Shoah was "invented" or that far fewer than six million Jews were killed.

Other IHRA Definition examples not among those listed above can operate by allusion or implication in the world of Western university faculty advocacy, such as "Using the symbols and images associated with classic antisemitism (e.g. claims of Jews killing Jesus or blood libel) to characterize Israel or Israelis." Such images are often reinvented without admitting (or perhaps even recognizing) the connection with classic antisemitic tropes. At other times, the echoes are obvious, as when faculty members or religious leaders like the West Bank Anglican prelate Naim Ateek invoke the claim that Palestinians are, in effect, being crucified by Israel throughout the West Bank: "It seems to many of us that Jesus is on the cross again with thousands of crucified Palestinians around him." Ateek has envisioned "hundreds of thousands of crosses throughout the land, Palestinian men, women, and children being crucified. Palestine has become one huge Golgotha. The Israeli government crucifixion system is operating daily" (Nelson and Gizzi 2021). There are other IHRA Definition examples one would not expect to find in the West outside hate groups, like "Calling for, aiding, or justifying the killing or harming of Jews in the name of a radical ideology or an extremist view of religion." Yet faculty like Judith Butler who discount Hamas's advocacy of killing Jews are acquiescing in the group's radical hostility. In a 2006 Q&A at a UC Berkeley teach-in, Butler notoriously remarked that "understanding Hamas, Hezbollah as social movements that are progressive, that are on the Left, that are part of a global Left, is extremely important."[8]

Faculty can advocate for the dissolution of the Jewish state while convincing themselves, mistakenly, that such a position has no antisemitic consequences. That is not to say that anti-Zionism is always driven by animus toward Jews, even though it can lead there. The IHRA Definition's examples are powerful warning signs that we may be dealing with antisemitism in a given case, but, as David Hirsh (2021c) argues, they are not an automatic, machine-like

---

8   See "Judith Butler: A Philosopher Promotes a One-State Fantasy," in Nelson (2019, 68–116).

classification system. As Eve Garrard (2021) points out, the Definition "is peppered with conditional verbs." Nor are the Definition's eleven examples intended to be a blueprint for speech codes or legal action. Yet they enable us to sort through and recognize specific forms of antisemitism in a world in which antisemitism steadily mutates and metastasizes. The examples describe prevalent manifestations of demonstrable antisemitism. They are indispensable if you want to make sense of the contemporary world.

At the same time, the IHRA Definition's examples are necessarily written at a level of generality designed to ensure they remain applicable for the foreseeable future. This means that people need to be prepared to recognize how evolving claims and accusations fit into the Definition's various categories. Michael Saenger and I have created our own list of more specific, more narrowly defined, antisemitic statements about Israel to supplement the IHRA Definition examples, perhaps increasing the evidence that there are indeed forms of anti-Zionism that constitute antisemitism:

- Promoting the false notion that Jews are not originally from the land that is now Israel.
- Representing Zionism as a fundamentally racist political project at its origin and throughout its history, ignoring its establishment as a movement for national liberation and self-determination.
- Claiming that Israel is *the premier modern instance* of settler-colonialism, while ignoring far more significant historical examples, like the settlement of the Americas, whose consequences persist today.
- Representing violence associated with the creation of Israel as unilateral and disproportionately hateful compared to other wars for independence (e.g. Greece, the United States, Canada, India, the Balkans, etc.).
- Falsifying Israeli history by deleting events such as the invasion of Israel mounted by five Arab states in 1948 or Jordan's sovereignty over the West Bank and Egypt's sovereignty over Gaza prior to the Six-Day War.
- Classifying all the population transfers of the period before, during, and immediately after Israel's War of Independence as "ethnic cleansing," while not designating as such the transfer of millions of Europeans during and after World War II.
- Treating the creation of the new nation of Israel or its establishment of its borders as illegitimate while normalizing the establishment of many new other national borders (for example between India and Pakistan) at the same historical moment.

- Pretending that Israelis have no historical warrant for identifying Jerusalem as their capital.
- Portraying Israel as particularly, even uniquely, responsible for political forces and problems that are demonstrably global, among them ultra-nationalism and religious nationalism.
- Characterizing worldwide ethnic, environmental, and economic issues as markedly dramatic, severe, and emotionally destructive in Israel.
- Inventing demonstrably false claims or conspiracy theories about Israeli actions.
- Blaming Israel exclusively for conflicts in Gaza, while discounting Hamas's role in initiating them with rocket barrages.
- Misrepresenting all progressive features of Israeli society, including its positive LGBTQ+ culture, as deceptive efforts to distract from or cover up Israeli crimes.
- Pretending that religious freedom does not exist in Israel.
- Substantially misrepresenting the legal system within Israel's pre-1967 borders.
- Insisting that Israel within its pre-1967 borders is an apartheid and undemocratic state.
- Placing sole responsibility for the failure of peace negotiations on Israel despite repeated Palestinian rejection of offers that were on the table.
- Characterizing conventional military uniforms, equipment, and training as particularly devious, cruel, menacing, or inhuman when the military is Israeli.
- Discriminating against the Hebrew language and Hebrew publishing by boycotting them, or disrupting theatrical and cultural performances in Hebrew.
- Invoking Israel's conduct to justify violence against Jews in Israel or worldwide.
- Blaming all Israelis for the policies of their government.
- Wildly exaggerating Israel's international political influence.
- Denying that Israeli Arabs—Arab-Palestinian citizens of Israel proper—possess basic human and political rights.
- Supporting the UN's selective investigation of and enforcement actions against Israel.
- Claiming that Israeli government actions or policies are equivalent to or worse than those of Nazi Germany.
- Arguing that Israeli laws are equal to or worse than those in apartheid South Africa.

- Asserting that Israel invokes the Holocaust to justify lethal violence against Palestinians.
- Promulgating the notion that Israelis enjoy killing Palestinian children.
- Claiming that Israel deprives Palestinian children of nourishment to stunt their growth.
- Claiming that Israel's occupation of the West Bank is genocidal or the world's single greatest crime against humanity.
- Maintaining that Israel's problems cannot be solved without the elimination of the Jewish state.
- Inventing malicious and even absurd accusations against Israel, such as the claim that Israel is responsible for or profiting from the COVID pandemic or that recipes for "Israeli hummus," which is part of traditional Oriental Jewish cuisine, are actually examples of cultural appropriation that prepare the ground for genocide.

The five IHRA Definition examples quoted earlier represent established, virtually consensual views in such disciplines or sub-disciplines as American, Middle East, ethnic, and women's studies; they represent apparent majority opinion in anthropology;[9] and minority but significant opinion in literary studies and history. If you attend an annual Middle East Studies Association (MESA) meeting, as I have, you will encounter overwhelming anti-Zionism among presenters and audience members alike.[10] In a number of smaller disciplines—among them African-American studies, Asian studies, and Native American studies—anti-Zionism is hugely influential. One obvious marker of anti-Zionism is when a disciplinary group calls for a boycott of Israeli universities.[11] In addition to the disciplines just named, some individual departments in other disciplines, including Jewish studies and political science, are dominated by anti-Zionists. The Jewish studies programs at UCLA and the University of Illinois at Urbana-Champaign are among those so dominated, as is the political science department at Ben-Gurion University of the Negev.

---

9 In the spring of 2016, the American Anthropological Association voted to defeat a resolution to boycott Israeli universities by a narrow margin of 2,423 to 2,384, with 51 percent of the members voting. In July 2023, the results of another boycott resolution were announced. This time, only 37 percent of the members voted, with 2,016 voting to boycott Israeli universities and 835 voting against (Jaschik 2023).

10 The US Commission on Civil Rights (2006) reported that "many university departments of Middle East studies provide one-sided, highly polemical academic presentations and some may repress legitimate debate concerning Israel." See also Kramer (2001).

11 For an analysis of various boycott resolutions, see Nelson and Brahm (2015).

3. Unwarranted fears, myths, and falsehoods about IHRA Definition-inspired "silencing"

If opponents bothered to engage with actual Definition-inspired practices, they might recognize that the brief opening definition, much criticized as being vague and unusable, is not actually being much used. In fact, it is not even meant to be used. It provides a general cultural context for what follows, while reminding us that the eleven examples cannot actually cover all varieties of antisemitism. It is the eleven examples of antisemitism that are being taught and applied—and with the discretion and attention to context that the Definition explicitly calls for. It is expected that the examples will help us recognize antisemitic statements, and we can test what we encounter against them. We are not encouraged to test events against the opening definition.

The protests against the Definition proceed in parallel with its widening adoption, though the two tracks rarely meet. Although there is a serious debate about the Definition, some of the clamor surrounding it belongs primarily to the general cultural and political project of demonizing and discrediting Zionism. That includes those who cite Stern not to oppose quasi-legal uses of the IHRA Definition but to condemn it entirely. In *The Conflict over the Conflict*, he reprints our joint op-ed warning against misuse of the Definition (Stern 2020a, 158–160), then goes on to list the ways it can help campus comprehension: "It is entirely proper for university administrators, scholars and students to reference the 'working definition' in identifying definite or possible instances of antisemitism on campus" (159). But his main emphasis otherwise is on the dangers the Definition presents.

Some anti-Zionist complaints regarding the Definition draw on a larger political phenomenon—false claims of victimhood from "silenced" members of both the political left and right. The most absurd versions of this trend bear no relation to the Israeli-Palestinian conflict; they come from politicians or academic groups with outsized megaphones that bellow "We will not be silenced!" whenever they face criticism. They equate being criticized with being silenced. It is a convenient way of avoiding serious debate. As an official BDS statement declares hyperbolically, "an ominous climate of bullying and repression has resulted from the proliferation of the so-called IHRA Working Definition of Antisemitism that conflates legitimate opposition to Israel's regime of apartheid, colonialism and illegal occupation with antisemitism."[12] Jonathan

---

12 "We Will Not Be Silenced," Palestinian BDS National Committee, December 2, 2020, https://bdsmovement.net/news/we-will-not-be-silenced.

Shamir (2020) adds a characteristic element of conspiracism: "A network of government-funded NGOs are pushing the definition in an effort to redefine antisemitism and quash Palestinian dissent."

Stern has repeatedly warned of a potential widespread chilling effect resulting from the adoption of the Definition, but criticism of Israeli policy and demonization of the Jewish state continue unabated. His fear that there will be a chilling effect on anti-Zionist speech on North American, British, and European campuses has not been borne out by reality, though that has not dissuaded him from repeating it. The fear has no real-world merit. In a December 2020 piece in *The Times of Israel*, he expands this claim: "For the past decade, Jewish groups have used the definition as a weapon to say anti-Zionist expressions are *inherently* anti-Semitic and must be suppressed" (Stern 2020b). Demands like this are not part of the Definition, and there is no evidence it can or will be used successfully in such a campaign. Although some Jewish groups have called for the suppression of certain forms of anti-Zionist speech that they consider antisemitic, they have not prevailed. Condemnation is not suppression.

Similarly, NGOs of many stripes routinely call on universities to censure or fire faculty for remarks of all kinds, but universities routinely dismiss those demands, except for part-time or contingent faculty, who are much more vulnerable. Rebecca Ruth Gould, a professor of Islamic studies at the University of Birmingham, claims that university administrators or legal counsel generally grant the Definition a form of quasi-legal status and use it to suppress expression that matches the eleven examples, an argument that others have echoed. A given university administrator or legal counsel could misinterpret the Definition, ignoring the fact, as Gould acknowledges, that it is "suffused with tentative language and caveats" (2022, 17), and try to limit expression in line with one of the eleven examples. Gould worries such actions could become standard practice, but I consider that highly unlikely. In the months following the British government's adoption of the Definition, a few higher education administrators overreacted and modified or cancelled events inappropriately, but respect for academic freedom has since prevailed.

Like a number of other IHRA Definition critics, Gould cites two early and misguided decisions to modify or cancel events that were considered to violate the Definition's guidelines. At the University of Manchester's 2017 Israeli Apartheid Week, an administrator accepted the argument that a presentation entitled "You're doing to the Palestinians what the Nazis did to me" would cause harm to Jewish students and retitled it "A Holocaust survivor's story and the Balfour declaration" (Gayle 2017). That was a violation of academic freedom. The original title should have been allowed, and instead a public discussion on why such analogies are painful and historically unwarranted should have been scheduled. Earlier in 2017, a University of Central Lancashire administrator cancelled an Israeli Apartheid Week panel both because it breached IHRA Definition guidelines and because it lacked the political balance required by British regulations, as detailed in my opening chapter (Doherty 2017). IHRA Definition guidelines did not mandate the panel's cancellation. The British requirement that events be politically balanced was relevant, though, as I have previously argued, I consider this to be an unfortunate rule.

In a search for cases of "silencing" to cite, other critics of the Definition have misrepresented or invented disciplinary actions taken against faculty members who have violated professional standards in the service of their anti-Zionism. Thus Jasmine Zine, a journalist and sociology professor at Wilfrid Laurier University, falsely claims that University of Michigan American studies professor John Cheney-Lippold was punished for criticizing Israel, when in fact he was punished for refusing to write a letter of recommendation for a student applying to study at Tel Aviv University, a student he regarded as well qualified (Zine 2020). She also tells us that universities have "cancelled events" that would have criticized Israel. As proof, she links only to an article about the scheduled November 2018 national conference of Students for Justice in Palestine, which did indeed meet with complaints beforehand. But the conference was held at UCLA as planned, two years before Zine published her piece, thus allowing her plenty of time to have found out what actually happened. As if these inaccurate examples were not enough to discredit a source, she adds that anti-Zionist students have been "expelled" from universities, which is certainly an extremely serious accusation. Her evidence is a link to a story reporting that Neal Sher, a former Justice Department official responsible from 1983 to 1994 for hunting former Nazis, told a reporter in 2018 that UC Berkeley students who equated the Pittsburgh synagogue murders with Israeli action in Gaza should be expelled, an intemperate statement that itself merits condemnation. But Sher was a private citizen whose government responsibilities had ended more than thirty years earlier. Indeed, he had been disbarred in the interim. Unsurprisingly, the students were not in fact expelled. Zine appears to have copied these citations, unacknowledged, from an article by Acadia University's Jeffrey Sachs.

Zine's irresponsible reproduction of these falsehoods was not the last step in their circulation. Two faculty members with long histories of anti-Zionism, Neve Gordon, a political scientist at Queen Mary University, and Mark LeVine, a historian from the University of California at Irvine, then cite Zine in an *Inside Higher Education* essay as evidence of Zionist political aggression. They were either too lazy or overwhelmed by confirmation bias to check her sources.

Distressed by the widening adoption of the Definition, Gordon and LeVine warn absurdly that Albert Einstein and Hannah Arendt could be judged antisemites by its criteria. They also wildly extend the Definition's silencing effects to claim it "is being wielded as a weapon to suppress a variety of progressive causes": "it allows conservative and even moderate political forces to discipline, silence and marginalize progressive voices against racism, poverty, the climate crisis, war and predatory capitalism" (Gordon and LeVine 2021). The editorial team at *Inside Higher Education* should have demanded evidence in support of these claims before publishing the essay. They might even have gone the extra mile and followed the links they supplied. I have published in *Inside Higher Education* many times; they always ask me to provide evidence if I haven't done so, and I appreciate their editorial care. I look forward to the evidence that the IHRA Definition is suppressing climate science.

Of course even a typically articulate NGO can get confused when talking about Israel. For a number of years, the Foundation for Individual Rights in Education (FIRE) has been a leader in defending academic freedom. When I was president of the American Association of University Professors (AAUP) from 2006 to 2012, I reversed an existing AAUP staff policy against collaborating with FIRE, and we worked closely together on several occasions. When my campus administration attempted to impose rules in violation of the First Amendment, FIRE's lawyers were essential in getting it to back down. But FIRE is among the groups condemning the IHRA Definition, guided, one suspects, by the prevailing left-wing bias against Israel.

FIRE's repeated criticism of the IHRA Definition falls dramatically short of its usual standards, though it does follow a pattern regarding Israel. One of the Definition's examples of antisemitism is "applying double standards by requiring of it [Israel] a behavior not expected or demanded of any other democratic nation." In response, FIRE tells us, "There is not—and there should not be—a law requiring those people to spend their time criticizing other regimes equally or else risk violating anti-discrimination laws" (Coward 2021). Who would disagree? The IHRA Definition does not make any such recommendation. It simply alerts us to a pattern of people and groups demanding that Israel honor principles and adopt practices that pretty much no one asks of other democratic countries. As Steven Lubet (2022c) writes, "That should be unobjectionable. A double standard is the essence of discrimination." It is absurd to suppose a "law" requiring anyone to criticize multiple regimes when they criticize one could pass muster in any democratic country. FIRE adds that "the Constitution affords people the freedom to be hypocritical in their analysis of other countries' policies" (Coward 2021). True again. But the First Amendment to the

US Constitution also permits us to recognize hypocrisy and condemn it. That's part of what the Definition helps us do. It does not propose a law against hypocrisy. What other than a predisposition against Israel could lead FIRE's lawyers to advance this ludicrous argument?

Other IHRA Definition critics have reformulated FIRE's objection to make it more plausible. Thus, Deckers and Coulter (2022) are concerned that the Definition suggests "it would not be fair to criticize the Israeli government for [human rights violations] unless one makes similar efforts to criticize other governments that also engage in human rights violations." But that is not the point. The point is that international principles for human rights and the pattern of accusations concerning human rights violations should govern complaints against Israeli policy. Deckers and Coulter press their concern further, suggesting that the Definition proposes that one will be "suspect of being motivated by antisemitism" unless "one speaks out against all injustices equally." That is indeed an absurdity, though not one inherent in the Definition, but rather one they have invented. Rights violations need to be specified, differentiated, and addressed by political critique and action. Thus, for example, the destructive Israeli policy of house demolitions denies a right and should be condemned. Palestinian farmers need protection from settler violence that also constitutes a human rights violation.

Similarly, some assert that the Definition's warning that "claiming that the existence of a State of Israel is a racist endeavor" can be considered antisemitic discredits the claim that a given policy is racist. But the warning is against assertions that Israel was founded as and remains a fundamentally racist enterprise, one presumably impossible to reform. The Definition does not block accusations that a particular Israeli policy is racist. Moreover, a presentation on campus could make the broader claim, though people would be free to dispute it. Or students and faculty could debate the claim that the State of Israel is a racist endeavor. What the Definition does is help empower those who want to argue that such a claim is antisemitic. It does not prohibit the resulting debate.

One universal complaint against the Definition, put forward in numerous articles excerpted by Lara Friedman, is that it treats all criticism of Israel as antisemitic and aims to suppress it. This complaint has been endlessly debunked, often by citing this passage from the Definition itself: "criticism of Israel similar to that leveled against any other country cannot be regarded as antisemitic." The Definition stipulates explicitly that criticizing Israeli government policy, something Israelis themselves do nonstop, does not constitute antisemitism. I have criticized Israeli policy on many fronts, and no one has declared me an antisemite. As Bernard Harrison of the University of Sussex and Lesley Klaff of Sheffield Hallam University write, "The 'examples' section of the Definition in no way restricts critical political debate concerning Israel; it merely restricts, by characterizing them correctly as antisemitic, certain lines of mendacious defamation, primarily of Israel, and secondarily of its supporters, Jewish and non-Jewish" (Harrison and Klaff 2021, 31). The Definition helps individuals, universities, NGOs, and governments take positions opposing contemporary examples of antisemitism, while preserving their right to make those same antisemitic claims. While one may hope that the Definition might discourage some hate speech, there is little reason to hope it can have a major impact on Israel's opponents. People can still say "Israel is the new Nazi Germany," a claim addressed below and by an IHRA Definition example. No one will be "silenced."

Joshua Shanes from the College of Charleston and Dov Waxman of UCLA take a different approach, turning the Definition's conditional wording, a feature others consider a strength, into a weakness, making its examples inadvertent weapons:

> This weaponization of the IHRA definition of anti-Semitism has been facilitated by its ambiguity. Although it does not simply equate anti-Zionism with anti-Semitism, or label all criticism of Israel to be anti-Semitic—as some opponents of the definition assert—its vague, conditional wording is open to misinterpretations and misuse. Its conditional phrasing—that criticism "could, taking into account the overall context" cross the line to anti-Semitism—is too often forgotten, or even purposefully ignored. Some of its examples relating to Israel are particularly prone to such problems. (Shanes and Waxman 2021)

As they acknowledge, some will inevitably misapply the examples in this or any other definition of antisemitism (or any other definition of a controversial concept). They find the Jerusalem Declaration, which I discuss below, an improvement. I do not. Either way, they are surely wrong in thinking that the Jerusalem Declaration, which also enumerates categories of antisemitic criticism of Israel, will be less susceptible to misapplication. The IHRA Definition has been and will continue to be misused, but far-right politicians such as former Trump administration official Secretary of State Mike Pompeo and former Trump presidential adviser Jared Kushner hardly require assistance from the Definition to hurl malicious accusations of antisemitism at their real or imagined opponents. Abuses of the Definition nonetheless need to be called out and condemned so as to preserve the document's core value.

4. Legislative use of the IHRA Definition

There is good reason to oppose legislative efforts to incorporate the IHRA Definition's examples into laws accompanied by punishments for individuals who transgress them. In the United States, the First Amendment to the US Constitution prohibits state punishment for antisemitic speech that does not urge violence. Within the academy worldwide, the principle of academic freedom creates boundaries that sanctions can easily cross. Moreover, accounting for the impact of context on potentially antisemitic statements, as the Definition requires, can be quite complicated. It is not merely difficult to imagine either public or university officials having the capacity to do so competently or honorably; it is inconceivable. I would not trust university officials to administer a punitive system based on the IHRA Definition. Unfortunately, the warnings some groups have issued against that danger have regularly incorporated misrepresentation of the Definition itself, along with misinformation about the topics it addresses. The Definition's opponents use the dangers of police state-empowered IHRA laws to indict all uses of the Definition, presumably save the record-keeping function. That slippage is not accidental; it is the whole point of the warning against legalization.

Such slippage is a key weapon of academic opponents of adopting the IHRA Definition. Nonetheless, limited adoption by colleges and universities for educational purposes is a serious benefit that needs to be promoted. Students, staff, and faculty with little understanding of antisemitism need education if they are to resist its proliferation. They need the Definition's examples if they are to comment on each other's behavior. They need guidance if they wish to understand and constrain their own impulses. A campus needs the Definition's examples if it is to categorize and keep track of instances of antisemitism and evaluate the local climate. All that can be accomplished without incorporating the Definition into speech codes or disciplinary regulations. But the problem of contemporary antisemitism cannot be successfully addressed without the imprimatur of formally adopting the Definition. We need the administrative and community prioritization that adoption can bring, along with the intelligibility the examples provide.

To give one telling instance of destructive slippage, one may turn to the AAUP's March 2022 statement of opposition to the Definition. For a hundred years, the AAUP has protected its political neutrality by not taking positions on controversial topics with no bearing on academic freedom. Academics on both sides of current political debates could thus see the organization as a defender of the core principles that define and underpin the academy, not as an advocate for a position that would otherwise divide its membership and weaken its core commitments. But the organization has recently compromised the tradition that has served it well for so many decades. Worse still, the very AAUP committee that has guarded and sustained that tradition—Committee A on Academic Freedom and Tenure—has taken sides on a hotly contested topic it should have scrupulously avoided: the definition of antisemitism. Committee A has decided to oppose the widely adopted IHRA Definition of antisemitism and how antisemitism bears on the Israeli-Palestinian conflict. The national AAUP is now officially behind the political assault on the Definition.

Given the anti-Zionist AAUP actions described in the first two chapters of this book, it is not surprising that the organization made this decision. But it is troubling nonetheless. Following the pattern just detailed, Committee A's March 2022 statement "Legislative Threats to Academic Freedom: Redefinitions of Antisemitism and Racism" frames its critique as an objection to legislative efforts to restrict how antisemitism and critical race theory are taught in universities, citing Florida legislation as a key example.[13] The project of protecting the university curriculum from legislative interference is not only laudable: it is also entirely in keeping with AAUP tradition. But Committee A's decision to link the very different topics of antisemitism and critical race theory is misguided and serves an ideological goal the Committee should not have embraced. It amounts to an indirect way of supporting the offensive claim that Zionism is a form of racism.

The Committee falsely claims that the IHRA Definition "equates criticism of the policies of the state of Israel with antisemitism," whereas the Definition, once again, specifies that criticism of Israeli policies comparable to those levied against other democratic nations are not antisemitic. The Definition also stipulates that demands that the Jewish state be eliminated can qualify as antisemitic, but such demands address Israel's right to exist, not its government policies. Committee A adds that the Definition "privileges the political interests of the state of Israel and suppresses discussion and activism on behalf of Palestinian rights," a claim that is untrue. There are many human rights abuses throughout the world that are available for comparison and potential application to Israel and other Middle East nations that are fully compatible with the Definition's principle. The debate about whether those comparisons are valid is not inhibited by the Definition's examples.

Florida's relevant 2019 legislation does draw on the IHRA Definition, but the AAUP goes beyond criticizing the legislation to attack the Definition itself as

13 See AAUP (2022).

"overly broad" and "discriminatory." The slippage here is more than ill advised: it is also deceptive. The Definition has been adopted by over 1,000 entities worldwide, including many universities. The AAUP pretends that it is only objecting to the legislative project and that it does not explicitly oppose university adoption of the Definition. But by opposing the Definition's supposed impact on human rights and by falsely implying it restricts academic freedom the AAUP has made its opposition clear. Moreover, the AAUP gratuitously expresses support for the Jerusalem Declaration on Antisemitism and for the BDS movement. As Steven Lubet (2022c) writes, especially

> troubling is the AAUP committee's gratuitous assertion that antisemitism should not be covered as a "special form of discrimination" in civil rights legislation but addressed only "as religious or race discrimination." This claim betrays either stunning ignorance or callous disregard for the uniquely protean history of antisemitism, a conspiracy-based ideology that shape-shifts among religious, racial, ethnic, national, cultural, genetic and other hatreds, whichever is most destructive at any particular time.

It is clear that the AAUP had no business seeking to define antisemitism. Hostility to Zionism did not make Committee A members experts in antisemitism. The AAUP's unfortunate action does, however, help us see how opposition to the Definition can embed a series of other political commitments.

5. Debates about the "quasi-legal" status of the IHRA Definition

Rebecca Ruth Gould, author of *Erasing Palestine: Free Speech and Palestinian Freedom* (2023), has published two long essays opposing the IHRA Definition.[14] Taken together, her essays and those by Peter Ullrich are among the most detailed critiques the Definition has received. The second of her essays, "Legal Form and Legal Legitimacy," adds another issue to attacks on the content of the Definition—the potential danger that it acquires quasi-legal status when it is adopted in an advisory capacity. Certainly, it has practical quasi-legal force if

---

14 Gould (2013) supports a cultural and academic boycott of Israel, but not a complete anti-normalization campaign that would prohibit all productive contact between individuals.

universities incorporate it into disciplinary regulations, turning it into a list of indictable offenses, or formalize it as a speech code. I oppose both; indeed, the Definition itself rejects such misuses, first by declaring itself not legally binding. In any case, there is no trend in that direction. Indeed, the adoption language I propose in this book's introduction is designed to bar such misuse.

Disciplinary procedures should embody the standard set in the 1994 investigative guidance of the US Department of Education's Office for Civil Rights (1994) regarding racial incidents and harassment: that an action is "sufficiently severe, pervasive, or persistent so as to interfere with or limit the ability of an individual to participate in or benefit from the services, activities, or privileges provided by a recipient." That standard is useful even in countries where it has no legal status. It is a long way from the Definition's concise list of examples to a conclusion that actions ignore this standard.

There is also considerable danger in supplementing the Definition by trying to assess the intent or motivation behind potentially antisemitic statements. The examples focus on verbal actions, not the motivations behind them. They do not tell us why people do what they do (Goldfeder 2021, 135). An analysis of intent or motivation can be either incriminating or exculpatory, but campus committees are not well qualified to adjudicate either.

"Quasi-legal norms," Gould writes, "compromise the rule of law when they rely on unauthorized deployment of the law's coercive force" (2022, 156). Fair enough. "By mimicking normative dimensions of the law," she adds, "quasi-laws ... empower special interest groups to act as proxies for the state." They "borrow from the coercive force of the law to silence their political opponents" (160). Once again, that is a common problem with the quasi-judicial practices that universities adopt. She points out that this parallels the problems that arise from "the implications of naming racism for legal purposes" (158). Gould attributes the risks to the character of the Definition, but I believe her anti-Zionism gets in the way of an objective analysis of the reasons for the risks of the Definition's misuse. She is writing in a British context, where the danger derives, I would argue, from the network of British laws and regulations, including those governing higher education, in which the Definition is entangled. I detail those in Chapter One.

But Gould goes beyond concern with quasi-legal uses of the Definition to attribute the problem to an internal quasi-legal character: "It is impossible to reconcile the IHRA document with the rule of law because, as a legal form, it asks institutions to penalize political speech" (166). When the Definition was adopted by the government, she argues, that fundamental character acquired legal, not quasi-legal, force: "universities are henceforth obliged to use the IHRA definition to limit every Israel-critical statement made by a student or staff" (168). The large staff needed to supervise this ambitious surveillance regime has yet to be appointed. Gould's fears of vast IHRA Definition overreach are unfounded fantasies.

Gould also displays a libertarian bias against "faith in the ability of positive legislation to combat racial hatred, and an arguably naïve belief in the capacity of the state to deliver social justice" (161). The state cannot deliver social justice tout court, but it can contribute mightily toward its observance. She entertains a radical suggestion that could make it impossible even to restrict calls for violence: "A purely democratic polity," she tells us, "would place the regulation of speech entirely outside the pale of its jurisdiction and would refuse to balance one civil liberty against another" (173). Instead, "the viewpoint selective censorship of controversial speech is part of the expanding remit of the state that is transpiring across many liberal democracies" (173). We are faced with "a neoliberal state that increasingly relies on informal institutions (including universities) to curtail civil liberties" (174). Thus "efforts to apply the definition as soft law have an overwhelming impact on freedom of expression" (172). Indeed, "censorious applications of the definition have caused lasting harm" (169). It would be challenging to prove these assertions. Yet all this eventually warrants the conclusion with which she opens: "the IHRA document cannot effectively combat antisemitism in the public sphere" (157). Time will answer that question. Meanwhile, her certainty that the civil liberties sky is falling is seriously overstated. The internet is giving us a taste of what truly unfettered speech means for social life. Our democratic institutions are more likely than the heavens above us to crumble as a consequence.

Gould's "Beyond Anti-Semitism" (2011) warns that "claiming the Holocaust as a holy event sanctifies the state of Israel and whitewashes its crimes," concluding that "perhaps the time has come to stop privileging the Holocaust as the central event in Jewish history" (Gould 2011, 2). "Jewish suffering," she adds, "will never be appeased by making Palestinians pay the price for the world community's silence half a century ago, when the Jews were being exterminated" (3). Readers may decide whether this implicates one of the Definition's examples of potential antisemitism: "Accusing the Jews as a people, or Israel as a state, of inventing or exaggerating the Holocaust." Perhaps a trace of her earlier sentiments survives in her 2022 complaint about the forced retitling of a University of Manchester event, "You're doing to the Palestinians what the Nazis did to me" (Gould 2022, 165), or in her claim that "a definition that was drafted to protect Jews has become an instrument for persecuting Palestinians and Jewish anti-Zionists" (185). The Definition has not become a means of persecution. Gould, however, may have embraced Holocaust inversion.

6. Does the IHRA Definition politicize antisemitism?

The Hebrew University's Eva Illouz is among those leveling the criticism that the IHRA Definition distorts and misapplies antisemitism by expressly politicizing it. It is worth focusing on her arguments because they are exceptionally clear, if misguided. "The struggle against antisemitism used to be above the fray of crass politics," she writes, "but during the last two decades, it has become politicized and subject to the same manipulations suffered by the ideological arena" (Illouz 2021). The argument, then, is that the Definition consolidates this trend and "weaponizes" it.

There are at least two problems with this claim. The first is definitional: what, exactly, is meant by politics? The second is historical: when was antisemitism first politicized and was there ever a moment of purity when antisemitism was wholly above the political fray? In a broad sense, politics covers all the ways cultural, religious, and more narrow political power structures institutions and relationships in a given society. More narrowly, it refers to the character of and struggle over the power of the state, including electoral politics. If antisemitism is a political force within a given society, can resistance to antisemitism, however principled, be entirely above the fray?

In both cases, the politicization of antisemitism dates roughly to its emergence within Christianity, to the process by which Christianity defined itself in opposition to Judaism. But its definitive realization came in the next century after the Roman Emperor Constantine I converted to Christianity and made it the state religion. The cross became a sword. In 315, a Roman edict made it illegal for Jews to proselytize. From 380 onwards, Christianity became increasingly linked with state power. In 388, it became a crime punishable by death for Jews to proselytize. Centuries followed in which antisemitism was enforced with the power of the state. The Nazis inherited that tradition and magnified it exponentially. But Illouz's golden age never existed. From the outset, antisemitism was both a cultural and a political phenomenon. To say so is not to politicize accusations of antisemitism; it is to describe and define their object.

The complaint that the IHRA Definition has politicized antisemitism rests on a common misunderstanding, namely that antisemitism always takes the simple form of an irrational dislike or hatred of Jews. From that perspective, antisemitism is an attitude that shapes both perception and behavior. But, as Bernard Harrison argues in "In Defense of the IHRA Definition," that hatred is frequently based on and rationalized by an integrated body of political theory, many elements of which are unique to Jews. He defines this contemporary version of antisemitism as "a delusive political theory concerning the allegedly crucial role played collectively by 'the Jews' in the direction of world affairs," then identifies its five main beliefs:

(i) the Jews are a people given to the pursuit of evil, and are behind every evil that besets the non-Jewish world, including all wars;

(ii) the Jews are gifted with quasi-demonic powers of conspiratorial organisation;

(iii) these extraordinary powers have allowed them to assume control of a vast range of supposedly non-Jewish organizations (the banks, the US Presidency, Hollywood, &c., &c.) and to subvert them to the service of Jewish goals;

(iv) because of the impossibility of negotiating with what is in effect a hidden and secret power, the only solution to these problems lies in the complete elimination of the Jews;

(v) once the elimination of the Jews is achieved, all problems will cease, and the non-Jewish world will return to the state of unbroken peace and happiness to which its manifest virtues evidently entitle it, and from which only the machinations of the Jews have been able to expel it. (Harrison 2022, 53)

One can hardly politicize something that is inherently and fundamentally political. You cannot address this phenomenon by positioning yourself above the fray of politics. Of course these conspiracy theories now have a new villain on which to focus, a Jewish state.

The key question for the IHRA Definition, then, is how it applies to attacks on the Jewish state. Although one may fairly decide that particular criticisms of Israel are antisemitic, it is difficult either in the West or in Israel to find rational people who actually say all criticism of Israel or Israeli policy is antisemitic. Illouz (2021) goes on to say that "by this logic, any and all criticism of Israel will always be illegitimate and reminiscent of demonization." But attributing that logic to the Definition itself is unwarranted. The potential for misuse of the Definition exists and should be condemned when it occurs. Illouz declares that the Definition "has been harnessed by the government as part of a vast campaign to whitewash its policies," which not only overstates the reality but also discounts the fact that any such campaign long pre-exists the Definition and does not depend on it. Illouz worries about "the semantic and moral dilution of the concept of 'antisemitism,'" though the manifestations of antisemitism have been so varied historically that the term may never have been altogether stable. It certainly cannot serve as a narrow and fixed referent either over time or in the contemporary moment.

Illouz would like to define antisemitism by claiming it "attributes a demonic nature and influence to the Jews as a whole or to Israel, and wants to rid the world of them." But that would eliminate a very wide range of beliefs and actions long classified as antisemitic. If anything short of that definition is excluded from antisemitism, much of the world's aggression against Jews would be protected from the accusation. Applying her definition to the Jewish state, she aims to draw "clear distinctions between a legitimate debate of opinion on Israeli policies and the essentialization of Jews as unpatriotic, evil or in control of the world," but it is not legitimate to collapse the whole spectrum of anti-Israel discourse into those stark, opposing categories.

That manufactured dichotomy makes it possible for Illouz to offer a particularly damning argument: "a critique of Israeli politics (an opinion) is transmuted into an essence and an identity (that of the antisemite), from which no politician or public figure can ever hope to recover" since it transforms "an opponent's opinions into a form of blasphemy." Now we have once again entered a fantasy realm. Politicians on the left in many countries who criticize Israeli policy regularly survive the antisemitic label to be re-elected. Indeed, in the United States that includes politicians who I believe *are* antisemitic. Accusations of antisemitism do not necessarily have a decisive impact on either a political or an academic career. The claim that criticism of Israeli policy translates into a basic character trait or a core antisemitic identity should not be mounted without convincing evidence.

Illouz declares furthermore that the Definition "lessens the commitment of Jews to their ethnicity and religion, and instead makes them increasingly define themselves in terms of their politics," but here too we are not faced with mutually exclusive alternatives but instead with multiple and coexisting features of personal identity. We may assume not only that Jews can walk and chew gum at the same time, that they can be primarily religious beings in one moment and political beings in another, but also that they can maintain both components of their identity simultaneously.

It is possible to debate with Illouz rationally. Some other proponents and opponents of the Definition, we will see, also engage their challengers substantively, important examples being *In Defence of the IHRA Working Definition of Antisemitism* (a 2021 *Fathom* eBook edited by Alan Johnson) and two statements published in March 2021: the Jerusalem Declaration on Antisemitism, which was developed at the Van Leer Institute in Jerusalem and signed by 200 academics worldwide, and the Nexus Document, which was drafted by a group organized through the University of Southern California's Annenberg School for Communication and Journalism. David Schraub (2021c) provides a helpful chart comparing the IHRA Definition with the Nexus Document and the Jerusalem Declaration. But first we need to consider a group of Arabs and Palestinians who mounted a still more hostile critique of the Definition, one leaving little room to imagine a two-state resolution to the general conflict.

7. The November 2020 statement of 122 Palestinian and Arab Intellectuals

Still greater concern is warranted by a November 2020 statement issued by a group of 122 Palestinian and Arab intellectuals entitled "Palestinian Rights and the IHRA Definition of Antisemitism."[15] Its claims, echoed by a number of speakers at the American-Arab Anti-Discrimination Committee's June 2023 convention, have become routine in pro-Palestinian objections to the Definition (Jacoby 2023). This document, comprising seven numbered objections to the IHRA Definition, seeks the elimination of any Jewish state throughout the Levant by defining what its authors consider "self-determination" to mean for Israelis and Palestinians in a unified territory from the Mediterranean to the border with Jordan. It claims that "the self-determination of a Jewish population in Palestine/Israel has been implemented in the form of an ethnic exclusivist and territorially expansionist state," thus casting Israel itself as illegitimate. To emphasize the point, it adds that "no right to self-determination should include the right to uproot another people and prevent them from returning to their land, or any other means of securing a demographic majority within the state." These principles, if realized, would invalidate not only the occupation of the West Bank but also the 1948 founding of Israel.

The November 2020 statement goes on to say that "the IHRA definition and the way it has been deployed prohibit any discussion of the Israeli state as based on ethno-religious discrimination," which is simply untrue: the Definition does not *prohibit* anything. Yet the Palestinian statement concludes that "the suppression of Palestinian rights in the IHRA definition betrays an attitude upholding

---

15 See "Palestinian Rights and the IHRA Definition of Antisemitism," letter to the *Guardian*, November 29, 2020, https://www.theguardian.com/news/2020/nov/29/palestinian-rights-and-the-ihra-definition-of-antisemitism.

Jewish privilege in Palestine instead of Jewish rights, and Jewish supremacy over Palestinians instead of Jewish safety" and thus that it "contravenes elementary justice and basic norms of human rights and international law." The authors will be aware that "supremacy" evokes white supremacy and thus racializes the conflict. The use of "privilege" is no doubt meant to suggest analogies with the concept of "white privilege." As writers seek to make an impression amid proliferating testimonies against the IHRA Definition and in support of the Jerusalem Declaration, the rhetoric escalates. Leiden University's Sai Englert (2021) writes that the Definition aims "to repress the historical facts of Palestinian dispossession, displacement and oppression" and thus decries "the repressive atmosphere" it creates. Comparably uncompromising condemnations of the Definition underlie the Jerusalem Declaration as well. Neither the statement by Arab intellectuals nor the Jerusalem Declaration anticipates either reconciliation or a peaceful resolution of the conflict.

Would the IHRA Definition lead us to regard "Palestinian Rights and the IHRA Definition of Antisemitism" as an antisemitic text? I believe so. Some opponents of the Definition treat the condemnation of calls to effectively eliminate Israel as a violation of human rights, disguising existential challenges to Israel's existence as "valid criticisms" or repudiations of "Jewish exceptionalism." For Barry Trachtenberg (2021), a historian at Wake Forest University and another endorser of the Jerusalem Declaration, it is time to push back "against the misguided belief" that antisemitism "is a unique and unparalleled form of hatred." Writing in *Tikkun*, a community psychologist named Donna Nevel (2021) presses the same point more bluntly: "We must not reinforce the notion that there is anything about criticism of Israel that requires 'special' attention." With a wave of her hand, two thousand years of history are swept away, as if the Jews never existed. She too feels "the IHRA definition goes full speed in conflating criticism of Israel and support for Palestinian justice with antisemitism." Nevel and Trachtenberg both praise the Jerusalem Declaration for pushing back. Trachtenberg then surprisingly tells us that "the IHRA definition has been used almost exclusively to silence Palestinians discussing their daily experiences of humiliation, violence, and dispossession under Israeli law."

8. The Jerusalem Declaration on Antisemitism

The text of the Jerusalem Declaration on Antisemitism (JDA) begins with a preamble that makes it clear that it was issued in explicit opposition to the IHRA Definition. But before then it offers a definition of antisemitism that serves as an epigraph: "Antisemitism is discrimination, prejudice, hostility or violence against Jews as Jews (or Jewish institutions as Jewish)." This definition—which operates like an extension of the minimalist dictionary definition "antisemitism is hatred of Jews"—has the virtue of clarity, but it is inadequate because it is excessively narrow and altogether blind to the ideological versions of antisemitism that have long been influential. What follows, moreover, actively promotes anti-Zionism and opens a space for some forms of antisemitism, among them the elimination of the Jewish state. (One can produce a concise history of antisemitism, but it is not so easy to combine a medieval claim that the Jews killed Jesus, Nazi racism, and a 1950s country club's refusal to accept Jewish members into one definition.) The Declaration's guidelines are divided into three sections: A, B, and C. The first is devoted to general observations about antisemitism; then come two contrasting sections devoted to Israel and Palestine.

The preamble includes one binding principle that the Declaration's supporters have found irresistible: "We hold that while antisemitism has certain distinctive features, the fight against it is inseparable from the overall fight against all forms of racial, ethnic, cultural, religious, and gender discrimination." The prime concept here is that the fight against antisemitism is part of the wider US debate on antiracism, that antisemitism is not really different from other forms of racism. As a matter of both principle and tactics, it is important that Jews join antiracist coalitions—so long as anti-Zionism is not the price of admission. But as David Hirsh and Dave Rich have shown, anti-Zionism is increasingly definitional for left-wing antiracism. The opening concession—"while antisemitism has certain distinctive features"—is condescending and dismissive, an impoverished gesture toward nearly two thousand years of Jewish history since Christianity coalesced. That history underlies our understanding of contemporary antisemitism and the identities of living Jews. The Declaration's core principle dissolves the fight against antisemitism into antiracism, discrediting and obliterating Jewish identity. Compare it with several equally unacceptable alternatives warranted by the Declaration's own list: "while anti-Black racism has certain distinctive features"; "while contempt toward Native Americans has certain distinctive features"; "while opposition to women's rights has certain distinctive features"; and so forth. The movements opposing these prejudices need dedicated historical awareness to make them effective. Hatred and a belief in inferiority are fundamental to many such histories. "Certain distinctive features" will not suffice to identify those histories with their defining traumas and triumphs; neither does it adequately characterize the history of the longest hatred.

Conceptual problems multiply as the Declaration proceeds. Section A oversimplifies matters by declaring that "what is particular in classic antisemitism is the idea that Jews are linked to the forces of evil." This idea is unquestionably integral to much Christian antisemitism, but it does not adequately account for antisemitic conspiracism, political antisemitism, Nazi Germany's racial theories, or other versions of Jew-hatred. Even for Christian antisemitism, accusations of Jewish evil are not always relevant. Christian supersessionism now commonly argues that God's covenant with the Jews has been "fulfilled" by the new covenant with the Church rather than having been voided by Jewish evil (Nelson and Gizzi 2021). Section B lists examples relating to Israel and Palestine "that, on the face of it, are antisemitic," whereas Section C covers examples relating to Israel and Palestine "that, on the face of it, are not antisemitic." This dichotomy makes a concession that even the IHRA Definition resists, as it insists on considering context when evaluating potential antisemitic statements. As University of Manchester philosopher Eve Garrard shows, the IHRA Definition "is peppered with conditional verbs" (2021, 47) that prevent its automatic application.

Section C of the Declaration relies on empty rhetorical strategies to disclaim antisemitic content. Notable among these is the thrice-repeated statement that certain claims, "even if contentious," "are not, in and of themselves, antisemitic." What the IHRA Definition makes clear instead is that certain categories of statements have a substantial history of being antisemitic. Yet they are probable indicators, not litmus tests. The Declaration absolves the anti-Zionist industry of any probable freight of hatred. It does so in part by seeming to defend a principle of free speech that discourages us from recognizing antisemitic effect when confronted by instances of "the new antisemitism."

Thus, it stipulates that "boycott, divestment and sanctions are commonplace, non-violent forms of political protest against states. In the Israeli case they are not, in and of themselves, antisemitic." The issue is not whether all boycott efforts are antisemitic "in and of themselves." Israelis commonly boycott West Bank products, a political choice that they have the freedom to make. The issue is whether the BDS *movement* is substantially antisemitic, given that its leaders advocate eliminating the Jewish state. By fudging the difference, the Declaration demolishes a straw man and confuses the issue.

Guideline 13 of the Declaration concludes "Thus, even if contentious, it is not antisemitic, in and of itself, to compare Israel with other cases, including settler-colonialism or apartheid." As Jeffrey Herf (2021) writes, "That phrase is written in bad faith. The BDS campaign does not merely 'compare' Israel to settler colonialism or South African apartheid. Rather it asserts that Israel is a case of one or the other or both. Of course, making comparisons is not 'in and of itself antisemitic' but in the actual world of political and academic debates of recent decades, the 'comparison' has amounted to an equation." Such comparisons carry inescapable political implications. Declaring Israel a settler-colonialist state sends a message that Israel in toto is occupied territory, established to exploit Palestinians and deprive them of their rights. It makes Israel a vestige of nineteenth-century imperialism and suggests that the inexorable movement of history has rendered the nation obsolete. One can deduce that Israel's eventual elimination is inevitable. Comparisons between South African apartheid and the policies in force on the West Bank elide the fundamental political and social differences between the two systems and misrepresent the Israeli-Palestinian conflict as a racial one. Moreover, those comparisons obfuscate the dangers inherent in formal annexation. Accusations that Israel within its pre-1967 boundaries is an apartheid state are both false and invidious. They are wielded to add a stronger moral imperative to an eliminationist motive: Israel, like apartheid South Africa, is a morally abhorrent entity that must be dissolved.

Yet the language of Guideline 13 is so general that it can include comparisons between Israel and South African apartheid that are manifestly untrue. The item opens by citing "evidence-based criticism of Israel as a state," suggesting this is all about sensible academic debate. In fact, denunciations of Israel as an apartheid state are largely neither reasoned nor evidence-based. When UCLA's Saree Makdisi declares that Israel's "apartheid regime" is actually worse than South Africa's, he indulges in pure invective, offering no proof. And when he falsely asserts that none of Israel's Basic Laws guarantee equality of citizenship, that there are no High Court rulings upholding equality as a right, and that "every major South African apartheid law has a direct equivalent in Israel and the occupied territories today" (Makdisi 2017, 310), his indifference to offering supportive evidence can be documented and his claims disproven, as I do at length in *Israel Denial*.

Herf reserves a still stronger critique for the Declaration's next guideline:

> The JDA's 14th point is the crux of the entire statement and the reason for its existence: "Boycott, divestment, and sanctions are commonplace, non-violent forms of political protest against states. In the Israeli case, they are not, in and of themselves, anti-semitic." In fact, the specific combination of boycott, divestment, and sanctions, that is, "BDS" is not "commonplace." Rather, the combination of those three words became famous as a marker of the specific Palestinian political warfare against the state of Israel waged primarily in British and American universities. The JDA statement seeks to separate the element of political warfare inherent in the BDS campaigns from the existence of actual war and terror that Israel faces, and the role that such campaigns have served in the past to justify terror. The most plausible reading

> of point 14 is that the JDA authors assert an absurdity, namely that the BDS campaigns of recent years aimed at the destruction of the Jewish state are not "in and of themselves," examples of antisemitism.

The Declaration's confusions multiply when we get to the opening of Guideline 15: "Political speech does not have to be measured, proportional, tempered, or reasonable to be protected...." People engaged in intemperate political speech should not be sanctioned, though autocratic regimes certainly do so. But intemperate political speech is not protected from criticism and condemnation. Unstated, but implied, is the familiar complaint that anti-Zionist advocacy is being silenced when it is simply being condemned.

The bland language referencing "other historical cases" obfuscates the signal omission here, an omission that is definitional for the Jerusalem Declaration. For the historical case that is really at issue, despite its absence from the Declaration, is Nazi Germany, a fact that should be obvious to any knowledgeable reader and to every one of the 200 people who endorsed the document. The IHRA Definition cites "drawing comparisons of contemporary Israeli policy to that of the Nazis" as one of its key examples of antisemitism. Indeed, such comparisons are really statements of equivalence. Some, like journalist Anthony Lawson, as Makdisi does with the South Africa analogy, insist that "Israel's policies are worse than Nazi Germany's ever were" (quoted in Harrison 2020, 150).

The rhetoric escalates, and it can have consequences, among them a belief that "large numbers of Jews must be as much enemies of humankind as were the Nazis, since they support, and are therefore presumably accessory to, the commission of these putatively equally egregious crimes" (Harrison 2020, 460). As Alan Johnson writes, "treating Israelis or Jews or Zionists as 'Nazis' is obscene; it verges on the demonic in its cruelty as it implicitly demands, as a matter of ethical obligation no less—and this after the rupture in world history that was the Shoah—the destruction of the Jewish homeland as a unique evil in the world, no better than the Third Reich, the perpetrator of the Shoah" (2021a, 54). The Declaration opens its second general guideline by stating: "What is particular in classic antisemitism is the idea that Jews are linked to the forces of evil." And yet the foremost contemporary manifestation of that association, the identification of the Jewish state with Nazi Germany, is one the Declaration never condemns as antisemitic.

Why? The omission is certainly deliberate. Among the signatories are Holocaust scholars Omer Bartov, Wolfgang Benz, Doris Bergen, Micha Brumlik, Amos Goldberg, Atina Grossmann, Wolfgang Gruner, Marianne Hirsch,

Marion Kaplan, Dominick LaCapra, Mark Roseman, Michael Rothberg, and Raz Segal, along with many other scholars of antisemitism and Jewish history who will have noted the omission. Perhaps it was thought impolitic to ask assent to the statement that calling Israelis and their Zionist supporters worldwide "Nazis" is not "on the face of it" antisemitic. Perhaps it was thought impolitic to ask those of the signatories who themselves have indulged in the Israel/Nazism comparison—indeed who insist on, highlight, and endorse that comparison—to classify their own work as antisemitic.

The phenomenon of a group of Holocaust scholars being alienated from and hostile to Israel, I should emphasize, is not new. It dates back at least a generation. The revival of antisemitism across the bloodlands of Eastern Europe, however reminiscent of the sorrows of the Shoah, has not, so far as I know, caused any of them to change their positions—even though the need for a Jewish homeland outside Europe seems urgent again. My former colleague Michael Rothberg has long been philosophically and politically opposed to the very concept of a Jewish state. Some Holocaust scholars have signed BDS petitions. Yet I believe harboring anti-Zionist convictions requires Holocaust scholars to manage inner contradictions of a special character; their emotions are not quite the same as those experienced by the average Jewish Voice for Peace member.

Perhaps such inner conflicts underlie Brown University's Omer Bartov's overwrought accusation about the IHRA Definition: "this definition and the kind of thinking it has come to embody enable Israel to justify its support for oppressive regimes that persecute minorities, suppress the opposition and even engage in antisemitic demagoguery, provided they don't criticize Israel's occupation policy" (Bartov 2021). It is neither responsible nor rational to lay Israel's sometimes ill-advised foreign policy at the feet of the Definition, let alone a vague "kind of thinking." Whatever kind of thinking is responsible did not originate with the Definition. For decades, Israel has been willing to maintain relationships with undemocratic regimes if they offered Israel support in the international arena or provided a market for Israeli products, including the products of its arms industry. That policy deserves to be debated, but the debate will only be confused by linking it to the Definition.

Like some other Holocaust scholars, Bartov seems enraged that the Definition is associated with the International Holocaust Remembrance Alliance, apparently determined to ensure that the Holocaust and contemporary antisemitism are regarded as unrelated phenomena. Eva Illouz, who was one of the Jerusalem Declaration's authors, worries that the IHRA Definition risks "cheapening the memory of the victims of antisemitism" (Illouz 2021), a concern Bartov seems to share. So he adds, without offering any evidence, that the kind of thinking at issue "diverts attention from the tendency toward Holocaust denial or distortion of Holocaust remembrance on the national level as in Hungary and Poland" (Bartov 2021). My own sense is that attention to Holocaust misrepresentation is increasing, not decreasing, partly as a result of attention given to the IHRA Definition.

Anti-Zionist Holocaust scholars can engage in their own odd version of Holocaust denial. I had one conversation with an internationally known Holocaust scholar who vehemently insisted that the Holocaust itself had nothing to do with the founding of the Jewish state. I was astonished at the idea that the UN vote had nothing to do with guilt over the Shoah, but he would not budge and refused to talk about it further.

The list of those signing the Jerusalem Declaration includes fierce and uncompromising anti-Zionists who cross a line into antisemitism, among them Richard Falk, along with a number of Jewish faculty who have grown disenchanted with Israel and now endorse the BDS movement but who may not yet be ready to demand Israel's dissolution. As David Schraub (2021a) writes in a piece about the Declaration, "Richard Falk is a signatory, even though he's endorsed materials which seem to cleanly fall under categories the Declaration deems antisemitic. Jackie Walker praised the JDA too even though her antisemitism likewise would be covered by the JDA." Falk has done far more than endorse other antisemites. In a report for the United Nations that he coauthored with Virginia Tilley, Israel is faulted for its "apparent annexationist, colonialist, and ethnic-cleansing goals" (Falk and Tilley 2017). In "Slouching toward a Palestinian Holocaust," he writes, "Is it an irresponsible overstatement to associate the treatment of Palestinians with this criminalized Nazi record of collective atrocity? I think not" (Falk 2007). In an interview with C. Gouridasan Nair, after rejecting the terrorist tactic of killing civilians, he allowed that "the armed settlers are an ambiguous category." Walker, who was cast out of the British Labour Party for antisemitic remarks, has praised the Declaration, but is not a signatory.

Sergio Luzzatto, a University of Connecticut historian who also signed the Declaration, has endorsed the despicable effort to revive the belief that medieval myths of Jews carrying out ritual murders of Christian children to obtain their blood for use in Passover preparations were true, most notoriously in his sympathetic review of Ariel Toaff's *Pasque di sangue* (Bloody Passovers), where he claimed that some Jews carried out human sacrifices several times (Loriga 2008). Luzzatto insisted that Jewish "confessions" obtained through torture should not be routinely discounted. As a colleague suggested, Luzzatto may well be the main person responsible for the revival of blood libel in the twenty-first century.

What would lead someone to sign a statement that amounts to a self-condemnation? Obviously rationalization and self-deception may play a role in the decision, but they cannot be decisive for everyone. Is it actually possible for Falk and Luzzatto to believe that they endorsed the Declaration to "strengthen the fight against antisemitism," a purpose the Declaration claims for itself? If not, others like them may well believe that by signing they are purging antisemitism of its inconvenient obsession with Israel and thereby, as Illouz puts it, making "the struggle against antisemitism regain its focus and moral clarity." It is an uplifting self-justification.

One collective motive seems comprehensible. Guideline 12 seeks to find a space ostensibly critical of antisemitism that can accommodate both established antisemites and less virulent anti-Zionists and in that way pardon them all:

> Criticizing or opposing Zionism as a form of nationalism, or arguing for a variety of constitutional arrangements for Jews and Palestinians in the area between the Jordan River and the Mediterranean. It is not antisemitic to support arrangements that accord full equality to all inhabitants "between the river and the sea," whether in two states, a binational state, unitary democratic state, federal state, or in whatever form.

Illouz (2021) describes this as a way to overcome a stark choice that seems to her as being reinforced by the IHRA:

> Faced with a complex and mined field, what is the Jewish intellectual to do? The alternative has been set up for him or her in an impossible way: either join the ranks of those who fight for a democratic Israel and run the risk of being dubbed an antisemite; or make the struggle against antisemitism the primary object of moral concern, at the expense of ignoring a historical injustice committed by Israelis against the Palestinians.

The Jerusalem Declaration aims "to make both struggles compatible." But they already are compatible for those who make that political and moral choice. The struggle for a two-state solution recognizes the rights of Palestinians while also defending the Jewish state against an antisemitic eliminationist agenda.

What does the Declaration offer instead? Setting aside the allusion to anti-Zionism's favorite slogan, "From the river to the sea, Palestine will be free," we are left with a principled-sounding "arguing for a variety of constitutional arrangements" that happen to contradict the constitution of the Jewish state. Such options would only be "constitutional" in Israel if the current constitution were scrapped. "Arguing for" is not simply a debating proposition; it is a political demand that one of a series of non-Jewish options be imposed on Israeli citizens. No provision is made for their right to decide their own political future.

This sleight of hand may have bamboozled some inattentive faculty into endorsing the Declaration. Others may have been drawn to join people they respect: "Michael Walzer signed; it must be OK." Walzer (2021) has since written in response that "I hope he [Nelson] is wrong to suggest that some people have signed on to the Jerusalem Declaration on Antisemitism (JDA) because I did." In any case, unlike those who drafted the Declaration, Walzer is not opposed to the IHRA Definition. Indeed, when it came under assault at University College London, he wrote publicly to express the hope that the IHRA Definition would retain its official status at UCL (Walzer 2021b).

The IHRA Definition includes "denying the Jewish people their right to self-determination" among its examples of antisemitism. In contrast, the Jerusalem Declaration endorses the antisemitic strategy of denying this fundamental Jewish right under the cover of offering multiple options. Illouz (2021) reduces explicit attempts to eliminate Israel to "thinking that Jews do not need a national home." That is the Declaration's main political intervention. And, "on the face of it," it presents a problem. It is not for a group of international academics to make that decision; it is for Israelis. Long-time anti-Zionist and Declaration coauthor Brian Klug of Oxford University, is among those falsely assuring us that, unlike the IHRA Definition, the Declaration "seeks to separate out the fight against anti-Semitism from partisan political argument. It has no political agenda regarding Zionism or the conflict over Israel/Palestine" (Klug 2021).

The Declaration offers modest criticism of antisemitism as a cover for endorsing the most antisemitic of all relevant political projects: eliminating the Jewish state. The blogger Elder of Ziyon (2021b) describes it as "an effort to carve out a space for anti-Zionists to advocate for the elimination of the Jewish state without being accused of anti-Semitism." In what is surely its most disingenuous declaration, it tells us it is antisemitic to deny "the right of Jews in the State of Israel to exist and flourish, collectively and individually, as Jews, in accordance with the principle of equality," a right that no realistic observer believes a Jewish minority in Palestine would enjoy. That is the fantasy, disingenuous or self-deluded, in which one-state enthusiasts invest their hopes. Few Israelis share their confidence. Perhaps some uneasiness about that imagined future is warranted by the Palestinian BDS National Committee's response to that passage in the Declaration:

> Some may abuse this to imply equal political rights for the colonizers and the colonized collectives in a settler-colonial reality, or for the dominant and the dominated collectives in an apartheid reality, thus perpetuating oppression…. Moreover, should Palestinian refugees be denied their UN-stipulated right to return home in order not to disturb some assumed "collective Jewish right" to demographic supremacy? What about justice, repatriation and reparations in accordance with international law and how they may impact certain assumed "rights" of Jewish-Israelis occupying Palestinian homes or lands?[16]

The opponents of the IHRA Definition cannot even agree as to what constitutes its main evil. On the other hand, despite its weaknesses, the next document I will review does at least show that it is possible to have a productive dialogue with the Definition.

9. The Nexus Document

Throughout the ten-year development and revision of the IHRA Definition it has been identified as a "working" document. The continuing assaults on its meaning and purpose may have discouraged some from attempting to clarify and amplify it. Instead, its supporters have defended it and promoted its adoption. Meanwhile, despite the controversy, people in state agencies, NGOs, and educational and religious institutions have gained a better and more grounded understanding of how antisemitism is manifested in the contemporary world. And the controversy has, as always in such cases, drawn more attention to the Definition.

But it is time for the Definition to acquire its own body of explanatory literature. Despite what some have said, that is not a weakness of the Definition. It is inherent to the genre of statements of principle or manifestos that seek wide, even international, endorsement. Too much detail and people raise objections.

---

16 "A Palestinian Civil Society Critique of the Jerusalem Declaration on Antisemitism," Palestinian BDS National Committee, March 25, 2021, https://bdsmovement.net/A-Palestinian-Civil-Society-Critique-JDA.

All the statements reviewed here are concise. In fact, it is remarkable that the Definition has won the level of support it has. The aforementioned *Fathom* collection—*In Defence of the IHRA Working Definition of Antisemitism*—is an important development in that process of elaboration. I consider the Nexus Document of February 2021 to be a partly friendly if problematic amendment to the original, even though it was not explicitly framed as a response. It was drafted by a working group, the Nexus Task Force, as a project of the Knight Program on Media and Religion at the Annenberg School for Communication and Journalism at the University of Southern California. Unlike the Jerusalem Declaration, the Nexus working group did not seek outside signatories. It offers a clear two-part definition, though it too emphasizes social, rather than political, antisemitism:

> Antisemitism consists of anti-Jewish beliefs, attitudes, actions or systemic conditions. It includes negative beliefs and feelings about Jews, hostile behavior directed against Jews (because they are Jews), and conditions that discriminate against Jews and significantly impede their ability to participate as equals in political, religious, cultural, economic, or social life.

> As an embodiment of collective Jewish organization and action, Israel can be a target of antisemitism and antisemitic behavior. Thus, it is important for Jews and their allies to understand what is and what is not antisemitic in relation to Israel.

Though I have significant disagreements with the Nexus Document, at least the examples that follow its definition are not expressly hostile to the IHRA Definition. But I believe it should at least add "theories" to its first sentence. Bernard Harrison would find this definition embodies social antisemitism but not political or ideological antisemitism. "One is indeed an emotional disposition: one consisting in hostility to individual Jews as Jews. The other is a body of explanatory pseudo-explanatory theory concerning the Jewish community considered as a supposedly coherently organized and unified political force" (Harrison 2020, 422). Social antisemitism "is not a theory of any kind but rather a state of mind" (423). The opening sentence of the IHRA Definition's basic definition—"Antisemitism is a certain perception of Jews, which may be expressed as hatred of Jews"—gives the same traditional emphasis to social antisemitism.

The Nexus Document's definition thus fails to account for the way in which contemporary antisemitism serves as a body of theory that claims to explain the world. The document subsequently offers two lists, entitled "What Is

Antisemitic" and "What Is Not Antisemitic." Both lists concentrate on Israel, as it represents the major disputed context for defining contemporary antisemitism. As in the case of the Jerusalem Declaration, the aim is not simply to address the area of maximum controversy. Both documents want to open a space for tolerable forms of anti-Zionism. But as Kahn-Harris (2021a) observes, "It is difficult to judge something as 'just' offensive and objectionable rather than antisemitic."

Writing as a contributor to the Nexus Document, David Schraub (2021b) provides an informative gloss on one of the guidelines in the first list:

> While the nexus between Israel and antisemitism often focuses predominantly on "left" critiques, it was important for us to articulate practices on the right with relation to Israel which have subjected many Jews to antisemitic abuse or harassment. It is antisemitic, we said, to "Denigrat[e] or deny the Jewish identity of certain Jews because they are perceived as holding the 'wrong' position (whether too critical or too favorable) on Israel." This is something that many liberal Jews (and in particular many Jews of color) have experienced, sometimes from other Jews, often from non-Jews, and it absolutely should be viewed as a form of antisemitism.

In the second list, the Nexus Document makes a special effort to define what kinds of anti-Israel commentary are not *necessarily* antisemitic, allowing that they sometimes may be. That effort is generally consistent with the IHRA Definition's insistence on considering the full context when evaluating statements. But the Nexus Document's attempt to provide more nuanced guidelines for determining what is and is not antisemitic inevitably raises complications. It tells us that "even contentious, strident, or harsh criticism of Israel for its policies and actions, including those that led to the creation of Israel, is not *per se* illegitimate or antisemitic." Journalist Ben Cohen (2021) points out that the authors give no examples of strident criticism that they find acceptable or unacceptable, making this abstract principle difficult to accept. They apparently did consider examples in the drafting process, but they are not cited, and the author I consulted could not recall them. In the real world, especially on social media, stridency gains attention for hate speech and anti-Zionism. It can make antisemitism more influential, amplifying its impact. Contrary to what the authors of the Nexus Document seem to believe, stridency is not easily separable from content. In evaluating a statement or a publication for its antisemitic character, stridency is not an independent variable, but it can be powerful evidence. The authors chose not to say so.

Other questions arise from the following guideline:

> Opposition to Zionism and/or Israel does not necessarily reflect specific anti-Jewish animus nor purposefully lead to antisemitic behaviors and conditions. (For example, someone might oppose the principle of nationalism or ethnonationalist ideology. Similarly, someone's personal or national experience may have been adversely affected by the creation of the State of Israel. These motivations or attitudes towards Israel and/or Zionism do not necessarily constitute antisemitic behavior.)

Critics of the Jewish state who want to see it dissolved, among them Judith Butler, sometimes announce that the era of the nation state has run its course, that nations will soon disappear from the earth. In reality, pernicious forms of nationalism are thriving. But surely it is significant that Butler and other anti-Zionists do not call for the elimination of the United States, Britain, Germany, France, India, Pakistan, Bangladesh, or other nations, including some whose establishment is linked to ethnic nationalism. They just want the forces of history to eliminate Israel. I am thus taking issue with those who only deny Jewish self-determination: their declarations do not represent the consistent application of the political theory they claim to advocate. It is hard to imagine a dedicated anarchist calling for the dissolution of Israel alone.

It is true, as the above-mentioned guideline implies, that personal experience of discrimination or injustice can trigger hostility to Zionism, but that does not eliminate a given statement's antisemitic meaning or effects. It helps explain a person's motivations, not necessarily the statement's content. Indeed, motivation is often irrelevant. That is especially clear in the case of brief anti-Zionist or antisemitic statements on social media. Like other brief comments, they can circulate in thoroughly impersonal and decontextualized forms. But even an anti-Zionist book need not arrive trailing its author's personal or family history. The case an argument makes needs to be evaluated on its own terms, not excused because of what its author may have felt. Sometimes an argument is inflected in ways that only personal experience can explain, but the Nexus Document is aiming for a general reason to excuse antisemitic anti-Zionism. As Kenneth Marcus (2023), writes, "The purpose of the Nexus Document is to completely insulate political anti-Zionism, even in some of its extreme forms, from being properly identified as an outgrowth of historical Jew-hatred."

The final guideline in the second list argues that "paying disproportionate attention to Israel and treating Israel differently than other countries is not prima facie proof of antisemitism." Given the "prima facie" modifier, that statement is fair. But it does not take a great deal of reflection to realize that the UN's hostile and exclusive obsession with Israel represents a form of anti-semitism. This guideline may be combined with one from the first list: "It is antisemitic to advocate a political solution that denies Jews the right to define themselves as a people, thereby denying them—because they are Jews—the right to self-determination." Although the authors had not seen the Jerusalem Declaration, the Nexus language demolishes the approval that the Declaration grants to the denial of Jewish self-determination. The IHRA Definition's argument that "applying double standards by requiring of it [Israel] a behavior not expected or demanded of any other democratic nation" is a form of antisemitism remains an essential qualification. One conclusion we can draw from this limited comment on the Nexus Document is that there are some benefits to be gleaned from putting the three texts in dialogue with one another.

10. Conclusion

It is a good thing overall to have people thinking about the nature of anti-semitism, what forms it takes, what its boundaries are. But the definition of antisemitism is now an enhanced arena of cultural struggle. Indeed, as a result of such critiques as those this chapter has documented, the meaning of the IHRA Definition's examples of antisemitic views about Israel has been com-plicated. Some people will be confused by the debate. Others will find their existing positions reinforced and hardened. Nor is this just an abstract debate about rhetorical options and definitions. The objections to the Definition are often fundamentally efforts to validate political and material assaults on the Jewish state itself. Those who care about antisemitism and Israel will have to engage in the conversation.

Other challenges and amplifications will follow, but the IHRA Definition will continue to hold its own and sustain the struggle against antisemitism. Meanwhile, we should also remain aware of the things the Definition cannot do. By classifying current examples of antisemitism, it can help identify the inspiration for antisemitic acts, including violent ones, but it does not attempt to unpack all the individual motivations behind them. Deborah Lipstadt has expressed her wish that, "if I call someone an antisemite, it should have the sting of a thousand cuts" (Ziri 2021), an effect that is one of the legacies of the Holocaust. Unfortunately, the internet and social media have contributed to the normalization of classic antisemitic tropes and have enabled antisemites to make contact with one another and replace isolation with a pernicious form of community. Neither trend can simply be laid at Israel's doorstep. It is not easy to see how we can recover the wider consensus that made the stigmatizing of antisemitism possible.

Indeed, the debate may yet intensify. At a webinar hosted by the US Campaign for the Academic and Cultural Boycott of Israel on April 6, 2021, entitled "Weaponizing Anti-Semitism: IHRA and Ending the Palestine Exception," Heike Schotten of the University of Massachusetts Boston read a collective position paper that offered a stark conclusion: "The dangers of IHRA cannot be overestimated."[17] Among the misguided assumptions she identifies as guiding the IHRA Definition are "that Jews comprise a unified 'people'; that an apartheid political structure can also, simultaneously, be a democratic national entity." Cornel West, who preceded Richard Falk as a speaker, had his own spin on the latter claim: "Whatever you call it, apartheid, neo-apartheid, crypto-apartheid, quasi-apartheid, it's a crime against humanity."

This event was followed by an anti-Definition webinar hosted by the Harvard Divinity School on April 20, 2021, entitled "The Politics of Defining: A Roundtable Discussion about the Jerusalem Declaration on Antisemitism."[18] Barnard's Nadia Abu El-Haj was a speaker and conceded that, in any settler nation, settlers gain some rights over time, but she then asked why a demand to expel them all on the face of it should be considered antisemitic. None of the other panelists—Seth Anziska, Lara Freidman, and Brian Klug—took issue with her. If such a demand were not to be considered antisemitic, perhaps it should simply be categorized as monstrous. In any case, we were unwittingly reminded of what work the IHRA Definition must do.

Contextualizing potentially antisemitic statements and documents, as the IHRA Definition insists we do, may nonetheless also involve substantial investigation and analysis, neither of which is facilitated by the hyperbolic warnings that the Definition's opponents have voiced. The attacks on the Definition also obscure the need to promote justice for both Israelis and Palestinians. There are no grand resolutions to the conflict in sight; instead, we can turn to reasoned advocacy and practical improvements in the material conditions of daily life. Being able to reject some arguments as antisemitic makes it possible to rule them inadmissible and establish a social and discursive space in which mutual respect can be promoted.

---

17 See https://usacbi.org/2021/04/video-weaponizing-anti-semitism-ihra-and-the-end-of-the-palestine-exception-usacbi-webinar/.

18 For a video and transcript of the roundtable, see https://rpl.hds.harvard.edu/news/2021/05/17/video-politics-defining-roundtable-discussion-about-jerusalem-declaration-antisemitism.

Chapter 9

Antisemitism and the IHRA Working Definition at University College London[1]

_____

Introduction

University College London (UCL), an institution that serves 40,000 students, of whom 55 percent are international, is in the midst of a well-organized multi-year campaign to convince the campus to withdraw its November 2019 adoption of the IHRA Working Definition of Antisemitism. A majority of English higher education institutions (70%) have adopted the Definition. UCL notably has the only Department of Hebrew and Jewish Studies in the United Kingdom, which gives both antisemitism and the IHRA Definition special academic relevance and application. The UCL campaign to withdraw the adoption of the Definition persists despite the fact, as UCL political scientist Brad Blitz (2022) pointed out in a November 2022 lecture, that the Definition has been in effect for three years without prompting the series of resulting complaints about curtailment of speech predicted by its opponents. Nonetheless, the anti-Definition campaign is conducted as though it were primarily a free speech issue. All that helps explain the pattern Kahn-Harris (2022) observes: "For opponents of IHRA, when a campaign against its

1   My thanks to John Hyman and Anthony Julius for providing me with essential documents and for suggestions concerning an earlier draft of this chapter.

adoption by a particular institution is unsuccessful, campaigning shifts to overturning it rather than to influencing how it is applied" (3). There is little impetus to debate how the Definition is applied if there are few if any local complaints about its application.

Rather than campaign to reverse a campus's adoption, a more productive strategy might be to complicate the Definition's actual implementation, overwhelming the potentially infinite requirement of contextualization and thereby rendering the Definition impractical. As Kahn-Harris writes, "there seems to be little appetite, for example, for leveraging the gnomic 'may' in the list of examples in order to render particular kinds of anti-Zionism as outside the definition's scope. To do so may require a level of cynicism that is hard to adopt; to pretend that a text that one views as fundamentally 'closed' is actually 'open' might be impossible for some" (3). Especially if "closed" actually means "demonic." But I suspect many of the Definition's opponents have little stomach for that kind of intricate engagement. Once again, as I pointed out in this book's introduction, intellectual debate lacks the gratification of symbolic politics.

Given that the number of such campaigns is likely to increase, the UCL case will remain instructive. The debate at UCL is also potentially of wide interest because the arguments and documents produced have been substantially more interesting and detailed than those forthcoming from other campuses. It thus offers an opportunity for timely education for all who confront a similar controversy.

Members of a UCL Academic Board Working Group questioned the Definition's usefulness, arguing that it presents a substantial danger to academic freedom. Indeed, all the Working Group members, save one, opposed the Definition, suggesting that their report may have been an exercise in confirmation bias. They repeatedly cite a challenge to a 2019 campus exhibition, which included a hand-embroidered map of Palestine that did not include Israel, as a telling example of the danger the Definition poses to academic freedom. Believing that this example has been misused by the Working Group and that it offers a teachable moment regarding how the conflict's complexity can be aired, contained, and mediated, I will begin this chapter there. I will then examine the arguments of the Working Group in detail, often finding them to be faulty and based on misrepresentations of the Definition, which I believe UCL should retain. As of mid-2023, the status of the Definition at UCL remains unchanged, though further news is likely.

1. Partisan maps of the area between the river and the sea

In the summer of 2014, I joined a faculty study tour of Israel sponsored by Brandeis University's Schusterman Center for Israel Studies. Before departing for Israel, the group spent three weeks in residence reading and discussing texts and attending lectures about the history and the contemporary issues at stake in the region. The tour was designed to give us direct experience of a variety of views about the Israeli-Palestinian conflict, which it did with significant degree of success. An Israeli tour service was hired to take us from place to place by bus, and, as it happened, this gave us our first material evidence of politicized understanding on the way in from Ben Gurion Airport. We were each given an illustrated map of Israel that had not been vetted by the Brandeis organizers. It depicted a greater Israel encompassing the West Bank. Neither the Palestinians nor the Palestinian Authority had any discernable place on the map.

The following year, traveling independently with a friend, the two of us spent a day in the well-known Ramallah antiquities shop and home of a Palestinian who had retired from the UN. In addition to several hours of political discussion, we took the opportunity to buy some gifts at the shop. My favorite purchases were antique jewelry. But we were also offered a quite collectible hand-embroidered map of Palestine. It was priced at several hundred dollars. A traditional aspirational craft item made after 1948 with a political message, it eliminated the State of Israel. There was only Palestine "free from the river to the sea," its Jewish presence erased.

I was startled in 2014 by what seemed such a blatant misrepresentation of reality, though I would encounter no few other examples of the same impulse on subsequent visits. By the time we saw the embroidered map the following year, I was prepared to recognize it as the other side of the same coin. Competing maps erasing one another's identity are a recurring feature of the conflict. They are the cartographic equivalent of the competing narratives embraced by Israelis and Palestinians. Years before the IHRA Definition was approved, Israelis and Palestinians complained about each other's maps. Anyone who wishes to learn about the conflict should see them.

Only a few years later, in February 2019, an exhibition entitled "Moving Objects: Stories of Displacement" opened in the Octagon Gallery at University College London. The form of displacement at issue was exile, and the exhibition's press release and website announced that it "draws together material objects, poems, visual pieces and archival materials selected, co-created, and analyzed by people with refugee backgrounds." Several pieces came from Palestinian refugees in Jordan, including an embroidered (traditional *tatreez*) map of historic Palestine. The panel accompanying the embroidered map (object no. 31) read as follows:[2]

> How do "we" and "others" carry a vision of home/homeland with us? How might such visions transform into new futures of promise? From ancient to modern times map-making acts as a powerful tool of possession, dispossession and repossession. Maps depicting what Edward Said referred to as a "tiny sliver of land in the Eastern Mediterranean", are often deeply contentious. Here a map embroidered by a refugee is rooted in a pre-1948 rural vision of Palestine transmitted across generations.

The description is clearly professionally done. It is not simply propagandistic—except for the counterfactual suggestion that there was a Palestinian Arab ambition for nationhood prior to the founding of Israel. These embroidered maps are often produced by children, which may be the case with this one as well. An account of the exhibition is included as an appendix to a UCL faculty Report of the Academic Board Working Group on Racism and Prejudice, which observes that "as an object that reflected their longing for home from the vantage point of the displaced, it had a Palestinian flag and did not make reference to Israel" (Working Group 2020, 79). A UCL community member complained to the university that this represented "hidden antisemitism." I would credit it to commonplace anti-Zionism, not antisemitism. And I would add that conservative Israelis and radical Palestinians each at times represent the political geography of the land between the river and the sea inaccurately.

Contrary to the lone complaint, these mutually antagonistic maps of erasure do not attempt to hide the messages they embody, alternately anti-Palestinian and anti-Israeli. While I was slightly drawn to the possibility of purchasing the *tatreez* map in 2015, I felt it belonged in the collection of someone who shared its aspirations, not in the home of someone for whom it was an educational souvenir. And, yes, decades of hostility were among the forces materializing in that intricately embroidered fabric. But *tatreez* in fact refers to the centuries-long tradition of Palestinian embroidery. A museum on the

---

2 The embroidered map is reproduced in a post opposing the exhibition. See Jonathan Hoffman, "Anti-Israel Propaganda in UCL's Refugees Exhibition," We Are the 99% of Jews (blog), August 19, 2019, https://onthedarkside410122300.wordpress.com/2019/08/19/anti-israel-propaganda-in-ucls-refugees-exhibition/.

grounds of the American Colony Hotel compound in East Jerusalem includes numerous exquisite examples of Palestinian embroidery, among them elaborate dresses intended for special occasions. Many are a hundred and more years old. The museum director was kind enough to grant me an exception to their rule and allow me to take photographs. The modest *tatreez* map that was part of the UCL exhibit channeled an ancient skill that has been passed down from mother to daughter over generations and has therefore only recently acquired its contemporary political valence.

Whether I could have persuaded the person who lodged the London complaint that it reflected an unfortunate element of historical ignorance I cannot guess. But I like to think that education would have complicated the response. Had I been a UCL faculty member and been consulted, I would have recommended not going forward with a formal complaint. In any event, a more widespread protest against the exhibition materialized that August. A petition organized from outside the university, calling to "correct the anti-Israel propaganda in UCL's refugees exhibition," gathered over 700 signatures. The *tatreez* map was cited as key evidence for the accusation of antisemitism. The complaint elicited a response from Fiona Ryland, UCL's Chief Operating Officer: "The stated purpose of the 'Moving Objects' exhibition was to provide a series of personal perspectives on the perception of displacement, and it was not intended or presented as an objective analysis of any issue." That rational observation should have closed the matter, but administrators prefer to cover themselves, so Ryland authorized an investigation.

During my twenty years in the elected leadership of the American Association of University Professors (AAUP), I saw many university investigations that should have been dismissed early on instead being allowed to proceed pointlessly. Most did not concern antisemitism, instead dealing with other sensitive issues that administrators did not want to take responsibility for resolving. Both then and since I have seen antisemitic incidents that should have been investigated being ignored instead. The price of addressing serious matters is that some frivolous ones will also enter a university's quasi-judicial system, at least until experience builds the will to embrace justice in a responsible manner.

The investigation of "Moving Objects" concluded by endorsing the exhibition and the work of its curators, though it detoured briefly and unwisely to suggest that an apologetic panel be added. But the overall controversy ended with a commitment to academic freedom. I agree with the authors of the Working Group report that the complaint against the exhibition is an instance of "unfounded accusations of harm" (Working Group 2020, 26). Where I do not agree is with the assessment that the controversy exemplifies the "stifling [of] legitimate academic debate" (26). The report overstates matters by claiming that "the review process lent credence (perhaps inadvertently) to defamatory accusations of antisemitic bias against these academics for presenting perspectives and by relevant interviewees that criticized or sidelined Israeli or Zionist narratives" (26). Had the exhibit been compromised—even by requiring inclusion of a "balancing" panel from a Zionist perspective—then legitimate historical research would have been compromised. But legitimate debate won out in the end. The complaint was discredited. The incident followed an acceptable pattern for academic debate. Sensitive subjects like antisemitism or racism more broadly will occasion campus disputes whether or not the Definition is adopted by a given institution.

UCL did not adopt the IHRA Definition until November 2019, but the controversy over "Moving Objects" is repeatedly cited by the Definition's opponents as a telling example of the kind of complaint that the Definition will justify and encourage. The whole incident is also a teaching opportunity. The anti-Definition position is that an increasing number of such complaints will have a chilling effect on academic expression, even though that has not happened at campuses that have adopted the IHRA Definition. Indeed, the right to document Palestinian opinion was strengthened by the UCL case. I actually think the collapse of a few frivolous and ill-informed complaints will discourage UCL from pursuing more of them. If the Definition is misused, institutions will learn from that experience and correct their practices accordingly. Meanwhile, the Definition gives the UCL community a rational reference point for future discussions.

But it will not suffice to rely on administrators alone to choose rationality as a route to establishing a community that stands against racism and antisemitism while protecting academic freedom. Idiosyncratic as the "Moving Objects" complaint may seem, in one critical respect it entirely resembles the way in which academic institutions prefer to handle all forms of harassment—racial, ethnic, antisemitic, Islamophobic, and sexual. Universities prefer to adjudicate trivial offenses and ignore serious cases of harassment that reflect badly on the institution because they demonstrate that the institution has failed to protect members of its community and allowed an environment that fosters abuses to persist. By substantially exaggerating the significance of this complaint, the report may have contributed to that pattern. Used thoughtfully as part of a university's overall commitment to educate its community about antisemitism, as the model adoption language in this book's introduction mandates, the IHRA Definition can help people understand and deal with the ways in which the world's oldest hatred manifests itself today, focusing on serious rather than incidental examples.

2. UCL and the debate over the adoption of the IHRA Definition

UCL's chief governing body, the UCL Council, formally adopted the IHRA Definition in November 2019. However, UCL's Academic Board is officially charged with advising the Council on "all academic matters and questions affecting the educational policy of the College, the organisation of teaching, examining, research, and courses of instruction," and all those responsibilities could be impacted by efforts to curtail antisemitism.[3] The Academic Board has about 1,700 members, including all full professors and several hundred permanent full-time faculty, senior administrative staff, and student representatives of each faculty.

Some members of the Academic Board had been agitating for months for a working group to be established to study and report on the consequences of adopting the Definition. Disputes about the group's proposed membership delayed its implementation, but an agreement about categories of representation in the group was negotiated. The Working Group on Racism and Prejudice was formed in December 2019 and issued a report opposed to the adoption of the IHRA Definition in December 2020. The report and its appended documents total 150 single-spaced pages. So far as I know, it is the most detailed faculty group critique of the Definition.

The Working Group report should be supplemented by two detailed anti-Definition documents issued by the UCL branch of the University and College Union (UCU), the trade union and professional association representing casualized researchers and teaching staff, as well as professional services personnel, across the British higher education sector. They are "Can the IHRA working definition be implemented?" and "FAQs: 16 questions on UCL and the IHRA definition of anti-Semitism."[4] The national UCU has a history of support for the BDS movement. The UCU at UCL is headed by Sean Wallis, a member of the Working Group who promoted a conspiracy theory disseminated to encourage the boycott of Israeli universities.[5]

---

3 See "Academic Board: Terms of Reference," University College London, accessed June 22, 2022, https://www.ucl.ac.uk/governance-compliance/academic-board/academic-board-terms-reference.

4 See UCL UCU (n.d.).

5 In 2009, Wallis spoke at a meeting organized by a UCU Congress group and accused lawyers backed by "bank balances from Lehman Brothers that can't be tracked down" of opposing the academic boycott. See "Jewish Jokes," CST Blog, June 10, 2009, https://cst.org.uk/news/blog/2009/06/10/jewish-jokes. Wallis denies any antisemitic intent. On his denial, see Schraub (2009).

He is one of two Working Group members who signed a letter in support of Bristol University conspiracy theorist and antisemite David Miller.[6] Saladin Meckled-Garcia, a UCU vice-president and the other Working Group member supporting Miller, served on the Academic Board's governance committee that established the process by which the Working Group was composed.

A number of these documents, which may prove influential on other campuses, should be of interest to anyone concerned with the fate and utility of the IHRA Definition. They contain a mix of repetition and variation, borrowing from each other's arguments while also introducing new elements to the discussion. However, the integrity of the Academic Board's report is compromised by the fact that not a single Jewish student was included in the Working Group. Of the two students appointed, information about only one is available; he supports the accusation that Israeli is an apartheid state. Only one Jewish student was even consulted. The Working Group's status as an objective body is further put in doubt by the fact that more than half of its members were already outspoken opponents of the Definition before the Working Group was established. Four of them had signed a detailed February 2019 letter, reproduced in the report, opposing UCL's adoption of the Definition (Working Group 2020, 105–108). In addition, the Working Group notably relied on existing documents, undertaking no research of its own on UCL's antisemitism problem.

It has been pretty much universally reported in the press that the Working Group's report was strongly supported and officially endorsed by the Academic Board. Yet only those members who attended the earlier meeting at which the Working Group presented its report and recommendations were eligible to participate in the online vote. In the end, only 334 ballots were cast, representing between 15 and 20 percent of the membership of the Board. Interpreting the result is precisely a matter of interpretation, as votes were cast as ranked choices among four options: (A) retain the IHRA Definition as is; (B) retain and amend with specified amendments; (C) replace through a specified procedure; (D) retract and return to the Equality Act alone. Ranked voting can work well with a list of candidates for office. In this context, it can be quite confusing. A statistical report circulated by the Secretary to the Board, Nick McGhee, was given graphic representation by UCL international politics and policy professor Brad Blitz (2021). Analysis of the numerical

---

6 See "Educators and Researchers in Support of Professor Miller," Support David Miller, accessed June 2022, https://supportmiller.org/educators-and-researchers.

data suggests that many ballots were contradictory: 40 percent voted for both B (retain with amendments) and D (retract completely), while 16 percent voted for both A (retain as is) and D (retract completely). Option C (replace) received the most first place votes, while B (retain in amended form) appeared on more ballots. The most one can conclude is that many of those who voted preferred some guidance specific to antisemitism. It is not justifiable to conclude that UCL faculty are united behind a demand to eliminate the IHRA Definition entirely. Indeed, it is significant that only one of the eleven members of the Working Group dissented from the report. The Working Group did not reflect the variety of opinion in the faculty as a whole.

3. Antisemitism at UCL

In December 2016, the UK government formally adopted the IHRA Working Definition of Antisemitism, including the eleven examples of antisemitism that follow the brief summary definition. British universities were first formally urged to adopt the Definition in a February 2017 letter from Universities Minister Jo Johnson to Universities UK (UUK) Chief Executive Nicola Dandridge.[7] Widely reported public incidents of invited campus lecturers being aggressively disrupted helped fuel awareness that action was needed.

The first relevant protest took place at King's College London on January 19, 2016, when protestors from King's College and other London universities disrupted a presentation by Ami Ayalon, a former head of the Shin Bet Israel's domestic security agency. After retiring, Ayalon became a peace activist, a Labor Party member of the Knesset, and a supporter of the two-state solution. He appeared in and helped organize the 2012 documentary *The Gatekeepers*, in which retired Shin Bet heads review Israeli security practices, critique Israeli government policy, and suggest routes toward peace. Protestors at his lecture apparently did not consider that history relevant. They adopted a tactic of repeatedly setting off building fire alarms to force the police to end the presentation, a tactic that eventually succeeded. The fire alarms were accompanied by protestors slamming chairs to the floor, chanting, and banging on windows, walls, and doors.

---

7   See "Universities Minister Calls on UK Universities to Tackle Anti-Semitism, Particularly in Context of 'Israel Apartheid Week,'" Conservative Friends of Israel, February 22 2017, https://cfoi.co.uk/universities-minister-calls-on-uk-universities-to-tackle-anti-semitism-particularly-in-context-of-israel-apartheid-week/.

On October 27, 2016, a former Israel Defense Forces (IDF) commander, Hen Mazzig, was scheduled to speak in a room in UCL's Archaeology Department. The event was advertised online, as was an organized effort to disrupt it. A detailed investigative report by Professor Geraint Rees reprints the protest notice that circulated online. It included these exhortations to action, including a distinctly antisemitic suggestion that every Israeli who serves in the IDF is an evil person with blood on his or her hands:

> Hen served as lieutenant in the Israeli Occupation Forces (IOF) for 5 years. That means he's complicit in the colonisation of Palestinian territory, protection of illegal Israeli settlements, and the murder and displacement of hundreds of innocent families.... We're just shocked and outraged that someone with the blood of innocent people on their hands can be given a platform at UCL to speak to students.... We're not about to sit back and let this happen. It's sick, wrong, and a grotesque violation of every mechanism in place to make sure we don't get evil people given a platform at our university. (Rees 2017, 8)

Protestors were urged to gather on the Main Quad hours in advance to be instructed on a plan for action. When security officers arrived at the lecture site an hour beforehand, protestors were already in the building. Soon shouting and chanting was accompanied by pushing and shoving as political opponents confronted one another. An effort was made to block attendees from entering the room, Meanwhile, protestors climbed through a window to gain access. The protestors used loudspeakers to aid in disrupting the event. Mazzig managed to talk for fifteen minutes, but then stopped because it was very difficult to hear him. A gauntlet of protestors repeated called out "Shame" to attendees who exited. Rees's report emphasizes that protestors successfully created an atmosphere of intimidation that clearly undermined academic freedom and "prevent[ed] the legitimate exercise of free speech" (15).

This widely reported episode alone made it clear that UCL had a problem with anti-Zionism and antisemitism. In 2017, Cathy Elliott, a UCL teaching fellow in political science, joined three of her students to conduct interviews with twenty-six Jewish UCL students about their experiences on campus. They produced a seven-episode podcast series narrating what the students had conveyed. Segments included "You Don't Look Jewish," "Talking about the Holocaust," "Jokes and Tropes," and "Talking about Israel." Elliott later summarized her findings in an essay, "Learning Lessons: The Articulation of Antisemitism on

Campus." She notes that, while most did not encounter daily antisemitism, they all had very troubling experiences to report:

> We came across many students who were afraid of disclosing that they were Jewish because of experiences of being called names or having to listen to jokes about Nazis, antisemitic tropes about rich Jews or stingy Jews, or Jews controlling the media or the supermarkets, or the world, or having to endure judgement about whether or not they "looked Jewish". Students who were bored of tedious jokes about eating pork. A student who had been chased down the street just outside our main quad, apparently because he was Jewish. Jokes about the Holocaust, patronising explanations of the Holocaust from non-Jews ("goysplaining"), crass comparisons between the Holocaust and unrelated issues such as animal rights. Doubts about the Holocaust's importance were in one case signaled by the question, "What do you think about the Holocaust?" The student on the receiving end had had family members murdered by the Nazis. We also came across belittling comments from tutors ranging from a refusal to make accommodations for religious festivals, to sexist remarks about women students being "good Jewish girls", to extraordinarily rude, antisemitic comments, such as "all you fucking Jews stick together, don't you?", to downplaying the horrors of the Holocaust in class. (Elliot 2019, 78)

Since the incidents reported often embodied traditional antisemitic tropes, code words, and dog whistles, Elliott concludes they are not connected to the "new antisemitism" organized around the Jewish state. She does not recognize the ways in which hostility toward Israel gives rise to a renewal of an ancient hatred, but her project is nonetheless an important part of the accumulating documentation of antisemitism at UCL.

It was not until October 2018 that UCL's senior management responded by agreeing to give the proposal to adopt the IHRA Definition full consideration. Significantly, in January 2019, UCL's Jewish Society surveyed Jewish students about their experience of antisemitism. In March, UCL Vice-Provost Lori Houlihan summarized its results in a paper on antisemitism at UCL:

> Comments reported by students covered a wide range of classic antisemitic tropes, including appearance ("you've got a small

nose for a Jew"), money ("Why don't you pay for my Uber Jew boy?", "You don't need an internship, you're guaranteed a job in a bank", "I'm not surprised, your people are so good with money"—said by a supervisor to their PhD student when he mentioned that he had identified a source of funding), and power (one student reports talking to a friend about antisemitic tropes about Jews controlling the media and being told "Well, it's not entirely untrue, is it?"). Strong feelings relating to Israel/Palestine also affect Jewish students on campus regardless of their views on or connection with Israel, with reported comments including "why do you like killing children?" and "You're Jewish? So you take all the water from Gaza?"[8]

These and other comments reported in the online poll map directly onto the examples included in the IHRA Definition, with some statements implicating more than one example. Moreover, the character of these instances of antisemitism is not seriously debatable. They represent harassment and expressions of hate, not political opinions protected by academic freedom. They demonstrate what even the UCL opponents of the Definition concede: "there is disturbing evidence that incidents of antisemitism have persisted in our university" (Working Group 2020, 3); "even classic antisemitic tropes are frequently not recognized as such" (36); "racism is part of the everyday experience of Jews, people of colour and Muslims" (64). As the Working Group's one dissenting member writes, "the IHRA was adopted by Council against a backdrop of rising antisemitic incidents at UCL and real concerns being voiced by the Jewish community about whether UCL was becoming an unsafe place for Jewish students" (66). There are other examples from the survey—among them "being told I am lying about the Holocaust having happened," "I've been told 'to go back to the gas chambers and die, you dirty f—ing Jew,'" "I've been told that I must have lice because all Jews do," "my friend has been called 'a smelly dirty Jew' because on shabbat he was walking around with a kippah," and "[I] have been told that by wearing a Star of David I support an apartheid state" (151)—but even those cited in Houlihan's summary suffice to warn there is a serious problem. The picture painted here is substantially worse than that presented at most American and Canadian campuses. The debate that ensued was over what to do about it.

---

8   Quoted in Working Group (2020, 116).

The "small nose for a Jew" remark matches the IHRA Definition's example of "using the symbols and images associated with classic antisemitism." The insults about money all reflect the example of "making mendacious, dehumanizing, or stereotypical allegations about Jews." The comments about killing children and taking Gaza's water embody the example of "holding Jews collectively responsible for actions of the state of Israel," but they do so fundamentally by way of slanders or misinformation about Israeli policy—in the first case perhaps reading homicidal malice and deliberate intent into the deaths of Gazan children who died from Israeli air strikes during 2014's Operation Protective Edge, in the second case ignorantly and falsely claiming that water shortages in Gaza are due to Israel "taking" the water. The Definition's examples help clarify why these comments are antisemitic. Beyond condemning them, a university might require offending students to take a course in the history of antisemitism. A student who persisted might be blocked from using university email if that medium had been the vehicle for the remarks. Oral harassment by students, staff, or faculty members could result in being barred from certain campus buildings.

UCL's Jewish Society has continued to collect testimony about antisemitic events on campus. A report compiled by Sam Goldstone and Rebecca Lyons (n.d.) documents incidents through January 2021. Thus, a student reports being "spat at for wearing a Star of David necklace," while another writes "when I was in uni members of the palsoc made jokes about the 3 boys that had been kidnapped and murdered in Israel and then told me it wasn't personal." Yet another writes, "As a Muslim student at UCL that is outspoken in my support of Jewish students on campus, I have often been subject to discrimination from other Muslim students on campus. In particular, I have been called a 'race traitor' and have been accused of engaging in 'respectability politics.'" It is worth mentioning a few examples that involve two other contexts—classroom incidents and overheard remarks. One student reported this incident during the 2019 academic year, once again an example of holding all Jews responsible for Israel's practices:

> Whilst reading postcolonial literature, I was personally singled-out by my professor in front of an entire lecture hall of students, and jokingly told to write my essay on the topic of "the Israeli colonisation of Palestine", with particular focus on "the ongoing Israeli torture of disabled Palestinians in the West Bank". This comment was entirely out of context with the texts relevant to my syllabus, and obviously directed towards me as a way of

> singling me, a Jew, as "other". I recall the humiliation and shock I felt, the stares of my peers, and the inability to confront a Professor who was my obvious superior.

There are several examples of overheard remarks; this one offers notable detail:

> During exam seasons in May 2018, I experienced anti-Semitism in the cruciform hub at UCL. I was studying in a shared room when I overheard a group of five people next to me starting to discuss Israel. They said things like "it's a sad world to be accused of antisemitism for being against Israel", then another student continued with "yes they should've all just burnt in the concentration camps". The whole group laughed out loud. I [have] graduated now but as a Jewish student listening to this, I did not feel safe.

The UK Equality Act 2010 has a sound definition of harassment: "intimidating, hostile, degrading, humiliating or offensive behavior, through means which have the purpose or effect of violating a person's dignity or creating an intimidating, hostile, degrading, or humiliating environment," a definition that UCL embraces. The Working Group insists that is all a university needs to address antisemitic harassment. Yet their report also points out that UCL overall displays "a lack of awareness about what antisemitism is and why it is a problem." The Equality Act gives no guidance in identifying actual instances of antisemitism or any other form of harassment involving protected categories. The gap between the Equality Act's generalizations and any action against antisemitism requires the additional information the Definition's examples provide.

Critics of the examples sometimes complain that they do not include the specific tactics for harassment regularly seen on campuses in a number of countries. Worse still, some argue, it does not categorize violent, even murderous, attacks on Jews, whether at the Hypercacher supermarket in Paris or the Tree of Life synagogue in Pittsburgh. That critique fundamentally misunderstands and misrepresents the purpose of the IHRA Definition. It identifies key examples of the political, ideological, and religious beliefs that underlie, motivate, or justify antisemitic statements and actions. That is the first step in recognizing and understanding contemporary antisemitism. Indeed, the Definition succeeds at identifying motivations behind both social and political antisemitism, categories Bernard Harrison has done much to clarify.

A much larger educational project should follow. The IHRA Definition is not the last word on antisemitism.

4. Working Group arguments opposing the IHRA Definition

As one of its general arguments against UCL or any other university adopting the IHRA Definition, the Working Group report repeatedly warns that it will both directly and indirectly compromise academic freedom. As proof that this fear is warranted, the report emphasizes both the objection to the "Moving Objects" exhibit and a request to prohibit Jackie Walker from speaking at a 2019 campus book launch for a book containing the proceedings of a conference held at UCL in 2017 to celebrate the legacy of Noam Chomsky's formative essay "The Responsibilities of Intellectuals."[9] Walker, a political activist and writer, is one of the contributors to the book. She had been suspended from the British Labour Party for antisemitic remarks in 2016, then reinstated, and was finally expelled in March 2019. As the report's authors acknowledge, Walker was approved for participation and the book launch proceeded.

The book launch is paired with the "Moving Objects" exhibition and characterized as one of two clear demonstrations of the dangers that the Definition will impose. Inconveniently for the purposes of the Working Group report, both events took place anyway, so the purported damage from the challenges to them is at best theoretical. The reputations of all involved in the projects may actually have been strengthened. It seems that the authors of the report want to milk the implications of trying to constrain a book launch at a research institution. The odds of successfully blocking one of a book's contributors from speaking at such an event are so minute as to defy calculation. However, one additional fact renders the calculation mathematically impossible: the book gathers together essays previously presented at a UCL conference.

In parallel to the "Moving Objects" protest, once again an administrator tried to impose a textual condition. This time speakers were asked to sign a set of guidelines identifying "tropes that UCL would find unacceptable to be repeated on its campus." "The Responsibilities of Intellectuals" echoes the title of a Noam Chomsky project and honors his work. Chomsky was shown the guidelines and given an opportunity to advise the speakers about

---

9   See Working Group (2020).

whether to sign. He is one of the world's best known anti-Zionists. Another mathematical impossibility: calculating the time delay between Chomsky receiving the guidelines and urging the speakers to refuse to sign them. The speakers then did refuse, and the requirement was dropped. While I object to the corrective panel proposed for "Moving Objects," I find these campus guidelines, which adapt IHRA Definition's examples, instructive, although I would not prohibit people from violating them on campus or require speakers to promise compliance.

> In the context of antisemitism, tropes that UCL would find unacceptable to be repeated on its campus include but are not limited to:
>
> – Suggestions (overt or implied) that Jews as a group or particular sections of the British Jewish community invent, exaggerate or "weaponise" incidents of antisemitism for political or other benefit
> – Suggestions (overt or implied) that Jews as a group or particular sections of the British Jewish community exploit or exaggerate the Holocaust for political or other benefit
> – Use (overt or implied) of "dual loyalty" tropes relating to Jews as a group or particular sections of the British Jewish community and the State of Israel—for example that they are "controlled" by Israel or are working on behalf of Israel to the detriment of Britain
> – Suggestions (overt or implied) that antisemitism is a less toxic form of racism than any other and/or that Jews are less vulnerable to discrimination than other minority groups
> – Repetition (overt or implied) of antisemitic tropes relating to Jews and money and/or Jewish financial involvement in historical events or injustices—for example that Jews financed wars, slavery, etc (Working Report 2020, 84)

It could be quite productive for the campus community to discuss whether it would be beneficial to air such views. Indeed, both the "Moving Objects" and the book launch examples demonstrate that the IHRA Definition presents no credible threat to academic freedom and no plausible prospect of a chilling effect on anti-Zionist speech. They are both frivolous complaints, but they are apparently the best the Working Group can offer. They would be a cause for concern only if you wish it were so. Despite that, I am willing to attribute their use in the report to a combination of confirmation bias and groupthink.

I cannot, however, regard the February 27, 2019, letter signed by Working Group chair Seth Anziska and forty-three other UCL faculty members with equal generosity. The letter's appendix lists what it calls "Documented Risks to Campus Free Speech Posed by the IHRA Definition in the US," six identified as "Threats against Professors/Classroom Curriculum" and three classified as "Threats against Student Clubs" (Working Group 2020, 109–110). I have written about several of these cases before, so I will just summarize them here. The letter by these UCL faculty willfully distorts and misrepresents these incidents, despite the fact that considerable factual information is available through an internet search.

The appendix implies that University of Michigan Professor John Cheney-Lippold was unfairly sanctioned because of a Zionist Organization of America (ZOA) demand following his refusal to write a letter of recommendation requested by one of his students who wished to study at Tel Aviv University. Cheney-Lippold made it clear the student was fully qualified, and he volunteered to write her a recommendation for any non-Israeli university. As I detail in Chapter Three, he was punished because his action was clearly discriminatory and in violation of his professional responsibilities. ZOA was but one of many organizations that commented on this widely debated case. Do Anziska and his colleagues actually believe the faculty member's blatantly discriminatory behavior is defensible?

Another example cited in the appendix to the letter concerns a student-taught UC Berkeley course on the Israeli-Palestinian conflict that was briefly suspended and then reinstated because it had not been subjected to the appropriate faculty review. I discuss the syllabus and the review process in detail in my book *Israel Denial*. The readings assigned were consistently anti-Zionist. The student was not qualified to answer the challenge that they were also antisemitic. Many of us who commented felt that uncredentialed undergraduates should not be teaching controversial political subjects for credit. That same consideration applied to the course at UC Riverside, which I discuss as well. Both students were taught, advised, and supervised by faculty members active in the boycott movement. The students were not exercising independent professional judgment in their teaching.

The appendix goes on to express concern over complaints about a national Students for Justice in Palestine (SJP) conference that was scheduled to take place at UCLA in 2018. Protests about such events will take place whether or not institutions adopt the IHRA Definition. In any case, like the events at UCL, the conference took place as planned.

Finally, and regrettably, the UCL faculty members address another event at UC Berkeley. As I wrote in *Fathom* (Nelson 2021a), Neal Sher, a former Justice Department official responsible from 1983–1994 for hunting former Nazis, told a reporter in 2018 that UC Berkeley students who equated the Pittsburgh synagogue murders with Israeli action in Gaza should be expelled, an intemperate statement that merits condemnation. But Sher was a private citizen whose government responsibilities had ended more than thirty years earlier. Indeed, he had been disbarred in the interim. Unsurprisingly, the students were not in fact expelled. The UCL faculty cite none of these details, presumably because one individual's irresponsible remark would seem unworthy of notice.

These remarkably weak anecdotes are not the only basis of the report's critique. It begins with the brief summary definition in the Definition's text: "Antisemitism is a certain perception of Jews, which may be expressed as hatred of Jews. Rhetorical and physical manifestations of antisemitism are directed toward Jewish or non-Jewish individuals and/or their property, toward Jewish community institutions and religious facilities." Curiously enough, both the Definition's supporters and its detractors take issue with these two sentences. The key fact regarding campus adoption, however, is not that it is dangerous to use this definition to identify potentially antisemitic statements or actions; the key fact, as I point out in Chapter Eight, is that it is impossible to do so. It has no practical uses. Critics and supporters of the Definition alike find the reliance on "a certain perception of Jews" to be disabling and unresolvable. Antisemitism is as likely to be based in beliefs and delusional explanatory theories as in perceptions. And they realize that even if it "may be expressed as hatred of Jews," it also may not be.

I regard the opening definition as a *preface* to the examples that form the functional part of the IHRA Definition. I prefer to see the opening definition supplemented by at least a couple of alternatives, emphasizing that no brief definition will be perfect. The Working Group quotes Holocaust scholar Helen Fein's definition of antisemitism, which I have used as well: "A persisting latent structure of hostile beliefs toward Jews as a collectivity manifested in individuals as attitudes, and in culture as myth, ideology, folklore, and imagery, and in actions—social or legal discrimination, political mobilization against Jews, and collective or state violence—which results in and/or is designed to distance, displace or destroy Jews as Jews." One of the virtues of her definition is that it recognizes that antisemitism is several things at once. Its latent persistence can erupt into a variety of manifest forms. A single unified definition accounting for the whole history of those manifestations is impossible.

5. Turning the IHRA Definition against itself

Most critics of the Definition regard the eleven examples as "the main problem." However, both the University College Union (UCU) and the Working Group insist on elevating the importance of the opening definition and treating it as a major condition for applying the eleven examples to real world behavior. Both the UCU and the Working Group characterize it as the "core" or "underlying" definition: "to qualify as antisemitic under the IHRA, it must fit the underlying definition of antisemitism" (Working Group 2020, 32), which is something that the Definition never asserts. In "Can the IHRA working definition be implemented?," UCU overreacts accordingly: "It invites investigative managers and panel members to ascribe beliefs to the accused, apparently on an all-or-nothing basis. Such allegations are liable to be libelous if unsupported by considerable evidence."[10]

Matters were not clarified when the UK Parliament's Home Affairs Select Committee, in an effort to ensure cautious use of the Definition, recommended adding two "caveats" supplementing the Definition, one of which reads as follows: "It is not antisemitic to hold the Israeli government to the same standards as other liberal democracies, or to take a particular interest in the Israeli government's policies or actions, without additional evidence to suggest antisemitic intent." That evidence can come from the overall context, which includes the surrounding debates about Israeli policies and actions. But it would be a mistake to infer that the use of antisemitic tropes without conscious or deliberate antisemitic intent avoids antisemitic consequences.

The caveat bringing "intent" into the discussion helped the Working Group read an insistence on "intent" back into the Definition. The Working Group thus falsely insists that the opening definition imposes intent on all manifestations of the eleven examples that follow (Working Group 2020, 33), something the Definition never maintains. The Definition rightly does not say that its examples only qualify as antisemitic if accompanied by a specific antisemitic intent. Nor in fact do the caveats specifically say this, despite the Working Group declaring that they require it. The Working Group report aims to convince us that the

---

10 See UCL UCU (n.d.).

Definition is constructed so that none of the examples are valid in application unless antisemitic intent can be demonstrated on every occasion.

Why should the cultural prevalence of "a certain perception of Jews" guarantee deliberate intent behind every antisemitic statement or action? The relevant perceptions can produce both conscious and unconscious dislike. They vary over time and from culture to culture and from community to community. It would have been a mistake for the Definition to insist on an intentional motivation for every antisemitic statement or action, and it does not do so. For better or worse, human beings often enough have no idea why they act as they do. Indeed, even the Working Group concedes that the Definition "otherwise make[s] no reference to the intent of the speaker" (33), but the initial definition does not take a stand on intent either. The sentence preceding the above-mentioned UCU statement is more accurate in its assessment of the opening definition: "In practice this is not a diagnostic tool that is readily employed." But that practical view contradicts the dire warnings that follow in UCU's position paper. Moreover, if the definition invites responsible parties to "ascribe beliefs to the accused," it is notable that no university I know of has required its community to do so over the years since the Definition was adopted by the IHRA. Intent plays a role in some cases but not in others.

The decision of the UCL's critics of the Definition to make intent such a central issue was not a product of disinterested or objective analysis. It was a political decision to seize on what was perceived to be a target of opportunity. First of all, it reflects the fact that intent is often impossible to determine with any certainty. The presumed "requirement" of intent thus disables the ability to identify most antisemitic statements or actions. Moreover, once this fictitious account of the Definition is announced, it can then be read into the examples. According to the Working Group, "the IHRA working definition says that antisemitic intent may be adduced from e.g. 'denying the Jewish people their right to self-determination' or by 'claiming that the existence of a State of Israel is a racist endeavor.'" (Working Group 2020, 35). Yet the Definition says nothing of the kind. The standard of analysis for years has been that such anti-Zionist statements have antisemitic effects, not antisemitic intent.

The artificially manufactured requirement of proven intent weaponizes the opening definition so that it can be turned against the eleven examples. The Definition then contradicts and deconstructs itself. The invented issue of intent also puts the Definition in conflict with the definition of harassment in the UK Equality Act 2010, a definition the Working Group purports to endorse: "This is a broader definition than the IHRA, as it covers not only statements but also *acts*, which furthermore need not be motivated by 'hatred'; moreover, it does not require intent to be demonstrated" (52). If either identification or enforcement is the goal, the Definition is in fact the Equality Act's partner, not its opponent. There is no "unavoidable tension" (54) between the two. The remarkable above-cited passage from the Working Group report is a layered collection of misrepresentations. The Definition highlights the beliefs that motivate antisemitic actions. It is not limited to explicit hatred, and it does not require evidence of intent. Moreover, the Equality Act gives no explicit guidance for defining instances of antisemitic harassment. The Definition meets that need.

The Working Group's highly debatable reasoning lets it appear to endorse five of the IHRA Definition's examples that address traditional forms of antisemitism unrelated to Israel (46–47), while disputing the Definition's ability to confirm them. The five examples are thus approved in principle only; if the principles are linked to the Definition, then we are powerless to use them. We are burdened with disabling conditions. But the conditions, again, are only artifacts of the Working Group's reasoning; the IHRA Definition itself gives us the authority to dismiss those conditions if we choose.

The chain of reasoning just outlined makes it possible for the Working Group to dismiss the Definition as "a tokenistic gesture rather than a rigorous and enforceable set of procedures and protocols" (4), even though the Definition makes no effort to design enforcement procedures. Those will depend on applicable national laws and institutional missions. Only if people believe the Working Group's reasoning can they accept its otherwise incomprehensible conclusion that "the IHRA working definition is unhelpful in identifying cases of harassment and is therefore a weak tool for effective university action" (5), indeed that its adoption "will actually undermine—rather than advance—efforts to tackle antisemitism" (45). We are to believe that the Definition is at one and the same time a powerful and dangerous tool destined to destroy academic freedom and a weak, self-contradictory document that should be contemptuously disregarded.

6. The Israel exception

As with all anti-Definition projects, the Working Group must turn to its main opponent: the seven examples that address the State of Israel, ultimately asking "whether *any* questioning of the existence of the State of Israel or its legitimacy is sufficient to constitute antisemitism" (2020, 35). A negative answer would be a stunning proposition in the light, among other examples, of the Hamas Charter which suggests that the unacceptable existence of Israel justifies the general killing of Jews. In the long history of the longest hatred, the Jewish people have never escaped the mutating hostility that has always kept them in view. But before 1948 the Jewish people did not have a Jewish state to draw antisemitic fire. Some would prefer to exclude Israel from discussions about antisemitism; then we could all agree on examples that are much easier to condemn. Yet even the Working Group has to concede that "contemporary antisemitism is often expressed in virulent criticism of the state of Israel" (46). The antisemitic attacks on Israel are at the center of what some designate as the "new antisemitism," though in truth there have been a succession of new antisemitisms over centuries. But the phenomenon of antisemitic anti-Zionism must be addressed whether or not it is seen to reconfigure antisemitism as a whole.

The IHRA Definition sets out a fundamental precondition for all consideration of whether anti-Israel sentiment is antisemitic: "criticism of Israel similar to that leveled against any other country cannot be regarded as antisemitic." This carefully worded condition is designed to mandate inclusion of a very wide range of attacks on Israeli policy and practices within acceptable political discourse. It deliberately opts to say "similar to," rather than "the same as." The "same as" would make the task of adjudicating examples much easier, but it would also classify many more criticisms of Israel as antisemitic. With that phrase, the Definition responsibly narrows the options for condemning criticisms of Israeli policy, reserving the accusation of antisemitism for attacks that treat Israel differently from other nation states. The Working Group worries that a course syllabus that "probe[s] how Israeli independence was intimately tied to Palestinian dispossession" (34) might be judged antisemitic, but the "similar to" criterion would admit comparisons with a significant number of modern nation states created by way of population transfers. And it would allow comparison or contrast as well with more violent dispossession, such as that central to the creation of Australia, Canada, Mexico, and the United States, among other countries. The whole range of potential comparisons is admitted to discussion, with the antisemitic designation available only to those judged not "similar to."

Like many other anti-Definition manifestoes, the Working Group's report complains that the Definition "fails to give adequate criteria for distinguishing" between criticisms "that are antisemitic from those that are not" (46), and it adds that "the notion of 'similar' ... is too vague and subjective to be useful as a neutral criterion" (50) for drawing the necessary distinctions. The Definition does indeed leave much of the work in making all these comparisons to the collective efforts of analysts across the world. The task is not appropriate to a concise Definition. Over time, after research and debate, general principles for comparisons among nation states related to antisemitism will be possible.

Meanwhile, the Definition sets a high bar for the antisemitism designation. Far from being irresponsibly "vague" or "imprecise," the Definition is determinedly ethical.

The above-mentioned precondition parallels one of the eleven examples of antisemitism: "Applying double standards by requiring of it [Israel] a behavior not expected or demanded of any other democratic nation." Indeed, it is helpful to pair the precondition with this example. This particular example has attracted remarkably confused and excited criticism. Once again, it requires serious comparative work by multiple scholars before it can be widely employed, but that necessity has just been addressed, and a great deal of that work has already been done. The Working Group regrettably quotes some decidedly confused reasoning to buttress its concerns. Thus it finds reasonable Lara Friedman's contention that the Definition concludes "it is anti-Semitic to challenge Israel's occupation of Palestinian lands—unless one is equally challenging occupation anywhere" (48). She seems to feel the Definition assigns this Herculean burden to everyone. The requirement instead is to contextualize criticism of Israel within the patterns of critique applied to other nations. That does not mean those patterns need to be specified. No one is required to elaborate on those comparisons as she says. We should be aware of the norms for nation state and policy critique when addressing Israeli policy, not create special demands of Israel alone among the nations. To do so, the Definition argues, may after analysis prove to be antisemitic.

The Working Group apparently also endorses Friedman's claim that the Definition implies boycotts of Israel are antisemitic "unless one is similarly boycotting every country guilty of violating the rights of any people, anywhere" (49), but no sane person has ever maintained that. On the other hand, when only one nation on earth, the one Jewish state, is subject to a continuing international boycott campaign, there is reason for concern that that nation's Jewish character may be at issue.

The parameters that the Definition sets for criticism of Israel are designed to protect robust critique while guarding against the far too frequent tendency for it to veer into demonization. When that happens Jewish students, staff, and faculty feel that the part of their identities that identifies with the Jewish state has been demonized as well. The available alternatives to the Definition, notably including the Jerusalem Declaration on Antisemitism, are structured to make demonization acceptable. That is not a sound basis for education. The Working Group may nonetheless reorganize as a new group dedicated to promoting the Jerusalem Declaration as a substitute for the IHRA Definition. Anziska is one of the people who drafted the Jerusalem Declaration. François Guesnet, another

Working Group member, cosigned it. Some British universities are considering adopting both the Definition and the Declaration, but the two documents would effectively cancel each other out and produce paralyzing confusion.

7. Conclusion

An increase in the number of cases of antisemitism worldwide, combined with an increase in the amount of attention devoted to antisemitism, has brought more frequent debate about antisemitism to campuses and the public sphere alike. There is, however, no evidence to support the fears expressed at UCL and by other opponents of the IHRA Definition that it has given or will give rise to a flood of restrictions and complaints that undermine academic freedom. Challenges will occur, and we will learn from them. As part of the debate over the Definition, UCL's provost recommended an annual report documenting and summarizing complaints and investigations. That would be a good way of assuring that local history and its lessons are not forgotten.

The Working Group report suggests "there is a real risk that members of the UCL community will be anxious about crossing a line when discussing topics like Israel and Palestine" (2020, 60). The reality is that the disciplines for which teaching and research about the Middle East is central are the very disciplines in which relentless anti-Zionism is pervasive. We are a long way from a culture in which those students and faculty would feel any hesitation about condemning Israel and pressing for its elimination. I do not see the adoption of the IHRA Definition changing that culture quickly; it certainly has not done so yet. The Definition can help orient the educational program that should be introduced, but it will not suffice on its own. Yet "Jewish students did report feeling safer on campus following its adoption" (42).

One-off event cancellations might have proven more likely, but the list of those is short. The University of Central Lancashire did cancel an event scheduled to be part of Israeli Apartheid Week early in 2017. The university first said that the panel on "Debunking Misconceptions on Palestine" violated IHRA Definition's guidelines, then said approval had not been requested on time. The *Legal Guide for Palestine Solidarity Student Activists* issued by the Palestine Solidarity Campaign in April 2021 cites the Central Lancashire cancellation, then adds:

> In withstanding attempts to mischaracterise and suppress the BDS movement for Palestinian rights, it is important to

remember that there is no other known case of any university directly citing the IHRA definition to close down an event that is legitimately critical of Israel and is therefore not anti-Semitic in the proper sense of manifesting hatred, discrimination or prejudice, towards Jewish people as Jews. If this were to occur this would be likely to be legally challengeable. (PSC 2021, 16)

Although the Working Group also concedes that the campus has not blocked a speaker (2020, 51), that fact does not make vigilance less necessary nor the issues less pressing. But it does suggest that the warnings issued and the rhetoric employed by the anti-Definition movement might benefit from some moderation. When UCL UCU (2021a) declares that "despite its length and complexity, the IHRA working definition (and all of its examples and caveats) adds barely a useful word to the Equality Act 2010 definition of harassment," it does not advance either understanding or productive debate. Similarly, the Working Group's concern for "the lecturer, who is forced to demonstrate time and again that he or she is not motivated by antisemitic intent" (2020, 54) is unfounded, not least because it would itself constitute harassment. The Working Group is also concerned that the Definition, once adopted, will function as "the final word on antisemitism" (54), a concern that has already been proven moot and one that would seem vanishingly small at any university.

In its "FAQs" document, UCL UCU (2021b) raises a quite justified concern that campus disciplinary procedures can take so long to resolve that they constitute punishment even for those judged innocent. We have already seen that happen repeatedly with false accusations leveled against Zionist students and faculty in the United States. A partial but key solution to that problem is to build into procedures ways to promptly reject frivolous complaints and cases that lack sufficient evidence.

The IHRA Definition is a powerful aid to both education and policy development. I hope that this review of its opponents' arguments will help promote its continued adoption. But that is not the issue at stake at UCL, where the Definition has been adopted and the Academic Board has been understood to demand its withdrawal. None of us have yet confronted a situation in which a campus that has very serious problems with antisemitism is actually seeking to abandon the Definition's eleven examples. That could well create a permissive campus atmosphere for antisemitism unlike anything we have recently seen in the West.

That is a danger faced by campuses well beyond UCL or Britain as a whole. It is a danger that hovers over all the events and disputes documented in this book. But the impact of the UCL debate will initially be felt in the United Kingdom. The British constituencies that are interested in seeing whether a campus's adoption of the IHRA Definition can be reversed are closely watching the process unfolding in London. If the Definition's opponents at UCL fail, its opponents elsewhere may lose heart. But the reverse is also true. Some of these battles are fought for all of us.

Conclusion

Augmented Debate

In the introduction to this book, I presented two documents that could be endorsed by a faculty senate and formally adopted by a campus's central administration. The first is a model for a campus policy on the use of the IHRA Working Definition of Antisemitism. Specifying how a campus may and may not apply the Definition, it prohibits some potential uses condemned by the Definition's critics and encourages other uses that would help educate a campus about antisemitism and diminish its presence. The second document is a model policy designed to prohibit official departmental statements taking positions on contested political issues, while leaving individual faculty members and groups of faculty free to do so. These documents offer practical solutions to disagreements presently dividing campuses on both sides of the Atlantic. It's unlikely that either document could entirely resolve current debates, but perhaps they demonstrate that rational analysis can offer a route to begin doing so. The rest of the book devotes substantial space to detailing the conditions that make the two proposed policies necessary. I cite the two documents again to invite their reconsideration now.

Since this book has carried on a dialogue with a number of AAUP policies, I also want to emphasize again that faculty participation in social media has put the AAUP's efforts to update academic freedom definitions under considerable stress. My own view is that the AAUP's policy of rejecting professional consequences for all social media posts should be withdrawn. Faculty often promote a view of academic freedom that serves their own narrow interests, not those of the academy or society at large. Since the AAUP rarely admits that it made a mistake, it is quite unlikely to adopt my recommendation. But at least I have made a case for the change.

Early in this book, I quote Michael Bérubé's and Jennifer Ruth's argument that the traditional liberal confidence—that more speech and better speech is the reliable answer to hateful speech—cannot survive the corrosive impact of online communication. They single out white supremacy, then recommend that campuses suppress it by firing tenured faculty who represent it. Surely they cannot imagine that white supremacy is the only category of reviled hate speech that would be so treated. I call their proposal "woke McCarthyism" because it recalls the purge of communists on campus in the 1950s. I have no love for white supremacy. The white supremacist mob in Charlottesville chanted "the Jews will not replace us" as they marched through the city with Nazi-style torches in 2017. But the competing values here require different solutions for higher education.

But I do share their concerns about the adverse impact of social media. Indeed, the London-based Community Security Trust reports that worldwide internet antisemitism often originates from the United States even if it seems to come from elsewhere. Americans thus have a special responsibility to respond to the challenge. Our free speech traditions are providing content and platforms for antisemitism worldwide. As the Community Security Trust has begun to document, online antisemitism is often exceptionally violent and vulgar. We must not underestimate its incitement potential.

As online antisemitism intensifies—and we can be certain it will—more of it will land in student inboxes. It will gain in impact and accustom the campus to both familiar and new, increasingly crude, examples of antisemitism. We must plan for continuing escalation of all forms of external hate speech and for its infiltration into campus communities. As students mimic some of the online rhetoric, we will find academic freedom protecting still more hate speech we would prefer never to encounter. It is crucial to prepare now. This will be a continuing war, not one that can be permanently won, but the price paid for ignoring it will rise.

Campuses with strong anti-Zionist movements will find productive debates increasingly blocked by those who embrace the BDS's anti-normalization protocol as a form of virtue-signaling. At the November 2022 University of the Pacific symposium on "Israel, Palestine, and the First Amendment" that I cited earlier, Palestine Legal's director Diana Khalid refused to participate on a virtual panel with Yehuda Kurtzer because he was affiliated with the US office of the Israel-based Shalom Hartman Institute—even though he was there to speak for himself as a scholar. Instead of wishing her the best of luck, the faculty organizer, Omar Dajani, provided her with an alternative session. After the official presentations in Kurtzer's session concluded, however, Dajani recognized Khalid to ask a question. Instead, she offered an "intervention" in the form of a detailed oral manifesto. In practice, she was on the same screen as the panelists for an extended presentation, thus managing to have her cake and eat it too. She declared her faux non-participation to be the moral and political equivalent of refusing to cross a picket line, then crossed it anyway. The whole performance was extraordinarily hypocritical.

As the anti-normalization agenda spreads, its advocates will try to transfer its analysis of asymmetric power relations on the West Bank to Western settings. This will involve claims of victimhood for Palestinian students and faculty on Western campuses comparable to the discrimination and political disempowerment that Palestinians face on the West Bank. The effort will be given a moral imperative. The claim that massive efforts are under way to "silence" pro-Palestinian voices on campus is largely a fiction, but a persistent one. Students and faculty sympathetic to Israel will be expected to confess their complicity in these and other human rights violations as a condition for participation in campus dialogue. Most will refuse. People should resist equating Western campuses with the occupied territories.

Two decades of BDS activism ensure that the anti-Zionist movement will continue to invent new tactics. These in turn will require fresh analysis and responses. Yet new tactics will exist alongside old ones that continue to be pursued. As I detailed earlier, we are seeing formal departmental politicization for the first time. In 2022, we saw officially recognized student groups, law student groups among them, pledge never to permit a Zionist speaker to address any topic whatsoever, including research topics unrelated to Israel or the Israeli-Palestinian conflict. Divestment resolutions and campaigns against the IHRA Definition meanwhile continue unabated. In November 2022, over one hundred faculty members signed a bizarre statement urging the United Nations not to adopt the Definition, pretending that it would compromise the organization's otherwise objective and disinterested approach to the Jewish state. In June 2023, the American Anthropological Association demonstrated that the drive for academic boycotts of Israel has not ended.

Although it originated at the University of Toronto in 2005 and spread to many other campuses within a few years, the Israeli Apartheid Week movement continues to grow after a period of relative stagnation. In the intervening years, the apartheid accusation has been repeatedly reinforced in faculty and NGO publications. The effort to normalize the accusation received an important boost with the 2022 publication of Amnesty International's *Israel's Apartheid against Palestinians: Cruel System of Domination and Crime Against Humanity*. This report has been subjected to an extensive and masterful critical analysis in Alan Johnson's *The Apartheid Smear* (2022) and a point-by-point forensic rebuttal in Salo Aizenberg's "Amnesty International's Cruel Assault on Israel" (2022). They demonstrate that the report consistently crosses the line into antisemitism. Amnesty's error-laden, polemical, and willfully deceptive report should have finally discredited the organization's anti-Zionist campaign, but it will no doubt instead persuade some faculty and students it is valid. We can expect Amnesty's counter-productive policy recommendations to seep into campus resolutions. Johnson's analysis details the report's likely political impact, concluding that it "will boost antisemitic anti-Zionism in the West, further poisoning campuses, civil society and politics, dividing communities and endangering Jews" (2022, 13).

Despite all these developments, I don't concede that the campus is no longer a forum for rational dialogue. But there is no guarantee that good will prevail, despite liberalism's contrary assumption. Though most social spaces are increasingly porous, campuses retain a degree of relative separation and self-enclosure. They can promote self-contained conversations that have an impact on the campus community. Higher education has practices that foster joint reading lists and shared contexts for debate. But matters cannot be left to chance, nor to any of the key constituencies. Free speech needs to be augmented with structured programs addressing racism and antisemitism.

That is one reason I urge campus adoption of the IHRA Definition, not as a code to punish speech but rather as a guide to understanding contemporary antisemitism. Formal campus endorsement gives the Definition the educational authority it needs. As an analytical frame for campus speech, it offers provisional coherence to the flood of internet messages, the pronouncements of campus groups, and the statements made by individual students and faculty. It does not provide definitive understanding, but it is a place to start, followed by the kind of contextualization the Definition considers necessary.

But the Definition is not a cure-all. In a highly polarized culture on and off campus, people with hardened political views are often unreachable. Campus efforts to silence views about the Israeli-Palestinian conflict come mostly from pro-Palestinian, anti-Zionist students. Comparable efforts from Zionist students are notably less common. In *The Conflict over the Conflict*, Kenneth Stern is devoted to proving that anti-Zionist and anti-Palestinian efforts to curtail speech are comparable, so he cites off-campus anti-Palestinian activism to make his case. The result sometimes has the character of a search for bad Jews.

Despite the combative character of campus debates, we should not block any duly invited speakers. It can be useful even to expose students to people with loathsome views if they are in leadership positions and have a constituency. Sixty years ago, the students at Antioch, my undergraduate college, invited Nazi leader George Lincoln Rockwell, who ended his remarks by vociferously cursing the audience, which remained silent in response. It did not endear him to anyone. I do not think Iranian president Mahmoud Ahmadinejad won over his Columbia University audience in 2007. He did not conclude by cursing, but he did unforgettably announce that there are no homosexuals in Iran. In cases where students might be susceptible to despicable views, we should plan multiple compensatory events embodying a comprehensive educational strategy, not a single rejoinder. The campus response to hate speech should not be as fleeting as a tweet or an afternoon panel. If you believe an Israeli or Palestinian speaker is a monster, educate the campus over time by explaining why. Unlike Bérubé and Ruth, I wouldn't ban white supremacists, in part because they represent a movement that seeks political power. We need to know who they are. At the same time, as I said in my opening chapters, I would not hire them or award them tenure, which would assign official merit to their hatreds. But if people turn toward darkness after tenure I would sanction them in such a way as to discredit them. Purging tenured white supremacists will eventually mean purging people representing other publicly despised ideologies. We will inevitably get it wrong, and academic freedom will suffer. I would handle clear antisemites the same way.

Finally, a note about a topic that I have addressed elsewhere, but that is outside the parameters of this book: models for achieving a two-state solution to the Israeli-Palestinian conflict and strategies for promoting them. I have addressed those topics repeatedly in earlier books. *Israel Denial* and *Peace and Faith* both have chapters devoted to specific steps that can be taken toward this end. As Alan Johnson observes, "this approach may not be well suited to winning applause from a campus audience, but it is well suited to encouraging a recommencement of the peace process down the line" (2022, 5). In addition, *Israel Denial* has a chapter condemning anti-Zionist teaching and a companion chapter about a course built around teaching Israeli and Palestinian poetry together to encourage empathy and mutual understanding instead. *Peace and Faith* addresses techniques for reconciliation and includes a chapter about shared society projects by Michael Gizzi. But there is scant cause for hope about political possibilities in either Israel or the United States, at least in the near term. Nonetheless, those in the West who care about peace can promote improvements in the quality of Palestinian daily life and support for guarantees of Israeli security. Meanwhile, everything must be done to deliver a message to Israeli governments opposing annexation of West Bank territory, the one step that is sure to kill a two-state solution. While some Israeli parties will press for annexation, others will be aware that annexation would not only provoke Palestinian violence but also likely torpedo efforts to bring more nations into the Abraham Accords and seriously damage Israel's international status in other ways. But de facto annexation will increasingly present a comparable challenge.

On some fronts, the present book charts a difficult way forward. National groups such as the American Association of University Professors (AAUP) remain mired in a view of faculty rights based on defending an outdated twentieth-century model of public communication, one that has been swept aside by online hate and misinformation, proliferating antisemitism being but one major consequence. I expect my recommendations regarding social media in Chapter Two to be quite controversial, especially given the AAUP's influence over policy. As this book was going to press, I spoke with a faculty member serving on a search committee that was prohibited from considering candidate views expressed on social media. This is an absurd restriction in my view.

Our understanding of academic freedom needs to be rebalanced with renewed commitment to the search for the truth and the need to balance faculty rights with responsibilities. These are not unrelated principles. The postmodern conviction that all truth is relative should be complicated by recognition that—however much history, culture, and bias mediate our understanding—there are truths to be found beyond the chimerical theater of representation. Academic disciplines need to be removed from their unwarranted pedestals, stripped of counterproductive idealization, and put in dialogue with multiple academic fields. Disciplinarity itself will need to be rethought in the process, not least to differentiate it from political advocacy. There is little reason to suppose faculty are ready to undertake any of these tasks. Debate will need to be augmented with education. The first necessity is to clarify the nature of the problem. That is part of what I have tried to do here.

References

AbuKhalil, As'ad. 2012. "A Critique of Norman Finkelstein on BDS." *Al Akhbar*, February 17, 2012.

Abunimah, Ali. 2014. *The Battle for Justice in Palestine*. Chicago: Haymarket Books.

Ain, Stewart. 2022. "Jewish Undergrads Targeted for Their Support for Israel File Civil Rights Complaint against New York College." *Forward*, August 18, 2022. https://forward.com/fast-forward/514862/jewish-students-antisemitism-suny-new-paltz-antisemitism/.

Aizenberg, Salo. 2022. *Amnesty International's Cruel Assault on Israel: Systematic Lies, Errors, Omissions and Double Standards in Amnesty's Apartheid Report*. Jerusalem: NGO Monitor. https://www.ngo-monitor.org/pdf/SaloAizenberg_Amnesty_Rebuttal.pdf.

Alliance for Academic Freedom. 2016. "The Blacklist in the Coal Mine." *Tablet*, October 26, 2016. https://www.tabletmag.com/sections/news/articles/the-blacklist-in-the-coal-mine-canary-missions-fear-mongering-agenda-college-campuses.

———. 2022. "On Excluding Zionists from Campus Groups." *The Third Narrative*, September 6, 2022. https://thirdnarrative.org/on-excluding-zionists-from-campus-groups/.

Alterman, Eric. 2022. *We Are Not One: A History of America's Fight Over Israel*. NY: Basic Books.

Alvarez, Maximillian. 2021. "Cornel West: 'My Ridiculous Situation at Harvard,'" *Chronicle of Higher Education*, February 22, 2021.

American Association of University Professors (AAUP). 2007. "Freedom in the Classroom." *Academe* (September-October): 54–61. https://www.aaup.org/file/ACASO07FreedomClassrmRpt.pdf.

———. 2009. "Protecting an Independent Faculty Voice: Academic Freedom after *Garcetti v. Caballos.*" *Academe* (November-December): 67–88, https://www.aaup.org/file/Protecting-Independent-Voice.pdf.

———. 2014. "Statement on the Case of Professor Steven G. Salaita." Media release, August 7, 2014. https://www.aaup.org/media-release/statement-case-steven-salaita#.YDrGhC2cbjA.

———. 2015a. *Academic Freedom and Tenure: The University of Illinois at Urbana-Champaign*. Washington, DC: AAUP. https://www.aaup.org/report/UIUC.

———. 2015b. *Policy Documents and Reports*. 11th ed. Washington, DC: AAUP; Baltimore: Johns Hopkins University Press.

———. 2020. "AAUP Announces 2020 Awards for Outstanding Faculty Activists." AAUP update, May 20, 2020. https://www.aaup.org/news/aaup-announces-2020-awards-outstanding-faculty-activists.

———. 2022. "Legislative Threats to Academic Freedom: Redefinitions of Antisemitism and Racism." Statement approved by the AAUP's Committee A on Academic Freedom and Tenure in March 2022. https://www.aaup.org/report/legislative-threats-academic-freedom-redefinitions-antisemitism-and-racism.

American Jewish Committee (AJC). 2020. "The Working Definition of Antisemitism: What Does It Mean, Why Is It Important, and What Should We Do With It?" Portal to articles about the IHRA Definition. https://www.ajc.org/the-working-definition-of-antisemitism.

Amnesty International. 2022. *Israel's Apartheid against Palestinians: Cruel System of Domination and Crime Against Humanity*. London: Amnesty International. https://www.amnestyusa.org/wp-content/uploads/2022/01/Full-Report.pdf.

Andermann, Hendrik-Zoltán, and Boris Zizek. 2022. "Reconstructing an Antisemitic Meme on Social Media through Objective Hermeneutics." In

Antisemitism on Social Media, edited by Monika Hübscher and Sabine von Mering, 151–66. New York: Routledge.

Anderson, Greta. 2020. "Tulane Postpones Discussion with "Life of a Klansman" Author." *Inside Higher Education*, August 9, 2020. https://www.insidehighered.com/quicktakes/2020/08/10/tulane-postpones-discussion-life-klansman-author.

Anti-Defamation League (ADL). 2020. "USC Student Leader Resigns after She's Branded a 'Racist' for Supporting Zionism." ADL Los Angeles, August 10, 2020. https://la.adl.org/news/usc-student-leader-resigns-after-shes-branded-a-racist-for-supporting-zionism/.

Applebaum, Anne, and Peter Pomerantsev. 2021. "The Internet Doesn't Have to Be Awful." *The Atlantic* (April): 40–49.

Aridan, Natan. 2019. "Israel Lobby." In "Word Crimes; Reclaiming the Language of the Israeli-Palestinian Conflict," edited by Donna Robinson Divine, Miriam F. Elman, and Asaf Romirowsky, special issue, *Israel Studies* 24, no. 2 (Summer): 128–43.

Arnold, Sina. 2022. "A Practical Definition." *Conflict & Communication Online* 21, no. 1. https://regener-online.de/journalcco/2022_1/pdf/arnold2022_engl.pdf.

Arnold, Steve. 2021. "Valentina Azarova Declines Job Offer from UofT Law School as the Faculty Group 'Pauses' Its Censure." *Canadian Jewish News*, September 17, 2021. https://thecjn.ca/news/azarova-declines-job-offer-from-uoft-law-school-as-the-faculty-group-pauses-its-censure/.

Azarova, Valentina. 2009a. "Who Is a Civilian in Gaza? The Dangers of Adopting a Membership Approach to 'Direct Participation in Hostilities.'" *International Law Observer*, March 3, 2009. https://internationallawobserver.eu/?s=who+is+a+civilian+in+Gaza.

———. 2009b. "Internationalisation and Attribution: The *Tadic* Analysis in the *Genocide in Bosnia* Case." Online Working Paper 2009/2, Westminster International Law and Theory Centre. https://www.westminster.ac.uk/sites/default/public-files/general-documents/ILTC-Working-Paper-Valentina-Azarov.pdf.

———. 2009c. "A Line of Selective Rhetoric: Israeli Supreme Court Fails to Enforce the Evacuation of 'Unauthorised Settlements' in the Occupied West Bank." *International Law Observer*, June 17, 2009. https://internationallawobserver.eu/?s=a+line+of+selective+rhetoric.

————. 2009d. "Israeli Supreme Court Decision on the Wall in Jayyus: Another Assault on the ICJ." *International Law Observer*, October 3, 2009. https://internationallawobserver.eu/israeli-supreme-court-decision-on-the-wall-in-jayyus-another-assault-on-the-icj.

————. 2009e. "The Security Paradigm in the Israeli Supreme Court." *International Law Observer*, October 30, 2009. https://internationallawobserver.eu/the-security-paradigm-in-the-israeli-supreme-court.

————. 2010. "Lost at Sea: Attacks on the Gaza Flotilla and the Siege on the Occupied Gaza Strip." *International Law Observer*, June 7, 2010. https://internationallawobserver.eu/lost-at-sea-attacks-on-gaza-flotilla-and-the-siege-on-the-occupied-gaza-strip.

————. 2011. *Al-Haq's Questions and Answers: Palestine's UN Initiatives and the Representation of the Palestinian People's Rights.* Ramallah: Al-Haq. https://www.alhaq.org/cached_uploads/download/alhaq_files/publications/UN.Initiatives.Q.A.pdf.

————. 2012a. "ICC Jurisdiction in Palestine: Blurring Law and Politics." *Jurist*, April 9, 2012. https://www.jurist.org/commentary/2012/04/valentina-azarov-icc-palestine/.

————. 2012b. "Disingenuous 'Disengagement': Israel's Occupation of the Gaza Strip and the Protective Function of the Law of Belligerent Occupation." *Opinio Juris*, April 24, 2012. http://opiniojuris.org/2012/04/24/disingenuous-disengagement-israels-occupation-of-the-gaza-strip-and-the-protective-function-of-the-law-of-belligerent-occupation/.

————. 2012c. "Shifting Paradigms: Israel, Palestinian Territory and International Law." *Jurist*, July 25, 2012. https://www.jurist.org/commentary/2012/07/valentina-azarov-israel-occupation/.

————. 2013a. *Institutionalized Impunity: Israel's Failure to Combat Settler Violence in the Occupied Palestinian Territory.* Ramallah: Al-Haq.

————. 2013b. "Backtracking on Responsibility: French Court Absolves Veolia for Unlawful Railway Construction in Occupied Territory." *Rights as Usual* (blog), May 1, 2013. https://rightsasusual.com/?p=414.

————. 2013c. "Israel's Loopy Logic of Exoneration." *Open Democracy*, May 3, 2013. https://www.opendemocracy.net/en/opensecurity/israels-loopy-logic-of-exoneration/.

—. 2013d. "Investigative or Political Barriers? Dutch Prosecutor Dismisses Criminal Complicity Case against Riwal." *Rights as Usual* (blog), May 29, 2013. http://rightsasusual.com//?s=investigative+or+political+barriers.

—. 2013e. *Securing Injustice: Legal Analysis of G4S Israel Operations in Occupied Palestinian Territory*. Jerusalem: Diakonia.

—. 2013f. "Making Human Rights Work for the Palestines of the World." *Open Democracy*, November 3, 2013. https://www.opendemocracy.net/en/openglobalrights-openpage/making-human-rights-work-for-palestines-of-world/.

—. 2014a. "An International Legal Demarche for Human Rights? Perils and Prospects of the Palestinian UN Bid." *International Journal of Human Rights* 18 (4–5): 527–44.

—. 2014b. "From Discretion to Necessity: Third State Responsibility for Israel's Control of Stay and Entry into Palestinian Territory." *Journal of Human Rights Practice* 6, no. 2 (July): 327–55.

—. 2014c. *Families Under The Rubble: Israeli Attacks on Inhabited Homes*. London: Amnesty International.

—. 2015a. "A Healthy Dose of Wartime Normative Realism." In *Palestine Yearbook of International Law* 18: 205–17. Leiden: Brill.

—. 2015b. "Introductory Note to *Chirago and Others v. Armenia*." *International Legal Materials* 54(6): 962–64.

—. 2015c. "Palestine's Day in Court? The Unexpected Effects of ICC Action." *Al-Shabaka*, April 1, 2015. https://al-shabaka.org/briefs/palestines-day-in-court-the-unexpected-effects-of-icc-action/.

—. 2015d. "Exploding Civilian Involvement and 'The People's Perspectives' Report," *Just Security*, June 18, 2015. https://www.justsecurity.org/24005/guest-post-exploding-civilian-involvement-comment-report-the-peoples-perspectives/.

—. 2015e. "The Trickle-Down Effects of Normative Power: The Role of International Courts in Advancing Palestine's Actual Independence." In *Palestine Yearbook of International Law* 17: 83–100. Leiden: Brill.

—. 2016a. "On Business and Human Rights in Illegal Territorial Regimes," *Opinio Juris*, January 26, 2016. http://opiniojuris.org/2016/01/26/guest-post-on-business-and-human-rights-in-illegal-territorial-regimes/.

———. 2016b. "Taking Forward the UN Commission of Inquiry Report on Gaza: Paths and Prospects for NGO Advocacy." EuroMed Rights 2016 NGO Briefing Paper on Accountability, Copenhagen, February 2016.

———. 2016c. "The International Criminal Court, Israel/Palestine and EU Support." EuroMed Rights 2016 NGO Briefing Paper on Accountability, Copenhagen, February 2016.

———. 2016d. "Boycotts, International Law Enforcement and the UK's 'Anti-Boycott' Note." *Jurist*, April 12, 2016. https://www.jurist.org/commentary/2016/04/valentina-azarova-uk-note/.

———. 2017a. "The Bounds of (Il)legality: Rethinking the Regulation of Transnational Corporate Wrongs." In *Human Rights and Power in Times of Globalisation*, edited by Ekaterina Yahyaoui Krivenko, 227–66. Leiden: Brill.

———. 2017b. "Israel's Unlawfully Prolonged Occupation: Consequences under an Integrated Legal Framework." Policy Brief, European Council on Foreign Relations, June 2017. https://css.ethz.ch/content/dam/ethz/special-interest/gess/cis/center-for-securities-studies/resources/docs/ECFR-Israel's%20Unlawfully%20Prolonged%20Occupation.p.

———. 2017c. "The Pathology of a Legal System: Israel's Military Justice System and International Law," *Questions of International Law*, Zoom-in 44 (2017): 5–20.

———. 2018a. "Business and Human Rights in Occupied Territory: The UN Database of Business Active in Israel's Settlements." *Business and Human Rights Journal* 3(2): 187–209.

———. 2018b. "Review Essay: Neo-colonial Transformations of Occupied Territory—and of the International Law of Occupation?" In *Palestine Yearbook of International Law* 19: 223–35. Leiden: Brill.

———. 2018c. "The Secret Life of Non-Recognition: EU-Israel Relations and the Obligation of Non-Recognition in International Law." *Global Affairs* 4(1): 23–37.

———. "The UN Database on Business in Israeli Settlements: Pitfalls and Opportunities." *Al-Shabaka*, May 29, 2018. https://al-shabaka.org/commentaries/the-un-database-on-business-in-israeli-settlements-pitfalls-and-opportunities/.

———. 2018e. "Tracking Businesses in Israeli Settlements." *U.S. News and World Report*, July 31, 2018. https://www.usnews.com/news/best-countries/articles/2018-07-31/why-the-un-is-tracking-companies-operating-in-israeli-settlements?context=amp.

———. 2019. "Towards a Counter-Hegemonic Law of Occupation: The Regulation of Predatory Interstate Acts in Contemporary International Law." In *Yearbook of International Law*, vol. 20, edited by Terry D. Gil, Tim McCormack, Robin Geiß, Heike Krieger, and Christophe Paulussen, 113–60. London: Springer.

———. 2020. "Adjudicators, Guardians, and Enforcers: Taking the Role of Non-Governmental Organisations in Customary International Law-Making Seriously." In *International Organisations, Non-State Actors and the Formation of Customary International Law*, edited by Jean d'Aspremont and Sufyan Droubi, 404–36. Manchester: Manchester University Press.

Azarova, Valentina, Amanda Danson Brown, and Itamar Mann. 2022. "The Enforced Disappearance of Migrants." *Boston University International Law Journal* 40(1): 133–204.

Ball, Edward. 1998. *Slaves in the Family*. NY: Farrar, Straus and Giroux.

Ball, Edward. 2020. *Life of a Klansman: A Family History of White Supremacy*. NY: Farrar, Straus and Giroux.

Baker, Rabbi Andrew, Deidre Berger, and Michael Whine. 2021. "The Origins of the Working Definition." In *In Defence of the IHRA Working Definition of Antisemitism* (eBook), edited by Alan Johnson, 8–11. London: Fathom. https://fathomjournal.org/wp-content/uploads/2021/02/In-Defence-of-the-IHRA-Working-Definition-of-Antisemitism-1.pdf.

Barghouti, Omar. 2007. "No State Has the Right to Exist as a Racist State." Interview by Sylvia Cattori. *Voltaire Network*, December 7, 2007. https://www.voltairenet.org/article153536.html.

Bartov, Omer. 2021. "Criticism of Israel and Its Policies Isn't Antisemitism." *Haaretz*, March 30, 2021.

Benesch, Susan, Cathy Buerger, Tonei Glavinic, Sean Manion, and Dan Bateyko. 2021. *Dangerous Speech: A Practical Guide*. Washington, DC: Dangerous Speech Project. https://dangerousspeech.org/guide/.

Bernstein, Rachel, and Alexis Timko. 2020. "USG Vice President Rose Ritch Resigns." *USC Annenberg Media*, August 5, 2020. https://www.uscannenbergmedia.com/2020/08/05/usg-vice-president-rose-ritch-resigns/.

Bérubé, Michael, and Jennifer Ruth. 2022. *It's Not Free Speech: Race, Democracy, and the Future of Academic Freedom*. Baltimore: Johns Hopkins University Press.

Blackmer, Corinne E. 2019. "Pinkwashing." In "Word Crimes; Reclaiming the Language of the Israeli-Palestinian Conflict," edited by Donna Robinson

Divine, Miriam F. Elman, and Asaf Romirowsky, special issue, *Israel Studies* 24, no. 2 (Summer): 171–81.

———. 2022. *Queering Anti-Zionism: Academic Freedom, LGBTQ Intellectuals, and Israel/Palestine Campus Activism*. Detroit: Wayne State University Press.

Blackmer, Corinne E., and Andrew Pessin, eds. 2021. *Poisoning the Wells: Antisemitism in Contemporary America*. New York: Institute for the Study of Global Antisemitism and Policy (ISGAP).

Blaff, Ari. 2019. "Settlements." In "Word Crimes; Reclaiming the Language of the Israeli-Palestinian Conflict," edited by Donna Robinson Divine, Miriam F. Elman, and Asaf Romirowsky, special issue, *Israel Studies* 24, no. 2 (Summer): 217–27.

Blitz, Brad. 2021. "Analysis of the UCL Academic Board Vote on the IHRA Working Definition of Antisemitism." Report circulated to UCL faculty.

———. 2022. "Struggles over the IHRA Definition at UCL." Zoom presentation, London Centre for the Study of Contemporary Antisemitism, November 30, 2022.

Brahm, Gabriel Noah. 2019. "Intersectionality." In "Word Crimes; Reclaiming the Language of the Israeli-Palestinian Conflict," edited by Donna Robinson Divine, Miriam F. Elman, and Asaf Romirowsky, special issue, *Israel Studies* 24, no. 2 (Summer): 157–70.

Butler, Judith. 2012. *Parting Ways: Jewishness and the Critique of Zionism*. New York: Columbia University Press.

Canadian Association of University Teachers. 2020. "CAUT Report on Academic Freedom at the Faculty of Law, University of Toronto." Report, October 2020. https://www.caut.ca/sites/default/files/caut-report-on-academic-freedom-at-the-faculty-of-law-university-of-toronto_2020-10_0.pdf.

Canadian Judicial Council (CJC). 2021. "Canadian Judicial Council Completes Its Review of the Matter Involving the Honourable D. E. Spiro." Press release, May 21, 2021. https://cjc-ccm.ca/en/news/canadian-judicial-council-completes-review-matter-involving-honourable-de-spiro.

Canadian Association of University Teachers (CAUT). 2021. "CAUT Council Imposes Rare Censure against University of Toronto over Azarova Hiring Controversy." News article, April 22, 2021. https://www.caut.ca/latest/2021/04/caut-council-imposes-rare-censure-against-university-toronto-over-azarova-hiring.

Canary Mission. 2023. "Lara Sheehi." Profile, last modified February 19, 2023. https://canarymission.org/professor/Lara_Sheehi.

Center for Countering Digital Hate (CCDH). 2022. "STAR Framework: A Global Standard for Regulating Social Media." Report, September 21, 2022. https://counterhate.com/research/star-framework/.

Chayka, Kyle. 2022. "What Fleeing Twitter Users Will—And Won't—Find on Mastodon." *New Yorker*, November 22, 2022.

Chesley, Kate. 2020. "Faculty Senate Condemns COVID-19 Actions of Hoover's Scott Atlas." *Stanford News*, November 20, 2020. https://news.stanford.edu/2020/11/20/faculty-senate-condemns-actions-hoover-fellow-scott-atlas/.

Christensen, Dusty. 2019. "Pink Floyd's Roger Waters, Activist Linda Sarsour to Talk Israel, Palestine at UMass Amherst." *Daily Hampshire Gazette*, April 23, 2019. https://www.gazettenet.com/Pink-Floyd-s-Roger-Waters-activist-Linda-Sarsour-part-of-upcoming-UMass-Amherst-panel-24853065.

Cohen, Ben. 2021. "Anti-Semitic or Just 'Strident?'" *Jewish News Syndicate*, March 19, 2021. https://www.jns.org/opinion/anti-semitic-or-just-strident/.

Commanders for Israeli Security. 2016. "Security First: Changing the Rules of the Game." Report, May 2016. http://en.cis.org.il/wp-content/uploads/2016/05/snpl_plan_eng.pdf.

Community Security Trust. 2020. *Hate Fuel: The Hidden Online World Fuelling Far Right Terror.* London: CST.

Cooper, Helene. 2021. "Pentagon Updates Its Rules on Extremism in the Military." *New York Times*, December 20, 2021. https://www.nytimes.com/2021/12/20/us/politics/pentagon-military-extremism-rules.html.

Coward, Tyler. 2021. "Biden Administration Commits to Anti-Semitism Definition That Could Stifle Campus Speech." Foundation for Individual Rights in Education (FIRE), March 19, 2021. https://www.thefire.org/news/biden-administration-commits-anti-semitism-definition-could-stifle-campus-speech.

Crowell, Thomas A. 2021. "Independent Review of the Search Process for the Directorship of the International Human Rights Program at the University of Toronto, Faculty of Law." Report, March 15, 2021. https://live-presidents-office.pantheonsite.io/wp-content/uploads/2021/12/Report-of-the-Hon-Thomas-A-Cromwell-CC-%E2%80%93-March-15-2021.pdf.

Czymmek, Quint. 2022. "The Impact of Antisemitic Content and Hate Speech on Social Media on Young Jewish Social Media Users." In *Antisemitism on Social Media*, edited by Monika Hübscher and Sabine von Mering, 181–92. New York: Routledge.

Deckers, Jan, and Jonathan Coulter. 2022. "What Is Wrong with the International Holocaust Remembrance Alliance's Definition of Antisemitism?" *Res Publica* 28: 733–52.

Dery, Mark. 2021. "The Professor of Paranoia." *Chronicle of Higher Education*, May 12, 2021.

Dirks, Nicholas. 2017. "Chancellor's Message on Campus Appearance by Milo Yiannopoulos." *Berkeley News*, January 26, 2017.

Divine, Donna Robinson. 2019. Introduction to "Word Crimes; Reclaiming the Language of the Israeli-Palestinian Conflict," edited by Donna Robinson Divine, Miriam F. Elman, and Asaf Romirowsky, special issue, *Israel Studies* 24, no. 2 (Summer): 1–16.

———. 2020. "The Uproar over 'Word Crimes': A Political Not Scholarly Agenda." *Journal of Contemporary Antisemitism* 3(2): 149–52.

Divine, Donna Robinson, Miriam F. Elman, and Asaf Romirowsky, eds. 2019. "Word Crimes: Reclaiming the Language of the Israel-Palestinian Conflict." Special issue, *Israel Studies* 24, no. 2 (Summer).

Doherty, Rosa. 2017. "University Cancels Israel Apartheid Week Event." *Jewish Chronicle*, February 21, 2017. https://www.thejc.com/news/uk/university-cancels-israel-apartheid-week-event-1.433123.

Dorning, Mike. 1993. "Debate over Farrakhan Book Engulfs College." *Chicago Tribune*, April 28, 1993. https://www.chicagotribune.com/news/ct-xpm-1993-04-28-9304280203-story.html.

Elder of Ziyon. 2012a. "The Problems with the 'Jerusalem Declaration' Definition of Antisemitism." *Elder of Ziyon* (blog), March 26, 2012. http://elderofziyon.blogspot.com/2021/03/the-problem-with-jerusalem-declaration.html.

———. 2012b. "Yet Another Attempt to Sanitize Anti-Zionism." *Elder of Ziyon* (blog), March 29, 2021. http://elderofziyon.blogspot.com/2021/03/0329-links-as-passover-begins-jews-feel.html.

Elliott, Cathy. 2019. "Learning Lessons: The Articulation of Antisemitism on Campus." *Renewal* 27(2): 75–87. https://renewal.org.uk/archive/vol-27-2019/learning-lessons-the-articulation-of-antisemitism-on-campus/.

Elliott, Cathy, et al. 2017. "The JewCL." UCL Student Podcast, 7 episodes, September 21–October 4, 2017. https://jewcl.libsyn.com.

Elman, Miriam F. 2015. "Jewish Voice for Peace—'Jew Washing' the Anti-Israel Movement." *Legal Insurrection*, July 12, 2015. https://legalinsurrection.com/2015/07/jewish-voice-for-peace-jew-washing-the-anti-israel-movement/.

———. 2019. "Islamophobia." In "Word Crimes; Reclaiming the Language of the Israeli-Palestinian Conflict," edited by Donna Robinson Divine, Miriam F. Elman, and Asaf Romirowsky, special issue, *Israel Studies* 24, no. 2 (Summer): 144–56.

Elman, R. Amy. 2022. "The Mainstreaming of American Antisemitism: The Defeat of an Ideal." *Journal of Contemporary Antisemitism* 5(1): 105–19.

Engler, Yves. 2021. "University of Toronto Reverses Block of Hire after Donor Influence Scandal." *Mondoweiss*, September 30, 2021. https://mondoweiss.net/2021/09/university-of-toronto-reverses-block-of-hire-after-donor-influence-scandal/.

Englert, Sai. 2021. "Jerusalem Declaration on Antisemitism: We Cannot Define Our Way Out of This Impasse." *Middle East Eye*, April 1, 2021. https://www.middleeasteye.net/opinion/jerusalem-declaration-antisemitism-we-cannot-define-our-way-out-impasse.

Equality Act 2010 (UK). https://www.legislation.gov.uk/ukpga/2010/15/contents.

European Commission. 2021. *Handbook for the Practical Use of the IHRA Working Definition of Antisemitism.* Luxembourg: Publications Office of the European Union. https://op.europa.eu/en/publication-detail/-/publication/d3006107-519b-11eb-b59f-01aa75ed71a1/language-en.

Faculty for Palestine Canada. 2015. "Open Letter: Defend Freedom of Speech." Statement, March 14, 2015. https://www.faculty4palestine.ca/wp-content/uploads/2015/03/F4P-Open-Letter-420.pdf.

Falk, Richard. 2007. "Slouching toward a Palestinian Holocaust." Transnational Foundation for Peace and Future Research (TFF), June 29, 2007. http://www.oldsite.transnational.org/Area_MiddleEast/2007/Falk_PalestineGenocide.html.

Falk, Richard, and Virginia Tilley. 2017. *Israeli Practices towards the Palestinian People and the Question of Apartheid.* Beirut: United Nations Economic and Social Commission for Western Asia. Available at

https://web.archive.org/web/20170316054753/https://www.unescwa.
org/sites/www.unescwa.org/files/publications/files/israeli-practices-
palestinian-people-apartheid-occupation-english.pdf.

Fein, Helen. 1987. "Dimensions of Antisemitism: Attitudes, Collective
Accusations, and Actions." In *The Persisting Question: Sociological Perspectives
and Social Contexts of Modern Antisemitism*, edited by Helen Fein, 67–85.
New York: Walter de Gruyter.

Feinberg, Ayal K. 2021. "From Scholarship to Swastikas: Explaining Campus
Antisemitic Effects." AEN Research Paper Series no. 2, Academic Engagement
Network, Washington, DC. https://academicengagement.org/wp-content/
uploads/2021/08/From-Scholarship-to-Swastikas-Explaining-Campus-
Antisemitic-Events_AEN_Ayal-Feinberg_2021.pdf.

Finkelstein, Joel, Corinne E. Blackmer, and Charles Rubin. 2021. "Holocaust
Denial on the Web: Confronting the Future of Antisemitism." In *Poisoning the
Wells: Antisemitism in Contemporary America*, edited by Corinne E. Blackmer
and Andrew Pessin, 71–85. New York: Institute for the Study of Global
Antisemitism and Policy (ISGAP).

Finkin, Matthew W., and Robert C. Post. 2009. *For the Common Good: Principles
of American Academic Freedom*. New Haven: Yale University Press.

Fisher, Max. 2022. *The Chaos Machine: The Inside Story of How Social Media
Rewired Our Minds and Our World*. New York: Little, Brown and Company.

Fitzsimmons, Emma G. 2014. "Condoleezza Rice Backs Out of Rutgers Speech
after Student Protests." *New York Times*, May 3, 2014. https://www.nytimes.
com/2014/05/04/nyregion/rice-backs-out-of-rutgers-speech-after-
student-protests.html.

Friedersdorf, Conor. 2016. "How Political Correctness Chills Speech on
Campus." *The Atlantic*, September 1, 2016.

———. 2017. "Judith Butler Overestimates the Power of Hateful Speech." *The
Atlantic*, December 12, 2017.

Friedman, Lara. 2022. Untitled presentation. "Israel, Palestine, and the First
Amendment: Defining the Boundaries of Freedom of Speech," symposium of
the University of the Pacific Law Review and the Global Center for Business
and Development at the McGeorge School of Law, November 4, 2022.

———. 2023. "Challenging the IHRA Definition of Antisemitism."
Foundation for Middle East Peace (FMEP), last updated April 24,
2023. https://fmep.org/wp/wp-content/uploads/Challenging-the-IHRA-
Definition-of-Antisemitism.pdf.

Fuller, Thomas. 2017. "A Free Speech Battle at the Birthplace of a Movement at Berkeley." *New York Times*, February 2, 2017. https://www.nytimes.com/2017/02/02/us/university-california-berkeley-free-speech-milo-yiannopoulos.html.

Garrard, Eve. 2021. "The IHRA Definition, Institutional Antisemitism, and Wittgenstein." In *In Defence of the IHRA Working Definition of Antisemitism* (eBook), edited by Alan Johnson, 46–50. London: Fathom. https://fathomjournal.org/wp-content/uploads/2021/02/In-Defence-of-the-IHRA-Working-Definition-of-Antisemitism-1.pdf.

Gayle, Damien. 2017. "UK University Censors Title of Holocaust Survivor's Speech Criticising Israel." *Guardian*, September 29, 2017. https://www.theguardian.com/education/2017/sep/29/manchester-university-censors-title-holocaust-survivor-speech-criticising-israel.

Gessen, Masha. 2021. "Did a University of Toronto Donor Block the Hiring of a Scholar for Her Writing on Palestine?" *New Yorker*, May 8, 2021. https://www.newyorker.com/news/our-columnists/did-a-university-of-toronto-donor-block-the-hiring-of-a-scholar-for-her-writing-on-palestine.

Goldfeder, Mark. 2021. "Defining Antisemitism." *Seton Hall Law Review* 52(1): 119–97.

Goldstein, Harry. 2020. "Antisemitism at UCL—the Working Party Report." *Medium*, December 22, 2020. https://harrygoldstein7.medium.com/antisemitism-at-ucl-the-working-party-report-d745c327684a.

Goldstone, Sam, and Rebecca Lyons. n.d. "Appendix: Testimonies from January 2018 to January 2021." Unpublished report prepared for UCL Jewish Society.

Goossen, Benjamin W. 2017. *Chosen Nation: Mennonites and Germany in a Global Era*. Princeton: Princeton University Press.

Gordon, Daniel. 2023. *What is Academic Freedom?* New York: Routledge.

Gordon, Neve, and Mark LeVine. 2021. "Was Einstein an Anti-Semite?" *Inside Higher Education*, March 26, 2021. https://www.insidehighered.com/views/2021/03/26/problems-increasingly-dominant-definition-anti-semitism-opinion.

Gould, Rebecca Ruth. 2011. "Beyond Anti-Semitism." *CounterPunch* 18, no. 19 (November 1–15, 2011). Available at https://www.researchgate.net/publication/228322693_Beyond_Anti-Semitism.

———. 2013. "To Boycott or Not? A Moral Conundrum." *Peace Review* 25(4): 584–89.

———. 2020. "The IHRA Definition of Antisemitism: Defining Antisemitism by Erasing Palestinians." *Political Quarterly* 91(4): 825–31.

———. 2022. "Legal Form and Legal Legitimacy: The IHRA Definition of Antisemitism as a Case Study in Censored Speech." *Law, Culture and the Humanities* 18(1): 153–86.

———. 2023. *Erasing Palestine: Free Speech and Palestinian Freedom*. London: Verso.

Grant, Nico. 2022. "Security Training Group Asks Musk to Rid Twitter of Antisemitism." *New York Times*, November 2, 2022. https://www.nytimes.com/2022/11/01/technology/musk-twitter-antisemitism-security-group.html.

Guhl, Jakob. 2022. "'Everyone I Know Isn't Antisemitic': Antisemitism in Facebook Pages Supportive of the UK Labour Party." In *Antisemitism on Social Media*, edited by Monika Hübscher and Sabine von Mering, chap. 4. New York: Routledge.

Harari, Yuval, Tristan Harris, and Aza Raskin. 2023. "If We Don't Master A.I., It Will Master Us." *New York Times*, March 24, 2023. https://www.nytimes.com/2023/03/24/opinion/yuval-harari-ai-chatgpt.html.

Harpham, Geoffrey. 2021. Letter to the editor. *Chronicle of Higher Education*, March 4, 2021.

Harrison, Bernard. 2020. *Blaming the Jews: Politics and Delusion*. Bloomington: Indiana University Press.

———. 2022. "In Defense of the IHRA Definition (Despite Its Defects as a Definition)." *Journal of Contemporary Antisemitism* 5(2): 4–65.

Harrison, Bernard, and Lesley Klaff. 2021. "In Defence of the IHRA Definition." In *In Defence of the IHRA Working Definition of Antisemitism* (eBook), edited by Alan Johnson, 27–33. London: Fathom. https://fathomjournal.org/wp-content/uploads/2021/02/In-Defence-of-the-IHRA-Working-Definition-of-Antisemitism-1.pdf.

Harvard Divinity School. 2021. "The Politics of Defining: A Roundtable Discussion about the Jerusalem Declaration on Antisemitism." April 20, 2021. Video and transcript published May 17, 2021. https://rpl.hds.harvard.edu/news/2021/05/17/video-politics-defining-roundtable-discussion-about-jerusalem-declaration-antisemitism.

Herf, Jeffrey. 2021. "IHRA and JDA: Examining Definitions of Antisemitism in 2021." *Fathom* (April 2021). https://fathomjournal.org/ihra-and-jda-examining-definitions-of-antisemitism-in-2021/.

Hirsh, David. 2017. *Contemporary Left Antisemitism*. London: Routledge.

———. 2021a. "It was the new phenomenon of Israel-focused antisemitism that required the new definition. David Hirsh responds to a recent 'call to reject' the IHRA." *Fathom* (January 2021). https://fathomjournal.org/it-was-the-new-phenomenon-of-israel-focused-antisemitism-that-required-the-new-definition-of-antisemitism-david-hirsh-responds-to-a-recent-call-to-reject-the-ihra/

———. 2021b. "The Meaning of David Miller." *Fathom* (March 2021). https://fathomjournal.org/fathom-long-read-the-meaning-of-david-miller/.

———. 2021c. "Jews Are Asking For Protection From Their Universities." In *In Defence of the IHRA Working Definition of Antisemitism* (eBook), edited by Alan Johnson, 34–37. London: Fathom. https://fathomjournal.org/wp-content/uploads/2021/02/In-Defence-of-the-IHRA-Working-Definition-of-Antisemitism-1.pdf.

———. 2023. "From a Critique of Zionism to an Anti-Jewish Worldview." In *Antisemitic Anti-Zionism: The Origins and Character of an Ideology*. London: Labour Friends of Israel, July 2023, 5-10, https://www.lfi.org.uk/wp-content/uploads/2023/07/Antisemitic-Anti-Zionism-1.pdf.

Home Affairs Committee. 2016. *Antisemitism in the UK: Tenth Report of Session 2016–17*. HC 136. Published on October 16, 2016, by authority of the House of Commons. https://publications.parliament.uk/pa/cm201617/cmselect/cmhaff/136/136.pdf.

Hübscher, Monika, and Sabine von Mering. 2022. "A Snapshot of Antisemitism on Social Media in 2021." In *Antisemitism on Social Media*, edited by Monika Hübscher and Sabine von Mering, 5–17. New York: Routledge.

Human Rights Voices. 2014. "UN Office in Geneva Holds 2-Day Israel-Bashing Confab." April 25, 2014. http://www.humanrightsvoices.org/site/developments/?d=12135.

Huszár, Ferenc, Sofia Ira Ktena, Conor O'Brien, Luca Belli, Andrew Schlaikjer, and Moritz Hardt. 2021. "Algorithmic Amplification of Politics on Twitter." *PNAS* 119, no. 1. https://www.pnas.org/doi/10.1073/pnas.2025334119.

Illouz, Eva. 2021. "Between Antisemitism and anti-Zionism: The Intellectual's Dilemma." *Haaretz*, April 15, 2021.

Independent Jewish Voices Canada (IJV). 2020. "Open Letter from 600+ Canadian Academics Opposing the IHRA Definition of Antisemitism." February 27, 2020. https://www.ijvcanada.org/open-letter-from-canadian-academics-opposing-the-ihra-definition-of-antisemitism/.

International Holocaust Remembrance Alliance (IHRA). 2016. Working Definition of Antisemitism. Adopted in Bucharest on May 26, 2016. https://www.holocaustremembrance.com/working-definition-antisemitism.

———. 2023. "Using Artificial Intelligence: Detecting Antisemitic Content and Hate Speech Online." July 21, 2023. https://www.holocaustremembrance.com/news-archive/using-artificial-intelligence-detecting-antisemitic-content-and-hate-speech-online.

International Jewish Anti-Zionist Network (IJAN). 2009. "Jewish Canadians Concerned about Suppression of Criticism of Israel." http://www.ijan.org/uncategorized/jewish-canadians-concerned-about-suppression-of-criticism-of-israel/.

Ionescu, Dana. 2022. "The IHRA Definition of Antisemitism in a Melee: A Critical Discussion of the Mobilizations against the First International Definition of Antisemitism." *Conflict & Communication Online* 21, no. 1. Available at https://regener-online.de/journalcco/.

Jacoby, Jenny. 2023. "How the IHRA Definition Limits Palestinian Voices." *Washington Report on Middle East Affairs,* July 17, 2023. https://www.wrmea.org/north-america/how-the-ihra-definition-limits-palestinian-voices.html.

Janofsky, Michael. 2020. "A USC Student Leader Resigns amid Accusations That Her Zionism 'Made Her Complicit in Racism.'" *Forward,* August 6, 2020.

Jaschik, Scott. 2016. "Uninvited for Being Israeli." *Inside Higher Education,* September 5, 2016. https://www.insidehighered.com/news/2016/09/06/syracuse-condemns-action-professor-rescind-invitation-israeli-scholar.

———. 2023. "Anthropologists Vote to Boycott Israeli Academic Institutions." *Inside Higher Education,* July 24, 2023. https://www.insidehighered.com/news/faculty-issues/2023/07/24/anthropologists-back-boycott-israeli-academic-institutions.

Jensen, Uffa. 2022. "Dangerously Close to a Correspondence Theory: The IHRA's Problematic Attempt to Define Antisemitism." *Conflict & Communication Online* 21, no. 1. Available at https://regener-online.de/journalcco/.

Jerusalem Declaration on Antisemitism. 2021. Adopted under the auspices of the Van Leer Institute, Jerusalem, on March 21, 2021. https://jerusalemdeclaration.org/.

Jewish Voice for Peace. n.d. "JVP's Approach to Zionism." Accessed July 2021. https://www.jewishvoiceforpeace.org/wp-content/uploads/2019/01/JVP%E2%80%99s-Approach-to-Zionism.pdf.

Jikeli, Gunther, David Axelrod, Rhonda Fischer, Elham Forouzesh, Weejeong Jeong, Daniel Miehling, and Katharina Soemer. 2022. "Differences between Antisemitic and non-Antisemitic English Language Tweets." *Computational and Mathematical Organization Theory* (2022). https://link.springer.com/article/10.1007/s10588-022-09363-2.

Jikeli, Günther, Damir Cavar, Weejeong Jeong, Daniel Miehling, Pauravi Wagh, and Denizhan Pak. 2022. "Towards an AI Definition of Antisemitism?" In *Antisemitism on Social Media*, edited by Monika Hübscher and Sabine von Mering, 193–212. New York: Routledge.

Jikeli, Gunther, Damir Cavar, and Daniel Miehling. 2019. "Annotating Antisemitic Content: Towards an Applicable Definition of Antisemitism." IUScholarWorks, Indiana University, October 2019. Available at https://arxiv.org/abs/1910.01214.

Jikeli, Gunther, and Katharina Soemer. 2022. "Conversations about Jews on Twitter: Recent Developments since the Takeover by Elon Musk." Institute for the Study of Contemporary Antisemitism (ISCA), Indiana University, November 2022. https://isca.indiana.edu/publication-research/social-media-project/Conversations-About-Jews-on-Twitter.-Recent-Developments-Since-the-Takeover-by-Elon-Musk.pdf.

Joffe, Alex. 2019. "Human Rights." In "Word Crimes; Reclaiming the Language of the Israeli-Palestinian Conflict," edited by Donna Robinson Divine, Miriam F. Elman, and Asaf Romirowsky, special issue, *Israel Studies* 24, no. 2 (Summer): 103–18.

Johnson, Alan. 2019. "Institutionally Antisemitic: Contemporary Left Antisemitism and the Crisis in the British Labour Party." *Fathom* (March 2019). https://fathomjournal.org/fathom-report-institutionally-antisemitic-contemporary-left-antisemitism-and-the-crisis-in-the-british-labour-party/.

———. 2021a. "The IHRA Definition Helps Us Understand and Combat the New Antisemitism." In *In Defence of the IHRA Working Definition of Antisemitism* (eBook), edited by Alan Johnson, 51–57. London: Fathom. https://fathomjournal.org/wp-content/uploads/2021/02/In-Defence-of-the-IHRA-Working-Definition-of-Antisemitism-1.pdf.

———, ed. 2021b. *In Defence of the IHRA Working Definition of Antisemitism* (eBook). London: Fathom. https://fathomjournal.org/wp-content/uploads/2021/02/In-Defence-of-the-IHRA-Working-Definition-of-Antisemitism-1.pdf.

———. 2022. *The Apartheid Smear*. London: Britain Israel Communications and Research Centre (BICOM). https://www.bicom.org.uk/wp-content/uploads/2022/11/BICOM-AS-Update-NOV-2022-3.pdf.

Joint Committee on Human Rights. 2018. "Free Speech: Guidance for Universities and Students Organizing Events." Annex to HC 589 and HL Paper 111. Published on March 27, 2018, by authority of the House of Commons and House of Lords. https://publications.parliament.uk/pa/jt201719/jtselect/jtrights/589/589-annex.pdf.

Julius, Anthony. 2022. "Willed Ignorance: Reflections on Academic Free Speech, Occasioned by the David Miller Case." *Current Legal Problems* 75(1): 1–44. https://academic.oup.com/clp/advance-article/doi/10.1093/clp/cuac001/6595637.

Kahn-Harris, Keith. 2021a. "Defining Antisemitism—Again, and Again…" *JewThink*, March 25, 2021. https://www.jewthink.org/2021/03/25/defining-antisemitism-again-and-again/.

———. 2021b. "Into the Flatlands with Professor David Miller." *JewThink*, February 21, 2021. https://www.jewthink.org/2021/02/22/into-the-flatlands-with-professor-david-miller/.

———. 2022. "What We Don't Know about IHRA: Practices of Subversion and Neglect." *Conflict & Communication Online* 21, no. 1. Available at https://regener-online.de/journalcco/.

Kampen, John. 2021. "Assessing the 2017 Mennonite Resolution on Israel/Palestine." In *Peace and Faith: Christian Churches and the Israeli-Palestinian Conflict*, edited by Cary Nelson and Michael C. Gizzi, 296–316. Philadelphia: Presbyterians for Middle East Peace. Distributed by Academic Studies Press.

Karni, Annie, Malika Khurana, and Stuart A. Thompson. 2022. "How Republicans Fed a Misinformation Loop about the Pelosi Attack." *New York Times*, November 5, 2022. https://www.nytimes.com/interactive/2022/11/05/us/politics/pelosi-attack-misinfo-republican-politicians.html.

Kang, Pyeng Hwa. 2018. "Constitutional Treatment of Hate Speech and Freedom of Expression: A Canada-U.S. Perspective." *La Revue des Droits l'Homme* 14 (2018). http://journals.openedition.org/revdh/4109.

Karsh, Efraim. 2019. "Occupation." In "Word Crimes; Reclaiming the Language of the Israeli-Palestinian Conflict," edited by Donna Robinson Divine, Miriam F. Elman, and Asaf Romirowsky, special issue, *Israel Studies* 24, no. 2 (Summer): 45–51.

Keane, David, and Valentina Azarova. 2013. "UNESCO, Palestine, and Archaeology in Conflict." *Denver Journal of International Law and Policy* 41(3): 309–43.

Kertzer, David. 2022. *The Pope at War: The Secret History of Pius XII, Mussolini, and Hitler.* New York: Random House.

Klaff, Lesley. 2019. "Holocaust Inversion." In "Word Crimes; Reclaiming the Language of the Israeli-Palestinian Conflict," edited by Donna Robinson Divine, Miriam F. Elman, and Asaf Romirowsky, special issue, *Israel Studies* 24, no. 2 (Summer): 73–90.

Klug, Brian. 2021. "The Jerusalem Declaration on Antisemitism." *The Nation,* April 1, 2021. https://www.thenation.com/article/society/jerusalem-declaration-antisemitism-ihra/.

Kozlowski, Kim. 2018. "UM Disciplines Prof over Israel Letter Controversy." *Detroit News,* October 9, 2018. https://www.detroitnews.com/story/news/local/michigan/2018/10/09/university-michigan-disciplines-professor-over-israel-letter-controversy/1580969002/.

Kramer, Martin. 2002. *Ivory Towers on Sand: The Failure of Middle Eastern Studies in America.* Washington, DC: Washington Institute for Near East Policy.

Kurtzer, Yehuda. 2022. Untitled presentation. "Israel, Palestine, and the First Amendment: Defining the Boundaries of Freedom of Speech," symposium of the University of the Pacific Law Review and Global Center for Business and Development at the McGeorge School of Law, November 4, 2022.

Landes, Richard, ed. 2020. *Salem on the Thames: Moral Panic, Anti-Zionism and the Triumph of Hate Speech at Connecticut College.* Boston: Academic Studies Press.

Landy, David, Ronit Lentin, and Conor McCarthy, eds. 2020. *Enforcing Silence: Academic Freedom, Palestine, and the Criticism of Israel.* London: Zed.

Laura Waxman. 2018. "SF State President Apologizes for Comments about Zionists." *San Francisco Examiner,* February 28, 2018. https://www.sfexaminer.com/news/sf-state-president-apologizes-for-comments-about-zionists/.

LeBlanc, Paul, and Jeremy Diamond. 2020. "Trump Coronavirus Adviser Scott Atlas Urges Michigan to 'Rise Up' against New Covid-19 Measures." *CNN,* November 15, 2020. https://www.cnn.com/2020/11/15/politics/scott-atlas-coronavirus-michigan.

Levitt, Matthew. 2007. "Teaching Terror: How Hamas Radicalizes Palestinian Society." Washington Institute for Near East Policy, February 12, 2007. https://www.washingtoninstitute.org/policy-analysis/teaching-terror-how-hamas-radicalizes-palestinian-society.

Linfield, Susie. 2019. *The Lion's Den: Zionism and the Left from Hannah Arendt to Noam Chomsky*. New Haven: Yale University Press.

Lockard, Joe. 2021. "Against Partisan Political Statements by Arizona Public University Departments." *Jewish News*, July 9, 2021. https://www.jewishaz.com/opinion/against-partisan-political-statements-by-arizona-public-university-departments/article_f1f57386-e0c8-11eb-b255-571436339dc7.html.

Loriga, Sabina. 2008. "The Controversies over the Publication of Ariel Toaff's 'Bloody Passovers.'" *Journal of the Historical Society* 8, no. 4 (December): 469–502.

Louis D. Brandeis Center. 2020. "University of Illinois Jewish Students File Complaint with U.S. Department of Education." Louis D. Brandeis Center for Human Rights Under Law, October 23, 2020. https://brandeiscenter.com/university-of-illinois-jewish-students-file-complaint-with-u-s-department-of-education/.

———. 2022. "Jewish Sexual Assault Victims Expelled from Support Group File Complaint with U.S. Department of Education." Louis D. Brandeis Center for Human Rights Under Law, August 18, 2022. https://brandeiscenter.com/jewish-sexual-assault-victims-expelled-from-support-group-file-complaint-with-u-s-department-of-education/.

Lubet, Steven. 2021. "Cornel West is Blaming His Problems on Israel—Again." *RealClearEducation*, March 3, 2021. https://www.realcleareducation.com/articles/2021/03/03/cornel_west_is_blaming_his_problems_on_israel__again_110544.html.

———. 2022a. "Antisemitic Conspiracy Theories Are Going Mainstream." *Daily Beast*, September 3, 2022. https://www.thedailybeast.com/antisemitic-conspiracy-theories-are-going-mainstream?ref=wrap.

———. 2022b. "The Squeaky Wheel of the Boycott Israel Movement." *RealClearEducation*, March 14, 2022. https://www.realcleareducation.com/articles/2022/03/14/the_squeaky_wheel_of_the_boycott_israel_movement_110711.html.

———. 2022c. "University Professors' Organization Misunderstands the Nature of Antisemitism." *The Hill*, August 24, 2022. https://thehill. com/opinion/education/3611324-university-professors-organization-misunderstands-the-nature-of-antisemitism/.

Mackenzie, Jonathan. 2020. "University of Toronto Law School Hiring Controversy Continues." *TheJ.ca*, November 18, 2020. https://www.thej. ca/2020/11/18/university-of-toronto-law-school-hiring-controversy-continues/.

Mahoney, Lynn. 2020. "Academic Freedom Debate Continues." President's Message, San Francisco State University Office of the President, September 23, 2020. Available at https://president.sfsu.edu/presidents-messages.

———. 2022. "Our Commitment to Academic Freedom." President's Message, San Francisco State University Office of the President, May 25, 2022. Available at https://president.sfsu.edu/presidents-messages.

Makdisi, Saree. 2010. *Palestine Inside Out: An Everyday Occupation*. New York: W. W. Norton.

———. 2018. "Apartheid / ~~Apartheid~~ / [   ]." *Critical Inquiry* 44, no. 2 (Winter): 304–30.

Marantz, Andrew. 2018. "How Social-Media Trolls Turned U.C. Berkeley into a Free Speech Circus." *New Yorker*, June 25, 2018. https://www. newyorker.com/magazine/2018/07/02/how-social-media-trolls-turned-uc-berkeley-into-a-free-speech-circus.

———. 2019. *Antisocial: Online Extremists, Techno-Utopians, and the Hijacking of the American Conversation*. New York: Viking.

Marcus, Kenneth L. 2013a. "Academic Freedom and Political Indoctrination." *Journal of College and University Law* 39(3): 725–46.

———. 2013b. "The Definition of Antisemitism." In *Global Antisemitism: A Crisis of Modernity*, edited by Charles Asher Small, 97–109. Leiden: Brill.

———. 2023. "Any Inclusion of Nexus Will Severely Undermine Biden's Antisemitism Plan." *Jewish Journal*, May 22, 2023. https://jewishjournal. com/commentary/opinion/358997/any-inclusion-of-nexus-will-severely-undermine-bidens-anti-semitism-plan/.

Matei, Liviu, and Shitij Kapur. 2022. "Academic Freedom Is Not Freedom of Speech for Academics." *Times Higher Education*, November 24, 2022.

https://www.timeshighereducation.com/opinion/academic-freedom-not-freedom-speech-academics.

Matas, David, and Aurel Braun. 2022. "The Avoidable Debacle at the University of Toronto." *Fathom* (February 2022). https://fathomjournal.org/rejecting-ihra-the-avoidable-debacle-at-the-university-of-toronto/.

Members of UC Berkeley Faculty. 2017. "Open Letters Calling for Cancellation of Milo Yiannopoulos Event." *Daily Californian*, January 10, 2017. https://www.dailycal.org/2017/01/10/open-letter-calling-cancellation-milo-yiannopolous-event.

Middle East Studies Association. 2022. "University of Denver Statement about Professor Nader Hashemi." Middle East Studies Association, September 2, 2022. https://mesana.org/advocacy/committee-on-academic-freedom/2022/09/02/university-of-denver-statement-about-professor-nader-hashemi.

Mills, Jon. 2023a. "Antisemitism at the APA? The Case of Lara Sheehi." *Areo*, February 7, 2023. https://areomagazine.com/2023/02/07/antisemitism-at-the-apa-the-case-of-lara-sheehi/.

———. 2023b. "The Politics of Division: Lara Sheehi, Antisemitism, and Antiwhite Racism in the American Psychological Association." Critical Theory Antidote, February 12, 2023. https://criticaltherapyantidote.org/2023/02/12/the-politics-of-division/.

Mohamed, Feisal. 2021. "I Love the Public Humanities, But …" *Chronicle of Higher Education*, July 28, 2021. https://www.chronicle.com/article/i-love-the-public-humanities-but?cid2=gen_login_refresh&cid=gen_sign_in.

Mondoweiss. 2022. "We Stand with Rabab Abdulhadi." *Mondoweiss*, September 12, 2022. https://mondoweiss.net/2022/09/we-stand-with-rabab-abdulhadi/.

Mor, Shany. 2019. "On Three Anti-Zionisms." In "Word Crimes; Reclaiming the Language of the Israeli-Palestinian Conflict," edited by Donna Robinson Divine, Miriam F. Elman, and Asaf Romirowsky, special issue, *Israel Studies* 24, no. 2 (Summer): 206–16.

Morris, Steven. 2015. "Germaine Greer Gives University Lecture Despite Campaign to Silence Her." *Guardian*, November 18, 2015. https://www.theguardian.com/books/2015/nov/18/transgender-activists-protest-germaine-greer-lecture-cardiff-university.

Nagourney, Adam. 2015. "In U.C.L.A. Debate over Jewish Student, Echoes on Campus of Old Biases." *New York Times*, March 5, 2015. https://www.nytimes.com/2015/03/06/us/debate-on-a-jewish-student-at-ucla.html.

Nair, C. Gouridasan. 2010. "Full Text of the Interview with Richard Falk." *The Hindu*, September 24, 2010. https://www.thehindu.com/news/resources/Full-text-of-the-interview-with-Richard-Falk-U.N.-Rapporteur-on-Human-Rights-in-the-Israeli-Occupied-Territories-of-Palestine/article16046050.ece.

Nelson, Cary. 2010. *No University is an Island: Saving Academic Freedom*. New York: NYU Press.

———. 2013. "Advocacy versus Indoctrination." *Journal of College and University Law* 39(3): 749–68.

———. 2016. *Dreams Deferred: A Concise Guide to the Israeli-Palestinian Conflict and the Movement to Boycott Israel*. Chicago: MLA Members for Scholars' Rights; Bloomington: Indiana University Press.

———. 2019. *Israel Denial: Anti-Zionism, Anti-Semitism, and the Faculty Campaign against the Jewish State*. Washington, DC: Academic Engagement Network; Bloomington: Indiana University Press.

———. 2021a. "Accommodating the New Antisemitism: A Critique of 'The Jerusalem Declaration.'" *Fathom* (April 2021). https://fathomjournal.org/fathom-long-read-accommodating-the-new-antisemitism-a-critique-of-the-jerusalem-declaration/.

———. 2021b. *Not in Kansas Anymore: Academic Freedom in Palestinian Universities*. Washington, DC: Academic Engagement Network. Distributed by Academic Studies Press.

———. 2023. "Lara Sheehi's Joyous Rage: Antisemitic Anti-Zionism, Advocacy Academia and Jewish Students' Nightmares at GWU." *Fathom* (April 2023). https://fathomjournal.org/lara-sheehis-joyous-rage-antisemitic-anti-zionism-advocacy-academia-and-jewish-students-nightmares-at-gwu.

Nelson, Cary, and Gabriel Brahm, eds. 2015. *The Case Against Academic Boycotts of Israel*. Chicago: MLA Members for Scholars' Rights; Detroit: Wayne State University Press.

Nelson, Cary, and Michael C. Gizzi, eds. 2021. *Peace and Faith: Christian Churches and the Israeli-Palestinian Conflict*. Philadelphia: Presbyterians for Middle East Peace. Distributed by Academic Studies Press.

Nelson, Cary, and Joe Lockard. 2022. "The Modern Language Association, Antisemitism and Anti-Zionism." *Fathom* (July 2022). https://fathomjournal. org/the-modern-language-association-antisemitism-and-anti-zionism/.

Nelson, Cary, and Steven Lubet. 2022. "The AAUP Explains Antisemitism and Gets It Wrong." *Inside Higher Education*, April 27, 2022. https:// www.insidehighered.com/views/2022/04/27/aaup-errs-taking-sides-defining-antisemitism-opinion.

Nelson, Cary, and Kenneth Stern. 2011. "Antisemitism on Campus." Open letter, April 20, 2011. Available at https://www.aaup.org/news/cary-nelson-and-kenneth-stern-pen-open-letter-campus-antisemitism#. YGInVC2cbUY.

Nelson, Cary, and Paula A. Treichler. 2019. "A Rejoinder to Gershon Shafir." *Fathom* (July 2019). https://fathomjournal.org/the-word-crimes-controversy-3-paula-a-treichler-and-cary-nelson-a-rejoinder-to-gershon-shafir/.

Nevel, Donna. 2021. "Challenging Antisemitism: Why Criticism of Israel Shouldn't be Singled Out & Our Interconnected Struggles for Justice." *Tikkun*, March 31, 2021. https://www.tikkun.org/ why-criticism-of-israel-should-not-be-singled-out-in-antisemitism/.

Nexus Document. 2021. Drafted by the Nexus Task Force as a project of the Knight Program in Media and Religion, Annenberg School for Communication and Journalism, University of Southern California, February 2021. https://israelandantisemitism.com/the-nexus-document/.

NGO Monitor. 2023. "HaMoked—Center for the Defense of the Individual." Online profile, last updated April 20, 2023. https://www.ngo-monitor.org/ ngos/hamoked_center_for_the_defense_of_the_individual/.

Oster, Marcy. 2016. "UAW Rejects Israel Boycott Vote by NYU Grad Student Union." *Forward*, June 29, 2016. https://forward.com/news/breaking-news/343959/united-auto-workers-rejects-nyu-graduate-student-union-vote-backing-israel/.

Oxnevad, Ian. 2023. *The Company They Keep: Organizational and Economic Dynamics of the BDS Movement.* NY: National Association of Scholars.

Palestine Solidarity Campaign (PSC). 2021. *Legal Guide for Palestine Solidarity Student Activists.* Adopted April 2021. https://www.palestinecampaign.org/ wp-content/uploads/Student-Legal-Support-Guide-2021-Revised-1.pdf.

Palestinian Feminist Collective. 2021. "Gender Studies Departments in Solidarity with Palestinian Feminist Collective." Statement issued on May 17, 2021. http://genderstudiespalestinesolidarity.weebly.com.

Patel, Vimal. 2022. "At Berkeley Law, a Debate Over Zionism, Free Speech and Campus Ideals." *New York Times*, December 21, 2022. https://www.nytimes.com/2022/12/21/us/uc-berkeley-free-speech.html.

Penslar, Derek. 2021. "Why I Signed the Jerusalem Declaration: A Response to Cary Nelson." *Fathom* (April 2021). https://fathomjournal.org/why-i-signed-the-jda-a-response-to-cary-nelson-2/.

Pessin, Andrew. 2016. "Palestinian Human Rights Activist Receives Death Threats from Anti-Israel Protesters During U of Chicago Lecture." *Algemeiner*, February 21, 2016. https://www.algemeiner.com/2016/02/21/palestinian-human-rights-activists-receives-death-threats-from-anti-israel-protesters-during-u-of-chicago-lecture-video/.

Pessin, Andrew, and Doron S. Ben-Atar, eds. 2018. *Anti-Zionism on Campus: The University, Free Speech, and BDS*. Bloomington: Indiana University Press.

Porat, Dina, Giovanni Quer, and Talia Naamat. 2021. "The IHRA Working Definition of Antisemitism: Criticism, Implementation, and Importance." Institute for National Security Studies (INSS) Special Publication, December 23, 2021. https://www.inss.org.il/publication/ihra/.

Post, Robert C. 2012. *Democracy, Expertise, Academic Freedom: A First Amendment Jurisprudence for the Modern State*. New Haven: Yale University Press.

Puar, Jasbir. 2017. *The Right to Maim: Debility, Capacity, Disability*. Durham: Duke University Press.

Quer, Giovanni Mateo. 2021. "Catholic Organizations and the Delegitimization of Israel." In *Peace and Faith: Christian Churches and the Israeli-Palestinian Conflict*, edited by Cary Nelson and Michael C. Gizzi, 189–206. Philadelphia: Presbyterians for Middle East Peace. Distributed by Academic Studies Press.

Ramirez, Chris. 2020. "Zoom Denies Service for Controversial Panel Featuring Leila Khaled." *Golden Gate Xpress*, September 22, 2020. https://goldengatexpress.org/94299/campus/zoom-denies-service-for-controversial-panel-featuring-leila-khaled-2/.

Rawnsley, Adam. 2023. "Jan. 6 Committee Experiment Found TikTok Went from Zero to Nazi in 75 Minutes." *Rolling Stone*, January 5, 2023. https://www.rollingstone.com/politics/politics-news/tiktok-served-nazi-propaganda-jan-6-committee-found-1234656268/.

Redden, Elizabeth. 2015. "Another Association Backs Israel Boycott." *Inside Higher Education*, December 1, 2015. https://www.insidehighered.com/news/2015/12/01/national-womens-studies-association-joins-israel-boycott-movement.

Rees, Geraint. 2017. "Investigation into the UCLU Friends of Israel Society Event on 27th October 2016 ('the Event')." University College London, January 2017. https://www.ucl.ac.uk/drupal/site_news/sites/news/files/Investigation_report.pdf.

Reichelmann, Ashley V., Stanislav Vysotsky, and Jack Levin. 2021. "The Perpetual Scapegoat: Antisemitism in the Ideology and Activities of Hate Groups in the United State pre- and post-Trump's Election." In *Poisoning the Wells: Antisemitism in Contemporary America*, edited by Corinne E. Blackmer and Andrew Pessin, 225–43. New York: Institute for the Study of Global Antisemitism and Policy (ISGAP).

Reichman, Henry. 2019. *The Future of Academic Freedom*. Baltimore: Johns Hopkins University Press.

Reichman, Hank. 2021a. "Academic Freedom and the Goldwater Rule." *Academe Blog*, March 26, 2021. https://academeblog.org/2021/03/26/academic-freedom-and-the-goldwater-rule/.

———. 2021b. "U. of California Faculty Call for Action on Academic Freedom and Policing." *Academe Blog*, May 2, 2021. https://academeblog.org/2021/05/02/u-of-california-faculty-call-for-action-on-academic-freedom-and-policing/.

Rich, Dave. 2018. *The Left's Jewish Problem: Jeremy Corbyn, Israel and Anti-Semitism*. London: Biteback Publishing.

———. 2021. "Why 'Academic Freedom' Is No Defence of the Bristol University Professor David Miller." *New Statesman*, March 23, 2021. https://www.newstatesman.com/politics/2021/03/why-academic-freedom-no-defence-bristol-university-professor-david-miller.

Ritch, Rose. 2020. "I Was Harassed and Persecuted on Campus Just for Being a Zionist." *Newsweek*, August 10, 2020. https://www.newsweek.com/i-was-harassed-persecuted-campus-just-being-zionist-opinion-1523873

Robertson, C. K., 2021. "Complexity and Contention: Four Decades of the Episcopal Church's Responses to the Israel-Palestine Question." In *Peace and Faith: Christian Churches and the Israeli-Palestinian Conflict*, edited by Cary Nelson and Michael C. Gizzi, 232–52. Philadelphia: Presbyterians for Middle East Peace. Distributed by Academic Studies Press.

Romirowsky, Asaf. 2019. "Arab-Palestinian Refugees." In "Word Crimes; Reclaiming the Language of the Israeli-Palestinian Conflict," edited by Donna Robinson Divine, Miriam F. Elman, and Asaf Romirowsky, special issue, *Israel Studies* 24, no. 2 (Summer): 91–102.

Rose, Hilary, and Steven Rose. 2002. "The Choice Is to Do Nothing or Try to Bring About Change: Why We Launched the Boycott of Israeli Institutions." *Guardian*, July 14, 2002. https://www.theguardian.com/world/2002/jul/15/comment.stevenrose.

Rosenbaum, Thane. 2019. "Zionism." In "Word Crimes; Reclaiming the Language of the Israeli-Palestinian Conflict," edited by Donna Robinson Divine, Miriam F. Elman, and Asaf Romirowsky, special issue, *Israel Studies* 24, no. 2 (Summer): 119–27.

Rossman-Benjamin, Tammi. 2009. "Campus Critics on Trial [on David Theo Goldberg and Saree Makdisi]." *The American Thinker*, November 1, 2009. Available at https://www.meforum.org/campus-watch/16350/campus-critics-on-trial-on-david-theo-goldberg.

———. 2013. "Identity Politics, the Pursuit of Social Justice, and the Rise of Campus Antisemitism." In *Resurgent Antisemitism: Global Perspectives*, edited by Alvin H. Rosenfeld, 482–520. Bloomington: Indiana University Press.

Rosenfeld, Alvin H., ed. 2013. *Resurgent Antisemitism: Global Perspectives*. Bloomington: Indiana University Press.

———, ed. 2015. *Deciphering the New Antisemitism*. Bloomington: Indiana University Press.

Ruth, Jennifer. 2022. "Statement in Support of The Harvard Crimson and Palestinian Liberation." *Academe Blog*, June 19, 2022. https://academeblog.org/2022/06/19/statement-in-support-of-the-harvard-crimson-and-palestinian-liberation/.

Sachs, Jeffrey. 2019. "Canada's New Definition of Anti-Semitism Is a Threat to Campus Free Speech." *University Affairs/Affaires universitaires*, September 10, 2019. https://www.universityaffairs.ca/opinion/in-my-opinion/canadas-new-definition-of-anti-semitism-is-a-threat-to-campus-free-speech/.

Said, Edward. 1996. "Identity, Authority, and Freedom: The Potentate and the Traveler." In *The Future of Academic Freedom*, edited by Louis Menand, 214–28. Chicago: University of Chicago Press.

Salaita, Steven. 2006a. *Anti-Arab Racism in the USA: Where It Comes From and What It Means for Politics Today*. London: Pluto Press.

———. 2006b. *The Holy Land in Transit: Colonialism and the Quest for Canaan*. Syracuse: Syracuse University Press.

———. 2011. *Israel's Dead Soul*. Philadelphia: Temple University Press.

———. 2015. *Uncivil Rites: Palestine and the Limits of Academic Freedom*. Chicago: Haymarket Books.

———. 2019. "My Lie as a Cautionary Tale: Probing the Limits of Academic Freedom." *The Chronicle Review*, August 28, 2019.

Samuels, Ben. 2021. "Cornel West Explains Why He's Convinced His Views on Israel Led Him Out of Harvard." *Haaretz*, March 14, 2021.

Scheper-Hughes, Nancy. 2011. "The Body of the Terrorist: Blood Libels, Bio-Piracy, and the Spoils of War at the Israeli Forensic Institute." *Social Research* 78, no. 3 (Fall): 849–86.

Scocca, Tom. 2020. "How the Awful Stuff Won." *New York Review of Books*, November 5, 2020, 55–57.

Schanzer, Jonathan. 2019. "Terrorism." In "Word Crimes; Reclaiming the Language of the Israeli-Palestinian Conflict," edited by Donna Robinson Divine, Miriam F. Elman, and Asaf Romirowsky, special issue, *Israel Studies* 24, no. 2 (Summer): 52–61.

Schneiderman, Jill S. 2018. "A Field Geologist in Politicized Terrain." In *Anti-Zionism on Campus: The University, Free Speech, and BDS*, edited by Andrew Pessin and Doron S. Ben-Atar, 317–22. Bloomington: Indiana University Press.

Schotten, C. Heike. 2020. "Against Academic Freedom: 'Terrorism,' Settler Colonialism, and Palestinian Liberation." In *Enforcing Silence: Academic Freedom, Palestine, and the Criticism of Israel*, edited by David Landy, Ronit Lentin, and Conor McCarthy, 282–309. London: Zed.

Scottish Council of Jewish Communities. 2013. "Church of Scotland Rejects Dialogue." Statement, May 23, 2013. https://www.scojec.org/news/2013/13v_cos/cos_4.html.

Schraub, David. 2009. "Wallis 'Refutes' Anti-Semitism Charge." *The Debate Link* (blog), June 2, 2009. http://dsadevil.blogspot.com/2009/06/wallis-refutes-anti-semitism-charge.html.

———. 2021a. "A New Challenger Approaches!: Evaluating the Jerusalem Declaration on Antisemitism." *The Debate Link* (blog), March 26, 2021. http://dsadevil.blogspot.com/2021_03_21_archive.html.

———. 2021b. "The Nexus in the Shadow of IHRA." *The Debate Link* (blog), March 17, 2021. http://dsadevil.blogspot.com/2021/03/the-nexus-in-shadow-of-ihra.html.

———. 2021c. "Three Definitions of Antisemitism: A Comparison." *The Third Narrative*, March 25, 2021. https://thirdnarrative.org/anti-zionism-antisemitism/three-definitions-of-antisemitism-a-comparison/.

———. 2022. "MESA Objects to the Most Milquetoast Possible Manner of Addressing Member's Conspiracy-Mongering." *The Debate Link* (blog), September 4, 2022. http://dsadevil.blogspot.com/2022/09/mesa-objects-to-most-milquetoast.html.

Shafir, Gershon. 2019. "The Word Crimes Controversy." *Fathom* (July 2019). https://fathomjournal.org/the-word-crimes-controversy-2-gershon-shafir-responds-to-cary-nelson/.

Shamir, Jonathan. 2020. "Israel Is Using the IHRA to Silence Its Critics." *Vashti Media*, December 18, 2020. https://vashtimedia.com/2020/12/18/issues/antisemitism/israel-ihra-antisemitism-definition-to-silence-palestinians/.

Shanes, Joshua, and Dov Waxman. 2021. "We Need a Better Definition of Anti-Semitism." *Slate*, March 26, 2021. https://slate.com/news-and-politics/2021/03/anti-semitism-better-definition-ihra.html.

Sheehi, Lara, and Stephen Sheehi. 2022. *Psychoanalysis under Occupation: Practicing Resistance in Palestine.* New York: Routledge.

Shivaram, Deepa. 2021. "Cornel West Has Announced He's Leaving Harvard and Says the School Has Lost Its Way." NPR, July 13, 202. https://www.npr.org/2021/07/13/1015632217/cornel-west-has-announced-hes-leaving-harvard-and-says-the-school-has-lost-its-w.

Shokirova, Dilshoda. 2019. "Palestine and International Legal Practice: Interview with Dr. Valentina Azarova (Manchester International Law Centre)." Istanbul Center for International Law, February 17, 2019. https://icil.org.tr/interview-with-dr-valentina-azarova-manchester-international-law-centre/.

Soave, Bobby. 2020. "Tulane Canceled a Talk by the Author of an Acclaimed Anti-Racism Book after Students Said the Event Was 'Violent.'" *Reason*, August 6, 2020.

Soucek, Brian. 2022. "Academic Freedom and Departmental Speech." *Academe* (Spring 2022). https://www.aaup.org/article/academic-freedom-and-departmental-speech#.Y5zVWi-B3gE.

Speyer, Lea, and Rachel Frommer. 2016. "Jewish Students at Texas U Cancel Lecture by Author Caroline Glick for Fear of 'Alienating' Anti-Zionists on Campus." *Algemeiner*, November 13, 2016. https://www.algemeiner.com/2016/11/13/pro-israel-jewish-groups-university-of-texas-austin-pull-sponsorship-caroline-glick-zionist-speaker-over-fear-alienating-students/.

Spyer, Jonathan. 2020. "Is the Popular Front for the Liberation of Palestine Back from the Dead?" *Jerusalem Post*, May 14, 2020. https://www.jpost.com/arab-israeli-conflict/is-the-popular-front-for-the-liberation-of-palestine-back-from-the-dead-628060.

Steinberg, Gerald M. 2019. "Uncivil Society: Tracking the Funders and Enablers of the Demonization of Israel." In "Word Crimes; Reclaiming the Language of the Israeli-Palestinian Conflict," edited by Donna Robinson Divine, Miriam F. Elman, and Asaf Romirowsky, special issue, *Israel Studies* 24, no. 2 (Summer): 182–205.

Stephens, Bret. 2023. "Three Falsehoods about Antisemitism—and One Truth." *Sapir* 10 (Summer 2023): 1–10. https://sapirjournal.org/antisemitism/2023/08/three-falsehoods-about-antisemitism-and-one-truth/.

Stern, Kenneth S. 2020a. *The Conflict over the Conflict: The Israel/Palestine Campus Debate*. Toronto: New Jewish Press.

———. 2020b. "Steering the Biden Administration Wrong on Anti-Semitism." *The Blogs* (blog), *Times of Israel*, December 10, 2020. https://blogs.timesofisrael.com/steering-the-biden-administration-wrong-on-anti-semitism/.

———. 2022a. "Yes It May Hurt, but Campus Groups Have the Right to Exclude Zionists." *The Blogs* (blog), *Times of Israel*, September 1, 2022. https://blogs.timesofisrael.com/yes-it-may-hurt-but-campus-groups-have-the-right-to-exclude-zionists/.

———. 2022b. Untitled presentation. "Israel, Palestine, and the First Amendment: Defining the Boundaries of Freedom of Speech," symposium of the University of the Pacific Law Review and Global Center for Business and Development at the McGeorge School of Law, November 4, 2022.

Strawson, John. 2019. "Colonialism." In "Word Crimes; Reclaiming the Language of the Israeli-Palestinian Conflict," edited by Donna Robinson Divine, Miriam F. Elman, and Asaf Romirowsky, special issue, *Israel Studies* 24, no. 2 (Summer): 33–43.

Tiede, Hans-Joerg. 2012. "Extramural Speech, Academic Freedom, and the AAUP: An Historical Account." In *Challenges to Academic Freedom*, edited by Joseph C. Hermanowicz, 104–31. Baltimore: Johns Hopkins University Press.

Topor, Lev. 2019. "Dark Hatred: Antisemitism on the Dark Web." *Journal of Contemporary Antisemitism* 2(2): 25–42.

———. 2023. *Phishing for Nazis: Conspiracies, Anonymous Communications and White Supremacy Networks on the Dark Web*. New York: Routledge.

Trachtenberg, Barry. 2021. "Why I Signed the Jerusalem Declaration on Antisemitism." *Jewish Currents*, March 26, 2021. https://jewishcurrents.org/why-i-signed-the-jerusalem-declaration-on-antisemitism/.

Troen, Ilan. 2019. "Ilan Troen Responds to Gershon Shafir." *Fathom* (July 2019). https://fathomjournal.org/the-word-crimes-controversy-4-ilan-troen-responds-to-gershon-shafir/.

Troen, Ilan, and Carol Troen. 2019. "Indigeneity." In "Word Crimes; Reclaiming the Language of the Israeli-Palestinian Conflict," edited by Donna Robinson Divine, Miriam F. Elman, and Asaf Romirowsky, special issue, *Israel Studies* 24, no. 2 (Summer): 17–32.

UCL UCU. n.d. "Can the IHRA working definition be implemented?" Accessed November 2022. https://www.ucl.ac.uk/ucu/campaigns/faqs-16-questions-ucl-and-ihra-definition-anti-semitism/can-ihra-working-definition-be.

———. n.d. "FAQs: 16 questions on UCL and the IHRA definition of anti-Semitism." Accessed November 2022. https://www.ucl.ac.uk/ucu/campaigns/faqs-16-questions-ucl-and-ihra-definition-anti-semitism.

UK Home Office. 2021. "Prevent Duty Guidance: For Higher Education Institutions in England and Wales." Updated April 1, 2021. https://www.gov.uk/government/publications/prevent-duty-guidance/prevent-duty-guidance-for-higher-education-institutions-in-england-and-wales.

Ullrich, Peter. 2019. "Expert Opinion on the 'Working Definition of Antisemitism' of the International Holocaust Remembrance Alliance." RLS Paper 3/2019, Rosa Luxemburg Stiftung, Berlin, September 2019. https://www.rosalux.de/fileadmin/rls_uploads/pdfs/rls_papers/Papers_3-2019_Antisemitism.pdf.

UNESCO. 1997. "Recommendation concerning the Status of Higher-Education Teaching Personnel." https://unesdoc.unesco.org/ark:/48223/pf0000113234.page=2.

UNICEF. 2017. "Table 2: Nutrition." In *The State of the World's Children 2017*, 158–61. https://www.unicef.org/media/48581/file/SOWC_2017_ENG.pdf.

United Nations Office for the Coordination of Humanitarian Affairs (OCHA). 2019. *Occupied Palestinian Territory—Humanitarian Atlas*. https://www.ochaopt.org/atlas2019/.

US Campaign for the Academic and Cultural Boycott of Israel. 2021. "Weaponizing Anti-Semitism: IHRA and Ending the Palestine Exception." Webinar, April 6, 2021. https://usacbi.org/2021/04/video-weaponizing-anti-semitism-ihra-and-the-end-of-the-palestine-exception-usacbi-webinar/.

US Commission on Civil Rights. 2006. "Findings and Recommendations of the US Commission on Civil Rights Regarding Campus Anti-Semitism." April 3, 2006. http://www.usccr.gov/pubs/050306FRUSCCRRCAS.pdf.

US Department of Education/Office for Civil Rights. 1994. "Racial Incidents and Harassment against Students at Educational Institutions; Investigative Guidance." 59 Fed. Reg. 47 (March 10, 1994). Available at https://www2.ed.gov/about/offices/list/ocr/docs/race394.html.

University of California. 2022. "Report of the Joint Senate-Administration Workgroup on the Role of the University and Its Units in Political and Social Action." Draft, May 2022. https://evcp.berkeley.edu/sites/default/files/joint_senate-admin_working_group_report_on_the_role_of_the_university_in_political_action_draft_202205.pdf.

Walker, Julian. 2018. "Hate Speech and Freedom of Expression: Legal Boundaries in Canada." Background paper, Library of Parliament, Ottawa, June 29, 2018. https://lop.parl.ca/sites/PublicWebsite/default/en_CA/ResearchPublications/201825E.

Wallach, Yair. 2019. "Concerns regarding the 'Word Crimes' Israel Studies Special Issue." *The Israel Studies Conversation* (blog), *Medium*, May 2, 2019. https://medium.com/the-israel-studies-conversation/concerns-regarding-the-word-crimes-israel-studies-special-issue-29ee2b1eb85.

Walsh, Joan. 2011. "Cornel West's Tragic Meltdown." *Salon*, May 19, 2011. https://www.salon.com/2011/05/19/cornel_west/.

Walzer, Michael. 2021a. "The Jerusalem Declaration: A Response to Cary Nelson." *Fathom* (April 2021). https://fathomjournal.org/the-jerusalem-declaration-a-response-to-cary-nelson/.

———. 2021b. "I Hope That UCL Faculty and Staff Will Defend IHRA, As I Would Do Were I with Them." *Fathom* (May 2021). https://fathomjournal.org/i-hope-that-ucl-faculty-and-staff-will-defend-ihra-as-i-would-do-were-i-with-them/.

Weber, Max. 1946. "Science as a Vocation." In *Max Weber: Essays in Sociology*, translated and edited by H. H. Gerth and C. Wright Mills, 129–56. New York: Oxford University Press. Citations refer to reprint available at: http://www.wisdom.weizmann.ac.il/~oded/X/WeberScienceVocation.pdf.

Weill, Sharon, and Valentina Azarova. 2015. "The 2014 Gaza War: Reflections on *jus ad bellum, jus in bello,* and Accountability." In *The War Report: Armed Conflict in 2014,* edited by Annyssa Bellal, 360–87. Oxford: Oxford University Press.

Weimann, Gabriel. 2022. "New Trends in Online Antisemitism." Keynote address at conference on Decoding Antisemitism, Berlin, October 19, 2022.

Weimannn, Gabriel, and Natalie Masri. 2022. "New Antisemitism on TikTok." In *Antisemitism on Social Media,* edited by Monika Hübscher and Sabine von Mering, 167–80. New York: Routledge.

Wilson, John. 2021. "In Defense of Departmental Academic Freedom." *Academe Blog,* June 7, 2021. https://academeblog.org/2021/06/07/in-defense-of-departmental-academic-freedom/.

Wong, Vincent. 2021. "What the IHRP Hiring Scandal Tells Us about Intersectional Privilege in Canadian Legal Institutions." *Opinio Juris,* April 6, 2021. http://opiniojuris.org/2021/04/06/what-the-ihrp-hiring-scandal-tells-us-about-intersectional-privilege-in-canadian-legal-institutions/.

Working Group on Racism and Prejudice. 2020. "Report of the Academic Board Working Group on Racism and Prejudice." University College London, December 16, 2020. https://www.ucl.ac.uk/ucu/sites/ucu/files/wg-racism-and-prejudice-report.pdf.

Yakira, Elhanan. 2018. "What Is It Like to Be an (Assertive) Academic Abroad?" In *Anti-Zionism on Campus: The University, Free Speech, and BDS,* edited by Andrew Pessin and Doron S. Ben-Atar, 348–54. Bloomington: Indiana University Press.

Zine, Jasmin. 2020. "Criticizing Israel Is Not Antisemitic—It's Academic Freedom." *The Conversation,* November 15, 2020. https://theconversation.com/criticizing-israel-is-not-antisemitic-its-academic-freedom-148864.

Ziri, Danielle. 2021. "U.S. Jewish Groups Want to Fight Antisemitism, but Struggle to Agree What It Is." *Haaretz,* February 21, 2021.

About the Author

Cary Nelson is Jubilee Professor of Liberal Arts and Sciences and Professor of English Emeritus at the University of Illinois at Urbana-Champaign. He is an affiliated faculty member at the University of Haifa and the recipient of an honorary doctorate from Ben Gurion University of the Negev.

He is the author or editor of thirty-six books and 400 essays. His books include *No University Is an Island: Saving Academic Freedom*, and six books about the intersections between anti-Zionism, antisemitism, and the Israeli-Palestinian conflict, including *Israel Denial: Anti-Zionism, Anti-Semitism, and the Faculty Campaign against the Jewish State; Not in Kansas Anymore: Academic Freedom in Palestinian Universities*; and *Peace and Faith: Christian Churches and the Israeli-Palestinian Conflict*. He has also written widely about modern poetry and about the politics and economics of higher education. His op-eds have appeared in the *New York Times*, the *Washington Post, Inside Higher Education*, the *Chronicle of Higher Education*, and elsewhere. He is presently completing *The Poetry of Hate*, a book focused on German antisemitic poetry from 1890 to 1945.

Nelson was president of the American Association of University Professors (AAUP) from 2006 to 2012, completing twenty years in the national organization's elected leadership. He served on the AAUP's Committee A on Academic Freedom and Tenure from 2006 to 2015. He presently serves as the chair of the Alliance for Academic Freedom, an organization comprising more than two hundred academics that is concerned with protecting academic freedom and free speech for all who are engaged in research, study, debate, or discussion about the Middle East conflict. He is a fellow of the Institute for the Study of Global Antisemitism and Policy (ISGAP) and serves on its Advisory Board and its Academic Steering Committee. He is also a research fellow at the London Centre for the Study of Contemporary Antisemitism.

Index

content provision on, 68–70, 76; coded
language in, 48; conspiracism through,
55; as corrosive force, 83; and the dark
web, 66–67; and faculty profiles, 106;
faculty's use of, 18, 65–67; and group
identification, 69; hate on, 21, 63–66,
77–83; and personnel decisions, 67–68,
73; regulation of, 65–66, 69, 83–84;
social media "ravings," 81; stridency on,
241. *See also* specific media
SodaStream, 186
Soros, George, 3
Soucek, Brian, 36–37
Southern Poverty Law Center, 70
speech cancellations: international
cancellations, 92–93; resistance to,
93–94; at Tulane and other universities,
91–92, 93–94; at UC Berkeley, 88–91
Spiro, David E., 168–70
StandWithUs, 76–77
Stanford University, 12, 18–19
STAR Framework, 83
State University of New York at New Paltz, 59
Steinberg, Gerald, "Uncivil Society," 134
Stephens, Bret, 45, 47, 58
Stern, Kenneth, 204, 206, 208, 216; *The
Conflict over the Conflict,* 205, 215,
274–75
Strawson, John, "Colonialism," 131
students: antisemitic by-laws for student
groups, 59–60; campaigns against, 54;
civil rights claims filed on behalf of,
59; student government resolutions on
boycott and divestment, 7–8; student
profiles, 10
Students for Justice in Palestine (SJP), 93, 97,
100, 155, 217, 261–62
Summers, Lawrence, 46
supersessionism, 145, 148, 150, 159, 232
Syracuse University, 92

T

tatreez, 248–49
teaching: academic freedom and course
content, 118–19; anti-Zionist courses,
118; classroom political advocacy, 49–52;
disciplinary standards in, 35
technology, promise of, 64
Telegram, 20, 69
terminology and connotative effects, 133
terrorism, 24–27, 31, 81
Terrorism Act (UK), 26
Threads, 66, 69
Tijani, Abeer, 99–100
TikTok, 65, 69, 81, 206

Tilley, Virginia, 236
Toaff, Ariel, *Pasque di sangue,* 236
Topor, Lev, 20, 64, 66; *Phishing for Nazis,* 206
Tor (The Onion Router), 67
Trachtenberg, Barry, 230
Treichler, Paula A., 129
Troen, Carol and Ian, "Indigeneity," 133
Troen, Ilan, 125
truth: and BDS claims, 111; and disciplinary
consensus, 35, 50, 57–58; faculty
and gross falsehoods, 76; norms for
distinguishing truth from fiction, 36;
and professional standards in the quest
for, 52–62; in scholarly debate, 122–23;
social media and, 78
Tulane University, 91–92, 101
Twitter, 64, 66, 69, 76, 83, 206–7

U

UCL. *See* University College London (UCL)
UCL Working Group on Racism and
Prejudice: and antisemitic harassment,
258; arguments opposing the IHRA
Definition, 259–63; claims by, 247;
on core definition of antisemitism,
263–65; formation of, 251; guidelines
for unacceptable antisemitism, 259–60;
and the Israel exception, 265–68; letter
on risks of IHRA Definition, 261–62;
makeup of, 251–52; and the "Moving
Objects" exhibition, 249
Ullrich, Peter, 200
UNESCO, Recommendation concerning the
Status of Higher-Education Teaching
Personnel, 20
UNICEF, 121; *The State of the World's
Children,* 122
United Kingdom: adoption of the IHRA
Definition, 253; anti-Zionism in, 153;
boycott resolutions in, 160; Equality
Act 2010, 29, 258, 264–65; "Free
Speech" (Parliament's Joint Committee
on Human Rights), 26; impact of UCL
debate on the IHRA Definition, 269–70;
laws on academic freedom, 26–27; laws
on discrimination, 29–30; "Prevent Duty
Guidance," 26–27; Public Order Act
1986, 27; suggested supplements to the
IHRA Definition, 263; view of Salaita's
tweets in, 73. *See also* University College
London
United Methodist Church, 155, 160
United Methodists for Constructive
Peacemaking in Israel and Palestine, 147
United Methodists for Kairos Response, 147